DATA BASE MANAGEMENT SYSTEMS

This is a volume in
COMPUTER SCIENCE AND APPLIED MATHEMATICS
A Series of Monographs and Textbooks

Editor: WERNER RHEINBOLDT

A complete list of titles in this series appears at the end of this volume.

Data Base
Management Systems

Dionysios C. Tsichritzis
Frederick H. Lochovsky

University of Toronto

A C A D E M I C   P R E S S   New York   San Francisco   London

A Subsidiary of Harcourt Brace Jovanovich, Publishers

ACADEMIC PRESS, INC.
111 Fifth Avenue, New York, New York 10003

United Kingdom Edition published by
ACADEMIC PRESS, INC. (LONDON) LTD.
24/28 Oval Road, London NW1

Library of Congress Cataloging in Publication Data

Tsichritzis, Dionysios C.
    Data base management systems.

    (Computer science and applied mathematics series)
    Bibliography: p.
    1.   Data base management.   I.   Lochovsky, Frederick H., joint
author.   II.   Title.
QA76.9.D3T74   001.6'442   76-13952
ISBN 0−12−701740−2

CONTENTS

PREFACE

Data base management systems or DBMS's have come into vogue in recent years. Their number and their usage have increased tremendously in a very short time. Many organizations have looked to a DBMS as a panacea for their data processing problems. Unfortunately, the claims made for and about DBMS's have sometimes exceeded their capabilities. In addition, it is very difficult for some organizations to take advantage of this new technology immediately. The rapid growth in the usage of DBMS's has created a shortage of personnel trained in the effective use of such systems. As a result, many organizations have found that instead of solving their data processing problems, DBMS's have sometimes created new ones [Cox, 1974].

As a first step toward resolving this situation, the user, or potential user, of a DBMS should have a firm grasp of DBMS concepts. These concepts include an understanding of the nature of data and data processing. They also deal with basic DBMS organizations and their capabilities and limitations. The first part of this book covers DBMS concepts. In Chapter 1, we examine briefly the history of data processing. We show how the need evolved for a unified approach to data management and how DBMS's help achieve this goal. The organization of data and the meaningful representation of data relationships via data models are presented in Chapter 2. Chapter 3 discusses data access via data languages in the context of the data models presented in Chapter 2. Chapter 4 discusses, in general, the facilities provided by DBMS's. Chapters 5, 6, and 7 describe respectively hierarchical, network, and relational systems. The description includes the respective data model, some data languages, and some example applications that demonstrate their use. Chapter 8 surveys implementation techniques. Finally, Chapter 9 discusses some operational requirements of DBMS's. With this background a user should be better able to evaluate various DBMS's and the claims made about them.

ix

As a second step, the prospective user should acquire some knowledge of the current state of the art in DBMS's. Commercial DBMS's should be investigated and their different features evaluated. The second part of this book serves this purpose by presenting a survey of various DBMS's. In this manner the user is not required to struggle with many sets of manuals containing completely different terminologies, attitudes, and approaches. In addition, the prospective user can appreciate how the abstract concepts discussed in the first part of the book are mapped into concrete system features.

As a third step, it is beneficial for the user to get some real "hands on" experience with a DBMS. Such experience is very valuable for alleviating a prospective user's "mental block" with respect to information systems in general and DBMS's in particular. In the Appendix we discuss a teaching environment that provides this type of experience.

Finally, the knowledgeable user may participate in the design, implementation, or maintenance of a real DBMS. However, we do not expect all our readers to go through this final step.

This book is written mainly for the DBMS user or prospective user. It is not a design manual for DBMS's nor a feature analysis of existing DBMS's. We hope to present the reader with an overall view of DBMS requirements, capabilities, and existing features. We have tried to present data base management as a unified subject and not as a collection of unrelated approaches and techniques. For this reason, we present some general, unifying concepts in Chapters 2–4, before we discuss the different approaches in Chapters 5–7. In addition, we present some implementation techniques in a unified manner in Chapter 8. We hope that the reader will find this organization helpful. It should enable him to grasp DBMS concepts as a unified approach and not as a fragmented set of ideas.

Implementation considerations are incorporated to provide some insight into the problems and resulting limitations of DBMS's. However, no detailed solutions to implementation problems are given. We concentrate mainly on the facilities provided by DBMS's and not on the details of their implementation. Such mechanisms are continually evolving, especially with hardware changes. New insights and techniques are emerging frequently. Any in-depth discussion of specific mechanisms would, of necessity, be incomplete and soon out of date.

We emphasize mainly the data-structuring aspect of DBMS's. Operational requirements such as security, integrity, and concurrency, which are an integral part of a successful system, are discussed briefly in Chapter 9. Although they deserve special attention, it is difficult to present general solutions concisely. Much research is still needed and is currently proceeding in these important areas.

In a book of this size it is not possible to present complete applications. However, since we feel that examples help illustrate the concepts discussed, we have included numerous examples of realistic applications. This book is not a programming manual. Some of our examples are neither complete nor particularly attractive programs. We try to deal with the applications and not with their particular representation in a programming language. Different languages are presented to illustrate features and concepts and not to promote any specific syntax for commands. The programs presented have been checked as thoroughly as possible for correctness. However, we did not ever intend to run them at any particular installation.

We strongly advise the reader to use a DBMS. It is a sobering experience to be confronted with the idiosyncrasies of a particular DBMS and to overcome them for a particular problem. Our DBMS teaching environment, described in the Appendix, is specifically designed for the purpose of exposing potential users to different DBMS approaches. However, for pedagogical use, any DBMS is adequate, provided it includes a wide range of facilities and operates within the budget of our readers.

We hope this book presents a concise overview of the DBMS area. We also hope that the material presented will not quickly become obsolete in the rapidly changing world of DBMS's. The first part of this book, which deals with basic concepts and organizations, will probably remain relevant for some time. The second part deals with particular systems which evolve continually. However, the investment of both manufacturers and users in these systems is so great that they will probably be with us for quite some time.

There is currently a debate among DBMS professionals concerning the advantages of each DBMS approach [Canning, 1972a; Ashenhurst, 1974; Bachman, 1974a; Codd and Date, 1974; Date and Codd, 1974; Sibley, 1974; Steel, 1975a]. The debate concerns not only specific, desirable features for a DBMS but also the possibility and desirability of a standardization [SPARC, 1974]. The different positions in this debate can be summarized as follows:

1. A group of proponents of network systems want the CODASYL DBTG proposal [CODASYL DBTG, 1971], with some possible modifications, to become a standard. Such standardization, they argue, will have the same beneficial effect on DBMS's as the standardization of COBOL had on EDP.

2. A group of independents strongly oppose any effort at standardization. They claim that it is too early to impose a standard in an area that is developing as rapidly as DBMS's. They would like to postpone any standardization effort. In this way, the successful commercial DBMS may become a *de facto* standard.

3. Some people prefer the relational model as a basic data model for DBMS's. They cite as advantages simplicity, data independence, etc. These people do not disregard hierarchies or networks for implementation, but simply prefer the user interface to be relational. Although they do not push for standardization, they would like DBMS development to be heavily influenced by the relational model.

4. Some people propose that a different, more flexible model should be the basis for DBMS's. Such a model is proposed as a *coexistence model*. It is a compromise between the hierarchical, network, and relational approaches, being identical to none, but able to accommodate all.

We shall try to avoid taking a particular position. We have our own prejudices which may show in this book; however, we think it would be unfortunate to base the book on a particular approach. We hope that time and maturity will eventually minimize the differences between the proponents of different approaches. At least the air will be cleared of misunderstandings, misconceptions, and differences of terminology which generate much of the controversy. The approaches are not really all that different [Stonebraker and Held, 1975]. In addition, none of them is a panacea. No approach by itself will solve all the problems associated with the design, implementation, and operation of DBMS's. The debate will probably evolve as an argument between efficiency and ease of programming. As such, it reminds one of the old controversy on the merits of different programming languages.

ACKNOWLEDGMENTS

We would like to thank Professor S. A. Schuster, Dr. E. A. Ozkarahan, J. Klebanoff, and all the people in the Data Base Group at the University of Toronto for many stimulating ideas and discussions.

Dr. P. A. Bernstein, Dr. H. A. Schmid, Dr. G. M. Nijssen, Professor W. R. Bezanson, B. Czarnik, M. L. Brodie, B. W. Wade, and J. R. Swenson provided us with many useful comments. Their criticism was helpful in turning a set of lecture notes into a book. We would also like to thank an Academic Press reviewer for his very helpful suggestions and comments.

The DBMS examples in Part II of this book were originally produced by R. Stark, S. Chan, D. Schafheitlin and B. Czarnik. The initial editing was done by J. Klebanoff. We would like to thank T. Cassidy and M. Kallaur for commenting on the original drafts of some of the descriptions. Their suggestions were very helpful in improving the content of the descriptions. We also acknowledge, with thanks, the help of the following organizations: IBM Canada Ltd., MRI Systems Corp., Cullinane Corp., Cincom Systems of Canada Ltd., and R. D. Nickel & Associates.

We would like to acknowledge, with thanks, many interesting discussions with persons at the IBM San Jose Data Base Group and the University of California at Berkeley Data Base Group.

Finally, we would like to thank I. Weber for typing the original draft of this book.

NOTES TO THE INSTRUCTOR

This book grew out of a course on DBMS's given since 1972 at the University of Toronto in the Department of Computer Science. The course is an introductory course aimed at the fourth-year undergraduate and first-year graduate level. It assumes that the student has some understanding of the basic principles of memory management and file organization techniques. In addition, the student should be aware of some basic searching techniques such as hashing, inverted lists, and multilists.

Besides providing students with a conceptual basis for DBMS's, the course also provides "hands on" experience with an educational DBMS. The Educational Data Base System (EDBS) is a DBMS designed and implemented at the University of Toronto. It is written in APL (I. P. Sharp APL level 4) and uses APL as a host language. The implementation is also compatible with APL*PLUS distributed by Scientific Time Sharing Corporation. EDBS is available for distribution from the Computer Systems Research Group of the University of Toronto.

EDBS is actually a family of three DBMS's that provide the user with either a hierarchical, network, or relational data model. Simple exercises, described in the Appendix, allow the user to become familiar with the three systems. The systems are then used to play the various games also described in the Appendix. The games are competitive to generate interest among the players. They also require the player to use a DBMS and thus, hopefully, to become familiar with its particular data model and data language facilities.

The importance of data in the educational world and in the commercial world is very different. Students write programs, considered to be important, and exercise them with token data, considered relatively unimportant. However, in commercial environments, a data base is more important than the programs that access it.

Programs can be replaced; data often cannot. Hopefully, the permanence and importance of the data bases in the games will give the student some appreciation for the importance of data.

The course provides a thorough examination of DBMS concepts, a look at some existing DBMS's, and "hands on" experience with a DBMS. We feel that these three components provide the student who completes the course with a good background in DBMS's. Hopefully, knowing the capabilities and limitations of DBMS's, the student will be able to make more effective and intelligent use of them in real-life data processing situations.

Part 1

DBMS CONCEPTS

Chapter 1

INFORMATION SYSTEMS AND
DATA BASE MANAGEMENT SYSTEMS

1.1 INFORMATION SYSTEMS

Decision-making is an integral part of our lives. Some of the decisions we make are trivial, e.g., what to wear today. Other decisions are much more complex and affect many people, e.g., should production be expanded? To help us make an intelligent decision in a given situation, we require information about the situation. Some people's occupation is supplying information for decision-making. For example, lawyers provide information concerning the law.

It is important to realize the distinction between data and information. *Data* are facts collected from observations or measurements. *Information* is the meaningful interpretation and correlation of data that allows one to make decisions. The data that are used by lawyers to provide information are available to everyone in law books. However, most people are not equipped to extract the information contained in the data. They require synthesis of the data, provided by a lawyer, which results in pertinent information about the law. Thus, even though people often have a great deal of data, they may lack information [Jardine, 1974].

Information is only of value so long as it influences the decision-making process and results in a better decision than would have been made otherwise. To be useful for decision-making, information must be

3

current. For information to be current, the data on which it is based must also be current. For example, a lawyer who dispenses advice based on obsolete laws will soon lose his clients.

To play a useful role in decision-making, data should be captured, processed, and stored so that they are available while still relevant. However, this process involves a cost/benefit trade-off. As the time between capture and availability of the data is reduced, the cost of supplying the data increases. On the other hand, if the time between capture and availability is too great, then the benefit of the data to the final decision-making process is reduced. Thus, it is important for an organization to realize the importance of data to its operation and to deal with it accordingly.

Data are actually one of an organization's three most important assets. The other two are money and people [Heydon, 1974]. The data portray the way an organization's business is conducted and provide information for planning. As such, data greatly influence the operation of an organization. In light of the importance of an organization's data, it is perhaps surprising to discover that it is only recently that many organizations regarded data as a resource at all [Jardine, 1974].

The lack of appreciation for the importance of data is best illustrated by its management in an organization. Whereas money and people are usually handled by distinct departments, data are often consigned to the comptroller's office. However, in some organizations, management of data has recently been recognized as a vital operation. In these organizations management of data is performed by a separate department whose head is often a vice-president who reports directly to the president.

In business, proper management of data, resulting in current, accurate information, can mean money to an organization. Consider the inventory of a manufacturing company. Storage facilities and transportation cost a considerable amount of money. On the one hand, the company tries to minimize the capital committed to its inventory. On the other hand, it should have enough inventory to satisfy the customers' needs. A good inventory control system can provide data on the levels of inventory of each product. These data can be correlated with marketing needs and plans. As a result, production schedules can be planned and orders of raw materials can be placed so as to minimize inventory and costs.

Current, accurate information is essential for the effective operation of an organization. Therefore, it is necessary to have a means of collecting, organizing, storing, and correlating the data, and extracting and distributing the information. A (*management*) *information system* is a means of supplying the information needed by an organization. It is an organized method of providing past, present, and projection information related to internal operations and external intelligence of an organization. It supports the planning, control, and operational function of an organization by furnishing uniform information in the proper time frame to assist in the decision-making process [Kennevan, 1970].

Within an organization, an information system can be used in a variety of ways to perform numerous functions. These functions can range both in scope and in complexity as the following examples illustrate. Some of the functions performed by information systems are

1. Fact retrieval, e.g., how many parts with part number 200 are in stock?
2. Briefing, e.g., how are sales doing?
3. Planning, e.g., how much money do we need to borrow?
4. Decision-making, e.g., if we want 50% growth how can we do it?
5. Design, e.g., display bridge design.
6. Business functions, e.g., payroll, billing, etc.

An organization usually consists of many different components performing various functions, e.g., marketing, manufacturing. An *application system* is the part of an information system that generates the information required to serve a specific component of an organization, e.g., accounting. An *application program* is the part of an application system that uses the processing services provided by an information system to perform a specific function, e.g., accounts payable, accounts receivable. The data needed by application programs and systems are stored in one or more *data bases*. Each application program and system may require the data of several data bases. Therefore, an information system must provide the communication facilities that tie the data bases together into an integrated unit to accommodate all the application systems of an organization [Hanold, 1972; Emery, 1973]. The application systems themselves can be highly integrated, sharing common resources, or only loosely connected. The following example illustrates the facilities of an information system and the functions of its application systems.

The University of Toronto has a system running on an IBM 370/158, for its administration of university affairs [IBM, 1971; University of Toronto, 1973]. The system has one million bytes of main memory and approximately 10 IBM 3330 disks on-line. It handles about 60,000 students in 200 departments and a total annual university operating budget of more than $150 million. The purpose of the system is to integrate all university functions in one information system. The system is designed to handle such requests as

1. a chairman asking for the department budget;
2. a professor inquiring about grants;
3. a registrar setting a program;
4. the comptroller requesting an analysis of the university's portfolios;
5. the government wanting to know statistical information about the staff.

The university information system actually consists of five separate application systems: UNIFACTS, UNISTAFF, UNISTARS, UNISPRING, and UNIMICS.

The University Financial Accounting Transaction System or UNIFACTS maintains all financial data of the university in various ledgers: operating expenditures, income, capital, trust funds, research grants, investments, accounts receivable/payable, and general ledger. The ledgers are updated daily. Detailed monthly statements of all accounts, vendor payments, petty cash, and reimbursements for expenses are produced. On a daily basis, purchase orders are processed and may be rejected due to insufficient funds. Overdrawn accounts are reported for review. Salary commitments are applied to accounts at the end of the month. Monthly statements are produced within three working days, and year-end statements within fifteen working days, with transactions complete to the last day of the period in each case. Various other reports of a statistical and control nature are also supplied. The UNIFACTS data base contains approximately 31,000 accounts.

The University Staff Records System or UNISTAFF maintains, on a daily basis, the personnel information from date of hiring to retirement. Payroll information for the various payroll groups and staff benefit information for approximately 20,000 employees is retained including terminations throughout the year. The system includes various analyses of payroll and personnel information, extraction of data for staff mailings, provision of data for government statistics services, and accommodation of legislative changes. There are two data bases in the UNISTAFF system. One contains the individual staff member records. The other contains information on staff members' accounts in banks, trust companies, etc., where their paychecks are deposited.

The University Student, Applicant and Alumni Records System or UNISTARS maintains personal, statistical, application, and student data on approximately 120,000 present and past students. A large number of output reports and statistics are produced for various internal and external users. The system incorporates various operations throughout the year. Among these are application recording, applicant selection and notification, registration, compulsory and optional course loading, student program preparation, weighted averages calculation, and grade reporting. Teleprocessing inquiry applications include the display of individual student records and the display of course enrollments and program registrants. There are three UNISTARS data bases: one for the individual personal records, one for the university programs in which students are registered, and one for the courses in which students are enrolled. These data bases are interrelated to provide access by program and by course. The UNISTARS data bases contain approximately 145,000 records of individuals, programs, and courses.

The University System for Physical Resources Information Generation or UNISPRING maintains physical resources information on approximately 200 buildings, 30,000 rooms, and 100,000 items of equipment and other fixed assets. Building, floor, and room data are available as well as equipment by class, and replacement and current cash values. The system allows a controlled distribution of assignable space and is the basis of building operating cost allocations. Access to available rooms is provided according to use and function. Reports prepared include building and room profiles, space inventory status reports, equipment revaluation ledgers, equipment confirmation reports, and departmental space profiles. There are six data bases in the system. They contain data on buildings, rooms, departments, fixed assets by class, and use of rooms and buildings.

Finally, the University Management Information and Control System or UNIMICS is a yearly summary system designed to provide executives with "global" information about the university. The system operates on data provided by the four systems—UNIFACTS, UNISTAFF, UNISTARS, and UNISPRING. A cost allocation technique is included in the system. Various reports are provided including Departmental Profile reports, describing a department's operation in the four aspects of finance; staff, students, and space; Program Costing reports; and Service Teaching Matrix reports. In addition, a wide range of special summary analyses are available.

The University of Toronto information system is an example of a fairly large, complex information system. However, information systems range both in scope and size depending on their information-supplying role in an organization. They can supply a very limited set of management reports or a fairly elaborate set of forecasts for planning and controlling an organization's operations. They can support only a few terminals or thousands of terminals. They can be implemented on minicomputers or large processors. For instance, one administrative system required four IBM 360/65's acting as front-ends, two IBM 360/85's doing the actual computations, and 40 IBM 2314 disk sets (each set consists of eight drives). A particular airline reservation system can handle 1200 terminals on-line. In another example, a bank is implementing a system that will handle about 4500 terminals scattered throughout Canada. Another bank plans to implement a distributed system using Digital Equipment Corporation PDP-11's for their extensive banking needs. Other examples of information systems can be found in the literature [Evans, 1973a,c,d; Huhn, 1974].

One of the most distinctive characteristics of an information system is that it is a man–machine system. People are required at the operational level to enter the data and to supervise the processing. At the managerial level, they are required to make the decisions. Although an information system does not necessarily imply computerization, today's computer technology makes information systems based on computers both feasible and cost effective. In addition, the rate at which data and information change makes the speed of computer data processing a necessity for quickly identifying and analyzing changing conditions. The part of an information system that is directly related to computerization is usually referred to as an *(electronic) data processing (EDP)* system.

Because an information system is a man–machine system, one can look at its functions from two viewpoints: the man or user viewpoint and the machine or system viewpoint. From both viewpoints, two broad categories of functions can be identified that are of major importance: data organization and data access. In the next section, some general aspects of data organization and access will be examined from the system's point of view. We will show how the system's view of these functions has changed to support the changing needs of users. Following this section, the rest of the book, except for Chapter 8, concentrates on the general aspects of data organization and access as they relate to the user's point of view.

1.2   DATA PROCESSING SYSTEMS

The objective of an information system is to provide the most accurate and current information available. From the system's viewpoint, the extent to which this objective is realized is sometimes greatly influenced by the data processing system used. To illustrate different approaches, an example application will be outlined and investigated using different data processing systems. The data processing systems are categorized according to the manner in which the data are organized and accessed.

As an example of an application, consider a department store's catalog sales operation. Customers place orders for items in person, at a catalog outlet, or by telephone. What are the data processing needs of this application? First, the orders must be collected in one place and processed. The warehouse must be informed of the order. If the item is out of stock, then the purchasing department must be notified to reorder the item. The customer must also be informed of this situation. If the item is in stock, then a delivery schedule must be established. The accounting department must bill the customer. If the item is to be charged, then the customer's credit must be checked. The marketing department may also have to be informed in order to perform sales analysis and planning. Thus, the data processing function should provide good customer service, maintain adequate stocks of merchandise, facilitate cash flow, and provide planning data, among other things.

1.2.1 Batch Processing

Batch processing is a method of collecting and ordering transactions so that they can be processed efficiently, as a group. Batch processing arises naturally, even in manual systems. For instance, an accountant may process accounts receivable one day, accounts payable the following day, etc. The objective is to collect similar transactions in batches and process them one after the other. This mode of operation is very plausible for data processing by computer, especially in a tape-oriented or sequential file system where the data are also organized in groups by type, e.g., customer billing file. In addition, such a system makes efficient use of the computer, even if this efficiency results in people's inconvenience. In a batch-processing system, the data processing function might be organized as shown in Fig. 1.2.1–1.

Source documents, order forms in the catalog sales application, are all gathered in one place and sorted according to type, e.g., clothing, hardware, toys. The documents are then forwarded to the appropriate store departments for manual processing. The departments validate, code, and prepare the documents for keypunching. This preparation process necessitates a high degree of interaction with manual files to

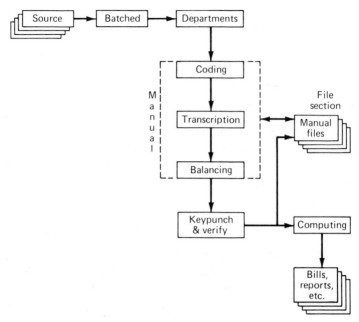

Fig. 1.2.1-1 Manual file batch processing system.

verify transactions and subsequently complete the coding, transcription, and balancing. The departments, in turn, produce new manual files from this process that need to be stored and maintained. The keypunching staff prepares the documents for input to the computer. More interaction with the manual files is sometimes needed to verify data. Finally, the transactions are again grouped, but according to the order in which they are to be run. The transactions are then processed and various reports are produced.

The processing cost per transaction in such a system is relatively low. In addition, many applications, such as payroll and billing, are easily handled since their processing needs are batch oriented. For example, a payroll is produced once a week and can be done all at one time. However, this type of batch-processing system has some disadvantages. A great deal of paperwork is involved in preparing source documents. Many duplicate forms are required to facilitate the distribution of orders to the different departments. The number of manual steps involved in processing source documents often results in a sizable delay between the initial batch step and the time the reports are ready. This can mean a delay of several days to detect, for instance, an out-of-stock condition. The manual nature of the system also makes it susceptible to the introduction of errors. These errors tend to propagate from step to step. As a result, the accuracy of reports produced by the system is often questionable. From a marketing standpoint, this can result in stocking items no longer in demand or a failure to stock high-demand items. Finally, the manual files are difficult to control. At any one time, they can be scattered over many departments resulting in problems of file accessibility, integrity, and security.

The problem of file control and data access can be alleviated by computerizing the manual files. This allows different departments to query the files freely while providing the centralized control necessary to maintain file integrity. However, updates to the files are still batched and are performed after the coding, transcription, and balancing are completed. Also, data entry now can be done during the coding phase. This leads to the batch-processing system illustrated in Fig. 1.2.1–2.

Other advantages of this processing system over the manual-file batch-processing system are that it is more transaction oriented and allows more rapid response for report generation. For example, an out-of-stock condition may be detected in a day or two as opposed to several days previously. It also allows preplanned procedures to be used for data entry and query. Since data entry and query are now comparatively simpler and faster, marketing analysis can be done more easily and inventory levels more closely controlled. However, files must now be readily available. In addition, they should be as up-to-date as possible. These requirements usually result in a higher cost per transaction.

Even with this more elaborate batch-processing system, only some of the problems have been solved. For many types of transactions, the batch nature of processing does not meet an organization's data proces-

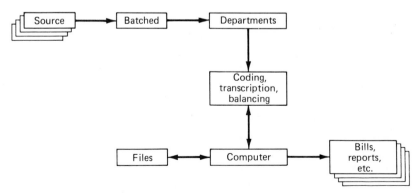

Fig. 1.2.1–2 Computerized file batch processing system.

sing needs! Most departments would like computing assistance at their convenience, not according to machine room schedules. For instance, it is unfortunate that a customer has to wait a day or two to find out that an item is out of stock. It would be nice if the information were available when the order is placed. Similarly, it would be convenient to schedule a delivery date at the same time as the order is placed.

'One of the drawbacks of batch processing is the way data enter the system. Every transaction involves a great deal of paperwork. Data entry consists of many manual steps and, as such, is a very expensive part of the system! For catalog sales, two different kinds of clerks are needed. One clerk writes the sales slip and the other transforms the data on the sales slip into machine-readable form. These two clerks work independently. It is advantageous if these two functions can be merged. In this way the clerk taking the orders enters the sales data for direct use by the processing system.

\ There are two approaches used to provide this service. In the first, called *key-to-tape* or *key-to-disk,* the data entered by the sales clerk are formatted, edited, validated, and stored for later processing. The entire transaction file is then processed later in a batch mode [Evans, 1973b]. In the second approach, called *on-line systems*, the transaction is processed immediately by the computer and no subsequent batch step is required. That is, the clerk is connected directly (on-line) with the data processing system. 'In the next section, on-line systems will be outlined and some of their technical difficulties discussed.

1.2.2   On-Line Processing

Early on-line systems were created mainly for high-return applications such as airline reservations. These systems often consisted of customized hardware, software, and communication links [Parker, 1965; Gray and Blair, 1975]. However, advances in hardware and software have allowed more versatile and flexible on-line systems.

An on-line processing system for the catalog sales application might be organized as shown in Fig. 1.2.2–1. Data are entered directly into the computer at the source, usually via CRT terminals. Queries, and sometimes updates, are done on-line.'The advantages of this system are that much of the paperwork and all the coding involved in data entry are eliminated. Data entry can be performed by sales people or clerks at the source!'Also, errors can be caught at data entry time and corrected on the spot by sales personnel, thereby reducing the processing cycle [Lias, 1974]. The data in such a system are up-to-date, resulting in

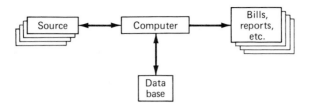

Fig. 1.2.2–1 On-line processing system.

much more effective data processing. For instance, when placing orders, customers interact with a clerk seated at a computer terminal. The clerk enters the order directly via the terminal. Any special condition, e.g., out of stock, can usually be detected immediately. The customer is billed and instructions for delivery are given directly by the system. No further data entry is necessary. In a more technically advanced system the clerks can be eliminated altogether [Canadian Datasystems, 1973]. Customers do their own order entry with the assistance of computer voice output directly through a Touch-Tone telephone. However, such a system lacks the nice human interaction that a clerk can provide for handling special situations.

Although on-line processing provides a very nice data entry and retrieval environment, it has its drawbacks. On-line systems are often very complex due to their need to communicate with, and control, many remote terminals [Huhn, 1974]. Expansion of terminal facilities is often difficult once installed. Similarly, concurrent use of a single resource, the data base, is a complex problem in a multiterminal (user) environment if the data base is subject to modification (see Section 9.4). Therefore, initial applications are usually inquiry only. On-line update, since it is far more complex, is added later, if at all.

On-line systems are often very expensive. Their cost is related, in part, to their complexity. Sometimes this complexity results in installation delays, which in turn result in budget overruns that add to costs. In addition, once an on-line system is installed, conversions become a way of life as installations try to take advantage of new technologies and improve performance.

On-line systems have a tendency of being below performance expectations. Typically, expected response times of 5 sec become 10 sec, etc. This situation is often due to the characteristics and requirements of on-line systems. For instance, CPU utilization is often quite low since on-line systems are heavily I/O bound. In addition, disks must be continuously available to obtain good performance and response time.

'Also, program testing and maintenance is more difficult in an on-line environment since the system must usually be available continuously and therefore cannot be shut down for extended periods.' Finally, recovery often is more complex since the state of all terminal communication must be restored. All these factors add considerable overhead to on-line systems, which can result in performance degradation.

As an illustration of on-line systems and some problems associated with them, consider the following on-line operation for the catalog sales example [Flynn, 1974]. An IBM 360/30 services IBM 2260 terminals in a single thread (one transaction at a time in the system) operation. The CPU constantly polls the terminals for valid ready messages. When a message is received, some editing and error checking is performed before an application program is selected to run. The application program is then given control by the system in order to access the data base, perhaps write some files, log the transaction, and format the answer. The answer then goes back to the user. Typical timings for a transaction can be broken down as follows:

Total message read time	0.5 sec
Total computation time	0.3 sec
Total I/O for data	1.2 sec
Total write response	1.0 sec
Minimum response time	3.0 sec

The timings indicate that the response time is fairly good. For example, with eight terminals, each transmitting a message every 30 sec, the maximum processing time required, within a 30 sec interval, is 8 × 3 or 24 sec. Thus, the system is being used 24 out of 30 sec or 80% of the time. However, suppose the system is now expanded to 12 terminals, each transmitting a message every 30 sec. The message-processing time needed within a 30 sec interval is now 12 × 3 or 36 sec. It should be obvious that it is impossible to service all twelve messages within a 30 sec interval. In addition, more messages will have arrived before the twelfth message in a group is processed. In such a situation, response time usually suffers as the system lags behind in processing the messages.

The preceding timing statistics also show that the CPU is actually used for only 0.3 out of the 3 sec or 10% of the total message-processing time. Thus, even though the system appears to be overloaded in one respect (message handling), it is in fact underutilized in another

(CPU utilization)! It is possible to improve the CPU utilization, and in turn the message-handling capacity of the system, by processing several transactions concurrently, rather than one at a time.

The introduction of a *Telecommunications Access Method* (TCAM), which is a method for accommodating several message processors, is one means of achieving some concurrency (Fig. 1.2.2–2). The message processors run in separate partitions sharing the CPU under the control of a supervisory program. Since there are several partitions, several messages can be processed concurrently. However, other problems now appear. First, the number of partitions available for message handling is usually limited. Also, there is a great deal of duplication of code if the programs are not reentrant. All terminal communication is still done by the CPU. Thus, as the number of terminals increases, the load on the CPU again rises. Eventually, a limit is reached on the number of terminals that the system can handle. In addition, such systems are usually only able to handle one type of terminal [Canning, 1973a; Gray and Blair, 1975].

Another way of achieving some concurrency is to use one or more front-ends. A *front-end* is a second, usually smaller, processor. The front-end relieves the CPU of all tasks related to terminal communication, message error checking, data conversion, etc. [Canning, 1973a; Reside and Seiter, 1974]. With the advent of cheap, reliable mini-computers, which can act as the front-ends, such an approach is becoming increasingly popular. In fact, it is possible to build a complete

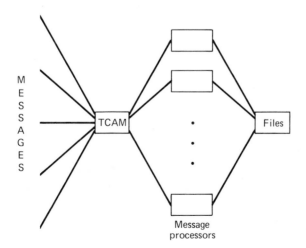

Fig. 1.2.2–2 Multiple-message processor.

data processing system using only minicomputers and a good data communication facility. The next section will outline how front-ends can be used to relieve a central computer of some of the processing load. Such a strategy can eventually lead to a distributed processing system.

1.2.3   Distributed Processing

Early data processing systems were characterized by the centralized nature of their facilities. Centralization of system facilities has been perpetuated by changes in computer architecture, operating systems, data communication, and data storage. These changes increased the versatility and cost effectiveness of centralized computer system configurations. In addition, the growth of on-line systems permitted convenient, remote access to a central facility [Canning, 1973b; Ashenhurst and Vonderohe, 1975]. Some specific advantages that are cited for centralized computer systems are [Canning, 1973b]

1. company-wide consolidation of operating results,
2. best use of scarce, qualified personnel,
3. ease of control of the data processing operation, and perhaps the most persuasive,
4. economies of scale, i.e., it is cheaper to do things in large batches.

For example, in the catalog sales application, all orders can be entered through a central installation. The central installation contains all the computer operations personnel, e.g., keypunch operators, computer operators, systems programmers. The terminals, in all the branch offices, are connected directly to the central installation.

A centralized operation, however, does pose several difficulties. To be able to handle all the local processing variations for various departments, application programs are usually quite large. These large programs present problems for the limited memory size of a given installation. The memory space problem is alleviated to some extent by multiprogramming and virtual memory. These solutions, on the other hand, involve some CPU overhead and thus lost computing power. Since all communication has to flow through the central computer, this can create a bottleneck. The teleprocessing overhead is often considerable. These types of problems are pushing the technological limits of current hardware.

One alternative to a centralized installation is a distributed system. A *distributed system* consists of [Canning, 1973b]

1. distributed processing,
2. distributed communication,
3. distributed data bases, and
4. system-wide rules.

Distributed processing means that the processing of a transaction occurs at its source. The transaction can be completely processed by a local processor or only partially processed. Partially processed transactions are sent to another processor for completion. The local processors are usually minicomputers. Some applications, such as process control, have always required local processing. In addition, applications needing a high degree of interaction with a computer tend toward decentralized facilities [Ashenhurst and Vonderohe, 1975].

Distributed communication consists of a communication network that removes the communication and device control functions from an application program. *Network* will be used here to mean a set of independent processors that are interconnected so as to permit communication and resource sharing. A *node* in the network is an independent processor or processing system. Communication in the network is performed in a standard format with all data conversions done by the individual node processors. Communication is further constrained by the network organization. There are three main ways of organizing a communication network.

A *hierarchical* or *star net* consists of a central node with various levels of minor nodes (Fig. 1.2.3−1) [Ashenhurst and Vonderohe, 1975]. The central node provides operational and developmental services on a shared basis. Each node can operate in stand-alone mode. In addition, each succeeding inner level provides some services that cannot be provided by an outer level. Usually, however, the outer level can provide most of the processing services needed by an application.

A *ring net* consists of a number of equal-capability nodes (Fig. 1.2.3−2) [Farber, 1975]. No single node is absolutely necessary for the operation of the system. Each node is capable of providing the same service as any other node. Therefore, the computing load can be distributed to nonbusy nodes when necessary. Each node can be relatively small and inexpensive. Real-time response is possible since there are usually several processors available.

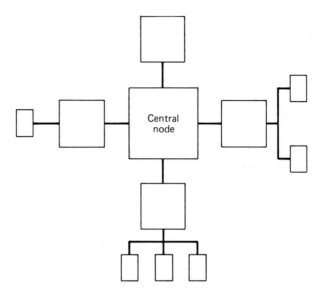

Fig. 1.2.3–1 A hierarchical net.

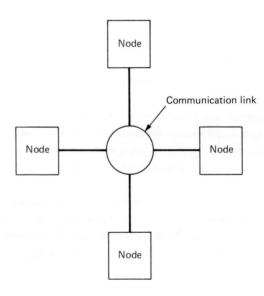

Fig. 1.2.3–2 A ring net.

A *topological net* consists of different-capability nodes (Fig. 1.2.3–3) [Canning, 1971]. Each node usually provides a specific (set of) service(s). One node, or several nodes, may be capable of providing the same service, but each node is not necessarily able to provide every service. A message may have to pass through several nodes to reach a node that is capable of responding to it.

It is possible to mix the various network organizations, e.g., a node in a ring or topological net may be a hierarchical net. In addition, each node can be a different type of processor.

A *distributed data base* is a data base in which the data are geographically distributed. The data reside near the location where their most frequent access occurs. All the data, however, can still be viewed as one data base and are available from all nodes subject to the access constraints of the network.

Although a system is distributed, it is *not* totally decentralized. A system-wide discipline is required and should be enforced at all times. Security, data access, data and program transfer between nodes, resource use, operating procedures, and data base definition are all centrally controlled.

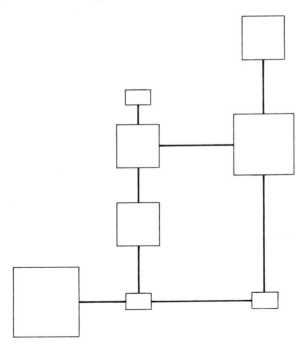

Fig. 1.2.3–3 A topological net. Equal size boxes indicate equal capability nodes.

Returning to the catalog sales application, a distributed system for this example can be organized as a hierarchical net. Each branch office has an intelligent terminal consisting of a CRT display and a small minicomputer system, perhaps only a CPU with a small amount of memory. These intelligent terminals are, in turn, connected to a more sophisticated minicomputer system located in a regional office. Finally, the regional offices are connected to a larger computer installation located at the head office. Each regional office may have a small warehouse where it stocks some items, but not all items. Therefore, some orders can be filled directly from the regional warehouse. Other orders have to be filled from the central warehouse, which is associated with the head office installation. In addition, the regional offices can handle the accounts of the customers in their region. In this way, a great deal of the day to day processing can be done at the regional installation without tying up the central installation. The central installation can be used for overall planning, market research, coordination, etc.

In summary, distributed systems offer an alternative to a centralized operation and have the following advantages [Canning, 1973a; Wulf and Levin, 1975] :

1. familiarity with, and fast response to, local problems;
2. profit–loss responsibility for the local operation;
3. modular growth for new applications;
4. reliability due to local processing capability and dynamic restructuring of resources in case of failure;
5. lower overall vulnerability than centralized systems;
6. incremental modernization since nodes can be changed or added and different hardware used without severely impacting the system.

With the advent of cheap, reliable, and flexible minicomputers and network data communication, the trend appears to be increasingly toward a distributed type of environment for data processing applications. In particular, distributed systems may be very advantageous for organizations that already have many local operations, e.g., large banks with many local bank branches.

1.3   DATA BASE MANAGEMENT SYSTEMS

Section 1.2 considered data organization and access, in an information system, from the system's viewpoint. However, information systems are meant to be used by people. Therefore, they should provide organization of data and access to the data that facilitate interaction with users.

Data, as stored in a data base, have a certain *physical organization* on physical storage media, such as tape or disk. For example, data on disks are stored according to cylinders, tracks, etc. However, the data also have a certain *logical organization* as seen at the user interface of an information system. A *data model* is a set of guidelines for the representation of the logical organization of the data in a data base. It is a pattern according to which the data, and the relationships among the data, can be logically organized. It consists of *named logical units of data* and the relationships among them.

As an example, consider the simple "flat-file" data model. This data model is commonly used in file processing. The data model consists of two logical units of data. A *data item* is the smallest logical unit of data. A *record type* is a collection of data items. For instance, consider employees in an organization and their number, name, address, age, department, skill, and salary. This application can be represented, using the flat-file data model, by the record type EMPLOYEE with seven data items: NUMBER, NAME, ADDRESS, AGE, DEPARTMENT, SKILL, and SALARY.

A data model does not specify the data in a data base. It merely indicates the ways the data may be logically organized and related. For example, the flat-file data model specifies that the data are to be organized according to record types and data items. For the EM-PLOYEE record type, this means that the data on each employee should be grouped to contain values corresponding to an employee's number, name, address, age, department, skill, and salary. An instance of such a group will be called a *record (occurrence)*. The instance of a data item will be called a *data item value*. For example, one EMPLOYEE record and its corresponding data item values might be '999', 'John Smith', '111 Main St.', '30', 'Production', 'Welder', and '250.00'.

Consider now a data base consisting only of the EMPLOYEE record type. Within an organization there may be several application programs using this data base. However, each application may require only part of the data base, i.e., part of an EMPLOYEE record. For example, suppose that part of the data base is required by both the payroll and the personnel departments. However, the payroll department requires only the employee's number, name, department, and salary. On the other hand, the personnel department is interested only in an employee's number, name, skill, and department.

A *view* is part of a data base as seen by an application program. The representation of data in a view is usually according to the data model of the data base. For instance, in the preceding example, the payroll department can define a view consisting of a PAYROLL record type with data items NUMBER, NAME, DEPARTMENT, and SALARY. Similarly, the personnel department can define a view containing the record type PERSONNEL with data items NUMBER, NAME, SKILL, and DEPARTMENT. The PAYROLL and PERSONNEL record types need not be implemented as separate physical storage structures. Instead, they can be defined as a subset of the EMPLOYEE record type and hence of the data base. A view "masks out" those parts of a data base not included in it. For example, an application using the PAYROLL record type would not have access to the data items ADDRESS, AGE, and SKILL. Indeed, the application may even be unaware that these data items exist!

Data models and views are completely logical. That is, no implementation in terms of a physical storage structure is implied. In fact, it is possible to implement the data base, containing the EMPLOYEE record type, in several ways.

One straightforward implementation is to make each record type correspond to a physical file, each record to a physical record in the file, and each data item to a field in a record (Fig. 1.3–1). This organization is rather simple to visualize since the physical storage structure is in one-to-one correspondence with the logical organization.

Another way of physically implementing the data base is to use a *transposed-file* organization (Fig. 1.3–2). In this organization, there is one file for each data item in the record type. Between files, there is a one-to-one correspondence of records. That is, the collection of each *i*th record in all the files corresponds to a record in the record type.

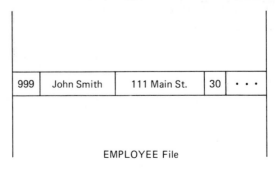

999	John Smith	111 Main St.	30	· · ·

EMPLOYEE File

Fig. 1.3–1 Straight-file implementation.

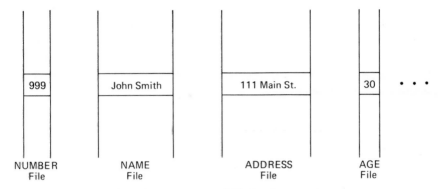

Fig. 1.3—2 Transposed-file implementation.

Such an organization can be useful for fast searches on a particular data item.

A third way of implementing the data base is to use a *data pool* organization (Fig. 1.3—3). In this organization, a record type is represented as a file. However, data item values are not stored directly in the file. Instead, they are stored in separate files, one for each data item in the record type. The records, in the record type file, contain a pointer for each data item. The pointers point to the location of the data item values in the appropriate data item file. Such an organization can be useful for reducing data duplication especially if many data item values occur frequently.

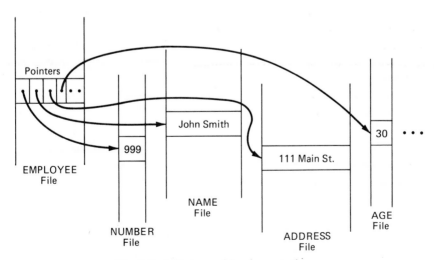

Fig. 1.3—3 Data pool implementation.

It should be obvious from the previous examples that there are many ways to implement a data base physically. In addition, the physical implementation of a data base can be very different from the representation required by the data model of the data base. Similarly, an application's view does not necessarily need to correspond to the physical storage structure of the data. For instance, the PAYROLL record type need not be stored as a physical record. For the preceding implementations, it is possible to write file access routines that convert the physical storage structure of an EMPLOYEE record into the view corresponding to a PAYROLL record. For example, in the straight-file implementation it is a simple matter merely to "mask out" data item values not in the view. The degree to which an application is insulated from the physical storage structure of its view is called _physical data independence_.

Physical data independence is desirable in a data processing environment for several reasons [Guide-Share, 1970; Engles, 1972; Date and Codd, 1974; Everest, 1974]. First, it allows the physical storage structure of the data to be changed without causing reprogramming of applications that use the data. In this way, the physical storage structure can be organized to take advantage of hardware features and usage of the data. However, since an application only sees its view, these changes do not affect it. Second, new hardware technologies can be introduced without causing application reprogramming. Third, data can be shared since different views can be provided for the same physical storage structure. In this way, data duplication is reduced. Fourth, application development is facilitated since applications can be programmed with respect to a view. They do not need to be concerned with physical storage structure or file access. Finally, unauthorized operations, such as update or deletion of data not in a view, can be prevented.

Some implementations of an application's view can defeat physical data independence. Consider an organization's data processing operations. There are usually many applications, e.g., payroll, personnel, sales, inventory, each requiring its own view. The simplest way to provide these views is to permit each application to implement its view directly in a physical storage structure (Fig. 1.3–4). However, such an approach completely defeats physical data independence. Since the physical storage structure for an application is unique to its needs, each application must contain its own file access routines. If the physical storage structure needs to be changed, or if the storage medium technology changes, then an application's file access routines must be

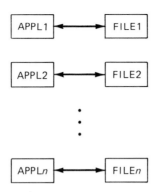

Fig. 1.3–4 Application and file dependence.

rewritten. Data sharing in such an environment is very difficult. All applications utilizing the same physical storage structure must be aware of the physical organization. An application cannot change the physical organization without affecting other applications. Unauthorized operations are difficult to detect since the same data may appear in many different physical organizations.

Each application system usually needs its own view. If there is a one-to-one correspondence between physical storage structure and views, then a proliferation of physical storage structures results. For example, suppose that the PAYROLL records discussed earlier need to be ordered by name and by department within name. On the other hand, the PERSONNEL records need to be ordered by skill and by department within skill. It is obvious that if the PAYROLL and PERSONNEL records are implemented by the same physical storage structure, then it is not possible to order the records physically to satisfy both requirements. In the past, the result was often two files containing essentially the same data, but organized as required by the application. In a typical installation, this proliferation of views requires many active tapes due to data duplication. A complicated application might necessitate from 10 to 50 tape mounts. As an organization accumulates more and more data and requires more and better information, these problems are compounded.

A logical step, therefore, to improve physical data independence, is to limit the number of different physical storage structures containing the same data. Applications are not allowed to define a physical storage structure corresponding to their view. Instead, all views and physical storage structures are defined by a central authority for use by many applications (Fig. 1.3–5). In this way, many views can be defined on

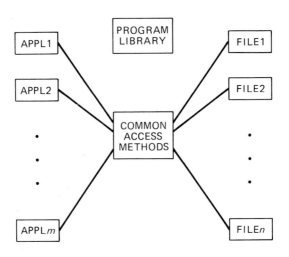

Fig. 1.3–5 File management systems.

the same physical storage structure. Similarly, the file access routines
are removed from the applications and consolidated into access
methods, which are then used by all applications to access data in their
view. Some common data query routines can also be standardized and
placed in a program library. This approach is essentially taken by file
management systems [Evans, 1971; Steig, 1972]. It provides some
degree of physical data independence since changes in physical storage
structure and storage medium technology can be incorporated into the
common access methods without affecting applications. Data sharing is
facilitated and data duplication reduced.

      However, problems remain. Each application still requires the data
structured according to its view. The view, as presented by the access
methods, may not be flexible enough to correspond to the view needed
by an application. Therefore, the application must restructure the data,
once they have been retrieved, to suit its needs. For example, recall that
the EMPLOYEE record type contained seven data items: NUMBER,
NAME, ADDRESS, AGE, DEPARTMENT, SKILL, and SALARY. A
payroll application might only need the NUMBER, NAME, ADDRESS,
DEPARTMENT, and SALARY data items. However, when accessing an
EMPLOYEE record, it must be aware that the AGE and SKILL data
items exist and where they are in the record.

      The ideal solution is to provide each application with its own view,
yet isolate the view completely from its physical storage structure. A
data base management system (DBMS) is a system that provides this

isolation by acting as an intermediary between an application's view and the physical storage structure (Fig. 1.3–6). A DBMS is a set of procedures and data structures that isolates the applications from the details of the creation, retrieval, storage, modification, security, and physical storage structure of computerized data bases. It presents an application with a view, as required by its processing needs, without consideration for the physical storage or access of the data.

The view required by an application may or may not exist as an actual physical storage structure. The important consideration is that no matter how the storage technology changes or how the data are organized or reorganized, the DBMS is always able to provide an application with the same view. How the DBMS materializes the view is irrelevant to an application. An application only requires that, when it asks to look at its data, it always sees them organized according to the same view.

A DBMS can also be considered as extending the amount of data that is accessible within a programming language. For example, suppose one is writing a computer program that at some point requires the salary of an employee. In file processing, the programmer has to know in what file and according to what format the salary is stored. The programmer has to open the file, find and retrieve the pertinent record, isolate the salary field, convert it, and assign it to a program variable. It would be much nicer just to say "Get the salary of John Smith." A DBMS allows one to do this. For example, a program may consist of a series of statements containing a statement of the form

SALARY = GET ('SALARY', 'NAME = JOHN SMITH').

The programming language compiler translates the GET statement into a request to the DBMS. Magically, the DBMS in turn brings in the right

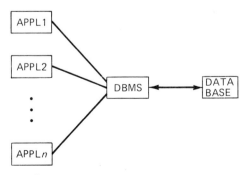

Fig. 1.3–6 Applications and DBMS.

data, in the right format, and assigns it to SALARY. The mechanics behind the GET operation are invisible to the programmer.

From a different viewpoint, all the application programs can be thought of as servants of the DBMS. The data have the central role. If an application program wants to do something with the data, it has to perform two actions. First, the pertinent data have to be isolated. Second, some procedures have to be used to manipulate the data to produce the desired result. The procedures themselves can be stored as data in the data base. In such a situation the data can influence the choice of the procedures.

1.4 CONCLUDING REMARKS

The characteristics and purpose of an information system can be summarized as follows [Murdick and Ross, 1971] :

> The interaction of a group of people, a set of manuals and data processing equipment to select, store, process and retrieve data to reduce the uncertainty in decision-making by yielding information for managers at the time they can most efficiently use it.

To achieve its goal, an information system requires a group of specialized persons. These persons formulate the requests to the system and evaluate the results. In addition, the system incorporates some specialized application programs. The application programs analyze the data and reduce them to a form that is natural for human understanding. However, the most critical part of any information system deals with the definition, storage, selection, and manipulation of the data. The proliferation of data is the main reason for the existence of information systems.

Originally the data of each program were handled individually. However, much duplication of effort and data resulted. In addition, data could not be easily shared among different applications. File systems were introduced to facilitate allocation of the data on physical devices and to permit some data sharing. Some standardized ways of accessing the data evolved in the form of access methods [Tsichritzis and Bernstein, 1974] .

However, all the methods were still based on properties of the physical allocation of data. The user had to understand some of the details of how the data were stored and retrieved. Usually application programs made many assumptions about such physical properties of the data as volume characteristics, record format, and file length. This situation made access to the data feasible only for the sophisticated user. In addition, programs were very dependent on the physical organization of the data. They had to be rewritten whenever files were reorganized. Different programs needed different files even if they accessed essentially the same data but required them organized in different ways.

Generalized DBMS's evolved to facilitate data organization and access. They serve as an interface between the user and the physical copies of the data. Users specify what data they want and in what form. They do not need to specify where the data reside or how to get them. Although a DBMS is by no means a necessity in an information system, it is becoming increasingly clear that a DBMS is required for effective data management in an information system environment.

The rest of Part I expands on the two major functions of DBMS's: data organization and data access. Most of the discussion is from the user's viewpoint. In particular, Chapter 2 discusses data organization in a DBMS environment while Chapter 3 concentrates on data access. Chapter 4 draws together the issues discussed in Chapters 2 and 3 in the context of facilities offered by DBMS's. Chapters 5, 6, and 7 examine specific ways of organizing and accessing data via DBMS's. In Chapter 8, we examine data organization and access in a DBMS from the system's point of view. Finally, Chapter 9 discusses data organization and access as it relates to the operational aspects of DBMS's.

EXERCISES

1.1 Identify a real-world information system where a data base is kept manually. Comment on the feasibility and desirability of implementing the system using a computer.

1.2 Comment on the desirability of producing a business report within

(a) 6 months   (d) 6 hours
(b) 6 weeks   (e) 6 minutes
(c) 6 days   (f) 6 seconds.

Associate some cost and operational characteristics with each time frame.

1.3 Identify three applications with the following properties:

(a) On-line operation is crucial.
(b) On-line operation is advantageous, but cost is crucial.
(c) On-line operation is only marginally advantageous.

1.4 There are three main ways to handle the terminals in an on-line system:

(a) through a software monitor running in the central installation,
(b) through a separate front-end computer, and
(c) through a set of several small front-end minicomputers.

Comment on the advantages of each approach.

1.5 Investigate an on-line data entry system. What problems were associated with the implementation and initial operation of the system?

1.6 Comment on the effect of new technologies in communication networks and trillion-bit mass storage on data base management [Houston, 1973].

1.7 Comment on the relative advantages of a centralized versus a decentralized operation. Concentrate especially on comparing a central versus a distributed data base. Give examples of applications that advantageously use each approach.

1.8 If a telephone, a TV set, and an LSI chip are combined to provide a readily available intelligent terminal in every home, how would you use such a capability?

1.9 Give a set of arguments designed to convince a business manager to take the DBMS approach for his information processing needs [Cuozzo and Kurtz, 1973].

1.10 Give a set of arguments designed to convince a business manager not to take the DBMS approach for his information processing needs.

1.11 Is the DBMS approach only applicable to large organizations? How important and realistic is the approach within a small business environment?

1.12 Very large data bases seem a reality. Isolate some examples of very large data bases. What problems become especially crucial in such an environment?

1.13 In our description of information systems we have concentrated mainly on the facilities they provide. However, an information system is not a panacea. What kinds of problems do you foresee information systems creating both for their implementors and users?

1.14 Information systems can come under attack for concentrating too much power, through the information they provide, in a small, select group of individuals. Do you foresee any social changes or dangers if information systems become all encompassing and powerful? What kind of controls would be necessary?

1.15   Outline the use of powerful information systems in

(a) the political campaign for election in a democratic society,

(b) the application of repressive measures in an autocratic society, and

(c) the organization and promotion of a radical movement.

Chapter 2

DATA MODELS

2.1 INTRODUCTION

This book is concerned mainly with the organization and access of data in computerized data bases from a user's point of view. The organization of the data is represented by a data model. A data model is an intellectual tool used to understand the logical organization of data. To understand data models fully, it is necessary to be aware of how people perceive data. Data can be discerned at several levels [Mealy, 1967; Engles, 1972; Schmid and Swenson, 1975]. At one level, people logically organize their perceptions of the real world. At another level, they interpret (give meaning to) the real world. Finally, they use data models to describe and record the interpretation of the world as data in their computers or perhaps in some other physical medium.

In the real world, one has a perception of the totality of events and occurrences, which corresponds to *reality*. As an aid to thought processes and communication with others, people use *models* of the real world. Within a model of the world, similar things are usually grouped into classes of objects called *object types* [Schmid and Swenson, 1975]. An example of an object type is the class of objects called houses. An object type is described by listing its *characteristics.* For instance, the object type houses has characteristics such as address, color, style, and price. It is possible for an object type to be a characteristic of another object type. For example, address is an object type whose characteristics include street number and street name. However, if the class of houses is added to a model of the world, then address is considered to be a characteristic of the object type houses. Finally, each characteristic can have many *instances*. For example, the style characteristic of houses has instances such as ranch house, bungalow, and duplex. The instances of the characteristics of an object type are generally used to distinguish between different instances of objects within the same object type. That is, the identity of a particular object type is known only insofar as the instances of the characteristics of its object type are given. A set of characteristics that uniquely identifies an object within its object type is referred to as a *key*. For example, if the address of a house can be used to identify each house uniquely, then the address characteristic is a key of the object type houses.

Having decided which object types and characteristics are relevant in a model of the world, it is necessary to place a certain interpretation on the model. The interpretation permits the extraction of *information* from the model of the world. For example, it is necessary to decide whether an object type will exist independently or only as a characteristic of another object type. Object types that have an *independent existence* and can be meaningfully considered *by themselves* are interpreted as *sets of entities* or *entity sets*. For example, the object type houses is an entity set. An entity set is meaningfully described in terms of its *attributes*. For example, the entity set houses is described by attributes such as address, color, and style. Notice that in this interpretation of a model of the real world, the object type address has been interpreted as a characteristic of the object type house and is therefore an attribute of the entity set houses. Address can also be interpreted as an entity set. However, in this case, it is not an attribute of the entity set houses since it has an existence of its own apart from houses. At any one time, an object type can be interpreted as an independent object type or as a characteristic of another object type, but not as both. However, the interpretation can be different at different times.

For each entity set, its attributes have certain values. For example, the color attribute has values such as red, green, and blue. The set of possible values of an attribute is called the *domain* of the attribute. It is possible for different attributes to share a single domain. For example, the attributes house size and lot number both assume values from the domain called nonnegative integers. A set of attributes that uniquely determine an instance of an entity is called a *key*. For instance, the attribute address is a key in the entity set houses, i.e., given a value for address, a house is uniquely identified.

Finally, it is necessary to choose a representation for the interpretation of a model of the world according to the data model provided by a DBMS. A *data model* is a pattern according to which data are logically organized. It consists of named logical units of data and expresses the relationships among the data as determined by the interpretation of a model of the world. One of several data models can be used to represent the interpretation of a model of the world. The main difference between them is the manner in which they represent certain relationships among the data. The next section will discuss, in detail, the types of relationships among data.

2.2 RELATIONSHIPS

Data values, by themselves, say nothing meaningful. A given set of values of house addresses and another of colors, as in Fig. 2.2–1, does not really communicate anything, except perhaps that the addresses and colors exist somewhere. However, if one is informed that the house at 125 Evelyn Ave. is painted red, the house at 4 Bridgetown Dr. is painted blue, etc., the two sets of values immediately convey some information. This information is available because a relationship has been established between the values of address and color.

A *relationship* is a correspondence, or mapping, between the members of two sets. For instance, the correspondence in Fig. 2.2–1 between address and color is given by writing them on the same line. There are many relationships that can be identified in our perception of the real world. For instance, each of "father of," "age of," and "residence of" defines relationships between a person and a person, age, and address, respectively. A relationship may be a 1:1, 1:N or N:M correspondence between the members of two sets. A 1:1 relationship, for example, is the relationship between an employee's personnel num-

address	color
125 Evelyn Ave.	Red
4 Bridgetown Dr.	Blue
190 St. George St.	White
15 Grove Park Cr.	Gray
56 Front St.	Green
101 Avenue Rd.	Yellow

Fig. 2.2–1 Two sets of data.

ber and social insurance number. Each employee has only one unique personnel number and one unique social insurance number. The relationship between an employee's personnel number and salary history is, in general, 1:N. An employee has only one unique personnel number, but may have had several different salaries. Finally, an N:M relationship is that between house color and house price. That is, houses with a certain color may sell at various prices and, similarly, houses at the same price may have various colors.

Consider two sets X and Y as in Fig. 2.2–2. The mapping properties of relationships can be defined formally if each relationship is considered as two mappings fx: $X \rightarrow Y$ and fy: $Y \rightarrow X$. A relationship is 1:1 if both mappings fx and fy are functional. A relationship is 1:N if one of the two mappings fx or fy is functional. A relationship is N:M if neither mapping fx or fy is functional. That is, for each x there can be many y's and vice versa. It is necessary to distinguish between partial functionality and total functionality. A mapping fx is *partially functional* if, for every X member, there is at most one (possibly none) Y member associated with it. A mapping fx is *totally functional* if, for every X member, there is exactly one Y member associated with it. In Fig. 2.2–2a, fx and fy are both totally functional. In Fig. 2.2–2b, only fy is totally functional. In Fig. 2.2–2c, neither fx nor fy is functional.

In our perception of the world, different relationships between entity sets and attributes can be identified. These relationships can be represented by a graph as in Fig. 2.2–3 [Abrial, 1974]. Each node represents an entity set, or an attribute. Each undirected arc specifies a relationship between the sets represented by the nodes. There can be many relationships, each one named explicitly, between nodes. A

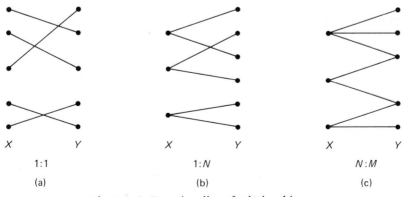

Fig. 2.2–2 Functionality of relationships.

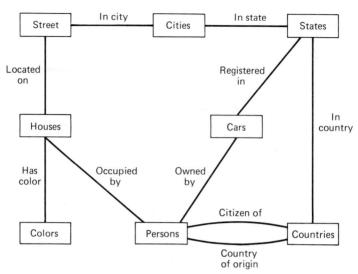

Fig. 2.2–3 Graph of relationships.

relationship can be either 1:1, 1:N, or N:M. There is no distinction as to the nature, meaning, or properties of each relationship.

It is, however, useful to distinguish between two types of relationships. The difference between them can be explained by the following examples [Schmid and Swenson, 1975]. A person's name and social insurance number are usually considered characteristics of the object type persons. They are characteristics since they usually describe a person and are of interest only so long as the person they describe exists. Therefore, a person's name and social insurance number are attributes of the entity set persons. In this case, the relationship between name and social insurance number defines an *attribute relationship, i.e., a relationship between* attributes of an entity set.

On the other hand, suppose that a person is the owner of a house. The house and the person each exist independently, whether or not the house is currently owned by the person. If the person sells the house, both the house and the person still exist although the relationship between them has changed. Therefore, houses and persons are considered as entity sets. In this case, the relationship between houses and persons defines a *relationship between entity sets.* Such a relationship is called an *association* [Schmid and Swenson, 1975]. Associations, since they are themselves relationships, can be 1:1, 1:N, or N:M. For instance, the association "owner" between persons and houses is N:M and can be represented graphically as in Fig. 2.2–4.

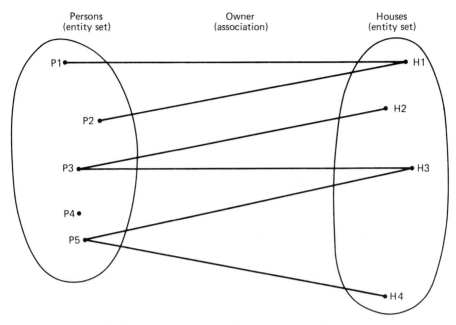

Fig. 2.2–4 An association between two entity sets.

Associations are not very different syntactically from attribute relationships, and sometimes it is difficult to differentiate between associations and attribute relationships. For instance, the relationship "married to" can be considered an association between two independent entity sets men and women. Alternatively, a person's entity set can have a spouse attribute. Thus, the relationship "married to" is represented as an attribute of a person. In any particular situation, people perceive a relationship either as an attribute relationship or as an association. However, this perception can change with time or if a different point of view is taken. After all, the difference between an attribute relationship and an association is a matter of interpretation, and interpretations are not static. In the real world, there may be a real distinction between object types and characteristics. However, when representing ideas about the real world by attributes and entity sets, this distinction is sometimes blurred. In addition, sometimes the representation chosen is dictated by the characteristics of the data model used. As we shall see, it may be necessary or more economical to represent certain relationships as attribute relationships and others as associations.

Attributes

Entities	Address	Color	Style	Price	Size
House 1	125 Evelyn Ave.	Red	Duplex	65,000	12
House 2	4 Bridgetown Dr.	Blue	Bungalow	45,000	6
House 3	190 St. George St.	White	Bungalow	45,000	6
House 4	15 Grove Park Cr.	Gray	Ranch	50,000	8
House 5	56 Front St.	Green	Duplex	65,000	12
House 6	101 Avenue Rd.	Yellow	Bungalow	45,000	6

Fig. 2.2–5 A five-set relationship.

So far, mainly binary relationships, i.e., relationships between two attributes or two entity sets, have been described. In fact, some data models are based on binary relationships [Senko *et al.*, 1973]. However, in general, it is possible to have relationships among the members of n sets. For example, an entity set can have several attributes. The entity set houses can be described by the relationships among the five attributes address, color, style, price, and size as represented in Fig. 2.2–5.

The data models used by DBMS's can be distinguished mainly as to how they represent relationships among data. Most data models handle attribute relationships in similar ways. However, associations are handled in different ways. There are two main approaches: the *network* and the *relational*. The rest of this chapter will present the details of only these two approaches. However, it should be noted that there are other very important data models proposed in the literature, e.g., the entity set data model [Senko *et al.*, 1973] and the set-theoretic data model [Childs, 1968]. In addition, there are some parallel concepts in the different data models [Chen, 1976; Kerschberg *et al.*, 1976].

2.3 THE NETWORK DATA MODEL

The *network data model* is a formal model for representing attribute relationships of an entity set and the associations between the entity sets. The data model consists of *record types* and *links*. Record types are used to represent the relationships among the attributes of an entity set. Links are used to represent the associations between entity sets.

A *record type* is a collection of data items. A *data item* is the smallest unit of logical data. Record types are generic since they represent a set of *record occurrences* consisting of *data item values*. A set of data items is called a *key* if its value uniquely determines an occurrence of a record. Record types allow duplication. That is, distinct record occurrences can be identical in that their corresponding data items have the same value. However, a key as defined here uniquely determines a record occurrence. For instance, consider the record type HOUSES with data items ADDRESS, COLOR, STYLE, PRICE, and SIZE. Assume that ADDRESS is a key. Given a value for ADDRESS, a record occurrence of HOUSES is uniquely determined. Therefore, the values for the data items COLOR, STYLE, PRICE, and SIZE are also determined. There can be no more than one record occurrence with the same value for the data item ADDRESS. The fact that ADDRESS is a key means that no two record occurrences are identical. Thus, if a record type has a key, then no duplication is allowed.

A record type can be used to represent an association. For instance, a record type OWNER can represent the association "owner" between the entity sets persons and houses. The record type OWNER would contain the data items OWNER NAME and HOME ADDRESS. However, while attribute relationships of an entity set are mapped into record types, associations are represented in a different manner.

In the network data model, associations are usually effected by explicit mappings between different record types. A *link* is defined as the representation of an association. In the same way that a record type represents an entity set, a link represents an association between entity sets. While an association is an abstraction corresponding to a perception of the world, a link is a concrete object representing the association in the network data model. For example, the association "owner" between the entity sets persons and houses can be represented by a link OWNER between the record types PERSONS and HOUSES. The link represents the two mappings that define the association between the entity sets houses and persons. One mapping maps houses to persons while the reverse mapping maps persons to houses.

Formally, a *link* L_{ij} defines a connection between two record types R_i and R_j [Tsichritzis, 1975a,b]. That is, for each record x of type R_i the link identifies a set of records (zero, one, or more) of type R_j, which are connected to x. In the opposite direction, for each record y of type R_j the link identifies a set of records of type R_i connected to y. In this way, a link represents an association between the entity sets represented by the record types R_i and R_j.

Links, since they define relationships, can be 1:1, 1:N, or N:M. For instance, the link LIVING IN between the record types PERSONS and

HOUSES is usually 1:N. The link OWNER is N:M if the possibility of joint ownership is considered. That is, each person can own many houses and each house can be owned by many persons. The link BUILT ON between the record types HOUSES and LOTS in a subdivision is usually 1:1. That is, a house occupies one lot and each lot has only one house.

Two kinds of links can be distinguished: information carrying and non-information carrying [Metaxides, 1975; Tsichritzis, 1975b]. *Information-carrying* links represent an association that cannot be expressed as a closed-form property between the attributes of the entity sets. For instance, if there is no OWNER data item in the HOUSES record type, then the link between PERSONS and HOUSES is information carrying. That is, it encodes some extra information not present in the data. On the other hand, if OWNER is one of the data items of the record type HOUSES, then the link between PERSONS and HOUSES is *non-information carrying*. It carries no information since the ownership information is supplied by the presence of a person's name as a data item in both the PERSONS and HOUSES record types.

The connections among the records according to information-carrying links are usually constructed *manually* by selecting records and explicitly connecting them. The connections among the records according to non-information-carrying links can be constructed algorithmically, once the user specifies the property among the attributes that defines the link. Such links are also called *automatic* because the connections can be algorithmically constructed and then automatically maintained.

Consider the relationship graph shown in Fig. 2.3–1. The nodes represent record types and the arcs represent links. All record types and links are explicitly named. In this way, more than one link can be defined between the same two record types. The links, in general, represent N:M relationships and form a network connecting the record types. For instance, the N:M relationship concerning the registration of companies in states can be represented by a link between the STATE and COMPANY record types.

In a general network data model, there are no restrictions on the relationships represented by the links. They can be 1:1, 1:N, or N:M. However, if links correspond only to 1:N relationships, then the arcs in the graph can be directed. The direction of an arc encodes the information about the 1:N (tail : head) direction of the relationship (Fig. 2.3–2). For instance, if a person can be a citizen of at most one

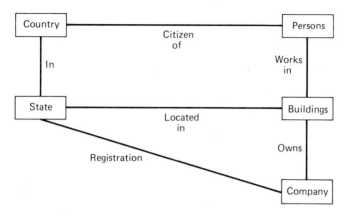

Fig. 2.3-1 A network of record types and links.

country, then the link CITIZEN OF is 1:*N* from COUNTRY to PER-
SONS. This implies that the link in the opposite direction is functional;
each person is a citizen of at most one country. Such a directed graph
representing record types and links is often called a *data structure*
diagram [Bachman, 1969] . The data structure diagram displays permissible connections between records of different records types, as exem-
plified in Fig. 2.3-3. Notice that a new record type REGISTRATION is
used to permit the representation of the *N*:*M* link by two 1:*N* links.
The representation of *N*:*M* links by 1:*N* links will be discussed in more
detail in Chapter 6.

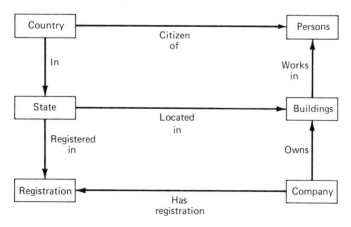

Fig. 2.3-2 A data structure diagram.

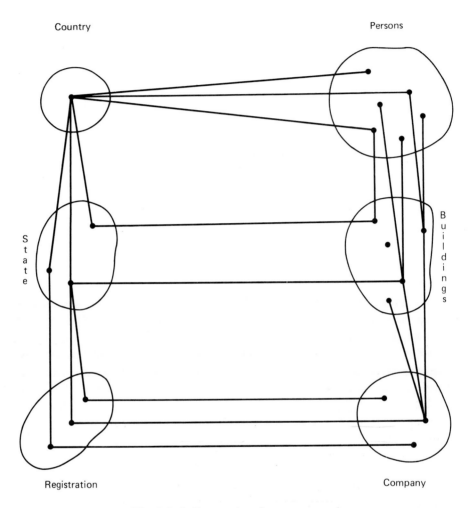

Fig. 2.3—3 Connections between records.

In summary, the network data model consists of a set of record types and links among the record types. The record types represent entity sets and the links represent associations between entity sets. Graphically, the record types and links are represented as nodes and arcs, respectively, in a relationship graph. In general, the relationship graph forms a network. A special case of the network data model restricts the links to be only 1:N. In this case, the links and record types can be represented by a directed graph called a data structure diagram.

2.4 THE RELATIONAL DATA MODEL

The *relational data model* is a formal model for representing relationships among attributes of an entity set and the associations between entity sets [Codd, 1970]. Consider a set of domains $S_1, S_2, \ldots, S_n$ (not necessarily distinct). R is a *relation* on these n sets if it is a set of *n-tuples* or simply *tuples* each of which has its first element from S_1, its second element from S_2, and so on. More concisely, R is a subset of the Cartesian product $S_1 \times S_2 \times \cdots \times S_n$. The set S_j will be referred to as the jth domain of R. As defined above, R is said to have *degree n*. Relations of degree 1 are often called *unary*, degree 2 *binary*, degree 3 *ternary*, and degree n *n-ary*. Figure 2.4–1 illustrates four relations, of different degree, corresponding to the entity sets courses, persons, and houses, and the association owner between persons and houses.

A relation represents an entity set both in terms of its *intension*, i.e., the entity set name, its attributes, and their properties, and in its valid *extension*, i.e., the possible values that the attributes may have. In addition, a data base relation is time varying. For instance, the entity set that the relation represents normally changes over time since entities are inserted, deleted, and modified. The time-varying nature of data base relations is one important aspect in which they differ from mathematical relations.

An *n*-ary relation can be represented as a table [Codd, 1970; Date, 1972a]. Each column of the table, called an *attribute*, corresponds to a domain of the relation. Each row corresponds to an *n*-tuple. For instance, if a relation represents an entity set, each column will correspond to an attribute and each row to an entity of the entity set. In addition, the ordering of the rows is immaterial and all rows are distinct, i.e., an entity cannot appear more than once in the table. These properties are immediate consequences of the fact that a relation is a set. Normally the ordering of columns is significant, representing as it does the ordering of the underlying domains. However, if each column is labeled with the name of its corresponding domain and

Unary relation	COURSES (SUBJECT)
Binary relation	PERSONS (NAME, ADDRESS)
Ternary relation	HOUSES (ADDRESS, PRICE, SIZE)
Binary relation	OWNER (PERSON NAME, HOUSE ADDRESS)

Fig. 2.4–1 Relations of different degrees.

referred to by this name rather than its relative position, then the ordering of the columns is also insignificant.

To ensure unique identification of an attribute (column), attribute names within relations must be unique. However, a difficulty arises when two or more attributes of a relation take their values from the same underlying domain. In the resulting relation, two or more attributes then have the same name. In such a situation the distinct *roles* played by each attribute can be distinguished by prefixing each appearance of the common attribute name with a distinct *role name*. In this way, attribute names of the relation remain unique. For example, consider the relation

   BUILDINGS (ADDRESS, MORTGAGE, MORTGAGE).

The meaning of BUILDINGS (X, Y, Z) is that the building at address X has two mortgages on it—a first and a second mortgage. The names FIRST and SECOND can be prefixed to MORTGAGE to form the relation

   BUILDINGS (ADDRESS, FIRST MORTGAGE, SECOND MORT-
       GAGE).

The prefixes identify the roles played by MORTGAGE in its two distinct appearances.

Normally the values of some subsets of the attributes of a relation uniquely identify each tuple of that relation. A *key* K of a relation R is a subset of attributes of R with the following time-independent properties [Codd, 1972a] :

P1. Unique Identification. In each tuple of R the value of K uniquely identifies that tuple.

P2. Nonredundancy. No attribute in K can be discarded without destroying property P1.

Obviously there always exists at least one key because the combination of all attributes of R possesses property P1. It is then a matter of looking for a subset with property P2 [Fadous and Forsyth, 1975]. A *prime attribute* of a relation R is any attribute that participates in at least one key of R. All other attributes of R are called *nonprime*.

So far, relations have been described in their capacity for representing attribute relationships. However, as shown in Fig. 2.4—1, an association can also be viewed as a relation in the same way that relationships among attributes are viewed as relations. For example, consider the association "owner" between the entity sets persons and houses. The entity sets persons and houses can be represented by the relations PERSONS and HOUSES, respectively. The association "owner" can be represented by another relation as follows. Two keys can be isolated from the relations PERSONS and HOUSES. Let PERSON NAME and HOUSE ADDRESS be the two keys. These attributes can now be used to form another relation, OWNER, which represents the association between entity sets persons and houses. The tuple (John Smith, 111 Main St.) in the new relation OWNER defines an association between a person and a house that the person owns.

In the relational data model all attribute relationships and all associations are represented as relations. There is no distinction, at least at the data model level, between different kinds of relations. Syntactically, all relations are the same. However, the data model does not preclude the introduction of additional semantic information to distinguish different relations according to their properties or intension.

2.5 NORMALIZATION

Suppose one is given some object types, and characteristics and relationships among them. That is, suppose one has to represent some part of the real world. How does one choose the appropriate relations? It would be nice if the relations represented the real world situation, the representation were efficient, and the data remained consistent. The same question can be asked with respect to the network data model. How does one choose the appropriate record types and decide which relationships will be represented by links? In both cases, the determining factors are the properties of the object types, characteristics, and relationships. In the sequel, these properties will be expounded and their impact discussed according to the relational data model. However, similar ideas apply to the network data model.

The problems encountered in choosing relations from a model of the world stem from the fact that the value of one attribute in a relation can completely determine the value of other attributes [Codd, 1972a]. Such relationships among attributes make it undesirable to group certain attributes together in one relation. Suppose that the value of the attribute BUILDER determines values for the attributes STYLE and PRICE and that the value for the attribute STYLE determines the

value for PRICE. Grouping these attributes together in the relation
HOMES1 (BUILDER, STYLE, PRICE) has several undesirable properties [Codd, 1972a; Heath, 1971].

First, the relationship between style and price is repeated in the
relation for each builder who builds a particular style of home. This
repetition creates difficulties. If a builder who happens to be the last
builder of a certain style home is deleted from the relation, then the
relationship between the style and its price also disappears from the
relation. This is called a *deletion anomaly*. Similarly, if a new builder
who happens to be the first builder of a certain style home is added,
then the relationship between a style of home and its price will also be
added, even though this was not the purpose of the insertion. This is
called an *insertion anomaly*. Such insertions and deletions are anomalous
because most such operations will not produce these side effects on the
style–price relationship. These anomalies are undesirable since the user
is not likely to realize the consequences of the insertion or deletion.
The user may inadvertently affect a relationship that was not intended
to be modified.

A second problem with this grouping is the effect of updates on the
consistency of the relation. An update may jeopardize consistency in
the following way. Suppose that the relationship between a style and its
price is changed, e.g., the price is increased. To maintain the consistency of the relation, the new style–price relationship should be
included for every builder of the style. A naive user may simply change
the relationship for only one builder. In a simple system this will be
inadequate for maintaining a consistent relation. A sophisticated
system, which understands the meaning of the builder–style–price
relationship, could make the proper inference and update the relationship for all builders of the style. In the latter case, it may still be ambiguous where a user's responsibilities begin and end in maintaining a
consistent relation [Bernstein, 1975].

Consistency and insertion/deletion anomalies are not problems
affecting all groupings of attributes. If the relation HOMES1 (BUILDER,
STYLE, PRICE) is normalized, then the consistency and anomaly
problems disappear. *Normalization* is a step-by-step reversible process
of replacing a given collection of relations by successive collections in
which the relations have a progressively simpler and more regular
structure [Codd, 1971a]. The simplifying process is based on nonstatis-
tical criteria. The reversibility guarantees that the original collection of
relations can be recovered and therefore no information has been lost.

The objectives of normalization are [Codd, 1970; Codd, 1972a] :

   1. to make it feasible to represent any relation in the data base;

   2. to obtain powerful retrieval algorithms based on a simpler collection of relational operations than would otherwise be necessary;

   3. to free relations from undesirable insertion, update, and deletion dependencies;

   4. to reduce the need for restructuring the relations as new types of data are introduced;

   5. to make the collection of relations neutral to the query statistics, where these statistics are liable to change as time goes by.

The first two objectives apply only to the first step (conversion to first normal form). The last three objectives apply to all normalization steps.

First normal form or *1NF* relates to the structure of the relation. Essentially, it requires that every attribute of a relation be based on a simple domain, i.e., a domain consisting of single, simple values.

First Normal Form (1NF). A relation is in 1NF if every attribute in the relation is based on a simple domain.

Consider the relation

HOMES (BUILDER, MODEL)

If MODEL is the relation MODEL (STYLE, PRICE) and a builder builds several model homes, then the HOMES relation violates 1NF. The relation can be represented as the 1NF relation

HOMES1 (BUILDER, STYLE, PRICE)

Any relation can be put into 1NF algorithmically by replacing a nonsimple domain by its constituent simple domains.

As mentioned previously, the problems in choosing relations from a model of the world are strongly tied to the fact that the values of some attributes completely determine the values of other attributes in a relation. This fact will be formalized as the concept of functional dependency. In order to do this, some terminology and notation will have to be introduced. The casual reader may wish to skip the rest of this section in order to avoid the more theoretical aspects of normalization.

Let A and B be attributes of a relation, let DOMAIN(A) be the domain of A and DOMAIN(B) be the domain of B, and let f be a time-varying function such that f: DOMAIN(A)→DOMAIN(B). In the precise mathematical sense, f is not a function because it is allowed to change over time in the same sense that data base relations are allowed to change over time. That is, if f is thought of as a set of ordered pairs $\{(a,b) \mid a$ in DOMAIN(A) and b in DOMAIN(B)$\}$, then at every point in time, for a given value of a in DOMAIN(A), there will be at most one value of b in DOMAIN(B). To distinguish f from a mathematical function, it is called a *functional dependency*. For notational convenience, the word DOMAIN is generally omitted and the notation f: A→B is used. If there is a functional dependency f: A→B, then B is said to be *functionally dependent* (or simply *dependent*) on A, and A is said to *functionally determine* (or simply *determine*) B. When there is only one functional dependency from A to B the notation A→B, i.e., A functionally determines B, is used as an abbreviation. The notation $A \not\to B$ means that there is no functional dependency between A and B. If both A→B and B→A hold, then at all times A and B are in 1:1 correspondence, and the notation A↔B is used.

Let f: $A_1, \ldots, A_n$→B and g: $A_1, \ldots, A_m$→B where $m < n$. Furthermore, assume $f(a_1, \ldots, a_n) = g(a_1, \ldots, a_m)$ for all a_i in A_i, $1 \leqslant i \leqslant n$. That is, the attributes $A_{m+1}, A_{m+2}, \ldots, A_n$ are extraneous in f. In this case, B is said to be *partially dependent* on $A_1, \ldots, A_n$. If there is no g with the above property, then B is *fully dependent* on $A_1, \ldots, A_n$. That is, there are no extraneous attributes in f. Partial dependencies can cause insertion/deletion anomalies and consistency problems. The second normalization step, conversion to *second normal form* or *2NF*, removes partial dependencies of nonprime attributes on keys.

Second Normal Form (2NF).   A relation R is in 2NF if R is in 1NF, and each nonprime attribute in R is fully dependent upon every key.

Given the relation (keys underlined)

HOUSES (ID, ADDRESS, LOT#, SUBDIV#, STYLE, BUILDER)

for a particular geographical area, there may be the following functional dependencies:

ID→ADDRESS	ADDRESS→ID	LOT#, SUBDIV#→ID
ID→LOT#	ADDRESS→LOT#	LOT#, SUBDIV#→ADDRESS
ID→SUBDIV#	ADDRESS→SUBDIV#	LOT#, SUBDIV#→STYLE
ID→STYLE	ADDRESS→STYLE	LOT#, SUBDIV#→BUILDER
ID→BUILDER	ADDRESS→BUILDER	SUBDIV#→BUILDER

In the HOUSES relation, the keys are <u>ID</u>, <u>ADDRESS</u>, and <u>LOT#, SUBDIV#</u>. The nonprime attributes are STYLE and BUILDER. The key LOT#, SUBDIV# has the functional dependency LOT#, SUBDIV#→BUILDER. However, it is also true that SUBDIV#→BUILDER. Thus, BUILDER is only partially dependent on LOT#, SUBDIV#. The relation is therefore not in 2NF. To place the HOUSES relation into 2NF, it is split into two relations:

HOUSES1 (<u>ID</u>, <u>ADDRESS</u>, <u>LOT#, SUBDIV#</u>, STYLE),
CONTRACTOR (<u>SUBDIV#</u>, BUILDER).

Access to the builder information is still possible from the HOUSES1 relation through the SUBDIV# attribute common to both relations. For example, to determine the builder of a certain house, the SUBDIV# attribute value is obtained from the appropriate tuple in the HOUSES1 relation. This value is then used to search the CONTRACTOR relation and determine the corresponding builder. Notice that it is possible to keep information about a builder for a subdivision independent of the HOUSES1 relation. This capability eliminates one of the insertion anomalies discussed earlier. Namely, in the HOUSES relation, the relationship between a builder and a subdivision was established as a side effect of inserting the first HOUSES tuple for a subdivision. Now the relationship between a builder and a subdivision is established explicitly as a result of inserting a tuple into the CONTRACTOR relation, and not as a side effect of an insertion into the HOUSES1 relation.

The next normalization step converts relations to *third normal form* or *3NF* by eliminating transitive dependence of nonprime attributes on keys. Suppose that A, B, and C are three subsets of attributes of a relation R (hence R is of degree three or more). Suppose further that the following time-independent conditions hold:

$$A \rightarrow B, \quad B \nrightarrow A, \quad B \rightarrow C, \quad A \rightarrow C, \quad C \nrightarrow A.$$

The entire set of conditions on A, B, and C can be represented by Fig. 2.5–1. Note that $C \rightarrow B$ is neither prohibited nor required.

If the above conditions hold then C is *transitively dependent* on A under R. In the special case where $C \rightarrow B$ also holds, both B and C are transitivity dependent on A under R [Codd, 1972a].

Transitive dependencies also lead to the insertion/deletion anoma-

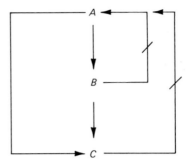

Fig. 2.5–1 Transitive dependence of C on A.

lies and consistency problems mentioned earlier. Recall the relation

HOMES1 (<u>BUILDER</u>, STYLE, PRICE).

Diagrammatically the dependencies are as shown in Fig. 2.5–2.

At a given point in time, the relation HOMES1 might contain the data shown in Fig. 2.5–3. Consider now the problem of changing the style of house that is built by a builder. A naive user may simply change the value of the STYLE attribute for a builder. However, this is not enough since there is a relationship between a style and its price. Normally, the value of the PRICE attribute also has to be changed. If it is not, then the data base will show an inconsistency.

Consider also the problem of inserting and deleting tuples. If a new HOMES1 tuple is inserted for a new style home, then the relationship between style and price is also created. Similarly, if a builder is deleted from the HOMES1 relation, and if this is the last or only builder of a particular style, then all information about the particular style–price relationship is also deleted.

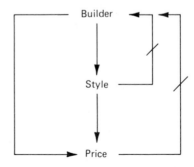

Fig. 2.5–2 Example of transitive dependence.

HOMES1 (<u>BUILDER</u>   STYLE   PRICE)

CADILLAC	Duplex	65000
DELZOTO	Duplex	65000
HOWLETT	Bungalow	45000
JOINT	Ranch	50000
METRO	Bungalow	45000
MONZA	Duplex	65000
TEREX	Ranch	50000
WIMPEY	Ranch	50000

Fig. 2.5-3 Instance of HOMES1 relation.

These problems arise because the dependency of price on builder can be derived indirectly due to the dependencies BUILDER→STYLE and STYLE→PRICE. The transitive dependency of BUILDER on PRICE can be eliminated by splitting the HOMES1 relation into the two relations

HOMES2 (<u>BUILDER</u>, STYLE),   COST (<u>STYLE</u>, PRICE).

These two relations cannot contain any transitive dependencies since they are each only of degree two. The example of Fig. 2.5-3 would now be as shown in Fig. 2.5-4.

The price now appears only once for each style. No information has been lost since the price of a style of house can be obtained by using the style value from the HOMES2 relation to access the COST relation. Both the HOMES2 and COST relations are in 3NF.

Third Normal Form (3NF). A relation R is in 3NF if R is in 2NF, and no nonprime attribute of R is transitively dependent on any key of R.

Any relation in 3NF has the property that every nonprime attribute of the relation is neither partially dependent nor transitively dependent

HOMES2 (<u>BUILDER</u>   STYLE)   COST (<u>STYLE</u>   PRICE)

CADILLAC	Duplex	Bungalow	45000
DELZOTO	Duplex	Duplex	65000
HOWLETT	Bungalow	Ranch	50000
JOINT	Ranch		
METRO	Bungalow		
MONZA	Duplex		
TEREX	Ranch		
WIMPEY	Ranch		

Fig. 2.5-4 Relations in third normal form.

on any key. This means that the nonprime attributes are independent of each other. If a value of a nonprime attribute is changed, this does not have any undesirable side effects as discussed previously. Note that only nonprime attributes of R need have these properties. Third normal form does not exclude prime attributes from exhibiting partial and transitive dependencies. It has been found that partial and transitive dependencies among prime attributes can also lead to consistency and update problems [Kent, 1973]. To eliminate these problems, the statement of 3NF has been reformulated to avoid reference to the concepts of prime attribute, full dependency, and transitive dependency [Codd, 1974b].

Boyce Codd Normal Form (BCNF). A relation R is in BCNF if it is in 1NF and, for every set of attributes C of R, if any attribute not in C is functionally dependent on C, then each and every attribute in R is functionally dependent on C.

This means that all attributes not in a key are independent of each other. In addition, all keys are independent of nonprime attributes and fully dependent on each other.

If a relation is in BCNF, it immediately follows that it is in 3NF. This consequence is due to the exclusion by definition of partial and transitive dependencies of any attributes (prime or nonprime) on a key. In addition, there are some examples of relations that are in 3NF, but not in BCNF [Date, 1975; Bernstein, 1975].

For example, consider a modified set of functional dependencies describing part of the HOUSES2 model shown in Fig. 2.5−5. Suppose that contracts are awarded to builders in various subdivisions. Within any subdivision a builder's contract specifies that only one style of house be built by the builder. Suppose further that for each subdivision in which a builder has a contract, the builder charges a fixed price per house. Also the price charged determines the subdivision. That is, a builder charges different prices for the same style house for each subdivision in which the builder has a contract. Now the relation HOUSES2 in Fig. 2.5−5 is a 3NF relation describing this small model.

BUILDER, SUBDIV#→STYLE
BUILDER, SUBDIV#→PRICE
PRICE→SUBDIV#

HOUSES2 (BUILDER, SUBDIV#, PRICE, STYLE)

Fig. 2.5−5   Relation in 3NF but not in BCNF.

However, something is amiss. The attribute SUBDIV# is now transitively dependent on the key BUILDER, SUBDIV# since BUILDER, SUBDIV#→PRICE, PRICE↛BUILDER, SUBDIV#, and PRICE→ SUBDIV#. Since SUBDIV# is prime, this is not a violation of 3NF, although it does violate BCNF. Nevertheless, this transitive dependency does create certain problems.

Suppose the price a builder charged in an old subdivision is also to be charged in a new subdivision, i.e., the PRICE→SUBDIV# dependency is modified. One might naively look for the BUILDER, SUBDIV# combination where the price used to occur, and change the SUBDIV# appropriately. This action, of course, is incorrect. First, the style of house assigned to the price's old BUILDER, SUBDIV# will automatically be assigned to the new one. This inference is improper. Second, it is possible that there are now two tuples, each with identical values for the key BUILDER, SUBDIV#. This whole problem resulted from the fact that the value of SUBDIV# for a given PRICE cannot be freely changed, even though the functional dependency PRICE→ SUBDIV# suggests that it is all right to do so.

A closer examination of BCNF can give us an alternative justification for normalized groupings of attributes [Bernstein, 1975]. In a BCNF relation R, every functional dependency in R must be of the form $K→A$, where K is a key and A is any attribute. The following can be asserted:

1. All nonprime attributes must be fully dependent on each key.
2. All prime attributes must be fully dependent on all keys of which they are not a part.
3. No attribute (prime or not) can be fully dependent on any set of attributes that is not a key.

All three restrictions follow directly from the definition of BCNF.

Since each key is fully dependent on every other key, the keys are functionally equivalent. That is, for every pair of keys there is a bijection, i.e., functions in both directions connecting them. By the first and last restrictions, all nonprime attributes are dependent only on the keys. Now, assume that a value for a nonprime attribute is altered in some tuple. Since the only functional dependencies that exist for that attribute are those mapping a key into that attribute and since each key value is unique within the relation, there can be no other tuples that are affected by the update. Thus, the value of each nonprime attribute in a tuple is independent with respect to all other tuples.

Prime attributes have no identity of their own within functional dependencies, but rather exist only as part of some key. Altering the value of a prime attribute in a tuple is therefore equivalent to altering the value of a key. Now assume that a value for a prime attribute is altered in some tuple. Equivalently, it can be assumed that a key value for that tuple has been altered. However, since all keys are by definition distinct, this change can only affect the tuple whose key value was changed. All other tuples have key values different from the one that was altered and therefore cannot be affected.

An example where such an alteration can matter will illustrate the point. Let $AB{\rightarrow}C$ and $B{\rightarrow}D$ be functional dependencies in the relation $R(A, B, C, D)$. AB is the only key for R. If a value of B is changed in one tuple, this changes the key for that tuple. However, it is possible that some other tuple is affected, since some other key value may have the same value of B as the one that was altered. If $B{\rightarrow}D$ is replaced by $AB{\rightarrow}D$, the problem disappears. Changing a value of B is now equivalent to changing the key value. Since no other tuple can have the same key value, then no other tuple can be affected.

It has been informally shown that an update to the value of any attribute in a BCNF relation affects only the tuple that was updated. Equivalently, all tuples are independent. Intuitively, one should be able to recognize that the independence of functional relationships in a BCNF relation makes it relatively easy to change values in one relationship without affecting others [Bernstein, 1975]. Figure 2.5–6 summarizes the normalization process.

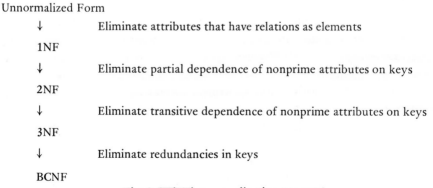

Unnormalized Form
    ↓   Eliminate attributes that have relations as elements
    1NF
    ↓   Eliminate partial dependence of nonprime attributes on keys
    2NF
    ↓   Eliminate transitive dependence of nonprime attributes on keys
    3NF
    ↓   Eliminate redundancies in keys
    BCNF

Fig. 2.5–6 The normalization process.

2.6 CONCLUDING REMARKS

Most DBMS's handle attribute relationships in similar ways, through record types or relations. However, the associations among entity sets can be handled with different mechanisms. These mechanisms are used to distinguish among the network and relational data models. Hence, DBMS's may be characterized by the mechanisms provided for representing associations [Fry and Sibley, 1976]. There are two main approaches, the *network* approach and the *relational* approach [Chamberlin, 1976; Taylor and Frank, 1976]. In the network approach, there is an explicit mechanism, links, for representing associations. This approach appears in most existing commercial systems [CODASYL, 1969; CODASYL, 1971]. An historic reason for its widespread use is that it evolved quite naturally from files representing record types and the ability to cross-link them.

The network approach can further be subdivided according to the restrictions on links. In almost all commercial network systems, the links are functional, at least in one direction. That is, the links are restricted to be $1:N$. However, for many systems further restrictions are imposed that enable the links between record types to be structured in a *hierarchical* fashion [Tsichritzis and Lochovsky, 1976]. Such systems are called hierarchical systems and will be discussed in detail in Chapter 5. The other network systems, which do not have the restrictions of hierarchical systems, will be discussed in detail in Chapter 6.

The relational approach uses relations to represent both attribute relationships and associations among entity sets. Relational systems themselves may use different mechanisms to implement different relationships, but such differences are transparent to the user. The user sees only relations, although semantically they may represent quite different relationships. Relational systems will be discussed in Chapter 7.

EXERCISES

2.1 There are two kinds of relationships between objects. One refers to attributes of the same entity set, e.g., house color and house address. The other refers to associations among entity sets, e.g., between houses and persons [Schmid and Swenson, 1975]. Try to formalize this distinction.

2.2 Investigate and compare different data models that portray the relationships between objects and their semantics. For instance, the DIAM model [Senko *et al.*, 1973], the relational model [Codd, 1970], Abrial's binary relation model [Abrial, 1974], and semantic networks [Schmid and Swenson, 1975; Roussopoulos and Mylopoulos, 1975].

2.3 Consider a link between two record types. The link can be 1:1, 1:*N*, or *N:M*. Comment on the relative difficulty of implementing a link in each case.

2.4 A link can be defined using an explicit property, for instance, between a HOUSE and a PERSON record if the person's name is the owner of the house. Comment on the desirability of maintaining such a link through an intermediate structure of pointers.

2.5 Given a relation explicitly as a table, outline an algorithm that obtains all the keys of the relation.

2.6 Consider a relation R. Show that

(a) The collection of attributes of R in a key K is a maximal functionally independent set, i.e., every proper subset of the attributes of K is functionally independent of every other proper subset of the attributes of K, and no other attributes of R can be added to K without destroying this functional independence.

(b) A maximal functionally independent set of attributes is not necessarily a key.

2.7 Consider files of records in the conventional sense. Are normal form ideas applicable in organizing the files and if so, in what ways?

2.8 Consider a data model allowing only binary relations among domains. Discuss the relative advantages of such an approach including ideas related to normalization.

2.9 Give specific algorithms to put a set of relations in 1NF, 2NF, 3NF, and BCNF.

2.10 Consider a set of domains { $A,B,C,D, \ldots$ } and functional dependencies relating them. Give algorithms to construct a set of 3NF or BCNF relations that incorporate all the given functional dependencies.

2.11 Consider the following relations and the functional dependencies among the attributes. Are the relations in 1NF, 2NF, or 3NF? Convert all relations to 3NF by following the normalization steps outlined in Section 2.5. Is the resulting set of relations also in BCNF? If not, convert them to BCNF.

(a) Relations   (b) Relations
     R1 (A, B, C, D) R1 (A, B, C, D, E)
     R2 (A, B, E) R2 (A, C, F)
     R3 (A, C, D, F)

     Functional Dependencies   Functional Dependencies
     $A{\to}B$ $A{\to}BC$
     $AC{\to}D$ $A{\to}D$
     $A{\to}E$ $A{\to}E$
     $B{\to}CD$ $AC{\to}F$
     $D{\to}F$ $BC{\to}E$
                                              $C{\to}E$
                                              $C{\to}A$

2.12 Consider a network of record types and links. Design an algorithm that will construct a set of relations that capture the same information. Handle information-bearing and non-information-bearing links separately. Prove that your algorithm captures all the information represented by the record types and links.

2.13 A certain property of a relation can be given in its definition (intension), or be present in the data representing the relation (extension). Discuss the difference of having functional dependencies, keys, normalization, etc., defined according to the intension or the extension of the relation involved.

Chapter 3

DATA LANGUAGES

3.1 INTRODUCTION

The data bases for an application are organized according to a data model as discussed in Chapter 2. The access to the data bases is provided by a data language. A *data language* is a set of operations that permit access to the data, as organized by a data model. The data language operations fall into two broad categories: retrieval and modification. Retrieval operations are concerned with obtaining data values or data relationships stored in a data base. Modification operations are concerned with changing the data values or data relationships of a data base. The data language features do not necessarily have to correspond to the physical access mechanisms of the DBMS.

A DBMS can be classified according to the way it provides a data language. A *host data language* is embedded in a host programming language, usually PL/1, COBOL, or an assembler language. In such systems, the data language is called a *data manipulation language* (DML) or a *data sublanguage* (DSL). The DML or DSL consists of a set of commands (operations) that can be issued from within a program written in the host language. Either a preprocessor or the programming language compiler interprets these commands as calls to the DBMS. During execution, the call is serviced in the environment of the DBMS, and the data are returned in the environment of the programming language. The commands can be either an integral part of the host

58

programming language or they can take the form of a procedure call with a list of parameters.

A *self-contained data language* is a complete programming language for both obtaining and manipulating data from a data base. The programming language exists only to support the data language. English-like, self-contained data languages are sometimes called *query languages*. Query languages usually enable an experienced user to formulate common requests with a simple, yet concise language. They provide a great deal of flexibility in terms of keywords, but the format of the commands is rather rigid. Even though they are called query languages, they also have modification operations.

Data languages can be either generalized or application oriented. Generalized data languages have general commands for extraction of data without any concern for the terminology used in the particular application. Application-oriented data languages follow closely the terminology and concepts used in a particular application, e.g., natural resources, medicine, law, real estate, or insurance. Often a data language can be customized by changing the keywords and/or the structure of the commands to fit a specific application. A *generator* (data language generating system) is able quickly to generate or adapt a data language according to users' applications or requirements [McKeeman *et al.*, 1970; Chan, 1974].

Data languages span a wide range of *procedurality* [Olle, 1974]. At one end, there are the more procedural data languages in which one has to specify what is wanted as well as how to obtain it. At the other end, there are less procedural data languages in which the programmer need only specify what is wanted and the system decides how to obtain it. The more procedural data languages are simpler to implement, since the programmer, in a sense, directs the DBMS step by step on how to obtain the data. The less procedural data languages, while somewhat more complicated to implement, allow the system to decide how to obtain the data and therefore how to optimize the search. However, the optimization of the search can be a complicated process [Palermo, 1972; Astrahan and Chamberlin, 1975]. The nonprocedural data languages are designed mainly for *casual users*. Casual users are people who want to use the facilities of a DBMS, but who, because of a lack of incentive and/or opportunity, do not want to know anything about computers [Codd, 1974a].

Nonprocedural data languages are related to two broad areas of computer science. On the one hand, the data management experts strive for better, easier, and more user-oriented data languages. These systems incorporate extensive dialogue facilities and general format commands, e.g., RENDEZVOUS [Codd, 1974a] and TORUS [Mylopoulos *et al.*, 1975]. On the other hand, artificial intelligence is moving slowly toward more applied problems using question-answering systems. The main purpose of these systems is to incorporate semantics and provide a natural language facility. For instance, they can support data retrieval for casual users in a particular application, e.g., LUNAR [Woods, 1973].

A typical dialogue for data retrieval in a casual-user oriented data language might go along the following lines [Codd, 1974a] :

Casual user: Give me a list of the part numbers, quantities, and suppliers of Houston parts.

System: Do you want quantities on hand, on order, or shipped?

Casual user: Quantities on order.

System: By Houston do you mean city, metro, warehouse, . . . [further clarification dialogue]

System: Does the following query specify what you want: "Find all combinations of part numbers, quantity on order, supplier name, and supplier city where the supplier supplied a part to a project located in Houston"?

Casual user: Yes.

System: Do you want all items on your terminal, or printed off-line?

Casual user: How many are there? [dialogue continues]

Such a system may need a natural language parsing and understanding facility coupled with a flexible data language.

3.2 DATA SELECTION

Data languages consist of a set of operations for accessing data in a data base. The operations are used mainly to process specific parts of a data base. However, before any operation can be performed, the pertinent data in the data base must be isolated. For instance, before any data retrieval can occur, the data must be located. In addition, before any data can be modified, the proper data again must be isolated.

Data selection is the process of identifying a subset of the data in a data base. The data are selected according to instructions given by the user. The user expresses an interest in some particular data by specifying some data values and, perhaps, some relationships among the data. The data values are used to select particular instances of units of data in a data base. The relationships are used to select other data related to the selected data. For instance, consider the request "Get the employees who have a salary of $50,000." Assume that there is a record type (relation) EMPLOYEE with a data item (attribute) SALARY in a company's data base. The request will probably be expressed in a data language as

GET EMPLOYEE WHERE SALARY = 50000.

The keyword GET specifies the operation, in this case retrieval. The phrase "EMPLOYEE WHERE SALARY = 50000" expresses directions for data selection. The DBMS is instructed to isolate EMPLOYEE records (tuples) on the basis of a specified data value. Namely, all those EMPLOYEE records (tuples) are to be selected where the SALARY data item (attribute) value is equal to $50,000.

The criterion according to which the DBMS selects data in a data base is called a *qualification.* The phrase "SALARY = 50000" is a simple case of a qualification. In general, a qualification consists of a set of *conditions* connected by *Boolean operators.* A *condition* is composed of the name of a logical unit of data, a conditional operator, and a data value. The logical unit of data is usually the smallest accessible unit of data in a data model. For the relational and network data models it would be an attribute and a data item, respectively. The usual conditional operators are $<, \leq, >, \geq, =$, and $\neq$, or equivalent mnemonic names. The data value must usually agree in type with that of the attribute or data item.

To illustrate these concepts, consider an EMPLOYEE record type (relation) with data items (attributes) NUMBER, NAME, ADDRESS, AGE, DEPARTMENT, SKILL, and SALARY. Some examples of conditions using the EMPLOYEE record type (relation) are

SKILL='WELDER'
AGE LESS THAN 30
DEPARTMENT≠'SALES'

Several conditions may be combined by means of *Boolean operators* such as AND, OR, NOT, NOR, IS ONE OF, or IS ALL OF. Usually some form of precedence rules apply to Boolean operators, e.g., AND has precedence over OR. In addition, the order of precedence may be changed by the use of parentheses. Examples of qualifications containing Boolean operators are

SKILL='WELDER' <u>AND</u> AGE<30
DEPARTMENT='SALES' <u>OR</u> DEPARTMENT='PRODUCTION'
DEPARTMENT <u>IS</u> <u>ONE</u> <u>OF</u> 'SALES', 'PRODUCTION'

The last two qualifications express the same selection criterion.

A qualification selects a subset of the data in a data base according to its contents. For example, one may be able to select EMPLOYEE records (tuples) because the SALARY data item (attribute) has a certain value. Usually, all the data items (attributes) related to the SALARY data item (attribute) through the record type (relation) EMPLOYEE, i.e., an entire EMPLOYEE record (tuple), will also be selected. This type of data selection is usually referred to as *content addressibility*. The implication is that once the data selection, using a qualification, is complete, the data related to the selected data, via a record type (relation), can be immediately obtained. Hence, the only problem is to identify (or address) the record (tuple) on the basis of its contents.

Content addressibility is related to a very basic problem in data processing, namely, *searching* [Knuth, 1973]. The searching problem can best be described by the mapping $M: v \rightarrow (i_1, i_2, \ldots, i_n)$. That is, given a value v for a data item (attribute), the mapping should give the record (tuple) identifiers (or addresses) $i_1, i_2, \ldots, i_n$ of the records (tuples) that have the value v as their contents. Many data structures can be used to implement such a mapping, e.g., lists or B-trees [Lefkovitz, 1969; Roberts, 1972; Martin, 1975].

The mechanism that implements $M: v \rightarrow (i_1, i_2, \ldots, i_n)$ is called an *inverted file*. For instance, consider the EMPLOYEE record type (relation) discussed earlier. Suppose an inverted file exists for the data item (attribute) AGE. The inverted file provides a mapping from a particular age to all EMPLOYEE records (tuples) with that age. The data item (attribute) corresponding to v is referred to as an *inverted* or *indexed* data item (attribute). It is also sometimes called a *secondary index*. This distinguishes the role of the *primary index* according to which records in the file are stored, e.g., employee number. An *index*, in general, implies a selection mechanism or a pointer structure to desired data. The term index is used in the literature in two ways. It can refer to the data item (attribute) that is inverted, e.g., AGE is an index. It can also sometimes refer to the mechanism that provides the inversion, e.g., the inverted file inverting AGE is an index. In this book, index will be used to refer to data items (attributes) supported by search-aiding mechanisms. A more detailed discussion of searching and its implementation in a DBMS will be presented in Chapter 8.

Content addressibility allows the selection of data in the data base according to its content. From the data so selected, it is possible to exploit attribute relationships, as represented by record types or relations, to select other related data. However, data may also be related via associations, for instance, through several links in the case of the network data model, or by using several existing relations in the case of the relational data model. When data selection is performed using associations, it is usually called *data relatability*.

Data relatability involves the ability to relate record types or relations on the basis of associations between them. For instance, consider the query "Get spouse name of John Smith." If the spouse name is grouped together with the data related to John Smith, say in an EMPLOYEE record type or relation, then the query would necessitate some content addressibility to find the John Smith EMPLOYEE record (tuple). On the other hand, if the spouse data are separate, say in a SPOUSE record type (relation), then the query would necessitate content addressibility to get to John Smith's EMPLOYEE record (tuple) and data relatability to get to his spouse's SPOUSE record (tuple). The data relatability can be provided via links in the network data model or via associations between relations in the relational data model.

Content addressibility and data relatibility are not that different. Both use the ability to select data on the basis of relationships. It is not very important whether the relationships are attribute relationships or associations. In addition, content addressibility and data relatability can be reduced to a common framework. Content addressibility can be thought of as relating the set of values for a particular data item (attribute) to the set of records (tuples) of a particular record type (relation). On the other hand, data relatibility relates each record (tuple) of a record type (relation) A to a set of records (tuples) of record type (relation) B. This relationship can be represented as the mapping $M: j \rightarrow (i_1, i_2, \ldots, i_n)$, where j is the record (tuple) identifier of a record (tuple) of record type (relation) A, and $i_1, i_2, \ldots, i_n$ are the record (tuple) identifiers of the records (tuples) of record type (relation) B related to record (tuple) j of record type (relation) A. However, this is exactly the representation that was given to the content addressibility problem. Namely, they can both be reduced to a searching problem. In the content addressibility case, a data item (attribute) value is mapped to a set of record (tuple) identifiers. In the data relatability case, a record (tuple) identifier is mapped to a set of record (tuple) identifiers.

Implementations of content addressibility and data relatability are sometimes referred to as *access paths*. *Access paths* are physical connections, e.g., pointers or adjacency, between data. The access paths implement a relationship or search-aiding data structure. DBMS's use access paths when selecting the appropriate data for a particular request. The implementation of access paths will be discussed in Chapter 8.

The result of a data selection will loosely be referred to as a *selection structure* [Earnest, 1975]. A selection structure can take several different forms. Consider as an example an EMPLOYEE record type or relation and the data selection EMPLOYEE WHERE SALARY = 50000. Three possible forms of the resulting selection structure will be outlined. First, a copy of the selected data can be made by creating a new file, independent of the data base, containing all selected records (tuples). This copy is quite independent, after its creation, of the data in the data base. Second, a data structure of pointers can be obtained, which point to the selected records (tuples) of the EMPLOYEE record type (relation) as they exist in the data base. The data selection result, in this case, can be affected by subsequent changes to the data base. Finally, the selected data can be defined as an addition to the user's view of the data base. For instance, a new record type (relation) RICH EMPLOYEE can be defined, which represents the selected records (tuples). In this case the new record type (relation) becomes an integral part of the data base. However, it is quite independent of other record types (relations) in the data base. The selection result in all cases will be referred to as a selection structure. The exact nature of the selection structure depends on the data model and the DBMS. The particular case of a named selection structure representing a subset of records (tuples) of a given record type (relation) will be called a *selector*. Selectors play an important role in representing intermediate data selection results or output to the user.

3.3 NETWORK SELECTION

In the network data model, attribute relationships are represented by record types while associations are represented by links connecting the record types. Data selection within a record type can be effected by content addressibility. Data selection among record types is effected by first isolating a set of records, via content addressibility, and then using data relatability to relate them to other records via the links connecting the record types. In this section, an example of a network data language will be outlined that provides operations for these types of data selection [Tsichritzis, 1976].

Consider a set of record types and links between them as in Fig. 3.3−1. The simplest form of data selection is one that selects a subset of records of a record type using a qualification. For example, the following statement selects the subset of houses that are priced above $100,000:

SELECT HOUSE
WHERE HOUSE.PRICE > 100000

The resulting selection structure represents all records of type HOUSE with PRICE greater than $100,000. However, the user may wish to mask some of the data items in the resulting selection structure. In this case, the data items to be selected can be specified explicitly:

SELECT HOUSE
WHERE HOUSE.COLOR = WHITE
KEEP HOUSE.OWNER

The result of the preceding statement is a selection structure representing only the names of owners of white houses. Let us suppose now that the user wants to select some houses and obtain the salaries of their occupants. In order to do this data selection, the user has to use the link connecting the HOUSE and PERSON record types. The follow-

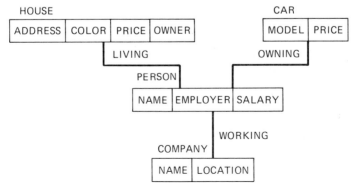

Fig. 3.3−1 Example network.

ing statement selects the records of all persons living in a house priced above $100,000:

SELECT HOUSE
WHERE HOUSE.PRICE > 100000

LINK TO PERSON

The selection structure represents only destination, i.e., PERSON, records and assumes that all data items are needed. If only the salaries of persons are wanted, then this is expressed as

SELECT HOUSE
WHERE HOUSE.PRICE > 100000

LINK TO PERSON

KEEP PERSON.SALARY

Suppose that the user wants a list of house prices, person's names, and their salaries. In order to effect this data selection, the DBMS has to represent in the selection structure some of the data pertaining to selected houses. This requirement can be expressed as

SELECT HOUSE
WHERE HOUSE.PRICE > 100000
KEEP HOUSE.PRICE

LINK TO PERSON

KEEP PERSON.NAME AND PERSON.SALARY

Suppose now that the user wants to exclude from the list of persons selected those people with salaries of $100,000 or more. This can be specified as

SELECT HOUSE
WHERE HOUSE.PRICE > 100000
KEEP HOUSE.PRICE

LINK TO PERSON

SELECT PERSON
WHERE PERSON.SALARY < 100000
KEEP PERSON.NAME AND PERSON.SALARY

The preceding queries assume that there is only one link between the HOUSE and PERSON record types. However, as shown in Chapter

2, there can be more than one explicitly named link between the same two record types. In general, therefore, the data selection should specify the particular link to be used as

SELECT HOUSE
WHERE HOUSE.PRICE > 100000
KEEP HOUSE.PRICE

LINK WITH LIVING TO PERSON

SELECT PERSON
WHERE PERSON.SALARY < 100000
KEEP PERSON.NAME AND PERSON.SALARY

In general, the data selection can be extended by following many links connecting different record types. This process is sometimes called navigation [Bachman, 1973b]. The result is a selection structure that contains all desired data. For example, suppose the user wants to list the car price in addition to the house price and salary. The data selection can be specified as

SELECT HOUSE
WHERE HOUSE.PRICE > 100000
KEEP HOUSE.PRICE

LINK WITH LIVING TO PERSON

SELECT PERSON
WHERE PERSON.SALARY < 100000
KEEP PERSON.NAME AND PERSON.SALARY

LINK WITH OWNING TO CAR

KEEP CAR.PRICE

So far, the data selection allows the user to traverse the network of links along a chain. In this particular example, the chain was HOUSE–LIVING–PERSON–OWNING–CAR. However, the network of links may have to be traversed in a more general way. Suppose, for example, that the user wants to obtain, in addition to the selection structure represented by the previous query, the location of the company where the person works. In this case, the data language must specify the data selection according to all three links, i.e., LIVING, OWNING, and WORKING. The data selection can be expressed by the statement

SELECT HOUSE
WHERE HOUSE.PRICE > 100000

KEEP HOUSE. PRICE

LINK WITH LIVING TO PERSON

SELECT PERSON
WHERE PERSON.SALARY < 100000
KEEP PERSON.NAME AND PERSON.SALARY

LINK WITH OWNING TO CAR

KEEP CAR.PRICE

LINK FROM PERSON WITH WORKING TO COMPANY

KEEP COMPANY.LOCATION

In this case, the links are not in a chain. Hence, in the next to last line of the statement, there is a need to specify from which record type (PERSON) previously used in the statement the link is to be effected after selecting CAR records. In the case where PERSON appears many times in the statement, there has to be a distinction from which instance of PERSON the link is to be effected. This distinction can be made by position or by using separate names for the different roles of the same record type. The details of the syntax are left as an exercise at the end of the chapter.

The form of the data selection in the preceding examples enables a user to traverse (navigate) according to the links of the network. In so doing, selection structures representing the result of a particular data selection can be constructed. These selection structures can be further manipulated using the facilities of a host programming language in the case of a host data language. However, to complete the discussion, some more capabilities will be presented that are needed for handling the selection structures. For instance, to distinguish between several selection structures, facilities have to be provided to name selection structures. Assume, without loss of generality, that the selection structures are defined again as record types. In this case, the selection structures can be named and defined as record types simultaneously. The form of the data selection has to be extended as follows to permit the naming of a new record type:

RECORD TYPE IS EXPENSIVE HOUSES
SELECT HOUSE
WHERE HOUSE.PRICE > 100000

Other operations that are necessary are the ability to merge selection structures, sort selection structures, eliminate duplicate records, etc. These operations can be defined as operations on record types, which in turn can represent selection structures. Examples of some operations can be specified as

RECORD TYPE IS <record name>
MERGE <record name> AND <record name>

RECORD TYPE IS <record name>
FROM <record name> ELIMINATE DUPLICATES

RECORD TYPE IS <record name>
FROM <record name> SUBTRACT <record name>

RECORD TYPE IS <record name>
FROM <record name> SORTED BY <data item name>

The preceding operations are outlined only syntactically. Care should be exercised in the exact specification of operations and their semantic properties. Since record types are allowed to have duplicate records, the operations of union, intersection, etc., are not necessarily set operations. However, all operations can be meaningfully defined.

Using the operations outlined in this section, a user can construct selection structures by navigating through a network data base. In addition, the selection structures can be named and manipulated. Therefore, it seems that the operations outlined form a complete set of operations for the network data model. The question of completeness will be discussed again in Section 3.5 following the presentation of a relational data language.

There are many variations for specifying data selection in the network data model. The example language presented in this section handles many records at a time and is applicable to the general network data model [Tsichritzis, 1976]. In Chapters 5 and 6, other data languages will be investigated that apply to particular versions of the network data model. However, in all data languages, data selection is present, although in different forms. In all cases, data are selected by qualifying certain records and relating them to some other records. This operation is effected according to the structure of the data expressed by the links among record types.

3.4 RELATIONAL ALGEBRA

In the relational data model, attribute relationships are represented by relations. However, unlike the network data model, the relational data model does not provide a different mechanism, such as links, to represent associations. Instead, another relation is used to represent an association.

Relations that represent associations can be existing relations in the data base or they can be generated (created) from existing relations by using relational operators. In addition, subsets of existing relations can also be generated with relational operators. All of the relational operators use only one data structure, the relation. A new relation, generated by relational operators, represents a subset of the relationships among the data in a user's view. For instance, there is a relationship between PERSON, HOUSE, and COMPANY relations expressed as "the houses of persons working for a company." Such relationships are expressed again as relations. In this particular example, the new relation is the result of a definition that relates the original three relations by the use of relational operators. The fact that the result is expressed again as a relation should not be surprising. After all, a relation can express any relationship.

In terms of data selection, a user usually specifies the data desired by giving a definition of the new relation. The selection structure in this case is the representation of the new relation. For instance, a user can specify, using relational operators, the definition of the relation to be isolated. The system responds by making such a relation available, either as a new relation in the user's view or as an output relation.

The relational operators can be described using either the relational algebra or the relational calculus [Codd, 1972b]. The relational algebra is a set of operators that constructs the required relation from given relations. The new relation is obtained by combining and subsetting the given relations and any intermediate relations that result. The relational calculus gives a definition of the desired relation. The definition is in the form of a predicate, which is the set of conditions that determines the shape and the membership of the resulting relation [Meltzer, 1974]. In this section, the relational operators will be discussed mainly in terms of the relational algebra. However, we will also give the relational calculus definition of the operators. The relational calculus will again be discussed in Chapter 7 in the context of the relational data language ALPHA [Codd, 1971b].

Before the operators themselves are discussed, it is necessary to introduce some terminology and definitions. The logical symbols $\exists$ (there exists), $\forall$ (for all), $\wedge$ (and), $\vee$ (or), $-$ (not, complement), $\in$ (belongs to, member of), $\subseteq$ (subset), ϕ (empty), and : (such that) will be used in their usual meaning. Delimiters used are [,], (, and). The following definitions will also be needed.

Definition 3.4–1 Given the tuples $r = \langle r_1, \ldots, r_m \rangle$ and $s = \langle s_1, \ldots, s_n \rangle$, the *concatenation* of r with s is the $(m+n)$-tuple defined by:

$$\widehat{r\,s} = \langle r_1, \ldots, r_m, s_1, \ldots, s_n \rangle.$$

For example, if $r = \langle 1,2,x \rangle$ and $s = \langle a,z,3 \rangle$ then $\widehat{r\,s} = \langle 1,2,x,a,z,3 \rangle$.

Definition 3.4–2 Let R be an n-ary relation, $r \in R$ a tuple of R, and $\{D_1, \ldots, D_n\}$ the domains of R; then

1. $r[D_i]$ designates the ith *component* (value of D_i) of r.
2. If $A \subseteq \{D_1, \ldots, D_n\}$, then
   (a) $r[A]$ is a tuple containing only those components specified by A, e.g., if $r = \langle a,2,f \rangle$ and R is $R(D_1, D_2, D_3)$, then $r[D_1, D_3] = \langle a,f \rangle$.
   (b) $R[A] = \{r[A] : r \in R\}$, e.g., if $R(D_1, D_2, D_3)$ is

$$R(D_1, D_2, D_3)$$

a	2	f
b	1	g
c	3	f
d	3	g
e	2	f

then

$R[D_1] = $	a	$R[D_3, D_2] = $	f	2
	b		g	1
	c		f	3
	d		g	3
	e		f	2

Definition 3.4–3 Let $T(x,y)$ be a binary relation. The *image set* of x under T is defined by

$$g_T(x) = \{y : \langle x,y \rangle \in T\}.$$

For example, if R is

$$R(D_1, D_2)$$

1	a
1	b
2	c
1	d

then

$$g_R \ (D_1 = 1) = \{ <a>, <b>, <d> \}$$
$$g_R \ (D_1 = 2) = \{ <c> \}$$
$$g_R \ (D_1 = 3) = \{ \phi \}$$

Definition 3.4–4 Given an n-ary relation R over a set of domains $\{D_1, \ldots, D_n\}$ and a k-tuple $(k \leqslant n)$ of domains A $(A \subseteq \{D_1, \ldots, D_n \})$ then

1. $\bar{A} = \{D_1, \ldots, D_n\} - A$ ($\bar{A}$ contains all domains *not* in A).
2. If r is an n-tuple of R, then

$$g_R \ (r[\bar{A}]) = \{ s: s \in R[A] \wedge <r[\bar{A}],s> \in R[\overparen{\bar{A} \ A}]\} .$$

If the relation R is

$$
\begin{array}{ccccc}
R(D_1, & D_2, & D_3, & D_4, & D_5) \\
1 & a & x & f & 2 \\
2 & a & y & g & 3 \\
1 & b & x & f & 2 \\
2 & c & y & h & 3 \\
3 & a & x & f & 1 \\
1 & b & y & f & 2 \\
2 & a & x & h & 3 \\
\end{array}
$$

and $A = \{D_3, D_2, D_4\}$, then $\bar{A} = \{D_1, D_5\}$. Let $r = <1,a,x,f,2>$; then $r[A] = <x,a,f>$, $r[\bar{A}] = <1,2>$, and

$$g_R \ (r[\bar{A}]) = g_R \ (<1,2>) = \{ <x,a,f>, <x,b,f>, <y,b,f> \}.$$

Definition 3.4–5 Two sets of attributes A and B are *compatible* if they are of the same degree and the corresponding domains are of the same data type.

The relational operators will be described by examples using the relations shown in Fig. 3.4–1. The relations depict the products manufactured by a company (their code, production cost, and selling price), and the buyers of those products (their names and the products they buy). Each operator will be discussed individually. However, since the result of each operator is another relation, it should be noted that the operators can be used in combination. The relational operators will also be defined formally. For each operator, the expression on the left-hand side of the equality sign is the relational algebra expression for the

BUYER (NAME,	ITEM)	PRODUCT (CODE,	COST,	PRICE)
SMITH	A	A	5	8
JONES	B	B	4	4
ADAMS	A	C	6	9
SMITH	B			
JONES	A			
SMITH	C			

Fig. 3.4—1 Example relations.

operator. The expression on the right-hand side is the relational calculus definition of the operator.

The first three relational operators are required to obtain any subset of a given relation. For example, suppose that a user wants those tuples in the PRODUCT relation where the PRICE attribute value is less than or equal to 8. The *restriction* operator can express this requirement as

PRODUCT[PRICE≤8] = (CODE, COST, PRICE)
                                    A   5   8
                                    B   4   4

More formally, restriction is defined as

$$R[A \ \theta \ v] = \{ r\colon r \in R \land (r[A] = v) \}$$

where A is an attribute of R, θ (theta) is one of the conditional operators $<, \leqslant, >, \geqslant, =$, or $\neq$, and v is a literal value.

The restriction operator is equivalent to a qualification, containing a single condition, on a single relation. It requires a specific data value (8 in the preceding example) in the condition. However, it is also possible to specify a condition involving two attributes of the same relation. For example, suppose that one would like to know which products are being sold at cost. The *selection* operator can specify this data selection as

PRODUCT[PRICE=COST] = (CODE, COST, PRICE)
                                        B   4   4

In this case, the qualification specifies a condition involving the two attributes PRICE and COST in the relation PRODUCT. The two attributes must be compatible. That is, they must be of the same data type. The result relation contains only those tuples of PRODUCT where the

COST attribute value is equal to the PRICE attribute value. More formally, selection is defined as

$$R[A \; \theta \; B] = \{r: r \in R \wedge (r[A] \; \theta \; r[B])\}.$$

The restriction and selection operators always select the values of all attributes in the tuples that are selected. However, a very common data selection is choosing only the values of certain attributes in a relation, or equivalently, masking the values of certain attributes. The *projection* operator can be used to perform this data selection. For example, if a user wants to know the names of all buyers of products, this data selection is specified as

BUYER[NAME] = (NAME)
                          SMITH
                          JONES
                          ADAMS

In the result relation, only the values of those attributes specified will appear. In addition, any duplicate tuples are also eliminated. More formally, projection is defined as

$$R[A] = \{r[A] : r \in R\}.$$

So far, the operators permit a user to select data from a single relation at a time. However, operators that exploit relationships between relations are also needed. In this way, data in different relations can be associated in a manner similar to links among record types.

The *cross-product* operator forms all possible combinations of the tuples of two relations. The result is a relation whose degree is the sum of the degrees of the original relations, and whose cardinality (number of tuples) is the product of the cardinality of the original relations. For example, the cross product of BUYER and PRODUCT is

BUYER $\otimes$ PRODUCT = (NAME, ITEM, CODE, COST, PRICE)

NAME	ITEM	CODE	COST	PRICE
SMITH	A	A	5	8
JONES	B	A	5	8
ADAMS	A	A	5	8
SMITH	B	A	5	8
JONES	A	A	5	8
SMITH	C	A	5	8
SMITH	A	B	4	4
JONES	B	B	4	4
ADAMS	A	B	4	4

SMITH	B	B	4	4
JONES	A	B	4	4
SMITH	C	B	4	4
SMITH	A	C	6	9
JONES	B	C	6	9
ADAMS	A	C	6	9
SMITH	B	C	6	9
JONES	A	C	6	9
SMITH	C	C	6	9

More formally, cross product is defined as

$$R \bigotimes S = \{ (\widehat{r\ s}) : r \in R \wedge s \in S \}.$$

Suppose now that a user wants a list of buyer names, the products they buy, and the cost and price of each product. The answer to this query is contained in two relations, BUYER and PRODUCT. A new relation, containing the answer to the query, can be constructed by taking the *join* of BUYER and PRODUCT according to a join condition. The result relation is constructed by taking each tuple in the BUYER relation, determining if it satisfies the join condition with each tuple in the PRODUCT relation, and forming a new tuple from the BUYER and PRODUCT tuples if it does. The join condition is expressed on two compatible attributes, one from each of the original relations. For example, the join of the BUYER and PRODUCT relation according to the join condition "ITEM attribute value equal to CODE attribute value" is

BUYER [ITEM=CODE] PRODUCT
= (NAME, ITEM, CODE, COST, PRICE)

SMITH	A	A	5	8
JONES	B	B	4	4
ADAMS	A	A	5	8
SMITH	B	B	4	4
JONES	A	A	5	8
SMITH	C	C	6	9

More formally, join is defined as

$$R [A \ \theta \ B] S = \{ (\widehat{r\ s}) : r \in R \wedge s \in S \wedge (r[A] \ \theta \ s[B]) \}$$

where θ again is one of $<, \leqslant, >, \geqslant, =$, or $\neq$. The attributes A and B must be compatible.

There are several types of joins. A *generalized join* forms a new tuple from a BUYER and PRODUCT tuple whenever the join condition is satisfied. Another way of looking at a generalized join is as a cross product and a selection. That is, the join of BUYER and PRODUCT on ITEM and CODE is the cross product of BUYER and PRODUCT from which only the tuples satisfying the join condition are selected. A *natural join* is a join where the conditional operator is equality. In addition, the common join attribute is not duplicated. Finally, *composition* is the natural join with the common join attribute deleted. The join in the preceding query is a generalized join. Note that join expresses a "for each" or "there exists" condition.

Consider now a query such as "Find the buyers who buy each type of product." In the relational algebra, this data selection can be represented by a *division* operator as

BUYER[ITEM÷CODE] PRODUCT = (NAME)
SMITH

More formally, division is defined as

$$R[A \div B] S = \{ r[\bar{A}] : r \in R \wedge S[B] \subseteq g_R (r[\bar{A}]) \}$$

where the attributes A and B are compatible.

The dividend relation (BUYER), dividend attribute (ITEM), divisor relation (PRODUCT), and divisor attribute (CODE) can be identified in a natural way. The result relation consists of the projection of the tuples in the dividend relation on those attributes (NAME) not in the dividend attribute that satisfy the division. One way of understanding division is to consider a construction algorithm for it as follows:

1. Consider the dividend relation as a binary relation consisting of the dividend attribute and nondividend attribute(s).
2. For each unique tuple in the projection of the dividend relation, on the nondividend attribute(s), do steps 3 and 4.
3. Select all tuples in the projection of the dividend relation on the dividend attribute that correspond in the dividend relation to the particular tuple selected in step 2. Call this set of tuples T.
4. If there is one tuple in T for every tuple in the projection of the division on the divisor attribute, then put the corresponding tuple selected in step 2 in the answer.

For the preceding example, the first step has no effect since the BUYER relation already is a binary relation consisting of dividend attribute ITEM and nondividend attribute NAME. However, if it were not, then the attributes would be grouped into two subsets as specified in step one. The projection in step two on the nondividend attribute NAME, results in three unique tuples as follows:

BUYER[NAME] = (NAME)
SMITH
JONES
ADAMS

The result T_i of step three for the ith tuple of the projection BUYER[NAME] is

1. (SMITH) $\rightarrow T_1 = \{(A), (B), (C)\}$
2. (JONES) $\rightarrow T_2 = \{(A), (B)\}$
3. (ADAMS) $\rightarrow T_3 = \{(A)\}$

Finally, the projection of PRODUCT on CODE is

PRODUCT[CODE] = (CODE)
A
B
C

Therefore, only T_1 contains a tuple for every tuple in the projection PRODUCT[CODE]. The tuple (SMITH), from the projection BUYER[NAME], is therefore placed in the answer. Note that the relational division is more like division in the partition sense (select those that match) than it is division in the arithmetic sense (how many goes into). Also, division expresses a "for all" condition (universal quantification). Contrast this with join, which expresses a "for each" or "there exists" condition (existential quantification) [Meltzer, 1974].

Finally, some additional operators are necessary for operating on relations as mathematical sets. These operators correspond to the set operators of union ($\cup$), intersection ($\cap$), and difference ($-$). They allow relations containing compatible tuples to be merged, complemented, etc. As an example of the combination of several operators, the query "Find those buyers who purchase products whose price is greater than 5 but less than 9" would be expressed as

(BUYER[ITEM=CODE] (PRODUCT[PRICE>5]
$\cap$PRODUCT[PRICE<9])) [NAME]

In addition to operations on relations, a relational data language should also provide facilities for naming the results of an operation.

These facilities will be discussed in Chapter 7 in the context of specific relational languages.

3.5 CONCLUDING REMARKS

The main facility of a data language is the ability to select pertinent data from the data base. Data selection is essentially effected in two ways. First, data are selected on the basis of some of their contents. Second, data are selected on the basis of relationships among them. A data language must provide operations that facilitate both types of data selection.

The first type of data selection can be handled by content addressibility. The second type of data selection requires data relatability. The way data relatability is effected depends on the data model. A network data language exploits the links that connect record types in a network. A relational data language constructs new relations from existing relations. In both cases, it is important to determine whether the data languages are "complete," that is, whether they provide a set of operations that are adequate to extract any data or data relationships in the data base.

Consider, for instance, the relational data model. The relational operations do not necessarily have to be based on the relational algebra. Instead, other equivalent operations can be provided that, in effect, enable the user to obtain any relation obtainable via the relational algebra. In order to be able to compare the capability of different relational data languages, a notion of equivalence between their capabilities is needed. A relational data language is defined to be *relationally complete* if it can perform the operations of the relational algebra. [Codd, 1972b]. This definition of completeness relates to the data selection and manipulation features of a data language.

Another equivalent definition can also be given. Consider a set of relations $R = \{R_1, R_2, \ldots, R_n\}$ and the set $C(R)$ of all relations obtained from them using relational algebra operators. The set $C(R)$ represents all the relationships that are present in the data base. If a data language can capture all the relationships expressed by $C(R)$, then it is called relationally complete.

The same issue of completeness also arises for operations on the network data model. Given a network data language, can it obtain all relationships represented in the data and structure of a network data base? The network data model is *structurally complete*, that is, it can represent any given relationship. However, this definition is not adequate. The issue of completeness is related not only to representation ability, but the ability to extract data relationships present in the data base. A notion of completeness parallel to relational completeness can be given in the following way. Consider a set of record types $T = \{T_1, T_2, \ldots, T_n\}$ and links $L = \{L_1, L_2, \ldots, L_k\}$. The record types have corresponding relations $RT = \{RT_1, RT_2, \ldots, RT_n\}$ in an obvious manner. Consider now the closure $C(RT)$ of the set of relations RT under relational operations. Given a data language for the network data model, its completeness can be investigated according to its ability to represent all relationships in $C(RT)$ for any set T of record types.

There are, however, two problems with this formulation. First, some joins used to obtain $C(RT)$ may have no corresponding links in the set L. Hence, there is no way that these joins can be used if the network data language does not have the ability to define new links. Second, there may be a link that is information carrying. The relations $C(RT)$ cannot be expected to contain the relationship represented by such a link. Both problems can be coped with rather easily. The first problem is handled by allowing new links to be defined in L, or else by restricting $C(RT)$ to joins already present in L. The second problem is handled by augmenting the set RT with relations corresponding to any information-carrying link in L. In this way, a definition of network completeness can be given similar to relational completeness. For instance, the network data language outlined in Section 3.3 is complete in this sense.

In the preceding discussion of completeness is the implied assumption that the informal abstract notion of completeness corresponds exactly to the rigorous definition of relational completeness. This claim can only be accepted as a thesis, i.e., a position in which to have faith. The claim cannot be proved since it relates a formal notion with an informal one. However, relational completeness seems to be a good thesis for two reasons. First, it corresponds fairly well to the informal notion of completeness. Second, different definitions of relational completeness, e.g., calculus and algebra oriented, have been proved to be equivalent [Codd, 1972b]. However, it should be pointed out that a data language may be complete in the formal sense and yet not allow some features that users want, e.g., average and sum operators on values. On the other hand, a language may be incomplete and still be a very good programming tool.

EXERCISES

3.1 Most commercial DBMS's have host data languages. Why?

3.2 Design a query language specifically oriented for data base queries in a particular application, e.g., airline reservation.

3.3 Consider the problem of interfacing a set-of-records or set-of-tuples data language with a host programming language handling only one record or tuple at a time. Propose a mechanism to do it.

3.4 How would you handle the problem of an unexpected null (no value) data item or attribute value in a host data language?

3.5 Propose a syntax for a network data language that distinguishes between different roles of the same record type in the same query.

3.6 Consider the following relations:

$$P(D_1 \quad D_2 \quad D_3) \quad Q(D_4 \quad D_5)$$

D_1	D_2	D_3	D_4	D_5
1	11	x	x	1
2	11	y	x	2
3	11	x	y	1
4	12	z		

What is the result of each of the following queries:

(a) $(P[D_3, D_1])-Q$
(b) $(P \bigotimes Q) [D_1 = D_5]$
(c) $P[D_1 < D_5] Q$
(d) $P[D_3 \div D_4] Q$
(e) $(P[D_2, D_3]) [D_3 \div D_4] Q$

3.7 Outline a series of algorithms to form joins. For each one, investigate its speed and general efficiency [Gotlieb, 1975].

3.8 The set of relational operators described in Section 3.4 is not a minimal set. For instance, the join operator can be expressed in terms of cross product, selection, and projection. Investigate different interdependencies among the operators. Propose a minimal set of operators.

3.9 Show that the network data language outlined in Section 3.3 is complete.

3.10 The data language outlined in Section 3.3 has the ability to link from a record type that is not necessarily the immediately preceding record type in a statement. This ability enables the user to link record types in a tree form rather than only in a chain form. Prove that this feature is necessary for completeness.

3.11 Compare the features of the network data language in Section 3.3 and the relational algebra in Section 3.4. Try to construct a table with corresponding features.

3.12 Compare the features of the network data language in Section 3.3 with the SEQUEL relational data language outlined in Chapter 7.

3.13 Suppose a DBMS provides complete content addressibility, i.e., all data items are inverted. Use the content addressibility also to provide data relatability.

Chapter 4

DBMS FACILITIES

4.1 SCHEMAS AND SUBSCHEMAS

A DBMS stores the data required by all applications in one or more data bases. It also provides a generalized data model for the data bases. Each application's view is usually patterned according to this generalized data model. The description of the view corresponding to a single data base is called a *schema* [CODASYL DBTG, 1971]. It names and describes all logical units of data in a data base, e.g., record types and relations. It defines the type of all data items or attributes, e.g., integer, real, and string. A schema expresses all possible logical relationships that exist between logical units of data in a data base. For example, it defines certain data items to be part of a record type. It may also express relationships between record types or relations. For example, between the record types (relations) PERSONS and HOUSES, it may express a "lives in" relationship. A schema may also describe some aspects of the mapping of logical units of data to a physical storage structure (see Section 4.3.2). Security and integrity measures, such as access restrictions to a certain logical unit of data, may also be specified in a schema.

A *subschema* describes the view used by an application [CODASYL DBTG, 1971]. It is a logical subset of a schema and thus of the view of an entire data base. A subschema may, in fact, be a view of an entire data base. It selects relevant parts of a schema and adds

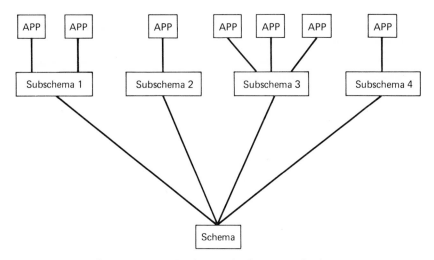

Fig. 4.1–1 Applications, subschemas, and schema.

necessary modifications to form an application's view. Some changes that could be made in a subschema are to omit entirely or change the organization of a logical unit of data, to change security or integrity measures, or to change the types of data items or attributes. It is the responsibility of the DBMS to materialize an application's view from a schema. An application invokes a particular subschema that meets its view requirements. Many applications may invoke the same subschema. The subschema acts as a declaration for the view allowing an application to access and manipulate the data within program variables according to the view. The relationship between applications, subschemas, and a schema is shown in Fig. 4.1–1. As discussed in Chapter 2, DBMS's can be distinguished according to the data model used for their schemas.

4.2 INTERFACES

A DBMS must provide facilities for two types of users, the *data base administrator* or *DBA* and *users* who wish to access a data base according to a view [Guide-Share, 1970]. The DBA is mainly concerned with the physical aspects of data organization and access. It is the DBA's responsibility to define schemas and subschemas and to create and maintain the physical storage structures that support the schemas and subschemas. The DBA is the decision-maker in a DBMS environment. All other people interfacing with the DBMS will simply be called users. Users are mainly concerned with the logical aspects of data organization and access. They interact with a data base via a view as defined by a subschema. Users require the facilities provided by a data language to access data in a data base.

4.2.1 Data Base Administrator

The DBA is a role that can be played by one person or several persons. For instance, the DBA's activities can be divided among different experts with the necessary coordination among them. Depending on the size of the computer installation, it can be an easy part-time occupation for one person, or it can be a whole department. In the sequel, the DBA will be referred to as a single individual without any particular implication about the composition of the role. In any case, the DBA role is critical for the smooth operation of a DBMS.

The DBA is responsible for the data processing operation of an organization. One of the DBA's primary functions is to determine the information requirements of the various applications and to provide the views they require. To perform this function, the DBA interacts with the applications' departments and acts as a liason between them and the system analysts and programmers. Another primary function of the DBA is to maximize the cost effectiveness of the data processing operation. To this end, the DBA should have knowledge of the current state of the art in DBMS's and computer hardware as well as some expertise in operations research. The specific duties of the DBA can be divided into four main areas: design, administration, operations, and monitoring [Canning, 1972b; Clark, 1974a,b].

In designing a data base, the DBA consults the various divisions of an organization to determine their information needs. The data base can then be designed and its rules of use determined. The schemas and subschemas are defined according to a data model. The physical storage structure of the data must be specified as well as the mapping between the physical storage structure and the different views. The organization and maintenance of the *data dictionary*, which defines the use and meaning of all names used in the schemas and subschemas, must also be specified. The DBA formulates security procedures, which are the rules by which the DBMS performs data protection, and the requirements for using the facilities of the DBMS. The integrity requirements of the data base, which may include backup and recovery procedures in case of system failure, must also be outlined. Finally, the DBA determines the software support that will be provided for applications. This consists of utility programs such as loading functions and report generators.

The DBA's administrative duties include interacting with the user community in order to determine their needs and complaints. As the custodian of the corporate data base, the DBA sets the standards for data representation and system documentation. The DBA also influences equipment selection for the computer installation.

The DBA has various operational duties. The DBA selects the most appropriate physical storage structure as well as the physical storage medium for a data base. As application needs or data usage characteristics change, the physical storage structure may need to be reorganized or the physical storage medium changed to maintain efficient access and cost-effective processing operations. Mechanisms for accessing and controlling access to a data base also need to be defined. The control mechanisms restrict access both by unauthorized users, and by authorized users during data base reconstruction, reorganization, or testing. The DBA creates integrity procedures for the data base. These procedures provide such functions as backup in case of system failure and controlled access to data during certain operations such as update. Mechanisms for controlling the storage of utility programs in program libraries are also provided. The mechanisms for controlling access to and maintenance of the dictionary of data base names are also specified by the DBA.

Monitoring in the system is oriented toward system accounting and performance to improve efficiency and cost effectiveness. It includes such things as determining the utilization of resources, determining bottlenecks, and measuring device performance. Monitoring is also oriented toward usage patterns of the data in a data base. It may reveal the need to reorganize the physical storage structure, to change the data access strategy, or to remove old or add new search-aiding data structures. The DBA interprets the performance measurement of the overall system in order to evaluate the efficiency of operations. Finally, the DBA determines the scheduling algorithm of the computer installation in an effort to maximize cost effectiveness.

4.2.2 User

A user's domain of interaction with a data base is defined by a subschema. A user presents data requirements to the DBA, e.g., view required, and the DBA defines a subschema that describes and implements the view. A user accesses the data and data relationships available in a view via a data language. There are various types of users having different data language capabilities and view requirements. For instance, data entry clerks may only be allowed to enter data, but never retrieve it. In such a case, they may not need a complicated view or data language. Report-browsing managers retrieve data, but never modify it. Their view is limited to report formats and their data language to simple report generation operations. Finally, application programmers need to be able both to enter and to retrieve data, and perhaps define subschemas. They require a wide range of view generation and data language capabilities.

It is projected that by the end of this century, the majority of DBMS applications will be oriented toward casual users [Codd, 1974a]. This category of user will represent the vast majority of the population. To supply the services of a DBMS to these users, a DBMS must eventually meet two requirements. First, it is essential that casual users be allowed to communicate with the DBMS in what they perceive to be their natural language. Second, the DBMS should be able to carry on a dialogue with the users to determine their information needs. In this way, the general public will be able to interact with a DBMS without the need for detailed knowledge of DBMS operations or facilities.

4.3 LANGUAGE FACILITIES

A DBMS usually supports two types of language facilities, a *data manipulation facility* (DMF) and a *data definition facility* (DDF). The DMF supports a data language and is used by a user for data selection and to cause the selected data to be transferred physically between a data base and an application program. The DDF is used to describe schemas and subschemas. It is provided mainly for the DBA. However, this distinction between the DMF and the DDF is somewhat blurred as some systems allow users to modify their subschema. The two types of facilities will be discussed separately, even though some of the functions can be combined.

4.3.1 Data Manipulation

A DMF is the main interface between a user and the DBMS. As such, it has to satisfy many requirements. First, it should be natural and easy to use. The semantics of the operations permitted on the data base should be simple and should reflect the intuition of the user. Second, it should be precise and complete. That is, it should have the power to specify without ambiguity any data or relationships among the data in a view as well as any operation on the data. Finally, it should facilitate an efficient implementation. The syntax of the data language does not have to reflect absolutely the architecture of the DBMS, but it should bear some relation to the basic primitives provided by the DBMS.

A DMF consists of certain primitive commands that correspond to the operations permitted on the data base. These commands perform the basic functions of informing the DBMS as to the kind of request to be made, retrieving data and returning it to the program environment, adding, changing and deleting data, and if necessary, releasing DBMS resources such as buffers. Associated with each primitive command, there may be a parameter list that specifies the data selection, names program variables into which the data are to be placed, and names error routines. There are three types of primitive commands: control, retrieval, and modification.

Control commands are concerned with identifying an application, determining which data base it wishes to access, allocating system resources such as files and buffers, and establishing the type of commands an application may use. In self-contained data languages, most of these functions are performed automatically by the DBMS once the application has been identified. In host data languages, a user must specifically perform most of these functions.

An *open* command signals a user's intention to begin accessing a data base. In response, the system must open physical files, allocate buffers and system tables, etc. On the other hand, a *close* command signals the DBMS to clean up processing by closing files and releasing storage areas used for data base access and communication.

A user is usually allowed to retrieve data, look at them, perhaps modify them, and then place the modified data back into the data base. In order to guarantee the integrity of the data base, the DBMS must prevent other users from manipulating the same data at the same time. To this end, a *hold* command may be provided that signals the DBMS to prevent access to the affected data until the user has finished modifying and replacing the data. The hold command may be combined with a retrieval command whereby access to the retrieved data by other users is prevented. For systems with a combined hold/retrieval command, a *release* command is a means of removing a hold if the modification is not to occur. This would then again permit access to the affected data by other users. The removal of a hold can also be automatic when any subsequent command is issued by the same user.

A *retrieval* command consists of data selection followed by some action on the selected data. The action to be taken after the data are selected can vary. The DBMS may be instructed simply to find the *location* of the selected data in the data base, but not to retrieve them physically at this time. In this case, the DBMS usually provides a set of pointers to the selected data. The user is then able to retrieve (gain *access* to) the selected data by means of these pointers. The pointers, as seen by the user, are usually logical, i.e., they cannot be explicitly manipulated by the user. The user asks, for example, for the "next" selected data. On the other hand, the DBMS can be instructed actually to retrieve (*locate and access*) all the selected data physically and place them either in a buffer or program variables.

In addition to retrieval of data contained specifically in the data base, statistical information for numeric data may be retrieved. Some common functions are counting the number in a set of selected data items, maximum and minimum of a set of values, average of a set of values, and sum of a set of values. Examples of such requests are number of employees with a salary of $20,000, average salary of all employees, and maximum salary.

A *modification* command refers to three types of operations on the data base: insertion, update, and deletion. An *insert* command adds new data to the data base. An *update* command changes data that currently exist in the data base. A *delete* command removes data that currently exist in the data base. Both an update and a delete command may require data selection to select the data to be updated or deleted.

4.3.2   Data Definition

Data definition is one of the most important functions of a DBMS. It is the means by which the data requirements of application systems and application programs are communicated to the DBMS [McGee, 1972]. Since the DBMS acts as the intermediary between applications and the physical data, data definition in a DBMS environment must satisfy three needs. First, it must specify the logical organization and characteristics of the data, according to a data model, as required by application systems and programs. Second, it must specify the physical organization of the data so that they can be placed on physical storage devices. Finally, it must specify a mapping between the physical and the logical organization of the data so that the DBMS is able to transform the physical organization into a logical one. All of these data definition facilities are provided by the DDF. In addition, the DDF also provides certain maintenance facilities to load data bases, specify integrity and monitoring mechanisms, reorganize parts of the data base, etc. These latter facilities are usually provided as utilities and will be discussed in more detail in Chapter 9.

The logical organization of the data in a data base is described by a schema and its subschemas. Schemas and subschemas are defined by means of a *data definition language* (DDL) [CODASYL DBTG, 1971]. A DDL is usually a self-contained language that provides the ability to [CODASYL DBTG, 1971; Engles, 1972]:

1. Specify the data model according to which the data base or a view of the data base is to be organized (if several data models are available).

2. Name the data base or view of the data base and all of the logical units of data, e.g., data items and record types.

3. Describe and perhaps name the relationships that exist between logical units of data, e.g., links between record types.

4. Specify the domain of values for the smallest units of logical data, e.g., integer or real.

5. Specify units of measurement for logical data, e.g., dollars, pounds, or feet.

6. Specify keys for certain logical units of data, e.g., record types or relations.

7. Specify integrity constraints on the data, e.g., an allowable range of values.

8. Specify access rules for the data, e.g., allow update only if a correct password is supplied.

This list is by no means exhaustive but is intended to convey some idea of possible logical descriptions of data.

The physical organization of the data in a data base is described by physical storage structures such as volumes, files, or bytes. Physical storage structures are defined by means of a *storage definition language* (SDL). The SDL provides the ability to:

1. Select the storage medium and perhaps a specific device.

2. Describe a mapping from logical data to a physical representation, e.g., record types map to files.

3. Specify indices for certain logical units of data, e.g., data items or attributes.

4. Specify a physical ordering for the data.

5. Specify a representation for physical data in the environment of a particular application.

6. Specify type conversion for data, e.g., binary to decimal.

7. Specify the form and/or placement of a data selection, e.g., buffers.

Again, this list is not exhaustive. It should be noted that in most existing DBMS's many of the functions of the SDL are performed by the DDL, while others are handled by utilities. Thus, most existing DBMS's do not have a separate, identifiable SDL. However, in order to provide a high degree of physical data independence, an SDL is a necessary part of a DBMS.

As an example of a simple schema definition using a hypothetical DDL and SDL, an EMPLOYEE record type will be defined.

```
SCHEMA COMPANY
    RECORD TYPE EMPLOYEE
        DATA ITEM NUMBER, DOMAIN IS INTEGER, KEY,
            ASSERT NUMBER > 0
        DATA ITEM NAME, DOMAIN IS CHARACTER
        DATA ITEM ADDRESS, DOMAIN IS ALPHANUMERIC
        DATA ITEM AGE, DOMAIN IS INTEGER, UNIT IS
            YEAR, ASSERT AGE IS 16 THRU 65
        DATA ITEM DEPARTMENT, DOMAIN IS CHARACTER
        DATA ITEM SKILL, DOMAIN IS CHARACTER
        DATA ITEM SALARY, DOMAIN IS REAL, UNIT IS
            DOLLARS, ASSERT SALARY IS 0 THRU 500
    END RECORD TYPE
END SCHEMA
STORAGE MODULE FOR SCHEMA COMPANY
    EMPLOYEE, CONTIGUOUS FILE, FILE NAME IS EMPFILE,
        MEDIUM IS DISK, DEVICE IS IBM 3330
    NUMBER, FIXED DECIMAL (3, 0), STORAGE KEY,
        SORT ASCENDING
    NAME, STRING (20)
    ADDRESS, STRING (15)
    AGE, BIT(8), INDEX USING B-TREE
    SALARY, FIXED DECIMAL (5, 2), INDEX USING
        POINTER ARRAY
    DEPARTMENT, STRING (10)
```

        SKILL, STRING 10, INDEX USING B-TREE
    END EMPLOYEE
END STORAGE MODULE

In the schema definition, the assertions such as ASSERT AGE IS 16 THRU 65 specify integrity constraints on the data. For this example, the DBMS is to check that the value of an AGE data item is always in the range 16 to 65. In the storage module, the representation CONTIGUOUS for the record type means that it should be implemented as a single file. Other possible representations could be TRANSPOSED, DATA POOL, etc. The INDEX characteristic means that the DBMS is to maintain a search-aiding data structure for the data item in the form specified. The mapping between the logical and physical data organizations is implied by matching the record type and data item names in the schema with the names used in the storage module. Note that the order of the data items as specified in the schema has been changed in the storage module. Such changes may reflect more efficient storage or access for the physical data. However, they do not affect a schema since the DBMS performs all physical to logical mappings.

A possible subschema definition for use in a PL/1 program by the personnel department might be

SUBSCHEMA PERSONNEL-VIEW OF SCHEMA COMPANY
    RECORD TYPE PERSONNEL OF RECORD TYPE
    EMPLOYEE
        ACCESS IS RETRIEVAL ONLY
        DATA ITEM NUMBER, KEY
        DATA ITEM NAME
        DATA ITEM ADDRESS
        DATA ITEM SKILL
        DATA ITEM DEPARTMENT
    END RECORD TYPE
END SUBSCHEMA

STORAGE MODULE FOR SUBSCHEMA PERSONNEL-VIEW
    HOST LANGUAGE IS PL/1
    BUFFER FOR EMPLOYEE IS STRUCTURE
        1 EMPLOYEE,
            2 NUMBER CHARACTER (3),
            2 NAME CHARACTER (20),
            2 ADDRESS CHARACTER (15),

2 SKILL CHARACTER (10),
2 DEPARTMENT CHARACTER (10);
END STORAGE MODULE

This subschema can be invoked, for example, from a PL/1 program. The invocation will cause a PL/1 structure having the above characteristics to be declared. The program can then access the data, after retrieval from the data base, via the PL/1 structure. The program need not be concerned with how the data are physically represented in the data base but only with the representation of the data in its environment. For example, an EMPLOYEE record type really has six data items and the DEPARTMENT data item comes before the SKILL data item. However, the program need not know this. The DBMS makes all necessary data conversions to conform to the user's view.

Schemas, subschemas, and storage modules are used by the DBMS whenever users access a data base. For example, consider the PERSONNEL-VIEW subschema and the query

GET EMPLOYEE WHERE SKILL = 'WELDER'.

In order to process this query, the DBMS must first check that it is formulated correctly and then locate and retrieve the pertinent data.

To check that the query is formulated correctly, the DBMS uses the PERSONNEL-VIEW subschema and its associated schema. Specifically, for the preceding query the DBMS checks that

1. The record type EMPLOYEE is the name of a record type that is known to the DBMS and that it is in fact a record type of the PERSONNEL-VIEW subschema.

2. The data item SKILL is the name of a data item of the record type EMPLOYEE.

3. The data value 'WELDER' is of the same data type as the data item SKILL and that its length does not exceed ten characters.

The DBMS may also have to perform additional checks using the subschema and schema depending on the query, e.g., check that a data value for AGE is between 16 and 65 when it is inserted or updated.

Once the query has been checked and validated, the storage modules are used to locate the data physically and return them to the application in a suitable format. For instance, if an index exists for the data item SKILL, then this is indicated in the schema storage module. The DBMS uses this information to select the pertinent EMPLOYEE records efficiently. The location of the physical file containing the

EMPLOYEE records is also stored in the schema storage module. Finally, the subschema storage module is used to format the retrieved data as required by the application.

The exact physical representation of schemas, subschemas, and storage modules as well as the data they contain can vary. The details of a physical representation are left as an exercise at the end of the chapter.

It may be desirable, in certain instances, to allow a user to use some of the DDF facilities. For instance, a user may want to define and name a specific relationship between record types. As an example, consider two record types HOUSES and PERSONS. A user may want to define a "lives in" relationship between HOUSES and PERSONS according to a common data item ADDRESS. However, users should be constrained from changing the physical structure of the data base as well as the view used by other users. Such actions should be performed by the DBA. Examples of other facilities that a user may need are the abilities to determine the view provided by a subschema and to inquire about the meaning of names as provided by a dictionary of data base names.

4.4 DATA INDEPENDENCE

The main reason for the existence of DBMS's is to provide data independence between the physical representation of data and a user's view. There are two aspects to data independence: physical data independence and logical data independence [Date and Hopewell, 1971a,b].

Physical data independence is a measure of how well an application is insulated from changes to the physical storage structure of the data. If an application program changes, then the storage structure should not have to change and vice versa. Physical data independence implies that users reference data by name and that searching for the data is a system function. In this way, a variety of search strategies and physical storage structures may be employed. The DBA is able to choose the best physical storage structure for all applications, and the DBMS is able to optimize the search strategy for a given request. Therefore, a user need not be concerned with the physical organization and accessing of data, or integrity and consistency requirements of the data base.

One problem associated with total physical data independence is binding [Sibley and Merten, 1973]. *Binding* is the firm association of an attribute of data, such as type and size, with a program variable.

Before data can be assigned to a program variable, in most programming languages the program must know the attributes of the data so that the appropriate storage space can be reserved and error checks performed. These attributes are usually specified in program declarations that name the variable and describe its attributes, e.g., PL/1 DECLARE statements. The language compiler is then able to reserve the appropriate storage space and perform some error checks at compile time. However, this implies that an application must know some of the physical attributes of data, e.g., character string length. Alternatively, the storage space allocation and error checking can be done at run time. However, this implies dynamic storage allocation, interpretation, and overall a more sophisticated and complex run time environment. Binding can take place at several points in the processing of an application, e.g., compile time, program load, or execution. The later the data are bound, the greater the physical data independence. However, very late binding implies multiple levels of indirection and interpretation at every access. Interpretation causes performance degradation due to the extra processing required [Meltzer, 1969]. Therefore, at some point there is a trade-off between physical data independence and DBMS performance.

Logical data independence is a measure of how well an application's view is insulated from changes in the schema of a data base. It is impossible to protect an application's view from changes to a schema that remove logical units of data that are part of the application's view. Since by definition, a subschema is a logical subset of a schema, removing logical units of data from a schema must also remove them from all subschemas. Any applications that formerly used the associated data will be affected. However, such changes usually imply that applications that accessed the deleted data are now obsolete and need to be changed anyway. The real problem in logical data independence is changes in a schema that add new logical units of data or modify relationships. For example, adding a new record type or data item to a schema should not affect an application's view. Logical data independence is a function of the flexibility of a data model in allowing very different views of the same data base and in allowing certain changes to the data base view.

Most existing DBMS's offer a certain degree of physical data independence, but very little in terms of logical data independence, which is much more difficult to achieve. It also cannot be attained in any general form, but is related to each particular data model. Different data models allow different forms of data relationships. Changing these data relationships without affecting user views is possible in most data models, but very difficult indeed.

4.5 CONCLUDING REMARKS

Up to this point the DBMS functions were discussed in an horizontal fashion. That is, all the pertinent commands were listed and outlined. However, data independence implies that the DBMS facilities are provided at different levels corresponding to the different levels of users. Consider, for instance, physical data independence. A DBMS provides a set of DML and DDL commands as outlined in Section 4.3 to instruct the system of the intentions and requirements of the user. These commands, however, need to be mapped into commands that perform physical data access and manipulation. During this mapping some of the DBA's instructions are followed to achieve better performance. It is implied, therefore, that the system has two levels. One level consists of the user-oriented commands dealing with the logical organization of data. These commands are then interpreted using facilities of an inner level, which deals with the physical organization of data. The presence of these two levels and the associated mapping provides the necessary indirection to achieve physical data independence.

Logical data independence is rather hard to achieve in just two levels. It implies the existence of indirection even among logical views of data. Consider a schema and the associated DML and DDL commands. If a user has logical data independence, it means that his view should be independent of the schema. It need not be exactly a subset of the schema. In this manner his view may change without necessitating schema changes. In addition, the schema may be modified without affecting the users' views. If the users' views are at a different level than the schema, then they can be mapped to the schema in the same manner that a schema is mapped to a physical representation. The mapping provides the indirection that can be used to achieve logical data independence.

It follows from this informal discussion that in order to achieve both logical and physical data independence the DBMS should be viewed as consisting of at least three levels. The outer level, closest to the user, provides the logical organization of data as a particular user or application wants to see it. The middle level provides a logical view of data, which is the common denominator among the varying requirements of the users. Finally, the inner level provides all the details of the physical structure of the data. The mapping between the outer and the middle levels provides logical data independence. The mapping between the middle and the inner levels provides physical data independence.

The idea of levels of a DBMS has been formally proposed as a framework for DBMS architecture [Bachman, 1974b; Sundgren, 1974; ANSI/X3/SPARC, 1975; Steel, 1975a; Yormark, 1976]. In their interim report the ANSI/X3/SPARC Study Group on Data Base Management Systems proposes three kinds of schemas, which correspond to our informal discussion of levels. At the outer level there are a number of *external schemas.* These correspond to the different users and applications. They can be very different in the way they view and logically organize the data. The different external schemas may even be organized according to different data models. At the middle level there is one *conceptual schema.* It corresponds to a common view of the data that is rather stable and encompasses all application systems. Finally, the *internal schema,* at the inner level, corresponds to the physical properties of the data as they are stored in the data base. In between the external, conceptual, and internal schemas, there are many mappings and interfaces that have been outlined in the ANSI/X3/SPARC report [ANSI/X3/SPARC, 1975].

Consider as an example a large enterprise, e.g., a manufacturing company. Each branch of activity of the enterprise has an application system that supports that function. Corresponding to the application system there is an external schema as outlined in Fig. 4.5—1. Each view according to an external schema can be quite different, e.g., one may be relational and another network oriented. All the external schemas are mapped into one conceptual schema that has an overall view of the logical data organization of the whole enterprise. Finally, the logical organization as presented in the conceptual schema is mapped into physical data structures as outlined in the internal schema. The internal schema contains all the details of the physical organization and is related to properties of the hardware and operating system of the DBMS.

The idea of organizing a system into levels is not new. It has been used extensively to provide structure and master complexity in other software systems, e.g., compilers [McKeeman *et al.,* 1970] and operating systems (OS) [Dijkstra, 1969]. The three levels, as outlined so far, are not a complete architecture. They are a guideline, or framework, for an architecture. In a realistic system architecture, the levels would be further subdivided in many more components. The idea of levels of a DBMS will be further explored in Chapter 8, in the discussion of DBMS implementation.

Most existing commercial DBMS's do not have any separation of their facilities into levels. They combine conceptual and internal schema facilities, and hardly provide any external schema views. This is

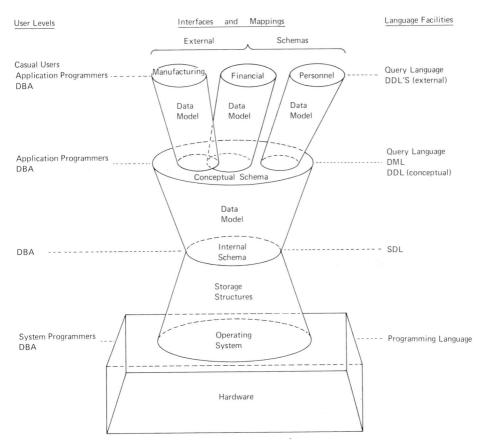

User Levels   Interfaces   and   Mappings   Language Facilities

Fig. 4.5—1 A DBMS architecture.

partly the reason that they only achieve a certain degree of physical data independence and almost no logical data independence. In the future, however, the ideas as presented in the ANSI/X3/SPARC report will be used to free the user both from the physical and, to some extent, from the logical characteristics of a data base. A user will be finally able to see the data in his way according to his data model. He will have the illusion that he is alone in using the data although there will be many users sharing the data at the same time. In this way, one of the most important goals of a DBMS will be achieved, i.e., to allow flexible sharing of the data.

EXERCISES

4.1 Compile a list of at least ten commercially available DBMS's with prices and main features.

4.2 It would be helpful if a schema incorporated some semantic information about a data base. Investigate the facilities needed for such a mechanism [Hammer and McLeod, 1975; Roussopoulos and Mylopoulos, 1975].

4.3 A schema and its subschemas contain information about the logical structure of a data base. Such information is often needed by the users. Propose a set of language facilities that enable an authorized user to obtain information about a schema and its subschemas.

4.4 One of the ways that a subschema can differ from a schema is in the type of the data items. Comment on the desirability and difficulty of providing automatic type conversion.

4.5 Outline a complete job description for a DBA. Do you, or anyone you know, come close to the qualifications you request?

4.6 Discuss the relative advantages of providing a combined *locate and access* retrieval command versus two separate retrieval commands *locate* and *access*.

4.7 Comment on the desirability and effectiveness of providing some DDF commands together with DMF commands for end-users. What types of commands would you provide?

4.8 The DDL may, in addition to type and structure descriptions, incorporate constraints that the data should adhere to, e.g., units or range of values. Design a set of language facilities that enable a user to specify these constraints. How would you implement the constraints?

4.9 Define formally a complete DDL and DML for the "flat-file" data model. Incorporate the DDL and DML in a programming language without file manipulation facilities, e.g., ALGOL or FORTRAN.

4.10 Design a physical representation for the COMPANY schema and storage module, and the PERSONNEL-VIEW subschema defined in Section 4.3.2.

4.11 Data independence can also refer to independence from the data model as it is used in a schema. Such independence could allow portability of application programs among different DBMS's. Comment on the desirability and difficulty of achieving this kind of independence.

4.12 The schema and subschemas for a particular data base are usually based on the same data model. Comment on the desirability and difficulty of providing a subschema that is based on a different data model than the schema. For instance, how would you provide a relational subschema based on a network schema?

Chapter 5

HIERARCHICAL SYSTEMS

5.1 HIERARCHICAL DATA MODEL

In Chapter 2, the network data model was introduced as a formal data model for representing attribute relationships of an entity set and the associations between entity sets. The network data model uses record types to represent attribute relationships and links to represent associations. For a particular application, the record types and the links between them can be displayed graphically as, respectively, nodes and arcs in a relationship graph. If all the links are 1:N, then the relationship graph is a directed graph called a data structure diagram.

Consider now the special case that the data structure diagram is an ordered tree as in Fig. 5.1—1. An *ordered tree* is a tree in which the relative order of the subtrees is important [Knuth, 1968]. For example, in Fig. 5.1—1 the fact that STATE is to the left of TERRITORY and CITY to the left of TOWN is significant. Such a restricted data structure diagram is called a *hierarchical definition tree.* Every node in the hierarchical definition tree represents a record type. Every arc represents a link between two record types. Since there can be at most one arc between any two nodes in a tree, the arcs do not have to be labeled to distinguish between them. That is, the links do not have to be explicitly named. A hierarchical definition tree is a template for the actual data base. The record types specify what types of records are allowed in the data base. The links specify the permissible connections between the record types.

In a hierarchical definition tree, there is one specially designated record type called the *root record type*. The other record types are called *dependent record types*. The *level* of a record type with respect to the root record type can be defined. The root record type is at level 1. Dependent record types are at lower levels (2, 3, etc.) in a hierarchical definition tree. For instance, in Fig. 5.1–1, the COUNTRY record type is a root record type and it is at level 1. The STATE and TERRITORY record types are dependent record types and they are both at level 2. Finally, the CITY and TOWN record types are also dependent record types and they are both at level 3.

A *hierarchical data base* is a collection, or *forest*, of disjoint trees with *record occurrences*, or simply *records*, as nodes. Each disjoint tree is called a *data base tree* and consists of one *root record* and all its *dependent records*. A root record is an occurrence of a root record type, while a dependent record is an occurrence of a dependent record type. All data base trees in a data base are constructed according to the connections between records permitted by the links in the hierarchical definition tree for the data base. Figure 5.1–2 is an instance of a hierarchical data base. It is organized according to the hierarchical definition tree of Fig. 5.1–1 and contains three data base trees.

In a hierarchical data base, *parents* and *children* among the records can be identified in a natural way according to the connections among the records. For example, in Fig. 5.1–2, a COUNTRY record may be connected to several STATE and TERRITORY records. In this case, the COUNTRY record is said to be the parent of the STATE and TERRITORY records. Conversely, the STATE and TERRITORY re-

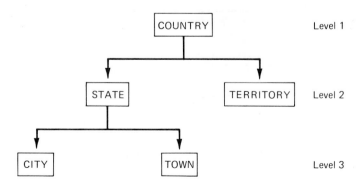

Fig. 5.1–1 A hierarchical definition tree.

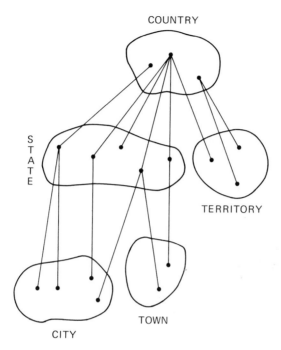

Fig. 5.1–2 A hierarchical data base.

cords are said to be children of the COUNTRY record. In addition, ancestors (parents, parents of parents, etc.) and descendants (children, children of children, etc.) among the records can also be identified in a natural way. A hierarchical path in the data base is a sequence of records, starting at a root record, in which the records are alternatively in a parent–child relationship. For example, the sequence COUNTRY record, STATE record, CITY record, specifies a hierarchical path.

In general, in a hierarchical data base, there can be a varying number of occurrences of each record type at each level in a data base tree. For example, in Fig. 5.1–2, there may be several COUNTRY records, each of which may be connected to several STATE records, each of which may in turn be connected to several CITY records. In addition, all connections between records, according to the links, are totally functional. That is, each record, except for a root record, must be connected to a parent record as constrained by the hierarchical definition tree. Furthermore, each record must be connected to at most one parent record. For example, in Fig. 5.1–2, there can be no "independent" occurrences of record types STATE, TERRITORY, CITY, and TOWN. However, there can be independent occurrences of the

COUNTRY record type since it is a root record type. In addition, each CITY and TOWN record must be connected to a STATE record, and each STATE and TERRITORY record must be connected to a COUNTRY record. However, each CITY record can be connected to only one STATE record, and each STATE record can be connected to only one COUNTRY record. A CITY or TOWN record cannot be connected to a TERRITORY record since this connection is not represented by a link in the hierarchical definition tree of Fig. 5.1–1.

There are two accepted notations for representing a hierarchical definition tree and a hierarchical data base. In one notation, shown in Fig. 5.1–3a and used up to this point, every node in a hierarchical definition tree represents a record type, and every node in a data base tree represents a record [IBM, 1975]. In the other notation, shown in Fig. 5.1–3b, only the terminal nodes (nodes that have no children) in a hierarchical definition tree and a data base tree represent, respectively, record types and records. The intermediate nodes (marked ⊙) serve only to maintain the hierarchical structure [Bleier, 1967; MRI, 1972].

In the first notation, since every node in a data base tree represents a record, the presence or absence of a record (node) determines the structure of the data base tree. For example, in Fig. 5.1–3a, a SUPPLIER record cannot exist in a data base tree if its associated PART record is not present. However, in the second notation, since only a terminal node represents a record, the intermediate nodes determine the structure of a data base tree. In this case, it is possible for a SUPPLIER record to exist in a data base tree even if its associated PART record is not present. This situation may arise if a supplier temporarily suspends supplying a part. In this way, it is still possible to represent the association of a SUPPLIER record with a DEPARTMENT record even if the PART record is not present.

In terms of representing the hierarchical structure of a data base, i.e., the hierarchical definition tree, the two notations are equivalent. Therefore, for simplicity and uniformity, only the former notation for representing a hierarchical definition tree will be used. However, it should be noted that, in terms of representing a hierarchical data base, i.e., the data base trees, the second notation has some advantages. These advantages are related to the association of dependent records with ancestor records and will be discussed again in Section 5.2.

The hierarchical data model provides no means for representing direct $N:M$ links between record types. However, an $N:M$ link between two record types can be represented by two hierarchical definition trees. In this case, each hierarchical definition tree represents a $1:N$

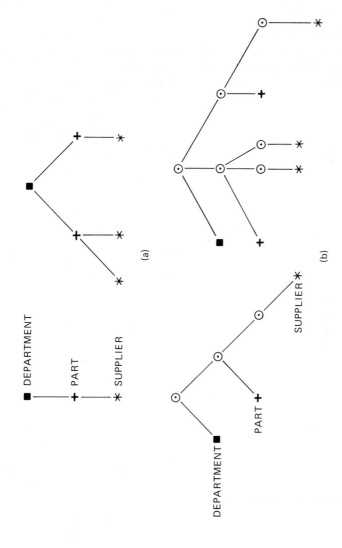

Fig. 5.1–3 Two data base hierarchies.

link. For instance, in the example of Fig. 2.3–1 the $N:M$ link REGIS-
TRATION between the record types STATE and COMPANY can be
represented by using two hierarchical definition trees, one with root
record type STATE and the other with root record type COMPANY as
in Fig. 5.1–4. The COMPANY REGISTRATION and STATE REGIS-
TRATION records need only contain enough data to identify their
respective COMPANY and STATE records.

An $N:M$ link between two record types can also be represented in a
single hierarchical definition tree. In this case, one record type is chosen
as the root record type and the other as the dependent record type.
However, a great deal of data duplication may be required. Consider
again the $N:M$ link REGISTRATION between the STATE and COM-
PANY record types. If the root record type is STATE, then a COM-
PANY record would have to be repeated under each state in which it is
registered. If the amount of data associated with each company is quite
large, then a great deal of storage space is required for data duplication.
In addition, symmetric queries are not handled in a symmetrical fashion. For example, a query such as "Find all companies located in state
S," is simple to answer; for state S, all company descendants are found.
However, the symmetric query, "Find all states in which company C is
located," cannot be answered by finding the descendants of the com-

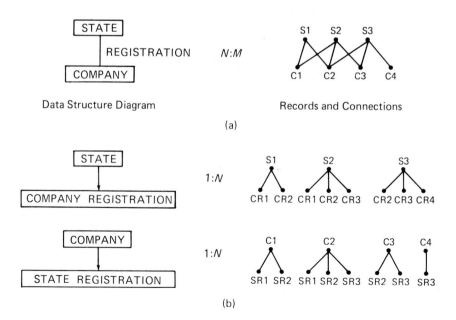

Fig. 5.1–4 Representing an $N:M$ link by two $1:N$ links.

pany C record. Instead, for every state, it is necessary to determine if company C is registered in the state.

To summarize, the *hierarchical data model* is a set of record types and links defined as follows:

1. There is a set of record types $\{R_1, R_2, \ldots, R_n\}$.

2. There is a set of links connecting all record types in one data structure diagram.

3. There is at most one link L_{ij} between any two record types R_i and R_j. Hence, links need not be named.

4. No link L_{ii} is defined for any i. That is, no connections between occurrences of the same record type are allowed.

5. The links, as expressed in the data structure diagram, form an ordered tree called a hierarchical definition tree.

6. Each link L_{ij} is totally functional in one direction. That is, for every R_j record occurrence there is *exactly one* R_i record occurrence connected to it, if the R_i record type is the parent record type of the R_j record type in the hierarchical definition tree.

7. There is a distinguished record type called the root record type, which has no parent record type.

5.2 HIERARCHICAL DATA LANGUAGES

A *hierarchical system* is a DBMS that organizes the data in a data base according to the hierarchical data model. In addition, it provides access to the data via a hierarchical data language. The hierarchical data language allows records in a hierarchical data base to be inserted, modified, deleted, and retrieved. Because of the nature of the links between record types in the hierarchical data model, inserting and deleting records require special consideration.

When a new record is inserted into a hierarchical data base (except for a root record), it has to be connected to a parent record. Usually, the parent record is selected by some form of data selection. The new record is then inserted as a child of the selected parent record. For example, in Fig. 5.1–2, to insert a new CITY record, a STATE record would first have to be selected. The CITY record is then stored in the data base and connected to the selected STATE record.

Deletion of a record in a hierarchical data base poses special problems. Usually, a dependent record in some sense owes its existence to an ancestor record. For example, consider the simple hierarchical definition tree in Fig. 5.2–1. A supplier is only associated with a

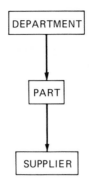

Fig. 5.2–1 Example of hierarchical definition tree.

department by virtue of the part(s) it supplies to the department. If a department no longer needs a part and the PART record is deleted, then logically the associated SUPPLIER record should also be deleted, since the connection to the DEPARTMENT record via the PART record is lost. However, one may want to keep the information that a supplier once supplied a department.

Recall that in Section 5.1 two notations for representing a hierarchical data base were discussed (Fig. 5.1–3). In the first notation, each node in a data base tree represented a record. In addition, the connections among the nodes represented the hierarchical structure. In the second notation, only the terminal nodes represented records. The intermediate nodes were used to represent the hierarchical structure. If only the terminal nodes represent records, then keeping a SUPPLIER record when a PART record is deleted is simple. Since the intermediate nodes maintain the hierarchical structure, it is possible to keep the association between a DEPARTMENT record and a SUPPLIER record even if a PART record is deleted. Only the necessary terminal node (PART record) is deleted. However, if every node in a data base tree represents a record, then deleting a record also changes the hierarchical structure. That is, all descendant records must be deleted since the connection with ancestor records is lost. Such a deletion operation is called a *triggered delete* since the deletion of a record triggers the deletion of its descendant records. The only way to keep descendant records in this case is to keep an empty record.

When retrieving records in a hierarchical data base, records are selected by a qualification and then related to other records according to the hierarchical structure. In general, the qualification can involve data items from any record type in the hierarchical definition tree.

However, almost all systems permit a qualification to contain data items only from record types whose records form a hierarchical path. In this way, they avoid the ambiguity that arises when the negation Boolean operator (NOT) is specified in a qualification [Hardgrave, 1972].

After a record has been selected by a qualification, other records may be selected according to the hierarchical structure. For example, every record has a unique set of ancestors in the data base. All ancestors of a selected record may also be selected for retrieval. In addition, a record may have a set of descendants. For example, in Fig. 5.1–2 a STATE record may have several CITY records connected to it. All descendants of a selected record may also be selected for retrieval. Notice that a selected record always has at most one ancestor record of each ancestor record type. That is, each record has at most one parent, which in turn has at most one parent, etc. However, in general, a selected record may have several descendant records of each descendant record type. That is, it may have several children, which in turn may have several children, etc. When selecting descendants, most systems allow descendants to be selected only along one hierarchical path. For instance, in Fig. 5.1–2, from a COUNTRY record one can select STATE records or TERRITORY records, but not both. Selecting ancestors of a record is called *upward hierarchical normalization*, while selecting descendants is called *downward hierarchical normalization* [Lowenthal, 1971].

Retrieval in a hierarchical data base may be performed in one of two ways. Using a *tree traversal* data language, a user explicitly uses the hierarchical structure of the data base to *traverse* the data base trees in a specified order. Using a *hierarchical selection* data language, a user selects records based on the relationships between the data items of the record types. In the case of hierarchical selection, although a user has to be aware of the hierarchical structure of the data base, he does not explicitly use this structure to retrieve records. Instead, the system utilizes the hierarchical structure to determine which records to select according to the data selection specified by the user. Each type of data language will be discussed in detail in the following sections.

5.2.1 Tree Traversal

Tree traversal hierarchical data languages allow the selection and retrieval of records in a hierarchical data base according to a systematic order. Several tree traversal methods are possible. In this section, two different methods will be examined: the first retrieves records according to a preorder data base tree traversal, and the second uses iteration to select data sequentially from all or certain records of a given type.

A preorder tree traversal is defined for binary trees [Knuth, 1968]. It can be extended to data base trees as follows:

1. Visit the record if it has not already been visited.
2. Else, visit the leftmost child not previously visited.
3. Else, if no children, grandchildren, etc., remain to be visited, go back to the parent record.

Starting with the root record, these steps are applied at each record of a data base tree whenever it is reached. It is assumed that the children of each parent are ordered according to the appearance of the child record type in the hierarchical definition tree, i.e., in Fig. 5.1–2, all STATE records under a COUNTRY record come before any TERRITORY records, etc.

The traversal begins at a root record and essentially visits all records in a data base tree in a top to bottom, left to right order. For example, for the data base tree given in Fig. 5.2.1–1, a preorder data base tree traversal would visit the records in the order indicated. Within a data base, all the data base trees are imagined to be connected to an imaginary head record, thus forming a single data base tree. In this way it is possible to visit all the records in the data base.

A tree traversal hierarchical data language that uses a preorder data base tree traversal will be outlined. It is based on IBM's Information Management System (IMS) Data Language/1 (DL/1) [IBM, 1975]. For pedagogical purposes, the syntax of the commands has been changed. (See Chapter 11 for the exact form of the IMS DL/1 commands.)

The retrieval commands are designed to facilitate a preorder data base tree traversal. Since the nature of the commands is sequential and one record at a time, it is necessary to maintain a pointer to the

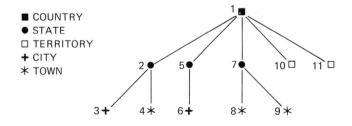

Fig. 5.2.1–1 Preorder tree traversal.

"current" record in the data base. The pointer marks a program's progress through the data base according to a preorder traversal of the data base trees. In the following examples, the data base shown in Figs. 5.2.1–2 and 5.2.1–3 is used.

A GET UNIQUE command retrieves a specific record of a specified type in the data base. The record retrieved is independent of the current position in the data base. Therefore, the GET UNIQUE command is used for nonsequential processing or to set the pointer to establish a start position for sequential processing of the data base. The start position may be set to a record of any type in the data base. The name GET UNIQUE is somewhat misleading since the record retrieved may not be unique. In general, the *leftmost* record in the data base trees satisfying the GET UNIQUE is selected. The selection of a record may be controlled by a qualification. In this case, the record selected is unique only if the qualification involves a unique key of the record type. Otherwise, the leftmost rule applies. For example, the query

GET UNIQUE DEPARTMENT WHERE (DEPTNAME=
   PRODUCTION)

retrieves the production DEPARTMENT record. The query

GET UNIQUE EMPLOYEE WHERE (DEPTNAME=RESEARCH)
   AND (SALARY=285)

retrieves the EMPLOYEE record (60, A BARTE, 285).

A GET NEXT command processes in a forward direction (to the right) from the current position in the data base, according to a preorder data base tree traversal. If the GET NEXT command does not specify a

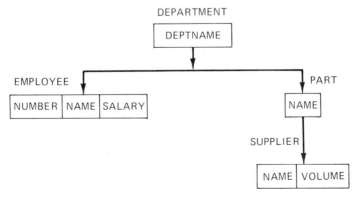

Fig. 5.2.1–2 Example of hierarchical definition tree.

record type or a qualification, i.e., is unqualified, then the next record in the data base according to a preorder data base tree traversal is retrieved. By starting at a root record, it is possible to retrieve every record in a data base tree. For example, for the data base tree of Fig. 5.2.1–3a, the records are retrieved in the order

(PRODUCTION)
(18, J GOULD, 285)
(23, D SMITH, 475)

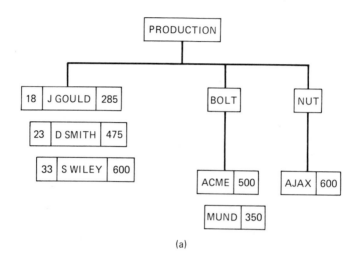

(a)

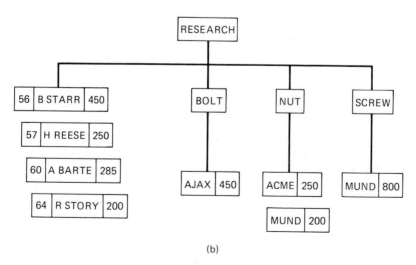

(b)

Fig. 5.2.1–3 Example of hierarchical data base.

(33, S WILEY, 600)
(BOLT)
(ACME, 500)
(MUND, 350)
(NUT)
(AJAX, 600).

The retrieval may be restricted only to records of one type. For example, the next EMPLOYEE record can be retrieved by the query

GET NEXT EMPLOYEE.

Starting at the current position in the data base tree, the next EM-PLOYEE record, according to a preorder data base tree traversal, is retrieved. Intervening records that are not of the specified type are skipped. In this way, it is possible to retrieve sequentially all records of one type within the data base. Finally, a qualification may further restrict the records to be retrieved. For example, the query

GET NEXT EMPLOYEE WHERE (SALARY>200)

retrieves the next EMPLOYEE record with a salary greater than $200. In all cases, the selection begins at the current position in the data base. All records that come "before" the current record, according to a preorder data base tree traversal, are automatically disqualified from consideration.

A GET NEXT WITHIN PARENT command obtains records within the family of a parent record according to a preorder data base tree traversal. The parent record is established by the last GET UNIQUE or GET NEXT command. The only difference between a GET NEXT and a GET NEXT WITHIN PARENT command is the result after the last child of a given parent is reached. The GET NEXT command continues retrieving records until the last record in the data base is reached. The GET NEXT WITHIN PARENT command signals that there are no more children. As for the GET NEXT command, the GET NEXT WITHIN PARENT command may be unqualified, qualified by a record type name, or qualified by a record type name and a qualification. An unqualified GET NEXT WITHIN PARENT command can be used to obtain all records within a parent. For example, suppose that the parent record is the PART record for Bolt in Fig. 5.2.1–3a. Two unqualified GET NEXT WITHIN PARENT commands would retrieve the records (ACME, 500) and (MUND, 350). A subsequent GET NEXT WITHIN PARENT command signals that there are no more children within the

parent record (Bolt). A GET NEXT WITHIN PARENT, qualified by a
record type name, retrieves only records of the specified type within
the parent. For example, if the parent record is a DEPARTMENT
record, then the query

GET NEXT WITHIN PARENT PART

retrieves only PART records within the parent. Finally, a qualification
may further restrict the records to be considered for retrieval. Again, all
records within the parent that come before the current record, according to a preorder data base tree traversal, are automatically disqualified
from consideration.

A HOLD feature can be combined with the previous commands in
the forms GET HOLD UNIQUE, GET HOLD NEXT, and GET HOLD
NEXT WITHIN PARENT. The HOLD feature allows only one user at a
time to modify a record by serializing access to the record.

To insert a new record, one must first select the parent-to-be of the
new record. The record is then inserted as the youngest child of the
parent by an INSERT command. The INSERT command both stores
the new record and connects it to its parent. This dual operation is
necessary since every record, except a root record, must have a parent.

A REPLACE command is used to update a record in the data base.
The record must first be selected by means of a retrieval command
using the HOLD feature.

A DELETE command deletes a record and all of its descendant
records. In order to delete a record, it must first be selected by means
of a retrieval command using the HOLD feature. The DELETE command is a triggered delete since the record selected and all its children
are deleted.

Another example of a hierarchical data language that uses a tree
traversal will be outlined. The language consists of a set of commands
that are part of an integrated, self-contained data language [Weiner *et
al*., 1975]. The main data selection feature of the language is the DO
FOR EACH statement, which has the following format:

DO loop-name FOR EACH record-name where-clause sort-clause;
.
.
.
END loop-name;

The loop-name, where-clause, and sort-clause are optional. The DO
FOR EACH statement selects all records of the type specified (record-
name) as controlled by a qualification (where-clause). However, since

the language is oriented to one-record-at-a-time processing, iteration is used to retrieve each selected record in turn and to process it. In addition, ancestor records are also available for processing since there is only one occurrence of each ancestor record type. However, descendant records are not available, since in general there may be several occurrences of each descendant record type. This restriction is a result of the one-record-at-a-time processing.

Consider the example of a company's data base shown in Figs. 5.2.1–2 and 5.2.1–3. Each employee is given a 10% raise as follows:

```
I=0;
DO RAISE FOR EACH EMPLOYEE;
    SALARY=1. 1*SALARY;
    I=I+1;
END RAISE;
```

The variable I is used to count the number of records accessed. If there are no EMPLOYEE records then the loop is not executed.

A DO FOR EACH statement will terminate after iterating through all selected records. In addition, there is an UNDO statement that can be used to cause termination of the loop. For instance, in the previous example, the loop is terminated after granting ten raises with the statement

```
IF I GT 10 THEN UNDO RAISE;
```

This statement is placed immediately after the DO FOR EACH statement so that only ten raises are granted.

Nesting of the DO FOR EACH statements allows descendant records to be selected and processed. In this case, the nested DO FOR EACH statement guarantees that only one descendant record is processed at one time. For example, the volume of bolts supplied by the ACME company to all departments is increased by 10% as follows:

```
DO FOR EACH PART WHERE NAME IS 'BOLT';
    DO FOR EACH SUPPLIER WHERE NAME OF SUPPLIER IS
    'ACME';
        VOLUME=1.1*VOLUME;
    END;
END;
```

The outer loop loops over each bolt PART record. The inner loop loops over each SUPPLIER record selecting only the Acme records. Note that increasing the level of nesting corresponds to descending a data

base tree along one path. That is, a DO FOR EACH statement contained within an outer DO FOR EACH statement accesses a record
lower in a data base tree than the one in the outer loop. Again one can
access ancestors during every iteration, but not descendants.

To summarize, DO FOR EACH statements conform to the following addressing rules [Weiner *et al.*, 1975] :

1. DO FOR EACH statements select only one type of record.

2. At each iteration, one can access one record of the specified
type. At the end of the iteration, the record is no longer accessible.

3. The ancestors of the selected record can be accessed during each
iteration.

4. A nested DO FOR EACH statement operates on the subtree
below the record selected in the immediately enclosing DO FOR EACH
statement. Nested loops have to go down a data base tree.

All data item names can be made unique by attaching IN or OF,
e.g.,

SALARY OF EMPLOYEE
SALARY IN COMPANY

The first example specifies SALARY to be a data item of the record
type EMPLOYEE. The second example states that the data item
SALARY is unique within the hierarchical definition tree. It is up to
the system to determine the appropriate record type.

Insertions are performed by means of a DO INSERT statement. An
empty record is first inserted and then filled with data within the DO
INSERT statement. The DO INSERT statement appears within a DO
FOR EACH statement or another DO INSERT statement. THE DO
FOR EACH statement or the preceding DO INSERT statement determines the parent of the new record. Only a DO INSERT for a root
record type need not appear within a DO FOR EACH or another DO
INSERT statement. The following is an example of the insertion of a
new employee:

```
DO FOR EACH DEPARTMENT WHERE NAME IS 'SALES';
    DO INSERT EMPLOYEE;
        NUMBER=35;
        NAME='C ADAMS';
        SALARY=550;
    END;
END;
```

A <u>DELETE</u> statement deletes a record and all of its descendants. The <u>DELETE</u> statement must appear inside a <u>DO</u> <u>FOR</u> <u>EACH</u> statement. The <u>DO</u> <u>FOR</u> <u>EACH</u> statement selects the record to be deleted.

The following program inserts a DEPARTMENT record and its EMPLOYEE records and then calculates the weekly department payroll. The % sign signifies a comment. External data input is performed via the procedure STRING_ INPUT.

```
DO EXAMPLE INSERT DEPARTMENT;
    DEPTNAME=STRING_INPUT;
    % INSERT EMPLOYEES.
    DO READ_ DATA FOREVER;
        LOCAL=STRING_ INPUT;
        IF LOCAL EQ '/ /' THEN UNDO READ_DATA;
        DO INSERT EMPLOYEE;
            NUMBER=STRING_ INPUT;
            NAME=STRING_ INPUT;
            SALARY=STRING_ INPUT;
        END;
    END READ_ DATA;
    % CALCULATE DEPARTMENT PAYROLL PER WEEK.
    PAYROLL=0 DOLLARS;
    DO PAY_ TOTAL FOR EACH EMPLOYEE;
        PAYROLL=PAYROLL+SALARY;
    END PAY_ TOTAL;
END EXAMPLE;
```

Tree traversal hierarchical data languages usually operate on one record at a time. As a result, although they operate on a tree, their nature is almost sequential. The nature of the commands influences their implementation. It would be nice if the logically next record in the hierarchy were also the physically next record in the underlying implementation. In this way, sequential processing of the data base trees is very efficient. On the other hand, it may well be that the nature of the tree traversal commands is related to some of their early, essentially sequential implementations.

5.2.2 Hierarchical Selection

Hierarchical selection data languages regard the records of a record type as sets of data item values. Records are selected and related according to the relationships among the data items of the record types. These relationships are determined by a hierarchical definition tree.

Consider, for instance, the hierarchical definition tree shown in Fig.
5.2.2—1. Each record type defines relationships among the data items of
the record type. In addition, there are relationships between data items
of different record types according to the hierarchical structure. For
instance, PROVINCE POPULATION and CITY POPULATION are
related according to the link between the PROVINCE and CITY record
types. This link essentially establishes a connection between the CITY
POPULATION of a city and the PROVINCE POPULATION of its
parent province. Any relationship between two data items in a hierarchical definition tree is given in a unique way by the links among the
corresponding record types. This property comes from the hierarchical
data model. However, the hierarchical data model does restrict the relationships between data items to be according to a hierarchical definition tree.

A qualification, in hierarchical selection data languages, is usually
specified by a WHERE clause. A WHERE clause consists of the keyword WHERE and a Boolean combination of conditions. The WHERE
clause specifies the records to be selected. Thereafter, upward and/or
downward hierarchical normalization can be performed. Downward
hierarchical normalization is usually restricted to one hierarchical path.

The features of hierarchical selection data languages will be illustrated by examples using SYSTEM 2000's "Natural Language" feature
[MRI, 1972]. This feature is an English-like, interactive query language.
The commands consist of two parts: an action part and a WHERE
clause. The action part specifies the operation to be performed, e.g.,
retrieval or update, and which data items should be operated on. The
basic retrieval command is the PRINT command.

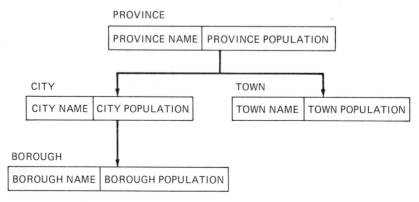

Fig. 5.2.2—1 Example of hierarchical definition tree.

The following query illustrates upward hierarchical normalization:

PRINT CITY NAME WHERE BOROUGH NAME EQ
   SCARBOROUGH:

This query specifies that the values of the CITY NAME data item in
CITY records are wanted. In addition, the CITY records must have a
BOROUGH descendant that satisfies the WHERE clause. Therefore, all
BOROUGH records satisfying the WHERE clause are selected and then
an upward hierarchical normalization is performed to select CITY
records. In general, several CITY records may be selected.

The next query illustrates downward hierarchical normalization:

PRINT BOROUGH NAME WHERE CITY NAME EQ TORONTO:

Examining CITY records, the records satisfying the WHERE clause
are selected. Again, in general, several records may be selected. A
downward hierarchical normalization is then performed to select
BOROUGH records. Many BOROUGH records may qualify. Note that
this and the preceding query are conceptually symmetric queries. However, they are not symmetric with respect to the hierarchical definition
tree. The query

PRINT CITY NAME WHERE CITY POPULATION GT 1,000,000:

involves neither upward nor downward hierarchical normalization. The
query is answered by selecting only CITY records. Again, several
records may be selected.

Now consider the query

PRINT PROVINCE NAME WHERE CITY NAME EQ TORONTO
   AND CITY NAME EQ OTTAWA:

The casual user would perhaps expect the response to this query to
be Ontario as the province that has both Toronto and Ottawa as cities.
However, the semantics of the WHERE clause, containing the AND
Boolean operator, are such that the answer to this query is null, i.e., no
PROVINCE record is selected. This problem arises because all Boolean
operations are performed at the same level at which records are selected
by the WHERE clause, i.e., on CITY records. Therefore, the intersection (AND) of two conditions in which a data item value must satisfy
two diametrically opposed criteria simultaneously must be null. That is,
the same record cannot have two different values for the same data
item.

If the Boolean operations are performed on selected records at a higher level, then the problem is overcome. The purpose of the HAS clause is to raise the level at which the Boolean operations are performed. This action is accomplished by performing an upward hierarchical normalization on the records selected by a WHERE clause and then applying the Boolean operations to the newly selected records. For instance, the query

> PRINT PROVINCE NAME WHERE PROVINCE NAME HAS CITY
> NAME EQ TORONTO AND PROVINCE NAME HAS CITY
> NAME EQ OTTAWA:

produces the answer Ontario as expected. In the previous query, using only the WHERE clause, the intersection (AND) is performed on CITY records. In this query, the intersection is performed on PROVINCE records since the level of Boolean operations is raised to PROVINCE records by means of the HAS clause. (The level to which upward hierarchical normalization is done is specified by the data item name preceding the keyword HAS.) In the first query, there is no CITY record satisfying both conditions of the WHERE clause. In the second query, there is at least one PROVINCE record that has CITY records satisfying the HAS clauses.

The HAS clause is also useful in other situations. For example, sometimes it is necessary to retrieve values from a record of one type based on the selection of a record of a different type at the same level. For instance, consider the query "Print the names of the cities located in a province that has a town called Last Chance." A WHERE clause does not permit this capability. However, a HAS clause does as follows:

> PRINT CITY NAME WHERE PROVINCE NAME HAS TOWN
> NAME EQ LAST CHANCE:

The appropriate TOWN record(s) is selected and then an upward hierarchical normalization is done to select PROVINCE records. A downward hierarchical normalization is then performed to select all CITY records connected to the PROVINCE record. It is also possible to retrieve town names based on the selection of BOROUGH records:

> PRINT TOWN NAME WHERE PROVINCE NAME HAS
> BOROUGH NAME EQ YORK:

Hierarchical selection data languages usually represent a hierarchical definition tree and a data base tree by using intermediate nodes to maintain the hierarchical structure. In this way, they are able to provide commands that delete a record, but not its descendants. In addition, data items in records may also be deleted without deleting the entire record. For example, in SYSTEM 2000, the <u>REMOVE</u> command deletes data item values from a record. The effect is to make the data item value null. Other data language operations, such as insertion and update, are similar in effect to corresponding tree traversal commands.

Hierarchical selection languages are very flexible. They use tree operations to select records in the data base. Records are selected because they are ancestors or descendants of other selected records. Queries that require movement up and down the data base tree can usually be handled in one command. As such, hierarchical selection data languages are more versatile than tree traversal data languages, which traverse the data base trees in a specific, sequential manner.

5.3 EXAMPLES OF APPLICATIONS

5.3.1 Payroll

A common example that seems to favor the hierarchical data model is a company's payroll application [Schafheitlin, 1974]. Information about an employee, such as income, deductions, and previous experience, is stored in the data base. The data can be grouped into the following entity sets.

Employee contains employee number, age, and address.

Pay contains pay period and income for it.

Type contains types of pay, i.e., regular, overtime, etc., and amount.

Deductions contains the deductions for a particular pay period.

Previous contains previous experience including place, leaving date, and salary.

The entity sets are easily organized according to a hierarchical data model. Between each employee and an employee's income, there exists a 1:N relationship, e.g., 1:26 for biweekly payments. For each pay period, its types of pay and deductions also form 1:N relationships. Similarly, previous experience forms the same type of relationship. The hierarchical definition tree shown in Fig. 5.3.1−1 is thus capable of handling the organization of the data.

IBM's Information Management System (IMS) DBMS will be used in this example. In IMS, record types are called segment types and data

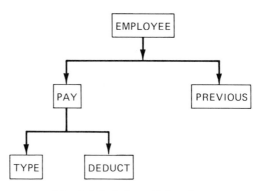

Fig. 5.3.1–1 Payroll data base.

items are called fields. The data base schema is defined by means of a Data Base Description or DBD. A subschema is defined by a Program Specification Block or PSB. Finally, access to the data base is via data base calls from PL/1, COBOL, or Assembler Language to Data Language/1 (DL/1). In this section, only enough detail is provided about IMS to comprehend the implementation of the application. For more information on the IMS DBMS see Chapter 11.

The first step is the schema definition. It will not be given in full as the intricacies of the data definition are not relevant to this example. The DBD for the data base is as follows:

DBD	NAME=PAYROLL,ACCESS=HDAM
DATASET	DD1=PAYHDAM,DEVICE=3330
SEGM	NAME=EMPLOYEE,BYTES=58
FIELD	NAME=(NUMBER,SEQ,U),BYTES=6,START=1
FIELD	NAME=NAME,BYTES=30,START=7
FIELD	NAME=AGE,BYTES=2,START=37
FIELD	NAME=ADDRESS,BYTES=20,START=39
SEGM	NAME=PAY,PARENT=EMPLOYEE,BYTES=6
FIELD	NAME=(PERIOD,SEQ,U),BYTES=2,START=1
FIELD	NAME=INCOME,BYTES=4,START=3
SEGM	NAME=TYPE,PARENT=PAY,BYTES=6
FIELD	NAME=(PAYTYPE,SEQ,U),BYTES=2,START=1
FIELD	NAME=AMOUNT,BYTES=4,START=3
SEGM	NAME=DEDUCT,PARENT=PAY,BYTES=7
FIELD	NAME=(KIND,SEQ,U),BYTES=3,START=1
FIELD	NAME=AMOUNT,BYTES=4,START=4

```
SEGM            NAME=PREVIOUS,PARENT=EMPLOYEE,
                  BYTES=37
FIELD           NAME=(PLACE,SEQ,M),BYTES=25,START=1
FIELD           NAME=DATE,BYTES=8,START=26
FIELD           NAME=SALARY,BYTES=4,START=34

DBDGEN
FINISH
END
```

The first set of statements assigns the data base the name PAY-ROLL, specifies the type of storage organization (HDAM), names the physical file (PAYHDAM), and specifies the type of storage device. The next five sets of statements define in turn the EMPLOYEE, PAY, TYPE, DEDUCT, and PREVIOUS record types. For each record type, the name, parent, and length in bytes are specified. For the data items within each record type, the name, length, and start position in the record are given. In addition, for each record type a key (SEQ) is specified.

Next, the subschema for the application is defined via a PSB. The PSB specifies some processing options and those record types which are required for an application. For the example application, only the EMPLOYEE, PAY, and DEDUCT records types will be needed:

```
PCB             TYPE=DB,DBDNAME=PAYROLL,PROCOPT=G,
                  KEYLEN=31
SENSEG          NAME=EMPLOYEE,PARENT=0
SENSEG          NAME=PAY,PARENT=EMPLOYEE
SENSEG          NAME=DEDUCT,PARENT=PAY
PSBGEN          LANG=PLI,PSBNAME=T4TAX
END
```

The application will be to obtain the data for the year end tax slip. It will be assumed, however, that only gross pay, pension, and income tax deductions are required.

This application involves essentially processing the left side of the data base trees. For each employee in the data base the pay must be totaled from all pay periods and for each pay period the pension and income tax deductions added to their respective totals. How these data are actually retrieved depends somewhat on the hierarchical data language used. In a hierarchical data language such as IMS's DL/1, which is used here, it is usually necessary to proceed down through the hierarchy processing a pay period, then its deductions, then another pay period, etc.

The various steps in the algorithm are as follows:

1. Get an employee.
2. Get a pay period and add pay to total.
3. For each pay period, get pension and tax deductions and add to totals.
4. Repeat (2) and (3) for each pay period.
5. Repeat (1) to (4) for each employee.

Before implementing these steps, several declarations internal to the application program are required. First, an outline of a mask for the Program Communication Block or PCB is required. The PCB is used to communicate between the application program and IMS. It returns a status code, specifies processing options, and provides feedback information. Only the parts relevant to the application will be given:

```
DECLARE 1 PCB BASED (TAX_ PCB),
          2  DATA_ BASE_ NAME CHAR(8),
                  .
                  .
                  .
          2  STATUS_ CODE CHAR(2),
                  .
                  .
                  .
          2  KEY_ FEEDBACK CHAR(11);
```

Next, the record buffers are declared. They are used to hold the record retrieved by IMS and to make it available to the host language program:

```
DECLARE EMPLOYEE_ IO_ AREA CHAR(58),
             1 EMPLOYEE DEFINED EMPLOYEE_ IO_ AREA,
                2 NUMBER CHAR(6),
                2 NAME,
                   3 LAST CHAR(19),
                   3 FIRST CHAR(10),
                   3 INITIAL CHAR(1),
                2 AGE CHAR(2),
                2 ADDRESS CHAR(20);
```

```
DECLARE PAY_ IO_ AREA CHAR(6),
        1 PAY DEFINED PAY_ IO_ AREA,
        2 PERIOD CHAR(2),
        2 INCOME FIXED DEC(7,2);

DECLARE DEDUCT_ IO_ AREA CHAR(7),
        1 DEDUCT DEFINED DEDUCT_ IO_ AREA,
        2 KIND CHAR(3),
        2 AMOUNT FIXED DEC(7,2);
```

For each record type, a *segment search argument (SSA)* must also be declared. It specifies a qualification involving the data items of a record type. Only the SSA_EMPLOYEE declaration is given. The other SSA's have a similar format:

```
DECLARE 1 SSA_ EMPLOYEE STATIC UNALIGNED,
          2 SEGMENT_ NAME CHAR(8) INIT('EMPLOYEE'),
          2 LEFT_ PARENTHESIS CHAR(1) INIT ('('),
          2 KEYFIELD_ NAME CHAR(8) INIT('NUMBER'),
          2 CONDITIONAL_ OPERATOR CHAR(2),
          2 SEARCH_ VALUE CHAR(6),
          2 RIGHT_ PARENTHESIS CHAR(1) INIT(')');
```

Finally, some necessary variables are declared:

```
DECLARE EMPLOYEE_ NO CHAR(6),
        FOUR FIXED BINARY(31) INIT(4),
        GU CHAR(4) INIT('GU  '),
        GN CHAR(4) INIT('GN  '),
        GNP CHAR(4) INIT ('GNP '),
        SUCCESSFUL CHAR(2) INIT (' '),
        TAXTOTAL,PENSIONTOTAL,PAYTOTAL FIXED
        DEC(7,2);
```

In the following program, calls to DL/1 are characterized by the starting sequence CALL PLITDLI. These calls may take a varying number of parameters. The first parameter indicates the number of parameters to follow. The second parameter indicates the type of command. In this application, it is either GU (GET UNIQUE), GN (GET NEXT), or GNP (GET NEXT WITHIN PARENT). The next parameter indicates the address of the PCB that IMS uses to obtain control information and to return status information. The fourth parameter specifies the address of the buffer where the retrieved record is to be placed. Finally, the remaining parameters specify the SSA's. There may be one SSA for each record type in the hierarchical path to the desired record.

The first step, in the program itself, is to obtain an EMPLOYEE record. Since the EMPLOYEE records are in ascending order (ordering done by IMS), the search value is initially set to the lowest possible value (LOW(6)) and the EMPLOYEE records are accessed in sequence.

The first part establishes a parent EMPLOYEE record. After each call to DL/1, the STATUS_CODE is checked. If it is not equal to SUCCESSFUL, then the end of the data base has been reached or some error has occurred and the program terminates. Otherwise, an employee's pay records are processed:

```
/*Set initial values*/
SSA_ EMPLOYEE.SEARCH_ VALUE=LOW(6);
SSA_ EMPLOYEE.CONDITIONAL_ OPERATOR=' >';
/*Get the first EMPLOYEE record*/
CALL PLITDLI (FOUR,GU,TAX_PCB,EMPLOYEE_IO_AREA,
    SSA_EMPLOYEE);
/*Do while not end of data base or error*/
DO WHILE(PCB.STATUS_ CODE=SUCCESSFUL);
    /*Set initial values*/
    EMPLOYEE_ NO=SUBSTR(PCB.KEY_ FEEDBACK,1,6);
    PAYTOTAL,PENSIONTOTAL,TAXTOTAL=0;
    /*Calculate pay and taxes*/
    CALL PROCESS_PAY;
    /*Output results*/
    CALL OUTPUT;
    /*Set the EMPLOYEE record search value*/
    SSA_EMPLOYEE.SEARCH_VALUE
        =SUBSTR (PCB.KEY_FEEDBACK,1,6);
    CALL PLITDLI (FOUR,GU,TAX_PCB,
        EMPLOYEE_IO_AREA, SSA_EMPLOYEE);
END;
```

The PROCESS_PAY procedure processes an employee's PAY records. Due to the nature of DL/1, a <u>GET</u> <u>NEXT</u> command must be used to establish a PAY record so that a <u>GET</u> <u>NEXT</u> <u>WITHIN</u> <u>PARENT</u> command may be used to retrieve deductions. The KEY_FEEDBACK area is checked to ensure that the employee number of the employee associated with a PAY record is correct. If it is, then the DEDUCT records are processed:

```
PROCESS_PAY:PROCEDURE;
    /*Get the first PAY record*/
    CALL PLITDLI (FOUR,GN,TAX_PCB,PAY_IO_AREA,'PAY');
    /*Continue processing PAY records until either*/
    /*a new employee is encountered or until no*/
    /*more PAY records remain in the data base*/
    DO WHILE ( (PCB.STATUS_CODE=SUCCESSFUL) &
        (SUBSTR(PCB.KEY_FEEDBACK,1,6)=
        EMPLOYEE_NO) );
            PAYTOTAL=PAYTOTAL+PAY.AMOUNT;
            CALL PROCESS_DEDUCTIONS;
            /*Get next PAY record*/
            CALL PLITDLI(FOUR,GN,TAX_PCB,
                PAY_IO_AREA,'PAY');
    END;
END PROCESS_PAY;
```

Finally, all deductions for a pay period are collected in the PROCESS_DEDUCTIONS procedure. No checks are performed to see if the deductions actually exist. However, if they do not, then the tax and pension totals remain unaltered. It is assumed that deductions are in order by their kind:

```
PROCESS_DEDUCTIONS:PROCEDURE;
    /*Set search value for income tax deductions*/
    SSA_DEDUCT.SEARCH_VALUE='001';
    CALL PLITDLI(FOUR,GNP,TAX_PCB,DEDUCT_IO_AREA,
        SSA_DEDUCT);
    /*Check if no tax deduction*/
    IF PCB.STATUS_CODE=SUCCESSFUL
        THEN TAXTOTAL=TAXTOTAL+DEDUCT.AMOUNT;
    /*Set search value for pension deductions*/
    SSA_DEDUCT.SEARCH_VALUE='005';
    CALL PLITDLI(FOUR,GNP,TAX_PCB,DEDUCT_IO_AREA,
        SSA_DEDUCT;
    /*Check if no pension deduction*/
    IF PCB.STATUS_CODE=SUCCESSFUL
        THEN PENSIONTOTAL=PENSIONTOTAL
            +DEDUCT.AMOUNT;
END PROCESS_DEDUCTIONS;
```

As the alert reader will have noticed, error checking in this application has been kept to a minimum. For instance, one might want to print an error message if there are no EMPLOYEE records, PAY records for an employee, or tax and pension deductions for a pay period. However, the purpose of this example is to demonstrate the nature of hierarchical processing, not error handling.

In this application the technique of establishing a parent and then processing its children was used at two different levels in the data base trees. This is a common procedure in hierarchical systems. At times the program may seem complex, but this is due more to the detailed procedural nature of the tree traversal commands than the hierarchical data model. In fact, for this problem the hierarchical data model seems quite natural.

There are, however, some difficulties in organizing the data according to the hierarchical data model. Consider a query such as "Obtain a list of all people who had deductions for Savings Bonds," or an update such as "Increase the amount deducted for a specific company pension plan by 10% for all employees who pay into it." Both of these applications require searches of the data base to produce complete solutions. Such searches are necessary because there are several occurrences of the required records, but in unknown locations. Content addressibility can be used to provide these locations directly if the appropriate data items are indexed.

5.3.2   Insurance Policy Processing

This example is a typical processing application for a life insurance company [Schafheitlin, 1974]. There are two data bases in this example: one policy oriented and the other client oriented. Both data bases will be structured according to a hierarchical data model. In an effort to simplify the real-life situation, hopefully without loss of generality, only nine dependent record types in the policy data base and three in the client data base are used. Typically, there are about forty dependent record types in the policy data base and ten dependent record types in the client data base in a real application.

The policy data base contains information on all policies issued. The entity sets, which will be represented by record types, are as follows:

Policy contains the policy number, the client's social insurance number, and the next activity to be performed for the policy.

Coverage contains the name of the insured.

Plan contains the type of coverage (life, term, endowment, etc.), the premium amount, the coverage amount, and the expiry date.

Annuity contains the total amount of the annuity and the benefit amount.

Prior contains the type, amount, and number of a prior policy.

Loans contains the balance, principal, and interest rate of a loan issued on a policy.

Suspensions contains the date of the suspension, when reestablished, and the reason for the suspension.

Billing contains currently paid to, previously paid to, and the number of months paid.

Method contains the method of billing (annual, semiannual, etc.) and the amount of payment.

Special contains a payment code and the amount for special billing.

The records are related according to the hierarchical definition tree in Fig. 5.3.2–1.

The client data base contains information on all clients of the company who have bought policies. Its entity sets, which will be represented by record types, are as follows.

Client contains the client name, address, social security number, and birthdate.

Insured contains the name and social security number of a person covered by a client's policy, e.g., a child of the client.

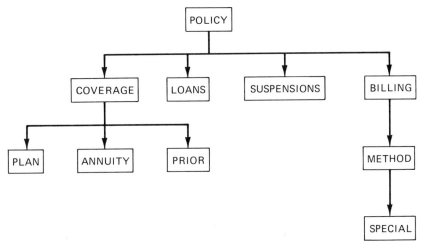

Fig. 5.3.2–1 Policy data base.

Policies contains the policy number of a policy under which the insured is covered.

Dependents contains the name, social security number, and birthdate of a client's dependent.

The hierarchical definition tree for the client data base is shown in Fig. 5.3.2—2. Although there is some duplication of data, it is necessary to allow access to the policy data base via a client.

In this example, another hierarchical system, SYSTEM 2000, will be used [MRI, 1972]. SYSTEM 2000 supports a hierarchical selection language. The definition of a schema consists of defining the record types and the data items. In SYSTEM 2000, dependent record types are denoted as repeating groups or RG. The hierarchical structure is displayed in the data base description by the indentations. If a data item is denoted as NON-KEY, then it is not indexed; otherwise, it is indexed.

DATABASE NAME IS POLICY:

1* POLICY NUMBER (INTEGER 9 (6)):
2* SIN (INTEGER 9 (9)):
3* NEXT ACTIVITY (DATE):
4* COVERAGE (REPEATING GROUP):
    5* COVERAGE NAME (NAME X(20) IN 4):
    6* PLAN (RG IN 4):
       7* TYPE (NON-KEY NAME X(4) IN 6):
       8* PREMIUM (NON-KEY MONEY IN 6):
       9* PLAN AMOUNT (NON-KEY MONEY IN 6):
       10*EXPIRY (DATE IN 6):
11*ANNUITY (RG IN 4):
       12*ANNUITY AMOUNT (NON-KEY MONEY IN 11):

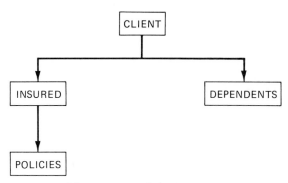

Fig. 5.3.2—2 Client data base.

13*BENEFIT (NON-KEY MONEY IN 11):
14*PRIOR (RG IN 4):
15*KIND (NON-KEY NAME X(5) IN 14):
16*PRIOR AMOUNT (NON-KEY MONEY IN 14):
17*PRIOR NUMBER (NON-KEY INTEGER 9(6) IN 14):
18*LOANS (RG):
19*BALANCE (NON-KEY MONEY IN 18):
20*PRINCIPAL (NON-KEY MONEY IN 18):
21*RATE (NON-KEY DECIMAL 9(3).9(1) IN 18):
22*SUSPENSIONS (RG):
23*SUSPENSION DATE (NON-KEY DATE IN 22):
24*REESTABLISHED DATE (NON-KEY DATE IN 22):
25*REASON (NON-KEY NAME X(10) IN 22):
26*BILLING (RG):
27*CURRENT (DATE IN 26):
28*PREVIOUS (NON-KEY DATE IN 26):
29*MONTHS PAID (NON-KEY INTEGER 9(3) IN 26):
30*METHOD (RG IN 26):
31*PAY METHOD (NON-KEY NAME X(2) IN 30):
32*METHOD AMOUNT (NON-KEY MONEY IN 30):
33*SPECIAL (RG IN 30):
34*CODE (NON-KEY NAME X(10) IN 33):
35*SPECIAL AMOUNT (NON-KEY MONEY IN 33):

DATABASE NAME IS CLIENT:

1* CLIENT NAME (NAME X(20)):
2* ADDRESS (NON-KEY NAME X(30)):
3* CLIENT SIN (INTEGER 9(9)):
4* CLIENT BIRTHDATE (NON-KEY DATE):
5* INSURED (RG):
6* INSURED NAME (NAME X(20) IN 5):
7* INSURED SIN (INTEGER 9(9) IN 5):
8* POLICIES (RG IN 5):
9* POLICY NUMBER (INTEGER 9(6) IN 8):
10*DEPENDENTS (RG):
11*DEPENDENT NAME (NAME X(20) IN 10):
12*DEPENDENT SIN (INTEGER 9(9) IN 10):
13*DEPENDENT BIRTHDATE (NON-KEY DATE IN 10):

A typical application is to remove the coverage for a person covered by a policy. An example is a family policy that covers the children until they turn twenty-one. To illustrate this application, the coverage for a specific person and for a specific policy is removed. The coverage for Jesse J. Jones is removed from policy number 320095. Using SYSTEM 2000's "Natural Language" feature the update is

REMOVE TREE COVERAGE WHERE POLICY NUMBER EQ
    320095 AND COVERAGE NAME EQ JESSE J. JONES:

Along with the COVERAGE record, any PLAN, ANNUITY, and PRIOR records under COVERAGE are also deleted. If one wants to retain these other records, then it is possible to delete only the COVERAGE record. The COVERAGE record is deleted by deleting all of its data item values as follows:

REMOVE COVERAGE NAME WHERE POLICY NUMBER EQ
    320095 AND COVERAGE NAME EQ JESSE J. JONES:

To provide a comparison, this application is also implemented using IMS [IBM, 1975]. Most declarations and initializations are omitted and error checking kept to a minimum to avoid confusing details. For convenience, the same names and hierarchies as declared in SYSTEM 2000 are used here. However, some of the names used would not be allowed in an IMS data base:

```
/*Set search arguments for POLICY and COVERAGE*/
SSA_POLICY SEARCH_VALUE='320095';
SSA_COVERAGE.SEARCH_VALUE='JESSE J. JONES';
/*Get and hold the record*/
CALL PLITDLI (FIVE, 'GHN',POLICY_PCB,
    COVERAGE_IO_AREA,SSA_POLICY, SSA_COVERAGE);
/*Check if record found*/
IF PCB.STATUS_CODE=SUCCESSFUL
    THEN CALL PLITDLI (THREE, 'DLET',POLICY_PCB,
    'COVERAGE'):
```

5.3.3 Student Records

The representation of an application according to the hierarchical data model is not always straightforward. There are some applications that favor a different data model. Although it is certainly plausible to implement them using the hierarchical data model, data duplication or inconvenience may result. A student records example illustrates some of these difficulties [Schafheitlin, 1974]. The same example is presented in Chapter 6 using the network data model. The reader is invited to compare the two implementations and to note the relative merits of each.

The example concerns information on the following entity sets:

Student contains student number, name, address, and year.
Teacher contains employee number and name.
Course contains course number and name.

In attempting to design a hierarchical definition tree for this application, some problems are immediately encountered. Course information is related both to students by the courses they take, and to teachers by the courses they teach. In addition, teachers are related to students by the students they teach, and students to teachers by the course taught to a student. It should be clear that, without a great deal of redundancy, it is not possible to represent all these relationships in a single hierarchy. Therefore, the solution adopted here is to use three hierarchies and to repeat part of the course information where necessary (Fig. 5.3.3–1).

The record types STUDENT, TEACHER, and COURSE contain data items corresponding to the attributes outlined previously. The remaining record types correspond to the following entity sets:

Student Course contains course number, section, and grade.
Teacher Course contains course number and section.
Dept contains department number (allows for cross appointments).
Section contains section identification and teacher number.

Notice that it is possible to obtain a student's teacher, but only with a bit of difficulty. The course number and section information from a STUDENT COURSE record have to be used to obtain the teacher numbers from the SECTION record. These teacher numbers are then used to access the teacher name in the TEACHER records. Similar difficulties arise when trying to find a teacher's students.

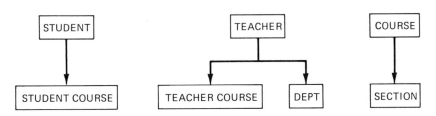

Fig. 5.3.3–1 Student records data base.

The data base is defined using SYSTEM 2000's DDF.

DATABASE NAME IS STUDENT:

1* STUDENT NUMBER (INTEGER 9(9)):
2* STUDENT NAME (NON-KEY NAME X(20)):
3* ADDRESS (NON-KEY NAME X(40)):
4* YEAR (NON-KEY INTEGER 9(2)):
5* STUDENT COURSE (RG):
    6* STUDENT COURSE NUMBER (INTEGER 9(5) IN 5):
    7* STUDENT COURSE SECTION (NON-KEY NAME X(1) IN 5):
    8* MARK (NON-KEY DECIMAL 9(3).9(1) IN 5):

DATABASE NAME IS TEACHER:

1* EMPLOYEE NO (INTEGER 9(9)):
2* TEACHER NAME (NON-KEY NAME X(20)):
3* TEACHER COURSE (RG):
    4* TEACHER COURSE NUMBER (INTEGER 9(5) IN 3):
    5* TEACHER COURSE SECTION (NON-KEY NAME X(1) IN 3):
6* DEPT (RG):
    7* DEPT NUMBER (INTEGER 9(5) IN 6):

DATABASE NAME IS COURSE:

1* COURSE NUMBER (INTEGER 9(5)):
2* COURSE NAME (NON-KEY NAME X(20)):
3* SECTION (RG):
    4* SECTION NUMBER (NAME X(1) IN 3):
    5* TEACHER NO (INTEGER 9(9) IN 3):

The example application will do two things:

1. Raise all course 2301 marks by 10%.
2. Delete teacher 03167895 from the data base.

The first update is specified as:

CHANGE MARK TO (MARKX1.1) WHERE STUDENT COURSE
    NUMBER EQ 2301:
LIST STUDENT NAME, MARK WHERE STUDENT COURSE
    NUMBER EQ 2301:

The simplicity of the update is due to the query language of SYSTEM 2000 and not the hierarchical data model. In fact, in many hierarchical systems, this update would be much more complex. The update involves searching the entire STUDENT data base and checking each student's courses to find the course 2301 marks.

In the second update, the problem of losing relevant data when deleting related information is present. It is desirable to maintain reference to sections taught by teacher 03167895, yet not the teacher record. Therefore, the teacher data item is deleted in the respective SECTION records, but the record is not deleted:

REMOVE TEACHER NO WHERE TEACHER NO EQ 03167895:
REMOVE TREE TEACHER WHERE EMPLOYEE NO EQ
     03167895:

One should note the duplication of data required in this example. In addition, the direct $N:M$ relationships that exist between the STUDENT, TEACHER, and COURSE record types have been lost. This problem can be alleviated if a hierarchical system allows pointers between data base trees as IMS and SYSTEM 2000 do [MRI, 1972; IBM, 1975]. In this approach, a record type can logically be associated with almost any other record type in the same or a different hierarchical definition tree. It essentially allows one to choose record types from existing hierarchical definition trees, and with some restrictions to form a new hierarchical definition tree representing a new view of the data base. However, the underlying storage structure is not altered to reflect the new view of the data base. Instead, pointers are used to materialize the new structure from existing storage structures. Thus data duplication is alleviated when trying to represent an $N:M$ relationship, although some pointer overhead is involved. This type of mechanism provides a very flexible subschema definition facility.

5.4 CONCLUDING REMARKS

Hierarchical systems have been available and well accepted for a long time [Bleier, 1967; CDC, 1970; UCS, 1970; Everett *et al.*, 1971; MRI, 1972; IBM, 1975]. In Part II of this book, two very successful hierarchical systems, Information Management System (IMS) and SYSTEM 2000, are outlined. It is difficult to relate a particular systems's success with its data model. There are many other parameters that influence the success of a commercial system. However, for some applications the hierarchical data model seems very natural. For instance, a corporate management structure is truly a hierarchical structure. In addition, most applications can be modeled according to the hierarchical data model, although some with more difficulty and redundancy than others.

Some specific advantages are widely accepted for the hierarchical data model. First, it is an easily understood data model and hierarchical systems provide the user with relatively few, easy to master commands. Second, because of the constraints on the types of relationships allowed, it seems to allow an easier implementation than some other data models. In fact, other data models such as the network and relational, may have to use hierarchical storage techniques for implementation purposes.

Some specific disadvantages are also associated with the hierarchical data model. The restrictions imposed force a sometimes unnatural organization of data. For instance, $N:M$ relationships can only be represented in a clumsy way. Because of the strict hierarchical ordering, operations such as insertion and deletion become quite complex. The triggered delete can lead to the loss of information present in the descendants. Users have to be careful when performing a triggered delete operation. Another disadvantage is that symmetrical queries are not represented in a similar fashion. Therefore, the view of the data base tends to reflect the needs of the applications, resulting in schema dependence.

Generally, the hierarchical data model does not seem to provide a great deal of flexibility for structuring data. It should be noted, however, that some hierarchical systems have facilities that essentially eliminate the basic rigidity of the hierarchical data model. For instance, they provide network structures by using logical pointers among hierarchies. They also provide logical hierarchical views that are different than the physically implemented structures [MRI, 1972; IBM, 1975]. Sometimes, hierarchical data languages are criticized as being too procedural. However, as shown in Section 5.2, higher level interfaces can be provided [MRI, 1972; Weiner *et al.*, 1975]. In this way, a casual user interface can be easily accommodated.

EXERCISES

5.1 Consider the relations defined by a hierarchical definition tree by using the data items as attributes of the relations. Investigate whether these relations are in 1NF, 2NF, or 3NF.

5.2 Consider the relations defined by a hierarchical definition tree as in Exercise 5.1. For all of the possible relations, is an update operation well defined? Is a delete operation well defined? Are any restrictions necessary on the types of operations allowed?

5.3 Consider two hierarchical definition trees. Define a hierarchical view that uses record types from both trees. Investigate the meaning of the different data language operations on the view in terms of the actual data language operations on the original data bases.

5.4 If a hierarchical view is defined as in Exercise 5.3, then when using a preorder data base tree traversal and issuing GET NEXT commands according to different views, a user can get into a cycle. How would you detect or avoid the possibility of such a situation?

5.5 Consider the application of suppliers and parts and the natural $N:M$ relationship between them. Implement this application using the hierarchical data model. What redundancy is needed? Give some examples of queries. How important is content addressibility?

5.6 Consider a different tree traversal than those discussed in Section 5.2.1. Design a language and outline its implementation based on this new tree traversal. What advantages (disadvantages) does your tree traversal have?

5.7 Outline a mnemonic hierarchical data language and a translation to IMS DL/I call statements [IBM, 1975]. How would you implement such a facility?

5.8 Consider the WHERE clause qualification in a hierarchical selection data language. The restriction can be made that a WHERE clause is well formed only if it contains data items appearing in the same path of a hierarchical definition tree. Why does this restriction work? Try to ease the restriction.

5.9 Design a manager-oriented simple query language. Outline its implementation in a hierarchical system.

5.10 Express the queries of the payroll example of Section 5.3.1 using the second tree traversal data language of Section 5.2.1. Compare the two languages in terms of procedurality and ease of use.

Chapter 6

NETWORK SYSTEMS

6.1 NETWORK DATA MODEL

In the general network data model discussed in Chapter 2, there were no restrictions on the relationships represented by links. In Chapter 5, the hierarchical data model was considered as a special case of the network data model. In the hierarchical data model, both the nature and the structure of the links were constrained. Links were restricted to be 1:N. In addition, they also had to be structured according to a tree and not a general network. In this chapter, another, less restrictive special case of the network data model will be considered. This data model will not be as general as the network data model discussed in Chapter 2. However, it will not be as restrictive as the hierarchical data model.

Consider the set of record types and links introduced in Section 2.3, Fig. 2.3–1. In a general network data model, there are no restrictions on the relationships represented by the links. They can be 1:1, 1:N, or N:M. However, some systems require specific restrictions on the links [CODASYL DBTG, 1971]. For instance, the links can be functional in one direction, that is, all links represent 1:N relationships. If this restriction is made, then the roles of the two record types connected by a 1:N link can be distinguished. For example, suppose that two record types R_i and R_j are connected by a 1:N link from R_i to R_j. Therefore, each R_i record is connected to many R_j records and no other R_i record is connected to the same R_j records. In this case, the R_i record is called the (owner) of the R_j records. Similarly, the unique set of R_j records connected to an R_i record are said to be *members* of the set of records owned by the R_i record. In the same manner, for every link the owner record type and the member record type can be identified. The separate roles of the owner and member record types can be represented in a relationship graph of the network by making the links directed from owner record type to member record type. Such a relationship graph is called a data structure diagram.

If only $1:N$ links are permitted between record types in the network, then the problem of handling $N:M$ links between record types arises. For example, consider the link REGISTRATION between the record types STATE and COMPANY in Fig. 2.3–1. In general, each state may have many companies registered in it and each company may be registered in many states. An example of such a situation is shown in Fig. 6.1–1. The fact that C2 is registered in both S1 and S2 makes this an $N:M$ relationship, rather than a $1:N$ relationship.

An $N:M$ relationship can be represented without using $N:M$ links between record types. Instead, an intermediate record type and two $1:N$ links can be used. In this way, a functional mapping is maintained. For example, for the $N:M$ link REGISTRATION between the STATE and COMPANY record types in Fig. 2.3–1, three record types (STATE, COMPANY, and REGISTRATION) and two links (REGISTERED IN between STATE and REGISTRATION and HAS REGISTRATION between COMPANY and REGISTRATION) are used as in Fig. 2.3–2. The two links and the intermediate record type represent the $N:M$ relationship between states and companies. The introduction of the

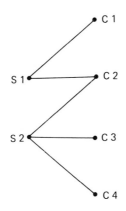

Fig. 6.1–1 State and company relationship.

intermediate record type is not always artificial. For instance, it can be used to contain data common to both states and companies.

In the hierarchical data model, links are unique between any two record types. Therefore, they do not have to be named to distinguish between them. However, given two different links between record types R_i and R_j, the links can still be distinguished by uniquely naming them. Hence, it is not difficult to handle many different links between two record types.

Recall that in the hierarchical data model, L_{ii} links were not allowed. There is nothing inherent in the general network data model that precludes the use of L_{ii} links. However, some systems disallow them to simplify navigation of a network data base. For example, consider an EMPLOYEE record type and a MANAGED BY link. The MANAGED BY link specifies an L_{ii} relationship for the record type EMPLOYEE. Suppose that one is at the record for a particular employee who also happens to be a manager. One arrived at this employee record by navigating through the data base from employee record to employee record. This particular employee record participates in a "managed by" relationship at two levels. First, the employee is one of perhaps several employees managed by another employee. Second, the employee, who is also a manager, manages perhaps several employees. If one now merely specifies that the next record according to the MANAGED BY link is wanted, one is at a loss as to which connection to pursue. However, if one also specifies the context, i.e., next employee MANAGED BY this employee, than the problem disappears. The need to specify the context of requests complicates navigation, which will be discussed in more detail in Section 6.3.

In Chapter 2, the general network data model was defined. It allowed any number of links between two record types. Also, there was no functionality requirement for the links, and L_{ii} links were allowed. Another, more restrictive form of the network data model can be defined [CODASYL DBTG, 1971]. The *DBTG network data model* is a set of record types and links defined as follows:

1. There is a set of record types $\{R_1, R_2, \ldots, R_n\}$.
2. There is a set of named links connecting the record types in a data structure diagram.
3. Every link is functional in at least one direction (partial functionality is allowed).
4. No link is of the form L_{ii} from a record type to itself.

Since most existing network systems also have restrictions 3 and 4, the rest of this chapter will examine, in detail, DBTG network systems.

The name DBTG is an acronym for the Data Base Task Group of the Conference on Data Systems Languages (CODASYL). In the next section, a network data model proposed by the DBTG will be discussed in detail. However, the reader should keep in mind that the general network data model can be another approach for the development of network DBMS's [Software AG, 1971].

6.2 CODASYL DBTG PROPOSAL

In this section the salient features of a data model for a network system proposed by the DBTG are presented. The terminology used will be according to the DBTG proposal [CODASYL DBTG, 1971].

One of the most important concepts introduced by the DBTG report is that of a *schema* and *subschema* as discussed in Chapter 4. All logical units of data are declared in a schema and its subschemas.

A *data item* is the smallest named logical unit of data as defined in Chapter 2. A *data aggregate* is a named collection of data items within a record type. There are two types of data aggregates allowed: vectors and repeating groups. A *vector* is a collection of data items all with the same characteristics. A *repeating group* is a collection of data items, vectors, or repeating groups occurring an arbitrary number of times.

A *record type* is a named collection of data items as defined in Chapter 2. In addition, data aggregates are also allowed to be a part of a record type. For example, CHILDREN can be thought of as a repeating group within a record type PERSON. Notice that the same logical relationship can be obtained by separating CHILDREN as another record type and connecting PERSON and CHILDREN records according to a link.

A *DBTG set* represents a named 1:N link among record types. It consists of one *owner* record type and one or more *member* record types (Fig. 6.2—1). A DBTG set can have many member record types, but the owner must be of a different type than any of its members. A DBTG set is not really a set in the mathematical sense. In the DBTG proposal, a DBTG set is called a set type. In addition, other alternative names have been proposed to avoid confusion with mathematical terminology.[1] Some of these other terms are coset for CODASYL set,

---

[1] The word "set" is the most overworked word in the English language, having 58 noun uses, 126 verbal uses, and 10 uses as a participial adjective ["Guinness Book of Records," p. 201 (McWhirter, N., and McWhirter, R., eds.), Sterling Publishing Co. Inc., New York, 1976]. Perhaps the DBMS community should refrain from giving the word set yet another use.

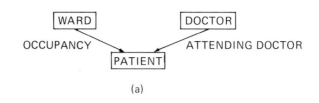

(a)

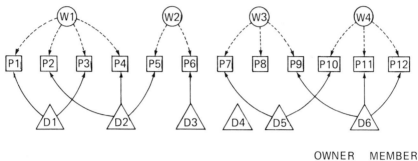

(b)

Fig. 6.2—1 Example of a network data base. (a) Data structure diagram. (b) Connections in the data base.

owner-coupled set, fan, etc. [Nijssen, 1975]. However, the term DBTG set will be used here to refer to the DBTG set type concept.

A set occurrence is the group of one owner record and several member records connected according to a DBTG set. It is usually identified by the owner record occurrence. Figure 6.2—1 shows four occurrences of OCCUPANCY and six occurrences of ATTENDING DOCTOR, one of which has no members. The capability of representing N:M relationships using DBTG sets derives from the ability of a member record type to be in more than one DBTG set at the same time, e.g., the PATIENT record type in Fig. 6.2—1. A DBTG set that has exactly one occurrence and is owned by the system is called a singular DBTG set. The type of set membership of records in set occurrences of a DBTG set must be specified in the schema. The options available are optional-manual, optional-automatic, mandatory-manual, and mandatory-automatic.

A record having *manual* set membership is made a member of a set occurrence only by explicitly including it in the set occurrence via data language operations. For example, in Fig. 6.2—1 the membership of a PATIENT record in an ATTENDING DOCTOR set occurrence can be specified as manual. Manual membership in this case means that a patient, e.g., P8 in Fig. 6.2—1, does not have to be assigned to a doctor (included in an ATTENDING DOCTOR set occurrence) at the time that he is admitted (that his PATIENT record is stored in the data base). The patient can be assigned to a doctor at any time after admission or not at all. A patient is assigned to a doctor (included in an ATTENDING DOCTOR set occurrence) by a data language command that connects his PATIENT record to the DOCTOR record of the doctor to whom he is assigned. The user must select the appropriate ATTENDING DOCTOR set occurrence by means of data language commands.

If the set membership is *automatic,* then at the time a member record is created, it is made a member of an occurrence of all the DBTG sets in which it is declared to be an automatic member. For example, in Fig. 6.2—1 the membership of a PATIENT record in an OCCUPANCY set occurrence can be specified as automatic. Automatic membership in this case means that a patient must be assigned to a ward (included in an OCCUPANCY set occurrence) at the time that he is admitted (that his PATIENT record is stored in the data base). The patient's PATIENT record is connected to the appropriate WARD record automatically when the PATIENT record is stored in the data base. No further action is required by the user to include the PATIENT record in an OCCU-PANCY set occurrence. The manner in which the DBMS selects the appropriate OCCUPANCY set occurrence will be discussed in Section 6.3.1.

Optional set membership implies that a record can be removed or inserted in a set occurrence by data language operations. For example, the membership of a PATIENT record in an ATTENDING DOCTOR set occurrence can be specified as optional. In this case, optional membership means that if a patient is assigned to a doctor (is a member in an ATTENDING DOCTOR set occurrence), then the patient can be discharged from the doctor's care (removed from the ATTENDING DOCTOR set occurrence). In addition, the patient does not have to be assigned to another doctor, although he may be. The patient is discharged from a doctor's care by removing his PATIENT record from the ATTENDING DOCTOR set occurrence via data language commands.

Mandatory membership means that once in a set occurrence, a record can never be removed from that set occurrence unless it is deleted or moved to another set occurrence. For example, the membership of a PATIENT record in an ATTENDING DOCTOR set occurrence can alternatively be specified as mandatory. In this case, mandatory membership means that once a patient is assigned to a doctor (included in an ATTENDING DOCTOR set occurrence) he cannot be discharged from the doctor's care (removed from the ATTENDING DOCTOR set occurrence) unless he is discharged from the hospital (his PATIENT record is deleted) or unless he is assigned to another doctor (removed from the current ATTENDING DOCTOR set occurrence and included in another ATTENDING DOCTOR set occurrence in one operation). In other words, once a patient is assigned to a doctor he must always be assigned to a doctor until he leaves the hospital.

It should be noted that set membership must always be specified in one of the combinations optional-manual, optional-automatic, mandatory-manual, or mandatory-automatic. Considering the ATTENDING DOCTOR DBTG set in Fig. 6.2—1 as an example, these combinations mean the following. Optional-manual set membership for the ATTENDING DOCTOR DBTG set means that a PATIENT record can be included in an ATTENDING DOCTOR set occurrence at any time after the PATIENT record has been stored in the data base. It does not have to be included at the time that it is stored. In addition, a PATIENT record can be removed from an ATTENDING DOCTOR set occurrence without deleting the PATIENT record and without including it in another ATTENDING DOCTOR set occurrence. Optional-automatic set membership for the ATTENDING DOCTOR DBTG set means that a PATIENT record must be included in an ATTENDING DOCTOR set occurrence at the time that the PATIENT record is stored in the data base. However, a PATIENT record may be removed from an ATTENDING DOCTOR set occurrence at any time without deleting the PATIENT record and without including it in another ATTENDING DOCTOR set occurrence. Mandatory-manual set membership for the ATTENDING DOCTOR DBTG set means that a PATIENT record can be included in an ATTENDING DOCTOR set occurrence at any time after the PATIENT record has been stored in the data base. However, once a PATIENT record has been included in an ATTENDING DOCTOR set occurrence it must remain a member in some ATTENDING DOCTOR set occurrence until it is deleted from the data base. Finally, mandatory-automatic set membership for the ATTENDING DOCTOR DBTG set means that a PATIENT record must be included in an ATTENDING DOCTOR set occurrence at the time that the PATIENT record is stored in the data base. In addition, it must remain a member in some ATTENDING DOCTOR set occurrence until it is deleted from the data base. Note that in a hierarchical data base, a record is inserted into a set occurrence (parent–child relationship) automatically since a record's creation and its inclusion in a set occurrence are performed in one operation. Also, records in a hierarchical data base must be related to a parent, which makes their set membership mandatory.

The DBTG placed two restrictions on DBTG sets. The report indicates that the restrictions simplify navigation in the data base. In addition, the restrictions somewhat facilitate implementation.

Restriction I The same record type cannot be both an owner record type and a member record type in the same DBTG set. In terms of links, it means that L_{ii} links are not allowed.

Restriction I is necessary to simplify navigation in the data base as discussed in Section 6.1 in the context of a MANAGED BY link between an EMPLOYEE record type. As another example, suppose that the DOCTOR record type is also a member of the ATTENDING DOCTOR DBTG set, i.e., a doctor can be the patient of another doctor. In this case, we can have the situation illustrated in Fig. 6.2–2, where the DOCTOR record D1 is a member in the ATTENDING DOCTOR set occurrence owned by the DOCTOR record D2. If we were navigating through this data base one record at a time according to the ATTENDING DOCTOR set occurrence owned by D2, we would expect to get the member records in the order (going clockwise) D1, P2, and P4. In the DBTG COBOL DML, which will be discussed in Section 6.3.1, this navigation would be specified by repeatedly issuing the command <u>FIND</u> <u>NEXT</u> <u>RECORD</u> <u>OF</u> ATTENDING DOCTOR <u>SET</u>. However, a problem arises when we reach member record D1. It also is an owner of an ATTENDING DOCTOR set occurrence, and therefore the <u>FIND</u> command might apply equally well to its set occurrence as to that owned by D2. Conversely, if we are navigating according to the ATTENDING

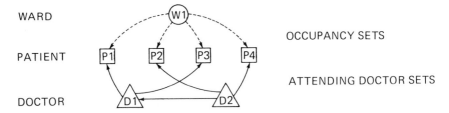

Fig. 6.2–2 Violation of Restriction I.

DOCTOR set occurrence owned by D1 and we start at D1, then the same problem arises. Without further guidance, the DBMS is at a loss as to the exact manner in which to interpret the <u>FIND</u> command. If more information is specified in the <u>FIND</u> command, then the dilemma could be resolved. However, the DBTG COBOL DML does not allow for this situation. Therefore, Restriction I is imposed.

Restriction II The same record occurrence cannot be in more than one set occurrence of a given DBTG set. In terms of links, it means that the links are (partially) functional in one direction. The partial feature comes from the mandatory-optional distinction of set membership.

The second restriction is necessary to ensure that every member record in a set occurrence has only one owner. This requirement is important for the applicability of the DBTG's COBOL DML one-record-at-a-time navigation. For example, suppose that a PATIENT record in Fig. 6.2—1 can be a member in two or more distinct ATTENDING DOCTOR set occurrences, i.e., a patient may be assigned to several doctors. In this case, we can have the situation illustrated in Fig. 6.2—3, where patient P2 is assigned to doctors D1 and D2. Therefore, the PATIENT record P2 is a member in the ATTENDING DOCTOR set occurrence owned by the DOCTOR record D1 and is a member in the ATTENDING DOCTOR set occurrence owned by the DOCTOR record D2. In the DBTG COBOL DML it is possible to retrieve the owner of a member record when navigating through the data base. However, because of the nature of navigation in the DBTG COBOL DML, at most one record can be retrieved at one time. Now, if we are at PATIENT record P2 in Fig. 6.2—3 and we ask for the owner of P2, then two DOCTOR records would have to be retrieved. To avoid this situation, Restriction II is imposed.

The preceding example is a case of an $N:M$ relationship between patients and doctors. Restriction II precludes the representation of direct $N:M$ relationships in a DBTG network data base. However, as

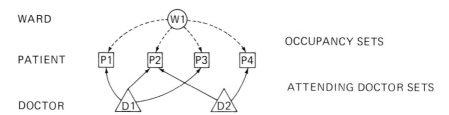

Fig. 6.2—3 Violation of Restriction II.

discussed in Section 6.1, such relationships can be represented by two 1:*N* relationships. This method involves the introduction of an intermediate record type into the data base. Figure 6.2–4 illustrates this method applied to the preceding example. It is now possible to assign a patient to several doctors. The intermediate record type ASSIGN is used to enforce Restriction II. It does not contain any data in this case, although it could be used to hold data that are common to both PATIENT and DOCTOR records. However, although it may not contain user data, in an actual implementation it may contain pointers that connect the PATIENT and DOCTOR records according to the links.

The DBTG report states that privacy locks can be declared in a schema to protect various logical units of data from unauthorized access. A privacy lock can be simply a password check or a procedure that performs security checks. The DBTG allows privacy locks to be declared for a schema and subschema, as well as most units of logical data. For a schema and subschema, privacy locks can be declared to prevent their alteration or display, copying parts of a schema into a subschema, and privacy locks from being displayed, changed, or created. Privacy locks on data bases can specify exclusive or protected retrieval and exclusive or protected update access. For DBTG sets and record types, privacy locks can restrict the use of each DML command that operates on a set occurrence or record occurrence. Finally, retrieval or modification privacy locks can be specified for data items.

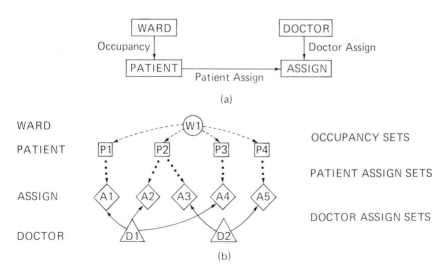

Fig. 6.2–4 Representation of *N:M* relationships. (a) Data structure diagram. (b) Connections in the data base.

In addition to a data model, the DBTG report also contains some proposals that have physical connotations or are related to implementation. An *area* is a named subdivision of storage in the data base containing occurrences of records and DBTG sets. It is defined as a logical unit of data although it has some physical connotations.

A *data-base-key* is a unique identifier assigned to each record of a record type and is used by the DBMS to uniquely identify a record occurrence within the data base. The definition of the data-base-key is left to the particular implementation.

The members in a set occurrence have a certain order that is declared in a schema. The members may be ordered in different ways, e.g., by data-base-key, by record type and designated fields in each record, chronologically by order of insertion, or by some user-defined ordering.

The DBTG report also described two *modes of a set*, essentially two ways of representing a set occurrence. In one of them, the member records are connected in a chain together with the owner. In the second mode, the member records are connected directly to the owner through a pointer array. The set mode is declared in the schema. It is one of the preceding, or it can be implementation defined. The set mode is essentially an implementation feature and will be discussed in more detail in Section 8.3.

According to the DBTG proposal, a data item may be an *actual* or *virtual result.* An *actual result* is physically stored, but a *virtual result* is produced by a procedure when accessed. For example, consider an employee's deductions for unemployment insurance. A data item, UIDEDUCTIONS, can be defined as an actual result and the amount of the deduction physically stored. However, whenever an employee's salary or the rate of deductions changes the UIDEDUCTIONS data item for the employee also has to be changed. On the other hand, UIDE-DUCTIONS can be defined as a virtual result. A procedure can then be defined that calculates the amount of the deductions based on the current unemployment insurance rate and the employee's salary. Notice that now if the rate changes only the procedure rather than each employee's deduction value needs to be changed. Similarly, a change in the employee's salary will automatically be reflected in the deducted amount. The advantage of this approach over a straight procedure for calculating the deduction is that the deduction amount is accessed as a data item of the employee's record. The application does not need to know that it is calculated by a procedure.

A data item may also be an *actual* or *virtual source*. This means that a data item in a member record is specified to have the same type and value as a data item in the owner record of a set occurrence. A *virtual source* is not physically stored in the member record, but derives its value from the owner record. An *actual source* is stored in the member record and the DBMS assures that its value is consistent with the value of the corresponding data item in the owner record. For example, suppose there are two record types EMPLOYEE and SALARYDATA and the DBTG set SALARYHISTORY with owner record type EMPLOYEE and member record type SALARYDATA. An employee's employee number might appear as a data item in both the EMPLOYEE and SALARYDATA records. If the employee number is declared to be an actual source in the SALARYDATA record, then it is physically stored as part of a SALARYDATA record. The DBMS guarantees that it has the same value in all member records of a set occurrence as it does in the owner record (EMPLOYEE record) of the set occurrence. If the employee number is declared as a virtual source, then it is physically stored only in the owner record. Whenever the employee number is accessed in a SALARYDATA record, the DBMS derives the value of the employee number from the owner record of the SALARY-HISTORY set occurrence.

6.3 NETWORK DATA LANGUAGES

A *network system* is a DBMS that organizes the data in a data base according to the network data model. In addition, it provides access to the data via a network data language. The network data language allows records in a network data base to be inserted, modified, deleted, and retrieved. It also allows connections between records to be created or destroyed according to the links among the record types.

In a hierarchical data base each child record cannot exist without a parent record. Also, each child record is connected to a unique parent record. Thus, when a new record is inserted, it can be connected to at most one existing record, namely its parent record. In a network data base, a record type can participate in many links with other record types. Thus, when a new record is inserted, it may have to be connected to several existing records. The connections between the records can be constructed manually or automatically. If the link is "information bearing," then when a record is inserted, it has to be explicitly (manually) connected to another record. If the link is "non-information bearing," then the record can be connected automatically by the DBMS. The connection can also be maintained by the DBMS. In addition, a record can have an independent existence apart from the links among record types. That is, a record does not have to be connected to another record even though a link is defined between the two record types. An independent existence for records is not allowed in a hierarchical data base except for root records.

Deletion of a record in a network data base does not necessarily trigger the deletion of all records connected to it, as it might in a hierarchical data base. Just as a record is explicitly connected to another record, it is possible to disconnect a record from another record. Therefore, it is possible first to remove all of the connections and then to delete the records. It is also possible to have the removal of certain connections implied by the deletion operation or to trigger the deletion of certain records connected to the deleted record. In a network data base, it is possible to combine deletion and removal of connections between records so that certain connections are automatically removed while other connections cause the associated records to be deleted. The creation and destruction of connections between records are operations that cannot be done explicitly in a hierarchical data base. Instead, they are implied by the insertion and deletion of a record.

A network data language must provide two basic data selection facilities. First, it must be able to locate, directly, some records in the data base. This facility is usually achieved by some form of content addressibility. A network data language must also be able to locate records based on the connections between records. That is, the data language must provide facilities for following the connections among the records according to the links.

A network data language can provide either one-record-at-a-time or many-records-at-a-time navigation facilities. In the one-record-at-a-time method, an application chains through the records one at a time and selects records connected to some specified record, according to a link. In the second method, an application uses the links to select, at one time, all records connected to some specified record. It is possible to follow several levels of links in both cases. However, in the first case an application has to be careful to select the right records to avoid backtracking. Backtracking may be necessary, for instance, if it is discovered that the prior selection of a particular path from several alternatives does not satisfy a program's navigation requirements. Backtracking may not be necessary in the second case because the multiple alternatives can be carried along and discarded if no longer necessary.

If only one record is selected at a time, then the queries are essentially of the nature "Give me the next record of type X connected to an instance of a record of type Y according to the link L." In this case, the DBMS maintains one record that is current at any point in time. These types of queries allow the data base to be traversed by navigating in the network from record to record [Bachman, 1973b]. In a many-records-at-a-time environment, the queries are of the form "Give me all records of type X connected to records of type Y according to the link L." In this case, the DBMS maintains a group of records that are current at any point in time. In the following sections, both one-record-at-a-time and many-records-at-a-time network data languages will be examined.

6.3.1 DBTG DML

As well as proposing a design for a DBMS, the DBTG was also concerned with developing a data language for COBOL. In this section some of the more important DML commands proposed by the DBTG for the COBOL interface are discussed. No attempt is made to provide a complete description of each command. Examples of the use of some of the commands can be found in this section and in Section 6.4.1. The notation used is similar to that of the DBTG report. The notation [item] means that the item may optionally appear. The notation {item, . . .} means select one of the items. For complete details concerning a particular command the interested reader is referred to the DBTG report [CODASYL DBTG, 1971].

In a hierarchical data base it is always possible to select related records (ancestors and/or descendants) simply by knowing the current record (position) in the data base. There is always a unique path from the current record to the root record and from the current record to any descendant record. In a DBTG network data base, however, there can be several paths from one record to another record. For example, in Fig. 6.2—4 it is possible to get from the WARD record W1 to the DOCTOR record D1 along several paths, e.g., (W1, P1, A1, D1), (W1, P2, A2, D1), or (W1, P3, A4, D1). Therefore, it is not possible to determine a unique path between two records in a DBTG network data base simply by knowing the current record (position) in the data base. It is necessary to have several current records (positions) in the data base. These current positions are called *currency indicators* by the

DBTG. Currency indicators are, in effect, pointers that mark a user's current position in the data base. In the DBTG DML there is one currency indicator, i.e., one current record, for each record type in the data base. However, most navigation in a DBTG network data base is according to set occurrences. For example, in Fig. 6.2−1 we may want to determine all the doctors that have patients in a particular ward, say W1. This query requires navigation according to the OCCUPANCY set occurrence to find all patients in ward W1 and navigation according to the ATTENDING DOCTOR set occurrences to find the doctors of the patients. To facilitate DBTG set navigation there is also one currency indicator, i.e., one current set occurrence, for each set type in the data base. In addition, there is one currency indicator for each area that marks the current record of the area and one currency indicator for the application that marks the most current record, i.e., the last record located, of all the current records. These currency indicators allow an application to keep track of where it is in the data base. Most commands refer to these indicators implicitly, but they may be explicitly used or suppressed.

In a DBTG network data base, in order to include a record in its proper set occurrence, the DBMS must be informed of how it is to select the set occurrence. For manual membership, an application first inserts a record and then procedurally selects a set occurrence and connects the record into the set. The application must thus preselect the desired set occurrence. For automatic membership, however, the DBMS selects the set occurrence according to a predefined procedure. This procedure is known as *set occurrence selection*. It is specified in the schema at the time that the DBTG set is defined.

Set occurrence selection is an algorithmic way of selecting a record, which then identifies a set occurrence. The *location mode* of a record type is a way of specifying the algorithm the DBMS has to use in selecting or storing a record. It has more the connotation of "store" than "find" since one of its major uses involves storing records. The location mode specifies the mapping algorithm to be invoked when records are stored. There are three types of location mode in DBTG:

1. DIRECT data-base-key. The record is assigned a data-base-key that determines its placement within an area and allows for fast retrieval of the record.

2. CALC [procedure] USING data-item1 [, data-item 2, . . .] DUPLICATES ARE [NOT] ALLOWED. A data-base-key is formed from data-item1, etc., using either a user- or a system-defined procedure.

3. **VIA** set-name **SET**. The record is to be stored on the basis of its membership in set-name.

When storing a record, the location mode controls the placement of the record in the data base. For example, the VIA set-name SET mode causes a record to be logically placed near other records in the same set occurrence. The DBMS must also be able to select the appropriate set-name set occurrence in this case. It does this by means of the *set occurrence selection* specified for set-name.

Set occurrence selection can be performed in two ways. First, if the set occurrence selection is

THRU CURRENT OF SET

then an application procedurally preselects the set occurrence that the DBMS will use. The DBMS implicitly uses the currency indicator for the DBTG set as set by the application to identify the appropriate set occurrence. A second way of selecting a set occurrence is by identifying the owner of the set occurrence. There are two methods for establishing an owner in this case.

The first method is analogous to upward hierarchical normalization, that is, given a set of records, one tries to determine a unique parent (owner) for the records. However, in the network case, the unique parent (owner) is then used to uniquely select one record from the original set of records. This record is the owner of the desired set occurrence. The set occurrence selection is specified as

THRU LOCATION MODE OF OWNER [USING data-item1
  [, data-item2, . . .]]

If the location mode of the owner is DIRECT or CALC, then the DBMS can immediately identify the owner. However, if the location mode is VIA set-name SET, then the DBMS must select the owner based on its membership in another set occurrence. This again involves a set occurrence selection for the set-name specified in the location mode. Such selection may continue to an arbitrary number of levels if the location mode is always specified as VIA set-name SET at each level. Eventually, though, the DBMS must be able to select only one record occurrence at some level. This record occurrence then determines a unique path back to an owner record for the DBTG set of interest. At each level of the selection process, many set occurrences may qualify. However, only one member within a set occurrence, as determined by the USING clause, may qualify. Eventually, at the last level only one set occurrence and one member within the set occurrence may be selected.

As an example, consider Fig. 6.2–1. One wishes to identify an occurrence of ATTENDING DOCTOR. The location mode for ATTENDING DOCTOR is

VIA OCCUPANCY SET.

Therefore, using the values of the data items specified in the USING clause, all occurrences of OCCUPANCY are scanned and those occurrences selected where a PATIENT member record has data item values matching those of data-item1, etc. Suppose the first PATIENT record in each occurrence of OCCUPANCY qualifies, i.e., P1, P5, P7, and P10. Since an ATTENDING DOCTOR set occurrence has not yet been uniquely identified, it is necessary to attempt to uniquely identify an occurrence of OCCUPANCY. Since the owner record type of OCCUPANCY is not a member type in any DBTG set, the set occurrence selection for OCCUPANCY must be either DIRECT or CALC. Therefore, an owner of an OCCUPANCY set occurrence can be uniquely identified. Suppose that the second OCCUPANCY set in Fig. 6.2–1 is selected, i.e., the set occurrence owned by W2. There is now a unique path back to an owner of an ATTENDING DOCTOR set, namely, the first PATIENT record in the second set occurrence of OCCUPANCY, i.e., (W2, P5, D2).

The second method of selecting the owner of a set is analogous to downward hierarchical normalization, that is, given a parent (owner) record, one tries to determine a unique descendant record at some level. The set occurrence selection is specified as

THRU set-name1 USING LOCATION MODE OF OWNER { set-
        name2 [USING data-item1 [,data-item2, . . .]]}

The owner of the set occurrence in question is identified by giving an explicit path to it through occurrences of other DBTG sets. At each level the DBMS must be able to uniquely identify an owner of a set occurrence (by means of the USING clause). The owner of the set occurrence at the final level is the owner of an occurrence of the DBTG set in question.

Consider now Fig. 6.2–4. One wishes to identify an occurrence of PATIENT ASSIGN. The location mode for PATIENT ASSIGN is specified as:

THRU OCCUPANCY USING LOCATION MODE OF OWNER
        PATIENT ASSIGN USING data-item1, . . .

Suppose the location mode for OCCUPANCY is CALC. Therefore, an owner of OCCUPANCY can be uniquely identified using the CALC location mode. Suppose that the first occurrence of OCCUPANCY in Fig. 6.2—4 is selected. Now, examining this OCCUPANCY set occurrence, a PATIENT member record that matches the data item values specified in the second USING clause is selected. Suppose the third member, i.e., P3, satisfies the USING clause. Thus, an owner of a PATIENT ASSIGN set occurrence has been selected.

The DBTG network data model allows cycles. Therefore, it is possible to get into an endless loop if the location mode is always VIA set-name SET. The DBTG foresaw this problem and limited the number of times a cycle could be traversed to one. Within that cycle, the set occurrence selection process must be completed.

A student—teacher—class example (due to D. D. Chamberlin) will be outlined here to illustrate in the following paragraphs the use of the DBTG COBOL DML commands. The data base consists of three record types and two DBTG sets. The schema is expressed in a simplified form of the DBTG COBOL DDL. For a more detailed example of a schema definition see Section 6.4.1.

    RECORD NAME IS STUDENT;
        LOCATION MODE IS CALC USING ID.
        2 ID; TYPE IS CHAR 25.
        2 SEX; TYPE IS CHAR 6.

    RECORD NAME IS CLASS;
        LOCATION MODE IS CALC USING SUBJECT.
        2 SUBJECT; TYPE IS CHAR 25.
        2 TEACHER; TYPE IS CHAR 25.

    RECORD NAME IS ENROLLMENT.
        2 SUBJECT; TYPE IS CHAR 25.
        2 GRADE; TYPE IS CHAR 1.

    SET NAME IS ROLL;
        OWNER IS CLASS.
        MEMBER IS ENROLLMENT.

    SET NAME IS SCHEDULE;
        OWNER IS STUDENT.
        MEMBER IS ENROLLMENT.

Part of this example data base is shown in Fig. 6.3.1—1. Record occurrences are connected via the ROLL and/or SCHEDULE set occurrences. In this simple case, the data base can be represented readily in

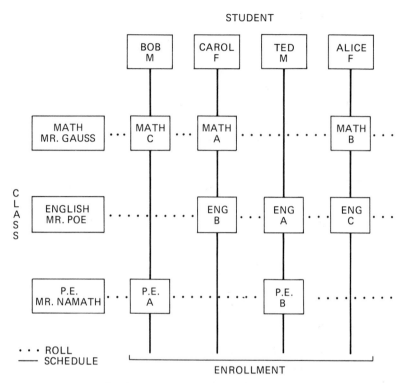

Fig. 6.3.1–1 Sample network data base.

two dimensions. For a more complicated data base with many DBTG sets, the graphical representation resembles a "bowl of spaghetti."

The major control commands in the DBTG proposal are <u>OPEN</u>, <u>CLOSE</u>, <u>KEEP</u>, and <u>FREE</u>. The <u>OPEN</u> command opens an area and determines a user's access rights for the area. One can optionally open an area for exclusive or protected retrieval or exclusive or protected update. The exclusive option prevents access to the area by other users. The protected option prevents concurrent update, but concurrent retrieval is allowed. Control over an area or all open areas is relinquished by the <u>CLOSE</u> command.

A <u>KEEP</u> command advises the DBMS of an application's intent to access again a record occurrence at a later time. Any subsequent access by the application is successful only if no other program has modified the record since the <u>KEEP</u> was executed. Other users may still modify the record while the <u>KEEP</u> is in effect. The <u>KEEP</u> merely serves to alert an application to an intervening modification by another application.

An implicit KEEP applies to the current record of an application. A FREE command cancels all or selected KEEP commands.

The DBTG COBOL DML separates the retrieval functions of location and access of a record into, respectively, the FIND and GET commands. When an application program invokes a subschema, the DBMS sets up a *User Working Area (UWA)*. The UWA essentially acts as a buffer area where data are placed after retrieval from the data base or before placement in the data base. Each data item included in a subschema is assigned a location in the UWA and may be referenced in the application by its name. The GET command transfers the contents of a record or certain data items from the data base to the UWA. The transferred record is the current record of the application as indicated by the currency indicator, that is, the one selected by the last FIND command executed by the application prior to the GET command. Hence, the GET command has no arguments except when only certain data items are transferred.

FIND commands can be divided into two major categories in terms of origin of access [Olle, 1975]. The first type accesses a record directly without use of currency indicators. It implies use of a data-base-key or index, e.g., DIRECT, CALC, or knowledge of the mapping to physical storage. The second type follows the connections of the set occurrences and uses the currency indicators. These types of commands provide the capability of *set switching*, that is, they provide the ability to select a set occurrence of a DBTG set S2, from a set occurrence of a DBTG set S1, via a record that is a member record in both the S1 and the S2 set occurrence. For example, in Fig. 6.3.1—1 one is able to get from a STUDENT record to a CLASS record via an ENROLLMENT record. In this way, one is able to navigate in the data base.

Before a FIND of the second type can be used in a program, it must be preceded by a FIND of the first type. The FIND command of the first type initializes the currency indicator(s). The FIND of the second type assumes that the currency indicator(s) has been properly positioned.

The FIND command has the additional side effect that all relevant currency indicators are updated as required, that is, a FIND command updates the appropriate record type, DBTG set (for all DBTG sets in which the record is an owner or participating member), and area currency indicators to the record located. The currency indicator of the application is always updated after every FIND command to the record located. However, the update of the other currency indicators can be suppressed selectively or totally by the SUPPRESS option of the FIND command. There are seven major formats of the FIND command and many options. The first two formats described are of the direct access type. The other five formats are of the second type.

1. FIND record-name USING key

A record-name record is located based on the value of *key*. The value of the variable *key* must contain the data-base-key of the desired record. Every record has a unique data-base-key assigned to it when it is created. The data-base-key uniquely identifies the record occurrence in the data base. A data item in a record type may be defined to hold a record occurrence's data-base-key if the data item was defined with a USAGE IS DATABASE-KEY clause in the schema. A data-base-key may be saved with the MOVE command. It may then be used later to locate the same record. For example, suppose that the data-base-key for the current STUDENT record is saved in the data item STUDENT-KEY, that has been properly declared in the schema, with the command

> MOVE CURRENCY STATUS FOR STUDENT RECORD TO
>   STUDENT-KEY.

The same STUDENT record can then be located at a later time with the command

> FIND STUDENT USING STUDENT-KEY.

The located record becomes the current record of the application, area, and the STUDENT record type as well as the current occurrence of the SCHEDULE DBTG set.

2. FIND [NEXT DUPLICATE WITHIN] record-name RECORD

When a record type was declared in the schema, possibly modified by the subschema, certain data items were designated as CALC keys. These data items are first initialized by an application. They are then used by the DBMS to scan the applicable area and to find the first or next duplicate occurrence of the named record type whose CALC keys match those specified by the application. For example, the data item ID is declared a CALC key for the STUDENT record type. Therefore, to locate the STUDENT record for Carol the user first sets ID equal to Carol and then executes the FIND command:

> MOVE 'CAROL' TO ID.
> FIND STUDENT RECORD.

The located record becomes the current record of the application, area, and the STUDENT record type as well as the current occurrence of the SCHEDULE DBTG set.

3. FIND [OWNER IN set-name OF] CURRENT OF { record-name RECORD, set-name SET, area-name AREA, RUN-UNIT }

The "current" record of the record type, DBTG set, area or application (RUN-UNIT) is located. This format permits revision of currency indicators that were previously suppressed. If the OWNER IN set-name OF option is specified, then the owner of the set-name DBTG set, as indicated by the "current" record of the record type, DBTG set or area of the application is located. For example, if the current record of the application is the ENROLLMENT record (Math, C), then the owner record STUDENT according to the SCHEDULE set occurrence is located with the command

FIND OWNER IN SCHEDULE OF CURRENT OF RUN-UNIT.

The located record becomes the current record of the application, area, and STUDENT record type as well as the current set occurrence of the SCHEDULE DBTG set.

4. FIND { NEXT, PRIOR, FIRST, LAST, integer } [record-name] RECORD OF name { SET, AREA }

The next, prior, first, last, or *n*th (integer) record of the named area or the "current" occurrence of the named DBTG set is located. Since a DBTG set may have more than one member record type and an area more than one record type, the record type to be retrieved may optionally be specified. As an example, consider the ROLL set occurrence owned by the CLASS record (English, Mr. Poe) in Fig. 6.3.1−1. Suppose that the ENROLLMENT record (Eng, A) is the current record of this ROLL set occurrence. The command

FIND NEXT RECORD OF ROLL SET.

would locate the ENROLLMENT record (Eng, C) connected to the current ENROLLMENT record. Conversely, the command

FIND PRIOR RECORD OF ROLL SET.

would locate the ENROLLMENT record (Eng, B). Note that in this example the command FIND FIRST would result in the same answer as FIND PRIOR. The located record becomes the current record of the application, area, ENROLLMENT record type, and the current occurrence of the ROLL and SCHEDULE DBTG sets.

5.   FIND OWNER RECORD OF set-name SET

The owner record of the "current" occurrence of the set-name DBTG set is located. For example, to find the owner record in the ROLL set occurrence of the preceding example, the command

FIND OWNER RECORD OF ROLL SET.

would be used. The CLASS record (English, Mr. Poe) would be located. This record becomes the current record of the application, area, and the CLASS record type as well as the current occurrence of the ROLL DBTG set. The ENROLLMENT record (Eng, A) remains the current record of the ENROLLMENT record type as well as the current occurrence of the SCHEDULE DBTG set.

6.   FIND record-name VIA [CURRENT OF] set-name [USING data-item1, data-item2, . . .]

If the CURRENT OF option is specified, then the "current" set occurrence of set-name is selected. The selection is based on the "current" record of the "current" set-name set occurrence (owner or member). The first record of the given type in this set occurrence is found. The order of the scan is determined by the set declaration in the schema. It may be in order of data-base-key, specified data items, chronological order of insertion, or determined by the program. If the CURRENT OF option is *not* specified, then the DBMS selects the appropriate set-name set occurrence using the set occurrence selection for set-name. If USING is specified, then the first record whose data items match the values given by data-item1, etc., is found. For example, suppose that the current occurrence of the SCHEDULE DBTG set is identified by the STUDENT record (Bob, M) in Fig. 6.3.1−1. To find the first ENROLLMENT record for Bob with a mark of A, the following commands would be used:

MOVE 'A' TO GRADE.
FIND ENROLLMENT VIA CURRENT OF SCHEDULE USING
    GRADE.

The ENROLLMENT record (P.E., A) connected to the STUDENT record (Bob, M) would be located. If the set occurrence selection for

SCHEDULE were declared as THRU LOCATION MODE OF OWNER, then the query can be answered as follows:

> MOVE 'BOB' TO ID.
> MOVE 'A' TO GRADE.
> FIND ENROLLMENT VIA SCHEDULE USING GRADE.

The DBMS uses the value of ID and the CALC location mode to select on occurrence of a SCHEDULE DBTG set in this case (Bob, M). It then scans this SCHEDULE set occurrence until it finds an ENROLLMENT record with a grade of A or until the end of the set occurrence is reached. The located record becomes the current record of the application, area, and ENROLLMENT record type as well as the current occurrence of the SCHEDULE and ROLL DBTG sets.

7. FIND NEXT DUPLICATE WITHIN set-name USING data-item1, data-item2, . . .

The "current" set occurrence of the set-name DBTG set is scanned. The next member record occurrence, which is of the same type as the "current" record of the set occurrence and has the same values for the data items as given by data-item1, etc., is found.

The modification commands can be divided into two categories, those concerned with record maintenance and those concerned with DBTG set maintenance. In the former category there is the ability to insert, delete, and modify records. The latter category includes the ability to add and remove members from set occurrences and to reorder the members in a set occurrence logically based on some key.

The STORE command places a new record in the data base and assigns it a data-base-key. The record is made a member in one occurrence of all DBTG sets for which its membership is automatic. The values of data items of records already in the data base are changed by the MODIFY command. Either all or selected data items in a record may be changed. The appropriate record must first be located with a FIND command.

A record is deleted from the data base by a DELETE command. A delete command may trigger other deletions depending on the option specified. If no option is specified, then the record is deleted only if all of the set occurrences of which it is an owner have no members. The ONLY option deletes the record along with all the mandatory members of set occurrences of which the record is an owner. Optional members only are removed. The SELECTIVE option is similar to ONLY except that optional members are also deleted, but only if they are not members in other set occurrences. Finally, the ALL option deletes all members regardless of their type of membership. In all cases, if a member record is an owner of another set occurrence, then the delete command applies to that set occurrence as if it had been specified for the owner of that set occurrence. This rule also applies for all subsequent owners of set occurrences encountered.

The two most important set manipulation commands are INSERT and REMOVE. The INSERT command is used to make a record a member of all or selected DBTG sets in which it has been declared a member. Membership must be manual. The membership of a record, in selected or all set occurrences in which it participates, is cancelled by the REMOVE command. This command may only be used on those records whose membership is optional.

Finally, some possible queries and updates are presented using COBOL and the DBTG COBOL DML. The keyword NOTE indicates a comment.

1. What grade did Ted get in English and who was his teacher?

NOTE Set the currency indicators for the STUDENT record and
    SCHEDULE set by locating Ted's STUDENT record.
MOVE 'TED' TO ID.
FIND STUDENT RECORD.
NOTE Set the current record of the program to Ted's ENROLL-
    MENT record in English.
MOVE 'ENGLISH' TO SUBJECT IN ENROLLMENT.
FIND ENROLLMENT VIA CURRENT OF SCHEDULE USING
    SUBJECT.
GET ENROLLMENT; GRADE.
NOTE Locate the owner of the ENROLLMENT record in the
    ROLL set to get the teacher's name.
FIND OWNER IN ROLL OF CURRENT OF ENROLLMENT
    RECORD.
GET CLASS; TEACHER.
STOP RUN.

2. Transfer Bob from Math to English, i.e., drop Math and add English.

NOTE Locate Bob's STUDENT record.
MOVE 'BOB' TO ID.

FIND STUDENT RECORD.
NOTE Find Bob's Math ENROLLMENT record and delete it.
MOVE 'MATH' TO SUBJECT IN ENROLLMENT.
FIND ENROLLMENT VIA CURRENT OF SCHEDULE USING
   SUBJECT.
DELETE.
NOTE Make English the current CLASS record.
MOVE 'ENGLISH' TO SUBJECT IN CLASS.
FIND CLASS RECORD.
NOTE Create and store a new ENROLLMENT record.
MOVE 'ENGLISH' TO SUBJECT IN ENROLLMENT.
MOVE 'U' TO GRADE.
STORE ENROLLMENT.
NOTE Include the new ENROLLMENT record in Bob's
   SCHEDULE and in the English ROLL.
INSERT INTO ROLL, SCHEDULE.
STOP RUN.

3. Are there any girls in the PE class?

NOTE Locate the PE CLASS record.
MOVE 'P.E.' TO SUBJECT IN CLASS.
FIND CLASS RECORD.
NOTE Look at the PE ENROLLMENT records until a girl is found
   or until no more PE ENROLLMENT records exist.
MOVE 'U' TO SEX.
PERFORM CHECK-NEXT-ENROLLMENT-RECORD UNTIL
   (ERROR-STATUS=0307) OR (SEX='F').
STOP RUN.

CHECK-NEXT-ENROLLMENT-RECORD.
   NOTE Locate the next Enrollment record in the ROLL set
      and check for the end of the set.
   FIND NEXT RECORD OF ROLL SET.
   IF ERROR-STATUS=0307
      PERFORM NO-GIRLS-IN-PE,
   ELSE
      NOTE Locate the STUDENT record in the SCHEDULE set
         and check if female.
      FIND OWNER IN SCHEDULE OF CURRENT OF ROLL
         SET,
      GET STUDENT,

<u>IF</u> SEX='F'
        <u>PERFORM</u> OUTPUT-GIRL-IN-PE-CLASS.

6.3.2   EDBS Network Language

As another example of a network language, the Educational Data Base System (EDBS) network language will be outlined [Kanfer, 1975]. EDBS is a host language system using APL both as host and implementation language. The EDBS network language is based on the DBTG proposal, but for ease of implementation and clarity of understanding, it has been greatly simplified. The data model and terminology is that of DBTG. No particular claims are made for this language. It is presented here because it offers a concise example of a network language. It also uses explicit operations on currency indicators for navigation. The DBTG proposal defines implicit currency indicator operations.

The EDBS network data model consists of record types and DBTG sets. Record types are composed of data items. A DBTG set consists of one owner record type and only one member record type. Owner and member record types must be of different type. Set membership for all DBTG sets is optional-manual as defined by the DBTG. No other type of membership is allowed. All other restrictions on DBTG sets and set membership, as outlined in the DBTG proposal, apply.

Currency indicators are maintained for all record types and all DBTG sets in the data base. A record pointer marks a record occurrence and a set pointer marks an owner or member record occurrence within a set occurrence. The pointers can be altered explicitly as a result of DML commands. In addition, DML commands implicitly alter at most either one record pointer or one set pointer.

The syntax presented here is not that used in the implementation. For pedagogical purposes, a pseudolanguage is used to present the commands. However, the semantics and the flavor of the commands are as presented here. For an example of the commands as they are used in APL, see Section 6.4.2. The notation [item] means that the item is optional. The notation {item} means select one of the items.

The EDBS network language combines the DBTG <u>FIND</u> and <u>GET</u> commands into a single <u>GET</u> command. The syntax and semantics are also simplified. Location mode in the schema has been replaced by where-clause qualification in the DML. Set occurrence selection is performed explicitly by manipulation of currency indicators. A <u>GET</u> command may also optionally place a hold on a record. This allows concurrent applications to access the data base, but does not allow modification commands by other applications to be used on the held record occurrence. The GET has two forms: one for record occurrence selection independent of DBTG sets and one for record occurrence selection within DBTG sets. Note that all record occurrences of a given type are assumed to be in a singular DBTG set owned by the system.

Records in a system-owned, singular DBTG set are retrieved by the command:

$$\underline{\text{GET}} \ [\underline{\text{HOLD}}] \left\{ \begin{array}{l} \underline{\text{NEXT}} \\ \underline{\text{PRIOR}} \\ \underline{\text{FIRST}} \\ \underline{\text{LAST}} \end{array} \right\} \text{record-name} \ \underline{\text{RECORD}} \ [\text{where-clause}]$$

A record of the specified type is retrieved from the data base and the record-name record pointer positioned to point at that record. Without a where-clause the next, prior, first, or last record-name record occurrence is retrieved. With a where-clause the next, prior, first, or last record-name record occurrence that satisfies the qualification specified on data items of the record type is retrieved. This command alters only the appropriate record pointer and has no effect on any set pointers.

Records are retrieved according to DBTG set set occurrences by the command:

$$\underline{\text{GET}} \ [\text{HOLD}] \left\{ \begin{array}{l} \underline{\text{OWNER}} \\ \underline{\text{NEXT}} \\ \underline{\text{PRIOR}} \\ \underline{\text{FIRST}} \\ \underline{\text{LAST}} \end{array} \right\} \text{set-name} \ \underline{\text{SET}} \ [\text{where-clause}]$$

A record within the specified DBTG set is retrieved from the data base and the set-name set pointer positioned to point at the record. Without a where-clause the next, prior, first, or last member record within a set-name set occurrence is retrieved. With a where-clause the next, prior, first, or last member record within a set-name set occurrence that meets the qualification of the where-clause is retrieved. If a where-clause is specified, then the owner is retrieved only if it meets the qualification of the where-clause. The set-name set occurrence is determined by the current position of the set-name set pointer. This command alters only the appropriate set pointer and has no effect on any record pointers.

To make set switching and selection more explicit, the EDBS network language allows an application to alter its currency indicators explicitly. The general format of the pointer manipulation command is

name1 CHANGE TO CURRENT name2

In general, the pointer value of name1 is changed to the pointer value of name2. Specifically, this command may only have three formats.

1. record-name CHANGE TO CURRENT set-name

The record-name record pointer is changed to point at the same record occurrence as the set-name set pointer. The set-name set pointer must currently point at a record occurrence of record-name record type.

2. set-name CHANGE TO CURRENT record-name

The set-name set pointer is changed to point at the same record occurrence as the record-name record pointer. The record-name must be an owner or a member record type of the DBTG set set-name.

In addition, the record occurrence pointed at by the record-name record pointer must be a member record in some occurrence of the set-name DBTG set.

3. set-name1 CHANGE TO CURRENT set-name2

The set-name1 set pointer is changed to point at the same record occurrence as the set-name2 set pointer. The set-name2 set pointer must point to a record type that is an owner or a member of DBTG set set-name1.

Note that it is only possible initially to select a set occurrence by a combination of retrieval and CHANGE TO CURRENT commands.

A new record is placed in a data base by the command

STORE record-name

The new record is established as an owner record occurrence for the DBTG sets in which it is an owner. A new record exists as a singleton or as an empty set occurrence. Upon completion of a STORE, the record-name pointer is set to the new record.

An existing record is deleted from a data base by the command

DELETE record-name

The record pointed at by the record-name record pointer is deleted and the record pointer is set to null. A member record can only be deleted after it has been removed from every set of which it is a member. An owner record can only be deleted after all its members have been removed.

The contents of a record in a data base are altered by the command

MODIFY

The record must have been obtained by a GET HOLD command prior to its modification.

A record occurrence is placed in a particular set occurrence by the command

INCLUDE set-name

The record pointed at by the record pointer of the member record type of set-name becomes a member of the set-name set occurrence pointed at by the set-name set pointer. The record occurrence to be included must not currently be a member in some set-name set occurrence. This command has no effect on the record or set pointers.

Finally, a record occurrence is taken out of a particular set occurrence by the command

REMOVE set-name

The record pointed at by the record pointer of the member record type is removed from the set-name set occurrence in which it is a member. Upon completion of the REMOVE command the record pointer and set pointer remain unaltered.

An example of an application showing the capabilities of the EDBS network language is given in Section 6.4.2.

6.3.3 Higher Level Interfaces

The network data languages discussed in Sections 6.3.1 and 6.3.2 only allow one-record-at-a-time navigation. In addition, the user has a great deal of flexibility in specifying options and guiding the system when navigating in the data base. However, this capability implies that a user needs much expertise and sophistication to use the navigation tools properly. The rather procedural approach of the DBTG COBOL DML and the EDBS network language is not inherent in a DBTG network system [Stonebraker and Held, 1975]. Other, much less procedural interfaces, for a DBTG network system, are possible.

One approach is to consider the relationships among the data items of a data structure diagram. Relationships among data items in a data structure diagram are defined by record types and across record types, according to the links, as in the hierarchical data model. However, unlike the hierarchical data model, which has unique links between record types, there can be more than one link between two record types in the DBTG network data model. Therefore, the links to be used in defining the relationship between data items in different record types have to be identified. The relationships can be defined by specifying the links that should be used to connect the record types. These relationships correspond to *selection structures* as discussed in Chapter 3.

Consider the data structure diagram in Fig. 2.3−2 again. The selection structure COUNTRY OF REGISTRATION is defined as

DEFINE COUNTRY OF REGISTRATION AS COUNTRY
LINKED WITH IN TO STATE
LINKED WITH REGISTERED IN TO REGISTRATION

The name COUNTRY OF REGISTRATION can be used to refer to the selection structure containing, as data items, all the data items of the record types COUNTRY, STATE, and REGISTRATION as connected by the links IN and REGISTERED IN. Data items of the record types COUNTRY, STATE, and REGISTRATION can be related in the same query. For instance, a possible query is

GET REGISTRATION.NUMBER
IN COUNTRY OF REGISTRATION
WHERE COUNTRY.NAME=U.S.A.

The DBTG network data model permits a wide variety of selection structures. Some of these selection structures have problems associated with modification operations. Consider the two selection structures, as shown in Fig. 6.3.3−1, according to Fig. 2.3−2.

In the case of Fig. 6.3.3−1a, the selection structure COMPANY REGISTERED IN STATE, defined by the relationships between the record types STATE, REGISTRATION, and COMPANY, does not present any problems. Consider a query of the form

GET COMPANY.NAME, STATE.NAME
IN COMPANY REGISTERED IN STATE
WHERE STATE.POPULATION>1000000
    AND COMPANY.SIZE>1000

This query can be evaluated by following the connections from STATE records to REGISTRATION records and from the COMPANY records to the REGISTRATION records, according to the two links REGISTERED IN and HAS REGISTRATION, separately. The REGIS-

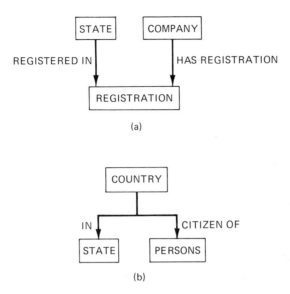

Fig. 6.3.3–1 Two selection structures.

TRATION records are then merged according to the Boolean operator in the qualification. In this particular example, STATE records with population greater than 1,000,000 are selected and connected to a set *A* of REGISTRATION records. COMPANY records with size greater than 1000 are also selected and connected to a set *B* of REGISTRATION records. The intersection *C* of *A* and *B* according to the AND Boolean operator is then obtained. From the set of records *C* the connections back to the STATE and COMPANY records, according to the links REGISTERED IN and HAS REGISTRATION, are followed to obtain the COMPANY.NAME and STATE.NAME for every REGISTRATION record in *C*.

The algorithm can be expanded to selection structures that are defined over a set of record types and links that have a "lowest" record type. That is, there is a record type in the selection structure which has, as direct or indirect owners, all the other record types. Furthermore, this record type is not owned by any other record having the same property [Earnest, 1975]. The selection structure so formed can be updated. Each update, insertion or deletion in the selection structure corresponds to a unique change in the record type or links used in the selection structure definition.

Consider now the selection structure STATES AND PERSONS IN COUNTRY among the data items of the record types STATE, COUN-

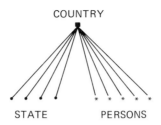

Fig. 6.3.3—2 Instance of STATES AND PERSONS IN COUNTRY selection structure.

TRY and PERSONS as defined by Fig. 6.3.3—1b. There are problems with selection structures formed in such a manner. For instance, suppose that the data base is as in Fig. 6.3.3—2. Changing the name of a state in one tuple of the selection structure should really trigger the change of the state names of all tuples with the same state name. Inserting a new tuple of STATES AND PERSONS IN COUNTRY may not be mirrored in a unique and well-formed change in the network data base. Therefore, it is better to constrain the operations to queries only in such selection structures. Updates can be done by looking at the data base in a network fashion and not according to the relationships among data items.

There are many advantages in defining a network selection interface on top of a DBTG network data base. A rather nice end-user query language is obtained. However, some constraints on the types of operations and selection structures allowed may be needed.

6.4   EXAMPLES OF APPLICATIONS

6.4.1   Student Records

The example of a student records data base introduced in Chapter 5 will again be examined [Schafheitlin, 1974]. The data base contains information concerning the students, the teachers, their courses, and course sections. There are N:M relationships between students, teachers, and courses. For instance, each student may have many teachers and each teacher many students. Because of these N:M relationships, the hierarchical data model does not seem natural for this example. In fact, a hierarchical data base requires duplication of data to represent all the relationships. The network data model is somewhat better suited for this application.

Figure 6.4.1–1 shows the data structure diagram for this example. It represents the relationships between the following four entity sets as embodied in record types.

Student contains student number, name, address, and year.
Teacher contains employee number, name, and department(s).
Course contains course number and name.
Section contains section name and student's mark.

To implement this example according to the DBTG proposal, duplicate SECTION records must be allowed. Duplicate SECTION records are needed since a record occurrence cannot be a member of more than one occurrence of the same DBTG set. In this case, several students may be in the same section. However, each occurrence of a SECTION record must be connected to only one student. Therefore, one section record is needed for each student in the same section. The individual SECTION record occurrences provide a natural place to maintain the student's mark.

For this application, the DBTG COBOL DDL and DML will be used. The schema is kept simple and only a brief outline is given in some cases. It is not the purpose of this description to expound on all the features of the DBTG COBOL DDL, but rather to examine a network example.

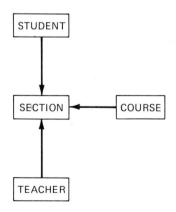

Fig. 6.4.1–1 Student records data structure diagram.

First, the schema name and two areas, STUDENT-AREA for the student and section records and TEACHER-AREA for the course and teacher records, are defined.

1   SCHEMA NAME IS STUDENT-RECORDS.
2   AREA NAME IS STUDENT-AREA.
3   AREA NAME IS TEACHER-AREA.

Next, each record type, its location mode, the area it is to be stored in, and its data items are defined. These definitions, for the most part, are self-explanatory.

4   RECORD NAME IS STUDENT;
5   LOCATION MODE IS CALC USING STUDENT-NO
6   DUPLICATES ARE NOT ALLOWED;
7   WITHIN STUDENT-AREA.
8   02 STUDENT-NO; TYPE IS FIXED DECIMAL 9.
9   02 NAME;   TYPE IS CHARACTER 20.
10   02 ADDRESS;   TYPE IS CHARACTER 40.
11   02 YEAR;   TYPE IS FIXED DECIMAL 2.

12 RECORD NAME IS TEACHER;
13   LOCATION MODE IS CALC USING EMPLOYEE-NO
14   DUPLICATES ARE NOT ALLOWED;
15   WITHIN TEACHER-AREA.
16   02 EMPLOYEE-NO;   TYPE IS FIXED DECIMAL 9.
17   02 NAME;   TYPE IS CHARACTER 20.
18   02 NO-OF-APPOINTMENTS; TYPE IS FIXED DECIMAL 2.
19   02 DEPARTMENT; OCCURS NO-OF-APPOINTMENTS
            TIMES.
20   03 DEPARTMENT-NAME; TYPE IS CHARACTER 20.
21   03 DEPARTMENT-NO;   TYPE IS FIXED DECIMAL 9.

DEPARTMENT is a repeating group that allows cross appointments of professors, i.e., professors can hold positions in several departments.

22 RECORD NAME IS COURSE;
23   LOCATION MODE IS CALC USING COURSE-NO;
24   WITHIN TEACHER-AREA.
25   02 COURSE-NO;   TYPE IS FIXED DECIMAL 5.
26   02 COURSE-NAME; TYPE IS CHARACTER 20.

27 RECORD NAME IS SECTION;
28   LOCATION MODE IS VIA COURSE-SECTION SET

```
29        DUPLICATES ARE ALLOWED;
30    WITHIN STUDENT-AREA.
31        02 SECTION-NAME; TYPE IS CHARACTER 2.
32        02 MARK;          TYPE IS FIXED DECIMAL 3;
33            CHECK IS RANGE OF 100 THRU 0.
```

The check on a mark ensures valid data for the MARK data item. Next, the DBTG sets are defined. The ordering LAST means that member records are to be ordered in chronological order of insertion. The ordering NEXT means that a member record is to be logically inserted after the record pointed at by the currency indicator for the DBTG set. The DBTG set currency indicator must be set correctly, by the user, prior to an insertion.

```
34  SET NAME IS STUDENT-COURSE;
35      ORDER IS LAST;
36      OWNER IS STUDENT.
37      MEMBER IS SECTION OPTIONAL MANUAL;
38          SET OCCURRENCE SELECTION IS THRU
39              LOCATION MODE OF OWNER.

40  SET NAME IS COURSE-SECTION;
41      ORDER IS SORTED INDEXED NAME IS SECTION-NAME
42          DUPLICATES ARE ALLOWED;
43      OWNER IS COURSE.
44      MEMBER IS SECTION OPTIONAL AUTOMATIC;
45          ASCENDING KEY IS SECTION-NAME;
46          SET OCCURRENCE SELECTION IS THRU
47              CURRENT OF SET.

48  SET NAME IS TEACHER-COURSE;
49      ORDER IS NEXT;
50      OWNER IS TEACHER.
51      MEMBER IS SECTION OPTIONAL MANUAL;
52          SET OCCURRENCE SELECTION IS THRU
53              CURRENT OF SET.
```

Next, the subschema for the application that will be implemented is defined. The definition is in terms of the host language, which is COBOL in this case. For the application, the subschema is the entire schema, but with parts of some records omitted. The COPY command specifies that the named unit of data is to be included in the subschema from the schema.

SUB-SCHEMA IDENTIFICATION DIVISION.

SUB-SCHEMA NAME IS GRADE OF SCHEMA STUDENT-RECORDS;

.

.

.

SUB-SCHEMA DATA DIVISION.

AREA SECTION.
COPY STUDENT-AREA, TEACHER-AREA.

RECORD SECTION.
01 STUDENT.
   02 STUDENT-NO; PICTURE IS 9(9).
   02 NAME;   PICTURE IS A(20).

01 TEACHER.
   02 EMPLOYEE-NO; PICTURE IS 9(9).
   02 NAME;   PICTURE IS A(20).

01 COURSE.
   02 COURSE-NO;   PICTURE IS 9(5).
   02 COURSE-NAME; PICTURE IS A(20).

01 SECTION.
   02 SECTION-NAME; PICTURE IS A(2).
   02 MARK;   PICTURE IS 9(3).

SET SECTION.
COPY STUDENT-COURSE, COURSE-SECTION,
   TEACHER-COURSE.

The application consists of two updates:

1. Raise all course 2301 marks by 10%.
2. Delete teacher 031678954 from the data base.

The algorithm for these two updates is as follows:

1. Find the COURSE record for course number 2301.
2. Chain through its SECTION records.
3. For each SECTION record modify its MARK, obtain the student's name and then print the name and mark.
4. Find the TEACHER record for teacher number 031678954 and delete it.

The first part of the COBOL program concerns the declaration of records, working storage, and facilities. Only the names of the sections required are listed.

IDENTIFICATION DIVISION.
.
.
.

ENVIRONMENT DIVISION.
.
.
.

DATA DIVISION.
.
.
.

PROCEDURE DIVISION.
OPEN STUDENT-AREA, TEACHER-AREA;
OPEN (non-DBTG files);
.
.
.

The first step in the implementation is to find the COURSE record for course number 2301. The record is found by using COURSE-NO as a direct access key. This establishes course 2301 as the current COURSE record and as the owner of a COURSE-SECTION set. The 0326 error-check checks for no occurrences of COURSE records for course number 2301. If no error occurs, then the marks are raised. Finally, the TEACHER record for teacher 031678954 is deleted. The error and output procedures are not given. Hopefully their function is obvious.

MOVE '2301' TO COURSE-NO.
FIND COURSE RECORD.
IF ERROR-STATUS=0326
        PERFORM ERROR-NOT-IN-DATA-BASE.
    ELSE
        PERFORM RAISE-MARK UNTIL ERROR-STATUS=0307.
PERFORM DELETE-TEACHER.
CLOSE (appropriate files).
STOP RUN.

In the RAISE-MARK procedure, all sections for course 2301 are found and each mark raised by 10%. First, the next SECTION record in the COURSE-SECTION set for owner COURSE record 2301 is obtained. If all members in the set (error-check 0307) have not been exhausted, then the mark of the SECTION record is modified. The STUDENT record associated with this SECTION record is then obtained via the STUDENT-COURSE set and the student name and mark printed.

```
RAISE-MARK.
    FIND NEXT SECTION RECORD OF COURSE-SECTION SET.
    IF ERROR-STATUS NOT EQUAL TO 0307
        GET SECTION; MARK,
        MULTIPLY 1.1 BY MARK,
        MODIFY SECTION; MARK,
        FIND OWNER IN STUDENT-COURSE OF CURRENT
            OF SECTION RECORD,
        IF ERROR-STATUS=0326
            PERFORM ERROR-NO-STUDENT-
                FOR-SECTION,
        ELSE
            GET STUDENT; NAME,
            PERFORM OUTPUT-NAME-AND-MARK.
```

Finally, teacher 031678954 is deleted. First, the TEACHER record is found using the EMPLOYEE-NO as a direct access key. The teacher is then deleted.

```
DELETE-TEACHER.
    MOVE '031678954' TO EMPLOYEE-NO.
    FIND TEACHER RECORD.
    IF ERROR-STATUS=0326
        PERFORM ERROR-NOT-IN-DATA-BASE.
    ELSE
        DELETE TEACHER ONLY.
```

This example is typical of how, in a one-record-at-a-time network language, such as DBTG COBOL DML, one chains through a set processing its members. It also demonstrates the ability to navigate through the data base. Processing starts on a record in one set and then switches to another set. Set switching is accomplished through a member record that is common to both sets as in the RAISE-MARK procedure. Processing then continues in the second set.

The question of deletion of a record in a network data base deserves attention. The problem that arises is what exactly the system should delete. If an owner record is deleted, what should happen to its member records? If they are only members of this one set occurrence, then probably they should be deleted when the owner is deleted. However, if they are members of several set occurrences, then perhaps the member records should only be removed from the set occurrence of the deleted owner, but remain members of the other set occurrences. Perhaps they must be deleted from all set occurrences. All possibilities are available in the DBTG COBOL DML through various combinations of the <u>DE-LETE</u> and <u>REMOVE</u> commands. Careful consideration must be given to these problems in a network system. In this example, by means of the ONLY option, the SECTION records in the TEACHER-COURSE set occurrence owned by teacher 031678954 are not deleted. They are removed from the TEACHER-COURSE set occurrence, but remain in the STUDENT-COURSE and COURSE-SECTION set occurrences.

6.4.2 Suppliers–Parts

This example appears often in the literature [Date and Codd, 1974]. It concerns a suppliers and parts data base. In general, each supplier may supply several parts and each part may be supplied by several suppliers. To represent such a network using the facilities proposed by the DBTG, two DBTG sets, S_SP (owned by record S) and P_SP (owned by record P) are required. In addition, an intermediate record type, SUPPLIER_PART, which is a member record type in both the S_SP and P_SP DBTG sets is required (Fig. 6.4.2–1).

The SUPPLIER_PART record type is necessary to represent the $N{:}M$ relationship between the supplier and part entity sets. DBTG restrictions I and II prohibit $N{:}M$ links between the SUPPLIER and

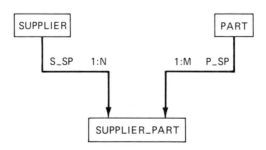

Fig. 6.4.2–1 Suppliers–parts data structure diagram.

PART record types. Thus, three record types and two DBTG sets are
needed. The entity sets that form the record types contain the following attributes:

Supplier contains supplier number, supplier name, status, and city.
Part contains part number, part name, color, and weight.
Supplier-part contains supplier number, part number, and quantity.

Notice that the supplier–part entity set explicitly includes the
appropriate supplier number and part number. This representation is
not required by the network data model. However, it does allow the
ordering of the SUPPLIER_PART record occurrences on part number
within each S_SP set occurrence and on a supplier number within each
P_SP set occurrence. The quantity of a part supplied by a supplier seems
to fit naturally in the SUPPLIER_PART record type since it is associated with both the SUPPLIER and PART record types. The schema
for the data base, using the EDBS DDL, follows [EDBS, 1975]. The
two sets S_SP and P_SP both have optional-manual set membership.

```
DATA BASE SUPPLIERS_PARTS NETWORK

    RECORD SUPPLIER
        DATA-ITEM SNUMBER, STRING 2 : KEY
        DATA-ITEM SNAME, STRING 10
        DATA-ITEM STATUS, NUMERIC(2,0)
        DATA-ITEM CITY, STRING 10
    END SUPPLIER

    RECORD PART
        DATA-ITEM PNUMBER, STRING 2 : KEY
        DATA-ITEM PNAME, STRING 10
        DATA-ITEM COLOUR, STRING 8
        DATA-ITEM WEIGHT, NUMERIC(3,0)
    END PART

    RECORD SUPPLIER_PART
        DATA-ITEM SNUMBER, STRING 2 : KEY
        DATA-ITEM PNUMBER, STRING 2 : KEY
        DATA-ITEM QUANTITY, NUMERIC(2,0)
    END SUPPLIER_PART

    SET S_SP
        OWNER IS SUPPLIER
        MEMBER IS SUPPLIER_PART
    END S_SP
```

    SET P_SP
        OWNER IS PART
        MEMBER IS SUPPLIER_PART
    END P_SP

END SUPPLIERS_PARTS

The queries and updates will be implemented using APL and the EDBS network language presented in Section 6.3.2. The same queries and updates can be found in the literature using DBTG COBOL DML [Date, 1972b, 1975; Date and Codd, 1974].

A sample data base is given in Fig. 6.4.2–2. This data base will be used to illustrate several queries and updates. The abbreviation CTC is used for the command CHANGE TO CURRENT described in Section 6.3.2.

1. Find the quantity of part P4 supplied by supplier S2.

    GET 'FIRST SUPPLIER RECORD WHERE (SNUMBER=S2)'
    'S_SP' CTC 'SUPPLIER'
    GET 'NEXT S_SP SET WHERE (PNUMBER=P4)'

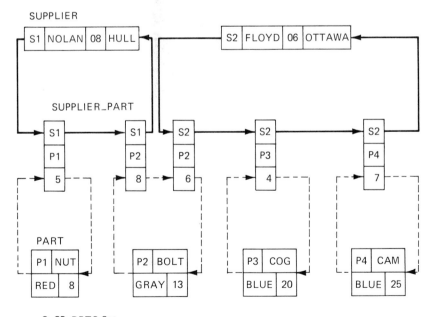

    —— S_SP DBTG Set
    --- P_SP DBTG Set

Fig. 6.4.2–2 Sample occurrence of suppliers–parts data base.

→NOTSUPPLIED <u>IF</u> STATUS=ENDOFSET
<u>READ</u> 'SUPPLIER_PART.QUANTITY'

The first thing to notice is that there is a strategy problem; does one start at supplier S2 and traverse the S_SP set occurrence or does one start at part P4 and traverse the P_SP set occurrence? The query implementation starts at supplier S2. The second <u>GET</u> command scans the current S_SP set occurrence, i.e., the one owned by supplier S2, for a SUPPLIER_PART record with a PNUMBER value qual to P4. The <u>READ</u> command displays the value of the quantity supplied on the user's APL terminal.

2.   Find the part numbers for parts supplied by supplier S2.

<u>GET</u> '<u>FIRST</u> SUPPLIER <u>RECORD</u> <u>WHERE</u> (SNUMBER=S2)'
'S_SP' CTC 'SUPPLIER'
NEXT:<u>GET</u> '<u>NEXT</u> S_SP <u>SET</u>'
→ALLFOUND <u>IF</u> STATUS=ENDOFSET
<u>READ</u> 'SUPPLIER_PART.PNUMBER'
→NEXT

Starting at the S2 SUPPLIER record, the S_SP set occurrence is followed to all SUPPLIER_PART member record occurrences and the PNUMBER for each SUPPLIER_PART record printed.

3.   Find the part numbers for all parts supplied by supplier S1 in quantities of one.

<u>GET</u> '<u>FIRST</u> SUPPLIER <u>RECORD</u> <u>WHERE</u> (SNUMBER=S1)'
'S_SP' <u>CTC</u> 'SUPPLIER'
NEXT: <u>GET</u> '<u>NEXT</u> S_SP <u>SET</u> <u>WHERE</u> (QUANTITY=1)'
→ALLFOUND <u>IF</u> STATUS=ENDOFSET
<u>READ</u> 'SUPPLIER_PART.PNUMBER'
→NEXT

This query is similar to the first query except that instead of searching for a specific part number in a SUPPLIER_PART record, a specific quantity in a SUPPLIER_PART record is wanted.

4.   Find all valid part-name/supplier-city pairs.

<u>GET</u> '<u>FIRST</u> PART <u>RECORD</u>'
SETPSP:'P_SP' <u>CTC</u> 'PART'
NEXTSP:<u>GET</u> '<u>NEXT</u> P_SP <u>SET</u>'
→NEXTP <u>IF</u> STATUS=ENDOFSET

'S_SP' <u>CTC</u> 'P_SP'
→NEXTSP <u>IF</u> STATUS=NOTINSET
<u>GET</u> 'OWNER S_SP <u>SET</u>'
<u>READ</u> 'PART.PNAME'
<u>READ</u> 'SUPPLIER.CITY'
→NEXTSP
NEXTP:<u>GET</u> '<u>NEXT</u> PART <u>RECORD</u>'
→SETPSP <u>IF</u> STATUS=SUCCESSFUL

Starting at the first PART record, all its members in the P_SP set are visited. At each SUPPLIER_PART record, its SUPPLIER owner record in the S_SP set is retrieved. The part name and city are then obtained. This operation is done for all PART records.

5. Add one to the quantity of part P4 supplied by S2.

<u>GET</u> '<u>FIRST</u> SUPPLIER <u>RECORD</u> <u>WHERE</u> (SNUMBER=S2)'
'S_SP' <u>CTC</u> 'SUPPLIER'
<u>GETHOLD</u> '<u>NEXT</u> S_SP <u>SET</u> <u>WHERE</u> (PNUMBER=P4)'
→NOTSUPPLIED <u>IF</u> STATUS=ENDOFSET
(1+<u>READ</u> 'SUPPLIER_PART. QUANTITY') <u>REWRITE</u>
   'SUPPLIER_PART.QUANTITY'
<u>MODIFY</u>
→ERROR <u>IF</u> STATUS≠SUCCESSFUL

The update involves retrieving the required record occurrence, altering it in the application program, and issuing a <u>MODIFY</u> command.

6. Remove the SUPPLIER_PART occurrence for supplier S2, part P4, from the S_SP set occurrence belonging to supplier S2.

<u>GET</u> '<u>FIRST</u> SUPPLIER <u>RECORD</u> <u>WHERE</u> (SNUMBER=S2)'
'S_SP' <u>CTC</u> 'SUPPLIER'
<u>GETHOLD</u> '<u>NEXT</u> S_SP <u>SET</u> <u>WHERE</u> (PNUMBER=P4)'
→NOTSUPPLIED <u>IF</u> STATUS=ENDOFSET
'SUPPLIER_PART' <u>CTC</u> 'S_SP'
<u>REMOVE</u> 'S_SP'
→ERROR <u>IF</u> STATUS≠SUCCESSFUL

The SUPPLIER_PART record occurrence still exists, but it is no longer a member in any S_SP set occurrence.

7. Create the SUPPLIER_PART record occurrence 'S2/P5/1'.

'S2, P5, 1' <u>WRITE</u> 'SUPPLIER_PART'

STORE 'SUPPLIER_PART'
→ERROR IF STATUS≠SUCCESSFUL

The WRITE command places the SUPPLIER_PART record into a buffer. The STORE command places it in the data base.

6.5 CONCLUDING REMARKS

The DBTG proposal provides the specifications for the logical user interface of a network system. It is intended to serve as a guideline for the implementation of network systems, although details of the implementation are left to the individual implementors. There are currently several network systems, which are based on the DBTG proposal, available on the market [Honeywell, 1972; Xerox, 1972; Datapro, 1972b; Gohren, 1973; Philips, 1974; Schubert, 1974; Cullinane, 1975; MacDonald, 1975; Robinson, 1975]. Not all systems are compatible with the DBTG proposal or with each other. In Part II of this book, two network systems, Total and IDMS, are described.

The DBTG was organized in 1968 to study DBMS's so as "to develop the specifications of a common language and functions for a unified data base system" [CODASYL, 1969]. The first result of the DBTG's work was a report published in October 1969 [CODASYL DBTG, 1969]. Its purpose was to solicit criticism and comment. About half of the 180 suggestions received were included in the second report of April 1971 [CODASYL DBTG, 1971]. The April 1971 DBTG report presents requirements for a network DBMS. It also proposed the DBTG network data model as an industry standard. In addition, the report describes a fairly detailed DDL and DML interface for COBOL.

Since the publication of the DBTG report, there have been several evaluations of the proposal from different viewpoints. Some have been favorable while others have offered extensive and sometimes detailed criticism. A summary of some of the important issues that have been raised will be presented [Engles, 1971; Canning, 1972a; Date and Codd, 1974].

The proposals of the DBTG that are favorably judged are those related to high-level design concepts. For example, the concept of a DBA is widely accepted. A data base system implies the sharing of a data base by many users. The DBA, by virtue of his centralized control of the data, is in a good position to understand, evaluate, and fulfil the different data requirements of users. Another widely accepted concept is the separation of a schema and its subschemas. This separation is important, in a multiple-user environment, both from an integrity and from a security standpoint. By means of a subschema, each user has his own view of the data base and has access only to those portions of a schema necessary for his processing requirements. The DBTG proposal introduced the important concept of a DDL to aid the DBA in the definition of schemas and subschemas. Finally, the concept of the DBTG set, as distinct from its use, is a good mechanism for representing complex relationships.

As a specific proposal for a data base design, the DBTG report was also subject to criticism. The most important areas of criticism are the DML, data structures, data privacy and integrity, and data independence.

The DML is criticized as being needlessly complex. For instance, currency indicators are a poor language design feature. Subtle side effects can be caused by certain DML commands on the currency indicators. The updating of the currency indicators must be suppressed in some cases for the correct operation of programs [Date, 1972b]. When using the DML, an application must know the location mode of a record type, e.g., CALC or direct, or the set occurrence selection for a DBTG set. A record type's location mode or a DBTG set's set occurrence selection cannot be changed without changing the application. Data-base-keys may be used explicitly in the DML, but are assigned to the implementor-defined portion of the architecture. This allows the implementor to make a poor choice, such as using physical addresses, for these keys. The area concept should not be part of the DML; it should only be a DBA tool. As proposed by the DBTG, an application must know how record occurrences and set occurrences are mapped into areas. It must provide area names in the code in order to access the records. The DBA may thus be restricted in the physical placement of records when the data base is reorganized.

The restrictions imposed on DBTG sets severely limit the ease with which they may be used. They prohibit the immediate representation of many common data structures, e.g., direct $N:M$ relationships. In addition, DBTG sets and repeating groups constitute redundant ways of representing $1:N$ relationships. A user must know how a relationship is represented since access to the data depends on the representation.

The data privacy and integrity facilities of the DBTG specifications are inadequate for a multiple-user environment. For instance, privacy can be improved by allowing a privacy lock to be sensitive to the content of a record. Also, the facilities for the exclusive use of an area should be applied to record types and DBTG sets as well. More explicit specification of the deadlock prevention mechanism is needed. For example, an application can be required to seize, in one command, all record types or DBTG sets of which it will need exclusive use. Another way of avoiding deadlock is to limit the time that one application can have exclusive or protected access to a unit of data. This limits the time a unit of data can be "tied up." Finally, the DBTG proposal does not eliminate concurrent update. Interference may not be detected and, even if it is detected no specific action is proposed. An application is free to ignore any warning of interference.

Specific features of the DBTG proposal defeat data independence. For instance, there is a dependency between the DDL location mode specification and the DML <u>STORE</u> command. When a schema definition is changed, applications may have to be changed. Different procedural steps must be taken in an application depending on whether set membership is automatic or manual, and on whether relationships are expressed as DBTG sets or repeating groups. Changes to a schema affecting location mode, set occurrence selection, etc., will thus require changes in applications. The DBA should be able to reorganize the data base without impacting the applications. Since applications open areas, and data-base-keys implicitly designate areas, the DBA is not always completely free to consolidate or rearrange areas. Some aspects of the proposal such as reference in the DML to areas and to date-base-keys may preclude the implementation of problem-oriented systems for use by nonprogrammers. Finally the <u>ORDER</u> command enables an application to dynamically change the ordering of record occurrences in a set occurrence. An application can thus cause the ordering of a set occurrence, as seen by another application, to change without notice. Reordering of sets is properly a function of the DBA rather than an application.

Some of the DBTG proposals may be modified in the future. They have come under much scrutiny lately because of a standardization effort. For instance, some suggestions for changes that have been made are [Douque and Nijssen, 1975; Steel, 1975b]

1. to allow owner and member record types to be the same in a DBTG set, that is, to allow L_{ii} links;

2. to restrict DBTG sets to only one member type;

3. to drop data aggregates, like vectors and repeating groups, from a schema;

4. to introduce a record identifier, such as a key, independent of record placement;

5. to prohibit the specification of a preferred access path (location mode) for a record type;

6. to simplify the set occurrence selection clauses.

In addition, many independent suggestions and/or criticisms have appeared in the literature [Huits, 1975; Kay, 1975; Nijssen, 1975; Olle, 1975; Taylor, 1975; Waghorn, 1975]. It is almost certain that many more recommendations will be made and some may be adopted.

The DBTG proposal has received much praise and a great deal of criticism. It represents a substantial effort at data base design. Even if one disagrees with some of its features, it has helped to focus attention on some very important problems. The DBTG proposal will have an important and continuing influence on the evolution of DBMS's.

EXERCISES

6.1 Survey at least five network systems and document any differences they have with the DBTG proposal.

6.2 Try to catalog all DBTG features into two categories relating to end-user facilities and system-oriented optimization features.

6.3 Investigate the importance, for implementation purposes, of restrictions I and II of the DBTG proposal concerning set membership.

6.4 What are the changes needed in the DBTG COBOL DML to accommodate links among record types of the form L_{ii}?

6.5 Compile a list of at least twenty different DBTG DDL or COBOL DML options. Propose an example for each option that uses it to advantage.

6.6 How would you modify Fig. 6.2−1 to permit a doctor to be assigned to a specific ward or wards? Show a data structure diagram and an example of connections in the data base.

6.7 How would you represent an L_{ii} link in a DBTG network data base? Demonstrate your solution using a MANAGED BY link between EMPLOYEE record types. Are there any practical problems with your solution?

6.8 Using COBOL, the DBTG COBOL DML, and the example data base in Fig. 6.3.1−1, write application programs that

(a) find all the students in Math who received a grade of A,

(b) insert a new STUDENT record (Tom, M) and enroll him in Math and English with a grade of U (undefined),

(c) remove Bob's ENROLLMENT records from all classes, i.e., from the ROLL DBTG set.

6.9 Construct an example that illustrates how one can get into an endless loop in a DBTG network data base. How would you design a system to recognize an endless loop during navigation of a data base?

6.10 Construct examples that make use of each format of the DBTG COBOL DML FIND command.

6.11 Express each of the FIND commands of DBTG COBOL DML using the features of the EDBS network language outlined in Section 6.3.2.

6.12 Propose a DML that provides all the facilities of the DBTG COBOL DML for another host language, e.g., PL/1.

6.13 According to the DBTG proposal, a GET command in an application refers to the record occurrence located by the immediately preceding FIND command. Prove that, in the general case, it is recursively unsolvable to determine which record occurrence the program will get.

6.14 Implement the example given in Section 6.4.1 using the EDBS network language outlined in Section 6.3.2.

6.15 Design a manager-oriented query language that is implemented using the DBTG proposal.

6.16 Propose a network system, complete with DML and DDL, that directly accommodates $N:M$ links between record types.

Chapter 7

RELATIONAL SYSTEMS

7.1 RELATIONAL DATA MODEL

Chapters 5 and 6 examined, respectively, the hierarchical and DBTG network data models. The main data-structuring facilities of these data models are record types and links connecting the record types. A record type represents the attribute relationships of an entity set. A link represents an association between two entity sets. Thus, two different concepts, record types and links, are used to represent relationships. In contrast, the relational data model uses only one concept, the relation, to represent relationships. Relations are used to represent both attribute relationships and associations.

As pointed out in Chapter 2, relations can be thought of as tables of data. The columns are called attributes and the rows are called tuples. A relation may have several keys. However, for each relation in a data base, one of its keys is arbitrarily designated as the *primary key*. The distinction between the primary key and other keys is only important for operational purposes. A primary key is not allowed to have an undefined value in any tuple of a relation. Any other keys or attributes may have undefined values. This restriction is imposed because of the vital role played by primary keys in search algorithms [Codd, 1972a].

Except for their tabular format, relations lack any inherent structure, such as links, at the data model level. The tabular form of relations is a very widely used and simple data structure. For example, files and record types can also be represented by tables. Hence, claims are made that some systems already support relations, or at least, can easily represent them. However, in considering the relational data model, it is important to consider the operations on relations as well as their representation. Files and record types are not exactly relations since the operations performed on files and record types are different from those performed on relations. For instance, one sorts record types and extends files, but these operations make no sense on relations. At the data model level, relations have no order or fixed length. In addition, some relational operators, such as join, are not provided for files or record types.

To summarize, the *relational data model* consists of relations that at any point in time conform to the accepted mathematical definition of relations. That is, a relation is a subset of the Cartesian product of its underlying domains. However, unlike mathematical relations, data base relations are time-varying since tuples may be inserted, deleted, or updated.

7.2   RELATIONAL DATA LANGUAGES

A *relational system* organizes the data, in a data base, according to the relational data model. In addition, it provides a relational data language for accessing a relational data base. The relational data language provides facilities capable of emulating the relational operators discussed in Chapter 3. The relational operators allow a user to construct new relations from existing relations.

In a relational system, several different kinds of relations can be distinguished. Some relations in the system have an independent existence. They are defined initially and tuples are inserted in them independently. Such relations will be called *primary* relations. In contrast, relations defined using relational operators on primary relations will be called *derived* relations [Tsichritzis, 1974]. For instance, the join of two primary relations is a derived relation.

Derived relations can have an independent existence after they are created. Such derived relations act like *snapshots* of the primary relation(s). They represent the data base as it existed at a particular point in time. Primary and snapshot relations will be referred to collectively as *base* relations. On the other hand, derived relations may continue to reflect changes to the primary relations. They abide by the definitions according to which they were derived, but they mirror changes to the data base. Such derived relations correspond to *evolving views* of the data base. For instance, a join of two primary relations can be defined to be a snapshot or an evolving view. If it is a snapshot, it becomes independent of the primary relations. If it is an evolving view, it will continue to reflect the changes made to the primary relations. That is, at any point in time, the evolving view will be exactly what would be obtained had the two primary relations just been joined [Boyce and Chamberlin, 1973; Chamberlin *et al.*, 1975].

A relational data language should allow any attributes in one relation to be associated with compatible attributes in other relations to get new derived relations. Derived relations provide data relatability. The ability to handle derived relations is an integral part of a relational system. A relational system that does not handle derived relations hardly deserves the name. It probably does not implement true relational operators.

Ideally, a relational data language should deal only with attributes (not relations) and the functional dependencies among the attributes. However, in some cases, the problem of associating two attributes in a relational schema has no easy solution [Parker and Jervis, 1972]. In general, there can be more than one set of relations relating two arbitrary attributes in the data base. This situation is analogous to the problem of several paths between two records in a DBTG network system. It is difficult, at the user level, to avoid naming the relations, i.e., the path, to be used in obtaining the answer. We illustrate this point by the following example.

Consider the relational schema in Fig. 7.2—1. The EMPLOYEE, DEPARTMENT, and SUPPLIER relations are fairly self-explanatory. The VOLUME attribute in the SUPPLIER relation indicates the total volume of the part supplied by the supplier to the enterprise. The USAGE and PROJECT relations require some explanation. The enterprise described in Fig. 7.2—1 uses two types of parts: externally

EMPLOYEE (NUMBER, NAME, SALARY, MGR)
DEPARTMENT (DEPT, MGR)
SUPPLIER (COMPANY, PART, VOLUME)
USAGE (DEPT, PART, VOLUME)
PROJECT (CODE, DEPT, PART, VOLUME)

Fig. 7.2—1 A relational schema.

supplied parts, which are supplied by a supplier who appears in the SUPPLIER relation, and internally supplied parts, which are supplied by a department to its projects by assembling externally supplied parts. Therefore, the USAGE relation gives the total volume of an externally supplied part used by a department. The PROJECT relation gives the total volume of each internally or externally supplied part that a department supplies to its projects.

Consider now the query "Find the immediate subordinates of the managers of the departments using parts that are supplied by company X." The difficulty with the preceding query, from the system's point of view, is determining which relations to use to answer the query. For example, from the schema alone, it is not clear whether the USAGE or PROJECT relation should be used to relate the COMPANY and the DEPT attributes. However, from the semantics of the relations, as discussed previously, it should be clear that the USAGE relation should be used. The system can choose the appropriate relations itself if it knows the semantics of the relations. However, most relational systems do not take into account the semantics of the relations. Therefore, the relations to be used in answering a query need to be specifically named. Using a relational data language, the preceding query is expressed as [Chamberlin and Boyce, 1974] :

```
SELECT NAME
FROM EMPLOYEE
WHERE MGR=
     SELECT MGR
     FROM DEPARTMENT
     WHERE DEPT=
          SELECT DEPT
          FROM USAGE
          WHERE PART=
               SELECT PART
               FROM SUPPLIER
               WHERE COMPANY='X'
```

This statement of the query specifies how the system is to answer the query. First, it is to scan the COMPANY attribute values in the SUPPLIER relation and select all parts supplied by company X. Then, using the parts selected, it is to scan the PART attribute values in the USAGE relation and select all departments that use any of the parts. Next, it is to scan the DEPARTMENT relation and select the MGR attribute values that manage a department selected in the previous step. Finally, it is to scan the MGR attribute values in the EMPLOYEE relation and select the names of employees who are managed by any of the managers selected in the previous step.

In this section, two different relational data languages will be considered. The features of each data language will be illustrated by examples. For economy of presentation, and by way of comparison, a common data base example and common queries will be used throughout this section. The data base consists of the relations and attributes shown in Fig. 7.2—1. The primary keys are underlined.

7.2.1 DSL ALPHA

In Chapter 3, the relational operators were presented in the context of the relational algebra. At that time, it was noted that the operators could also be expressed in terms of the relational calculus. In this section, a relational data language based on the relational calculus will be outlined.

DSL (*Data Sub-Language*) ALPHA is based on an applied predicate calculus [Codd, 1971b]. It is intended to operate within a host programming language such as PL/1, COBOL, or FORTRAN. Data is retrieved from and placed into the data base via *user workspaces*, essentially buffer areas. The data in a workspace has a representation similar to that for a relation, i.e., as a table. A user may have many active workspaces and these are referenced by user-specified names. Columns (attributes) of the relation in a workspace are referenced by means of a workspace attribute name, which is usually inherited from the data base relation. The syntax of the commands presented here is for pedagogical purposes only. The actual syntax would depend on the particular host language.

The ALPHA retrieval command has the general format

GET INTO workspace-name (target-list) option-list

The workspace-name is the name of the workspace into which the retrieved data are to be placed. A target-list is generally composed of elements each of which is of one of the forms:

relation name.attribute name
tuple variable.attribute name
relation name
tuple variable

In the last two cases, the omission of an attribute name indicates that complete tuples are to be retrieved from the corresponding relation. The option-list may have a qualification of the form

WHERE (qualification)

The option-list may also specify an ordering on the tuples retrieved.

The projection operator in ALPHA is illustrated by the following query.

1. Find all the part numbers of parts being supplied.

GET INTO W (SUPPLIER.PART)

A more complicated query, involving a qualification, is the following.

2. Find the names of employees who make more than $12,000.

GET INTO W (EMPLOYEE.NAME) WHERE (EMPLOYEE. SALARY>12000)

Suppose a user is beginning a terminal session or is writing an application program in which frequent reference is to be made to the EMPLOYEE relation. A range declaration of the form

RANGE EMPLOYEE E

can be used to tell the system that the user wants to talk about employees and is going to use E to designate a typical tuple of the EMPLOYEE relation. Query 2 can now be expressed as

GET INTO W (E.NAME) WHERE (E.SALARY>12000)

The purpose of the RANGE command is to force the user to state the context of requests. It also makes queries whose answer is essentially the entire data base, or some other equally unreasonable request, difficult to ask.

A workspace relation can be used in a query as the next example demonstrates.

3. Find the salary of Jones' manager.

RANGE EMPLOYEE E
GET INTO W1 (E.MGR) WHERE (E.NAME='JONES')
RANGE W1 X
GET INTO W2 (E.SALARY) WHERE (E.NUMBER=X.MGR)

Existential ($\exists$) and universal ($\forall$) quantifiers may appear in the qualification. Existential quantification is used to check for existence conditions when using the join operator. Universal quantification is used to check for membership conditions.

4. Find the companies who supply the types of parts used in the research department.

RANGE SUPPLIER S
RANGE USAGE U
GET INTO W (S.COMPANY) WHERE $\exists$U ((S.PART=U.PART) &
 (U.DEPT='RESEARCH'))

The expression S.PART=U.PART is called a *join term*. The attributes over which the join is to occur must be compatible.

Quantifiers may be moved to the RANGE statements by using SOME for $\exists$ and ALL for $\forall$, e.g.,

RANGE SUPPLIER S
RANGE USAGE U SOME
GET INTO W (S.COMPANY) WHERE ((S.PART=U.PART) &
 (U.DEPT='RESEARCH'))

Queries may reference more than one relation in the target-list. The qualification may also be quite complex.

5. For company ACME, obtain a list of those parts supplied in quantities greater than 1000 and departments using those types of parts.

RANGE SUPPLIER S
RANGE USAGE U
GET INTO W (S.PART, U.DEPT) WHERE ((U.PART=S.PART) &
 (S.COMPANY='ACME') & (S.VOLUME>1000))

Next, the universal quantifier is used to express the division operator.

6. Find the companies, each of which supplies every type of part used in the Research department.

RANGE USAGE U
RANGE SUPPLIER S
RANGE SUPPLIER T
GET INTO W (S.COMPANY) WHERE $\forall$U$\exists$T((U.PART=T.PART)
 & (T.COMPANY=S.COMPANY) & (U.DEPT='RESEARCH'))

ALPHA provides certain library functions that are useful in a data base environment for extending the selective capability of queries. Some of these are COUNT, MAX, MIN, and TOTAL [Codd, 1971b].

7. List the name and salary of every manager who manages more than ten employees.

```
GET INTO W1 (EMPLOYEE.MGR)
DO I=1 TO SIZE(W1)                              (host language)
    MGR_NO=W1 (I)                               (host language)
    GET INTO W2 (COUNT(EMPLOYEE.NUMBER) )
        WHERE (EMPLOYEE.MGR=MGR_NO)
    IF W2(1) > 10 THEN                          (host language)
        GET INTO W3 (EMPLOYEE.NAME, EMPLOYEE.SALARY)
            WHERE (EMPLOYEE.NUMBER=MGR_NO)
        OUTPUT(W3)                              (host language)
END                                             (host language)
```

The ALPHA insertion command, to insert new tuples into a relation, has the general format

PUT workspace-name relation-name options

The data in the workspace, given by workspace-name, is inserted into the relation specified by relation-name. Various options are available as shown by the following examples.

8. Insert into the ternary relation SUPPLIER the 3-tuple 'AJAX', 123, 0.

```
INPUT W (COMPANY='AJAX',
    PART=123, VOLUME=0)                         (host language)
PUT W SUPPLIER
```

Not all values need be specified. Missing values for non-primary key attributes are assumed to be null.

9. Insert into USAGE the values DEPT='SALES' and PART=84.

```
INPUT W (DEPT='SALES', PART=84)                 (host language)
PUT W USAGE. (DEPT, PART)
```

The delete command has the format

DELETE relation-name WHERE (qualification)

A single delete command removes tuples from precisely one data base relation. However, the qualification in the <u>DELETE</u> can involve any number of relations and quantifiers.

10. Delete the tuple for employee Smith from the EMPLOYEE relation.

<u>DELETE</u> EMPLOYEE <u>WHERE</u> (EMPLOYEE.NAME='SMITH')

The update command has the format

<u>UPDATE</u> workspace-name

The update command must be preceded by a <u>HOLD</u> command. The <u>HOLD</u> command has the same effect as a corresponding <u>GET</u> in regard to the data made available in the specified workspace. An additional effect of the <u>HOLD</u> command is that it warns the DBMS to be prepared to return modified data to the elements supplying the retrieved data. A pending modification may be cancelled by means of a <u>RELEASE</u> command.

The ALPHA <u>HOLD</u> command, unlike the <u>GET</u>, may only specify a single relation in its target-list. This avoids unwarranted complexity in the update process.

11. Give a 10% raise to all employees who make less than $12,000.

```
RANGE EMPLOYEE E
HOLD INTO W (E.SALARY) WHERE (E.SALARY<12000)
DO I=1 TO SIZE(W)                        (host language)
    W(I).SALARY=1.1*W(I).SALARY          (host language)
END                                      (host language)
UPDATE W
```

12. Add DELTA to the volume of PART 123 supplied by company ACME.

```
RANGE SUPPLIER S
HOLD INTO W (S.VOLUME) WHERE (S.COMPANY='ACME')
    & (S.PART=123)
W.VOLUME=W.VOLUME+DELTA                   (host language)
UPDATE W
```

In both of the preceding examples, the system retains enough primary key information so that it can perform the update properly.

In this section, a calculus-based relational data language, DSL ALPHA, was presented. Only the salient features of the language were discussed. In addition, the predicates used in the examples were quite simple. Much more complex predicates can be constructed [Codd, 1971b; Date, 1975]. The language has been shown to be complete [Codd, 1972b].

7.2.2 SEQUEL

SEQUEL (*S*tructural *E*nglish *Que*ry *L*anguage) is an English-like, set-oriented relational data language that is part of the System R relational data base management system [Chamberlin and Boyce, 1974; Astrahan *et al.,* 1976]. In processing queries, the effect is as if one scanned the column(s) of the relation looking for a value or set of values. The tuples, or portions thereof, in which the value(s) is found are returned as the result. Contrast this with DSL ALPHA, which is tuple-oriented. One selects a tuple and applies a predicate to it; if true then the tuple, or a portion thereof, is returned as the result. One iterates in this manner over all tuples of a relation. SEQUEL also eliminates the need for quantifiers and "linking terms" needed to correlate several relations.

SEQUEL is based on a notational relational data language called SQUARE (*S*pecifying *Que*ries *as* *R*elational *E*xpressions) [Boyce *et al.,* 1974]. The difference between SQUARE and SEQUEL is similar to the difference between the statements "3 + 5" and "add three and five". Both statements express the same intent. However, the former is notational while the latter is English-like.

A retrieval operation is specified in SEQUEL by a SELECT statement. A SELECT statement has the general form

```
SELECT [UNIQUE] attribute-list
FROM relation-list
[WHERE qualification]
[GROUP BY attribute-name [HAVING qualification] ]
```

where [   ] indicates optional items. The attribute-list specifies from which attributes values are to be selected. An asterisk (*) indicates that all attribute values are to be selected. The relation-list specifies one or more relations from which the attribute values are to be selected. The relations may be assigned identifiers in the FROM clause. These identifiers may then be used in the WHERE clause to resolve ambiguities (for instance, where a relation name appears more than once in a query; see Section 7.3.1 for an example). The qualification is used to specify the criterion for selecting tuples from one or several relations. Finally, the <u>GROUP BY</u> clause can be used to group rows of a relation according to some criterion. We will illustrate the facilities of the <u>SELECT</u> statement by examples.

1. Find all the part numbers of parts being supplied.

<u>SELECT</u> PART
<u>FROM</u> SUPPLIER

This returns the SUPPLIER relation projected on PART.
Query 2 illustrates the use of the qualification in SEQUEL.

2. Find the names of employees who make more than $12,000.

<u>SELECT</u> NAME
<u>FROM</u> EMPLOYEE
<u>WHERE</u> SALARY>12000

The result of one <u>SELECT</u> statement can be used in the qualification of another <u>SELECT</u> statement by nesting <u>SELECT</u> statements. The result of the innermost <u>SELECT</u> statement is used as an argument to the containing <u>SELECT</u> statement. This facility is used to express a join operation. A relation may either be joined with itself as in Query 3 or two or more relations may be joined as in Queries 4 and 5.

3. Find the salary of Jones' manager.

<u>SELECT</u> SALARY
<u>FROM</u> EMPLOYEE
<u>WHERE</u> NUMBER=
    <u>SELECT</u> MGR
    <u>FROM</u> EMPLOYEE
    <u>WHERE</u> NAME='JONES'

4. Find the companies who supply the types of parts used in the Research department.

<u>SELECT</u> COMPANY
<u>FROM</u> SUPPLIER
<u>WHERE</u> PART=
    <u>SELECT</u> PART

```
FROM USAGE
WHERE DEPT='RESEARCH'
```

5. For company ACME, obtain a list of those parts supplied in quantities greater than 1000 and departments using those types of parts.

```
SELECT DEPT, PART
FROM USAGE
WHERE PART=
    SELECT PART
    FROM SUPPLIER
    WHERE COMPANY='ACME'
    AND VOLUME>1000
```

Nested SELECT statements normally specify a disjunctive mapping between the inner SELECT statement and the containing SELECT statement. For example, in Query 4 a COMPANY value is selected from the SUPPLIER relation if the matching PART value appears on the list selected by the inner SELECT statement. That is, the company is selected if it supplies *any* part on the list selected by the inner SELECT statement. It need not supply *all* parts on the list. If we wanted only those companies that supply all the parts on a given list, then this would require a conjunctive mapping. Conjunctive mapping is equivalent to a division operation and is specified by the keyword SET in SEQUEL. In Query 6, a COMPANY value is selected only if it supplies all of the parts on the list selected by the inner SELECT statement.

6. Find the companies, each of which supplies every type of part used in the research department.

```
SELECT COMPANY
FROM SUPPLIER
WHERE SET PART=
    SELECT PART
    FROM USAGE
    WHERE DEPT='RESEARCH'
```

Sometimes it is necessary to correlate information pertaining to a specific row in a table with another row or set of rows from some table. Consequently, SEQUEL uses a GROUP BY clause, which groups rows of a relation according to the value of an attribute in the relation. For example, Query 7 groups rows of the EMPLOYEE relation according to those rows that have the same MGR value.

7. List the name and salary of every manager who manages more than ten employees.

```
SELECT NAME, SALARY
FROM EMPLOYEE
WHERE NUMBER=
    SELECT MGR
    FROM EMPLOYEE
    GROUP BY MGR
    HAVING COUNT (*)>10
```

The query also shows the use of one of the built-in functions of SEQUEL–COUNT. Others are SUM, AVG, MAX, and MIN [Boyce *et al.*, 1974; Chamberlin and Boyce, 1974].

It is possible to assign the result of a query in SEQUEL to a variable name. The effect is to create a *snapshot* of the relation(s) from which the result is taken.

SEQUEL also provide facilities for inserting, deleting, and updating tuples of a relation. The insert statement in SEQUEL has the general format:

INSERT INTO relation-name (attribute-list):<value-list>

The values for the attributes listed in attribute-list are given by value-list. Any attributes omitted are set to null. Queries 8 and 9 illustrate insertion.

8. Insert into the ternary relation SUPPLIER the 3-tuple 'AJAX', 123, 0.

INSERT INTO SUPPLIER (COMPANY, PART, VOLUME):
  <'AJAX', 123, 0>

9. Insert into USAGE the values DEPT='SALES' and PART=84.

INSERT INTO USAGE (DEPT, PART):<'SALES', 84>

The syntax of the SEQUEL delete statement is

DELETE relation-name
WHERE qualification

The relation is searched for tuples that match the qualification. All matching tuples are deleted.

10. Delete the tuple for employee Smith from the EMPLOYEE relation.

DELETE EMPLOYEE
WHERE NAME='SMITH'

An update is more complex. It is necessary, in general, to select the rows to be updated and to specify the update to be done. The general SEQUEL syntax is

UPDATE relation-name
SET attribute-name=update-value
WHERE qualification

11. Give a 10% raise to all employees who make less than $12,000.

UPDATE EMPLOYEE
SET SALARY=1.1*SALARY
WHERE SALARY<12000

12. Add DELTA to the volume of PART 123 supplied by company ACME.

UPDATE SUPPLIER
SET VOLUME=VOLUME+DELTA
WHERE COMPANY='ACME'
AND PART=123

In this section, the relational data language SEQUEL was discussed. The language is not based on the relational algebra or the relational calculus. Instead, it is set-oriented and provides set-oriented operations. SEQUEL has been shown to be complete [Boyce *et al.*, 1974].

7.3   EXAMPLES OF APPLICATIONS

7.3.1   Insurance Policy Processing

This is an example of a general processing application for life insurance [Schafheitlin, 1974], which is similar to the example examined in Chapter 5. Here, it will be implemented using the relational data model and SEQUEL DDF and DMF [Boyce and Chamberlin, 1973; Chamberlin and Boyce, 1974]. The typical entity sets that might exist in such a company are the following:

General policy contains policy number, social insurance number, previous status change, next activity code, and date.

Policy plan contains policy number, plan code, issue date, expiry date, amount, annual premiums, and next change date.

Client contains social insurance number, name, address, and birthdate.

Agents contains agent number, name, and area.

Agents' commission contains policy number, agent number, and commission rate.

Billing contains policy number, how paid, amount, number of months paid, and currently paid to.

Loans contains policy number, principal, interest, current balance, and next payment date.

Actuarial factors contains policy number, rank or series code, statistical units, net premium per unit, and terminal reserves.

The relations used in this example will be defined using SEQUEL DDF. Some explanation of the terms used is necessary. A *table* is an independent, generic relation. The *scope* of an attribute is a specification of the range of possible values, e.g., integer from 0 to 100 or string where length is 6. The *domain* of an attribute is its comparability domain. The domain is the basic unit that determines if it is semantically meaningful to compare two values. Two values can be compared if and only if they have the same domain. The *representation* of an attribute is its physical machine representation, e.g., FIXED BINARY(32,0) for integers. Finally, the *unit* of an attribute is a standard of measurement, e.g., dollars, marks, or pounds.

```
DEFINE POLICY TABLE AS:
    POLICY_ NO (SCOPE=DIGIT, DOMAIN=NUMBER,
        REPR=CHAR(9) ),
    SIN LIKE POLICY_ NO,
    STATUS_ CHANGE (SCOPE=ALPHA(8), DOMAIN=DATE,
        REPR=CHAR(8) ),
    NEXT_ ACTIVITY_ CODE (SCOPE=ALPHA(2),
        DOMAIN=CODE, REPR=CHAR(2) ),
    NEXT_ ACTIVITY_ DATE LIKE STATUS_ CHANGE;
```

The LIKE facility of SEQUEL means, for example, that SIN has the same characteristics as POLICY_NO, although not necessarily the same values.

DEFINE POLICY_PLAN TABLE AS:
   POLICY_NO LIKE POLICY.POLICY_NO,
   PLAN_CODE LIKE POLICY.NEXT_ACTIVITY_CODE,
   ISSUED LIKE POLICY.STATUS_CHANGE,
   EXPIRES LIKE ISSUED,
   AMOUNT (SCOPE=INTEGER, DOMAIN=MONEY,
     REPR=FIXED DEC(6,2)),
   ANNUAL_ PREMIUM (SCOPE=REAL, DOMAIN=MONEY,
     REPR=FIXED DEC(7,2), UNITS=DOLLARS),
   NEXT_ CHANGE_ DATE LIKE POLICY.STATUS_ CHANGE;

In POLICY_ PLAN, AMOUNT is in thousands of dollars as $1000 is the basic unit of life insurance policies.

DEFINE CLIENT TABLE AS:
   SIN LIKE POLICY.SIN,
   NAME (SCOPE=ALPHA(25), DOMAIN=NAME,
     REPR=CHAR(25)),
   ADDRESS (SCOPE=ALPHA(40), DOMAIN=ADDRESS,
     REPR=CHAR(40)),
   BIRTHDATE LIKE POLICY.STATUS_ CHANGE;

DEFINE AGENT TABLE AS:
   AGENT_NO LIKE POLICY.POLICY_NO,
   NAME LIKE CLIENT.NAME,
   AREA (SCOPE=DIGIT, DOMAIN=AREANO,
     REPR=CHAR(3));

DEFINE COMMISSION TABLE AS:
   POLICY_ NO LIKE POLICY.POLICY_ NO,
   AGENT_NO LIKE AGENT.AGENT_ NO,
   RATE (SCOPE=REAL, DOMAIN=RATE,
     REPR=FIXED(5,2));

DEFINE BILLING TABLE AS:
   POLICY_ NO LIKE POLICY.POLICY_ NO,
   PAY_ METHOD LIKE POLICY.NEXT_ ACTIVITY_ CODE,
   AMOUNT LIKE POLICY_ PLAN.AMOUNT,
   MONTHS_ PAID (SCOPE=INTEGER, DOMAIN=MONTHS,
     REPR=FIXED DEC(4)),
   PAID_ TO LIKE POLICY.STATUS_ CHANGE;

In this case, AMOUNT does not necessarily equal POLICY_

PLAN.AMOUNT as premiums could be paid quarterly or semiannually, etc.

```
DEFINE LOAN TABLE AS:
    POLICY_NO LIKE POLICY.POLICY_NO,
    PRINCIPAL (SCOPE=REAL, DOMAIN=MONEY,
        REPR=FIXED(8,2), UNITS=DOLLARS),
    INTEREST LIKE COMMISSION.RATE,
    BALANCE LIKE PRINCIPAL,
    NEXT_PAYMENT_DATE LIKE POLICY.STATUS_CHANGE;

DEFINE ACTUARIAL TABLE AS:
    POLICY_NO LIKE POLICY.POLICY_NO,
    CODE LIKE POLICY.NEXT_ACTIVITY_CODE,
    UNITS (SCOPE=REAL, DOMAIN=STATISTICS,
        REPR=CHAR(3) ),
    PREMIUM_UNIT LIKE POLICY_PLAN.AMOUNT,
    TERM_RESERVES LIKE PREMIUM_UNIT;
```

Several associations exist between these relations. They can be implemented as required by the queries and updates, or they can be implemented as permanent joins. Permanent joins play the same role in relational systems as links do in hierarchical and network systems. This example will demonstrate one permanent join, that of POLICY and CLIENT on social insurance number. This permanent join allows a client's name to be mapped to the policy number(s) of policies held by the client.

A *net* in SEQUEL is a named collection of directional paths that connect each tuple of a source relation to zero or more tuples of a target relation [Boyce and Chamberlin, 1973]. There may be only one loop-free path between any two relations in a net. A SEQUEL net corresponds to joins that are permanently kept and maintained by the system. Other joins may be formed implicitly while servicing SEQUEL query statements. However, nets are given names and defined explicitly. The concept of nets and permanent joins will be clarified when discussing implementation in Chapter 8.

The net between POLICY and CLIENT is defined as

```
DEFINE NET POLICY_CLIENT:
    BRANCH POLICY TO CLIENT:
        (FROM POLICY
        WHERE SIN IS
            SELECT SIN
```

```
                FROM CLIENT)
        BRANCH CLIENT TO POLICY:
            (FROM CLIENT
            WHERE SIN IS
                SELECT SIN
                FROM POLICY)
    END;
```

This net is bidirectional. That is, it specifies a path (BRANCH) in both directions. A shorthand notation for a bidirectional branch is the LINK concept:

```
    DEFINE NET POLICY_CLIENT:
        LINK POLICY TO CLIENT BY SIN;
    END;
```

The LINK concept corresponds to the conceptual links defined in Chapter 2 for the network data model.

Several straightforward queries and updates will be given as well as one more complex update. The first query demonstrates the collection of data from various tables. It is a typical sale statistics gathering query. The query is "Determine the number of policies sold in area 100 of type 45." The policy numbers for policies sold by agents in area 100 are obtained from the COMMISSION and AGENT relations. These policy numbers are then used to search the POLICY_PLAN relation and select those policies with POLICY_ CODE equal to 45. All policy numbers are counted only once by the system.

```
    SELECT COUNT (UNIQUE POLICY_NO)
    FROM POLICY_PLAN
    WHERE PLAN_CODE='45'
    AND POLICY_NO IS IN
        SELECT POLICY_NO
        FROM COMMISSION
        WHERE AGENT_NO=
            SELECT AGENT_NO
            FROM AGENT
            WHERE AREA='100'
```

The next update modifies the value of an attribute. It involves changing the interest rates on all loans that are currently at 11 to 12.5%. Because all loans are in one relation, and any attribute may be specified in the qualification, this update is trivial.

<u>UPDATE</u> LOAN
<u>SET</u> INTEREST=12.50
<u>WHERE</u> INTEREST=11.00

The next query combines the ability to relate and modify data in various tables. "Change all Ted Jones' policies from annual premium payment to semiannual." The policy numbers of Ted's policies are determined from the net POLICY_CLIENT. These policy numbers are then used to access the BILLING relation.

<u>UPDATE</u> BILLING
<u>SET</u> PAY_METHOD='SA', AMOUNT=.52*AMOUNT
<u>WHERE</u> POLICY_NO=
   <u>SELECT</u> POLICY_NO
   <u>FROM</u> POLICY_CLIENT
   <u>WHERE</u> NAME='TED JONES'
   <u>AND</u> PAY_METHOD='AN'

The AMOUNT attribute value is multiplied by 0.52 instead of 0.50 to allow for installment charges.

An example of a simple, but rather awkward update is the deletion of a policy. This update requires six delete statements. Besides the POLICY relation there are five other relations in which there may be one or more related tuples for the policy to be deleted. A deletion in one relation could automatically cause the deletion of related data in another relation. However, it is not clear that this is always what is wanted. It may be necessary, in some cases, to retain some of the related data. The type of delete operation provided would probably depend very much on the application and the sophistication of the system.

As a final example, consider a more complicated update. "For all policies for which the next activity date is today update the next activity date and code in the POLICY relation." To do this update, it is necessary to determine two things:

1. The policy numbers of policies whose next activity date is today.
2. The next activity for each policy selected in step one.

The next activity for a policy can be one of: billing (code BL), loan payment (code LO), or policy change (code PL). To determine which action is next, the BILLING, LOAN, and POLICY_PLAN relations must be examined. For each type of activity, the next earliest date for the

activity must be chosen, i.e., PAID_TO in BILLING, NEXT_PAYMENT
_DATE in LOAN, or NEXT_CHANGE_DATE in POLICY_PLAN. Since
each policy may have several billing methods, loans, or plan types, the
earliest next date for each type of activity, for each policy, must be
determined. Finally, from the earliest next date for each activity, the
earliest next date of the three must be determined for each policy. This
date is then used to update the NEXT_ACTIVITY_DATE in the
POLICY relation and to set the NEXT_ACTIVITY_CODE for each
policy.

The first step is to determine the next earliest date for each type of
activity. A snapshot relation, MIN_BILLING, MIN_LOAN, and MIN
_POLICY_PLAN, is created for each type of activity. Each relation
contains the policy number and next earliest date for the activity for
each policy. The tuples in the BILLING, LOAN, and POLICY_PLAN
relations are grouped by POLICY_NO, and the minimum date in each
group is chosen. The policy numbers are selected by joining the BILL-
ING, LOAN, and POLICY_PLAN relations with the POLICY relation
where the next activity date is today ('yy/mm/dd').

```
MIN_BILLING (POLICY_NO, BILL_DATE) ←
    SELECT POLICY_NO, MIN (PAID_TO)
    FROM BILLING
    WHERE POLICY_NO=
        SELECT POLICY_NO
        FROM POLICY
        WHERE NEXT_ACTIVITY_DATE='yy/mm/dd'
    GROUP BY POLICY_NO

MIN_LOAN (POLICY_NO, LOAN_DATE) ←
    SELECT POLICY_NO, MIN (NEXT_PAYMENT_DATE)
    FROM LOAN
    WHERE POLICY_NO=
        SELECT POLICY_NO
        FROM POLICY
        WHERE NEXT_ACTIVITY_DATE='yy/mm/dd'
    GROUP BY POLICY_NO

MIN_POLICY_PLAN (POLICY_NO, POLICY_PLAN_DATE) ←
    SELECT POLICY_NO, MIN (NEXT_CHANGE_DATE)
    FROM POLICY_PLAN
    WHERE POLICY_NO=
        SELECT POLICY_NO
```

<u>FROM</u> POLICY
<u>WHERE</u> NEXT_ACTIVITY_DATE='yy/mm/dd'
<u>GROUP BY</u> POLICY_NO

Each of the three new relations now contains the earliest next date for that particular activity. It is now necessary to determine which activity, for each policy, has the next earliest date. This is done by comparing the dates in all three relations, for a given policy, and for each activity, and placing a tuple in the result relation if the date for the activity is the next earliest. Three snapshot relations are created corresponding to those policies for which billing, loan payment, or policy plan changes are the next activity. It is necessary to create these relations because if only the earliest next date for each policy is found, then there is no way of knowing what the next activity is. The following queries also demonstrate the use of variable names (B, L, and P) to correlate tuples in different relations [Astrahan *et al.,* 1976].

BILLING_NEXT (POLICY_NO, DATE) ←
    <u>SELECT</u> POLICY_NO, BILLING_DATE
    <u>FROM</u> MIN_BILLING B
    <u>WHERE</u> BILLING_DATE<
        <u>SELECT</u> LOAN_DATE
        <u>FROM</u> MIN_LOAN
        <u>WHERE</u> POLICY_NO=B.POLICY_NO
    <u>AND</u> BILLING_DATE<
        <u>SELECT</u> POLICY_PLAN_DATE
        <u>FROM</u> MIN_POLICY_PLAN
        <u>WHERE</u> POLICY_NO=B.POLICY_NO

LOAN_NEXT (POLICY_NO, DATE) ←
    <u>SELECT</u> POLICY_NO, LOAN_DATE
    <u>FROM</u> MIN_LOAN L
    <u>WHERE</u> LOAN_DATE<
        <u>SELECT</u> BILLING_DATE
        <u>FROM</u> MIN_BILLING
        <u>WHERE</u> POLICY_NO=L.POLICY_NO
    <u>AND</u> LOAN_DATE<
        <u>SELECT</u> POLICY_PLAN_DATE
        <u>FROM</u> MIN_POLICY_PLAN
        <u>WHERE</u> POLICY_NO=L.POLICY_NO

POLICY_PLAN_NEXT (POLICY_NO, DATE) ←
    <u>SELECT</u> POLICY_NO, POLICY_PLAN_DATE

```
FROM MIN_POLICY_PLAN P
WHERE POLICY_PLAN_DATE<
    SELECT BILLING_DATE
    FROM MIN BILLING
    WHERE POLICY_NO=P.POLICY_NO
AND POLICY_PLAN_DATE<
    SELECT LOAN_DATE
    FROM MIN LOAN
    WHERE POLICY_NO=P.POLICY_NO
```

Finally, the POLICY relation is updated from the BILLING_NEXT, LOAN_NEXT, and POLICY_PLAN_NEXT relations.

```
UPDATE  POLICY P
SET NEXT_ACTIVITY_CODE='BL', NEXT_ACTIVITY_DATE=
    SELECT DATE
    FROM BILLING_NEXT
    WHERE POLICY_NO=P.POLICY_NO
WHERE POLICY_NO=
    SELECT POLICY_NO
    FROM BILLING_NEXT

UPDATE POLICY P
SET NEXT_ACTIVITY_CODE='LO', NEXT_ACTIVITY_DATE=
    SELECT DATE
    FROM LOAN NEXT
    WHERE POLICY_NO=P. POLICY_NO
WHERE POLICY_NO=
    SELECT POLICY_NO
    FROM LOAN NEXT

UPDATE POLICY P
SET NEXT_ACTIVITY_CODE='PL', NEXT_ACTIVITY_DATE=
    SELECT DATE
    FROM POLICY_PLAN_NEXT
    WHERE POLICY_NO=P.POLICY_NO
WHERE POLICY_NO=
    SELECT POLICY_NO
    FROM POLICY_PLAN_NEXT
```

The outlined implementation of the update is not a particularly good solution to the problem. There are, in fact, problems with the implementation. If the values of the attributes PAID_TO, NEXT_PAY-

MENT_DATE, and NEXT_CHANGE_DATE are all equal for a given policy number, then the update of the NEXT_ACTIVITY_DATE and NEXT_ACTIVITY_CODE attributes in the POLICY relation will not be performed at all. Also, it is assumed that every policy has a LOAN and POLICY_PLAN tuple in the LOAN and POLICY_PLAN relations. A policy may, of course, have no loans outstanding against it. However, the purpose of this example is to demonstrate a complex update. It also shows that relational queries or updates are not always simple, one-statement requests.

7.3.2 Personnel

This example illustrates the use of permanent joins between relations. The result is a set of relations connected by links represented as permanent joins. The example is essentially a manufacturing company's personnel data base [Frank and Sibley, 1973; Schafheitlin, 1974]. It contains data about the employees such as their medical history, education, and skills, as well as data concerning the machines, jobs, and the scheduling of the workloads. These data can logically be organized into several entity sets:

Person contains an identification number, name, birthdate, and salary.

Medical contains an absence date range, the illness, and comments.

Job contains a jobcode, start date, finish date, and performance rating.

Education contains a degree, start date, graduation date, and the school.

Machine contains a machine number and type, and the skills needed to operate it.

Schedule contains a job code, scheduled start date, scheduled completion date, and worker identification number.

Skill contains the skills possessed by employees of the company and the pay rate for the skill.

These entity sets will form relations. Once the relations are defined, some associations between them can be defined. Examining the relationships among the entity sets, persons should be related to their medical record(s), their job(s), their education, and any skills they have. Thus, persons form simple, i.e., 1:N, relationships with their medical, job, skill, and education data. However, any skill may be related to several people, i.e., several people may have the same skill. Similarly, several skill classifications may be capable of operating a machine, and one skill classification may be authorized to operate several machines. Thus, there exist *N:M* relationships between persons and skills, and between skills and machines. Finally, it seems natural to relate a machine to its scheduling data and persons to their scheduled machines. Thus, Fig. 7.3.2−1 expresses the relationships among the entity sets.

In SEQUEL these relationships may take the form of nets or they may be expressed in the actual query. It is assumed that these relationships are used frequently, and thus they are implemented as nets. To accomplish this, the relations to be joined must have a compatible attribute. Consequently MEDICAL, JOB, SKILL, and EDUCATION require the additional attribute of identification number (SCHEDULE already contains such an attribute called WORKER_ID). Also MACHINE will require a SKILL_CODE attribute and SCHEDULE a MACHINE_NUMBER attribute. This results in the following relations with their primary key underlined:

PERSON (<u>ID NUMBER</u>, NAME, BIRTHDATE, SALARY)
MEDICAL (<u>ID NUMBER, ABSENCE</u>, ILLNESS, COMMENTS)
JOB (<u>ID NUMBER, JOB CODE</u>, START_DATE, FINISH_DATE,
      PERFORMANCE)
EDUCATION (<u>ID NUMBER, DEGREE</u>, START_DATE,
      GRADUATION_DATE, SCHOOL)
MACHINE (<u>MACHINE NO, SKILL CODE</u>, MACHINE_TYPE)
SCHEDULE (<u>MACHINE NO, JOB CODE</u>, START_DATE,
      COMPLETE_DATE, WORKER_ID)
SKILL (<u>SKILL CODE, ID NUMBER</u>, JOB_RATE)

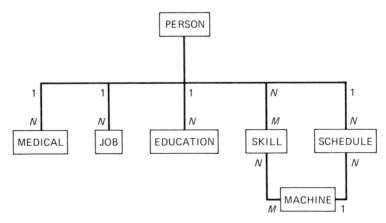

Fig. 7.3.2−1 Personnel relationship graph.

It is assumed that each machine is only scheduled once per job. This assumption is necessary to allow MACHINE_NUMBER, JOB_CODE to be the primary key in the SCHEDULE relation. If this assumption is not valid, another key has to be chosen.

The SEQUEL definition for the generic relations (tables) will not be given. However, the nets will be defined. The nets in this example form a networklike data base. A net can consist of branches involving several relations. For example, it is possible to link JOB, MEDICAL, and EDUCATION to PERSON in one net. However, it is not clear that this is the best approach. Most queries will probably not require all the data available in the net. Also, from an implementation viewpoint, it may be better to create several nets corresponding to the data required by frequently used queries. Therefore, several nets are created.

The net PERSON_JOB between PERSON and JOB is defined in SEQUEL DDF as

```
DEFINE NET PERSON_JOB:
    BRANCH JOB TO PERSON:
        (FROM PERSON WHERE ID_NUMBER IS
            SELECT ID_NUMBER FROM JOB)
    END;
```

The nets PERSON_MEDICAL between PERSON and MEDICAL and PERSON_EDUCATION between PERSON and EDUCATION are defined in a similar manner. These nets all represent $1:N$ relationships.

The next net involves $N:M$ relationships. It uses the relations PERSON, SKILL, and MACHINE. There is an $N:M$ relationship between PERSON and SKILL and between SKILL and MACHINE as discussed previously. The definition of the net is

```
DEFINE NET PSM:
    LINK PERSON TO SKILL BY ID_NUMBER;
    LINK MACHINE TO SKILL BY SKILL_CODE;
    END;
```

The final two nets are PERSON_SCHEDULE and MACHINE _SCHEDULE, both involving $1:N$ relationships.

The following example will be implemented [Frank and Sibley, 1973]:

For a specified period of time (in the future) find a person who is capable of running a particular machine, but who is not presently scheduled for that time. Schedule that person to work on the machine.

The problem is essentially to find and schedule someone who is capable of running a given machine and is free at the specified time. Figure 7.3.2–2 shows the view of the data base relevant to this example.

The major algorithm steps involved in answering the query are:

1. Initialize required input values. I/O is certainly important, but not particularly relevant to this example. It will be assumed that the machine number is '00001', the starting date 'XXXXXXXX', the completion date 'YYYYYYYY', and the job code 'ABCD'. These values will be used directly in the implementation.

2. Find all possible candidates, i.e., persons, who could be available for the specified time and who have the required skill.

3. Eliminate all persons who are already scheduled during the specified time on another machine.

4. Schedule one of the remaining candidates to work on the machine.

To make the implementation easier to understand, each step will be implemented separately and the result stored in a temporary relation. However, it is possible to merge most of the individual steps. The implementation will use the SEQUEL language.

The first step is to find all possible persons who have the required skill to operate machine '00001'.

        CANDIDATE (ID_NUMBER)←
            SELECT UNIQUE ID_NUMBER
            FROM PSM
            WHERE MACHINE_NO='00001'

The id numbers of all persons who have the skill required to operate machine '00001' are stored in a temporary relation called CANDIDATE. The relation CANDIDATE contains one attribute ID_NUMBER.

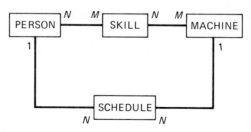

Fig. 7.3.2–2 A view of the personnel data base.

Duplicate id numbers are eliminated by the system. They arise because a person is capable of having two or more skills, each of which could run the machine. It is assumed that only a person who has the skill required to operate the machine in question will be considered.

In the next step, those persons already scheduled on some machine during the required time are identified. It should be remembered that a person selected in the previous step may also possess the skill required to operate some other machine and thus already be scheduled on it.

ALREADY_SCHEDULED (ID_NUMBER)←
    SELECT UNIQUE ID_NUMBER
    FROM PERSON_SCHEDULE
    WHERE ID_NUMBER=
        SELECT ID_NUMBER
        FROM CANDIDATE
        WHERE START_DATE<'XXXXXXXX'
        AND COMPLETE_DATE⩾'XXXXXXXX'
    OR ID_NUMBER=
        SELECT ID_NUMBER
        FROM CANDIDATE
        WHERE START_DATE⩾'XXXXXXXX'
        AND COMPLETE_DATE⩽'YYYYYYYY'

All ID_NUMBERs in PERSON_SCHEDULE that are also in CANDIDATE are checked to see if they are already scheduled. A person is scheduled if the start date is less than 'XXXXXXXX' and the complete date is greater than or equal to 'XXXXXXXX' or if the start date is greater than or equal to 'XXXXXXXX' and less than or equal to 'YYYYYYYY'.

To determine the remaining eligible candidates, ALREADY_SCHEDULED is subtracted from CANDIDATE.

    ELIGIBLE_CANDIDATES (ID_NUMBER)←
        SELECT ID_NUMBER
        FROM CANDIDATE

        MINUS

        SELECT ID_NUMBER
        FROM ALREADY_SCHEDULED

Finally, one of the eligible candidates is scheduled. To schedule a person, a tuple must be inserted into the SCHEDULE relation.

INSERT INTO SCHEDULE:
<'00001', 'ABCD', 'XXXXXXXX', 'YYYYYYYY',
SELECT MIN ID_NUMBER
FROM ELIGIBLE_CANDIDATES>

The function MIN returns the first person from ELIGIBLE_CANDIDATES, assuming that the original ordering of PERSON was extended to ELIGIBLE_CANDIDATES. In any case, any function that returns one ID_NUMBER suffices.

It is interesting to compare this implementation with a network implementation using the DBTG proposal [Frank and Sibley, 1973]. At first glance the relational implementation appears more concise. However, by the use of nets, the relational structure looks very much like a network. The real noticeable difference is the query language SEQUEL versus the procedural DBTG COBOL DML. However, comparing only data languages is unfair since SEQUEL and DBTG COBOL DML are oriented toward different user characteristics. DBMS approaches should not be compared only by the data languages they provide. For example, a data language, implemented on a DBTG network system and oriented toward casual users, will certainly not look like DBTG COBOL DML. Such a data language would probably have characteristics resembling SEQUEL rather than DBTG COBOL DML.

7.4 CONCLUDING REMARKS

In this section, we will present a brief summary comparison of the hierarchical, network, and relational approaches [Codd and Date, 1974; Date and Codd, 1974; Earnest, 1974; Michaels *et al.,* 1976]. The comparison is at the data model level, not at the implementation level. No inference should be drawn as to the advantages of one of the approaches over another from an implementation standpoint. In addition, comparing approaches has nothing to do with comparing actual systems.

The hierarchical and network data models both have links and record types. The multiplicity of structures can cause confusion. On the other hand, the relational data model uses only relations. Relations closely resemble flat files and tables, which have traditionally existed and with which a user is probably familiar. Attribute relationships and associations are separate concepts in the network and the hierarchical data models. However, the relational data model makes no distinction between attribute relationships and associations.

There are two types of data independence as discussed in Chapter 4: physical and logical. The relational data model makes no reference to any physical storage structure at all. The network data model on the other hand is predicated on navigation through the data base. The connections between records, according to the links, are usually provided by some form of access path in the implementation, e.g., the set mode of the DBTG proposal. This limits the degree of variation possible in the physical storage structure. However, it should be kept in mind that relational systems, as opposed to the relational data model, may allude to the existence of access paths between relations, e.g., the nets in SEQUEL. In addition, as discussed in Chapters 5 and 6, hierarchical and network systems may allow views that do not have physical access path counterparts. Adding a new relation to the data base or a new attribute to a relation does not impact existing application programs. The same is not always true in the hierarchical or network case [Date and Codd, 1974].

DBMS's should be designed with the casual user in mind [Codd, 1974b], who will probably be the biggest user of these systems in the future. For this reason, it seems that navigation through the data base should be automatic according to well-charted routes. The user thus becomes a "pilot" flying by instruments. The user tells the system the destination and lets the system choose the best route. Relational systems seem to offer such an environment for data base management.

EXERCISES

7.1 Represent a hierarchical definition tree using a relational schema. For instance, implement the payroll example of Chapter 5 using the relational data model. Comment on the relative advantages of such a representation.

7.2 Define, formally, a mapping from the hierarchical and network data models to the relational data model. What restrictions are necessary?

7.3 Given an application, outline a series of steps for choosing your primary relations. What considerations are important (e.g., normal form, dynamic properties)?

7.4 Some derived relations, formed by a series of joins between several relations, may not be meaningful. Give an example of such a situation. How would you limit the formation of such meaningless relations by a user?

7.5 Try to define a query language for use by casual users that is very different from relational languages. You can use sets, functions, or any other tools as long as the resulting language is easy to understand [Earley, 1973].

7.6 Compare a long query in SQUARE and SEQUEL. Draw some conclusions regarding English-like languages.

7.7 Compare the following relational languages: ALPHA, SQUARE, SEQUEL, and QUEL. The QUEL language was developed for the INGRES system at the University of California at Berkeley [Held *et al.*, 1975]. Provide mappings between features of the languages.

7.8 Outline a relational COBOL DML [Westgaard, 1975]. Compare it with the general flavor of COBOL and with the DBTG COBOL DML.

7.9 Compare the SEQUEL language as outlined in this chapter with the general network data language as outlined in Chapter 3.

7.10 Normalization was not discussed in connection with any of the relational languages outlined in this chapter. Why?

7.11 Represent the supplier-parts example outlined in Section 6.3.2 by the relational data model. Express each of the queries in Section 6.3.2 in SEQUEL using your relational schema.

7.12 Attempt to provide a common host language framework that is compatible with all three approaches, hierarchical, network, and relational [Date, 1976].

Chapter 8

IMPLEMENTATION CONSIDERATIONS

8.1 SEARCHING

The main data access facilities provided by DBMS's are retrieval, insertion, update, and deletion. A function common to all of these facilities is data selection. However, data selection invariably involves searching. *Searching*, in its traditional sense, is defined as a method of determining whether a particular item is a member of a set. Searching is an important function in many applications. For instance, it is needed to determine whether a particular symbol is in a symbol table. In a DBMS searching is obviously required for retrieval. That is, it is necessary to determine if the pertinent data are in the data base, and their location in the data base. For insertion, update, and deletion, searching is also important. In some systems, when inserting data, it is necesary to find the correct place to insert the data. Searching is also necessary to locate data that are to be updated or deleted. Therefore, searching mechanisms can be considered as basic techniques that must be included in the implementation of any DBMS.

Searching can be represented as the mapping $T: X \rightarrow \{$found, not found$\}$. That is, given a value for the variable X, it is either found or not found in a particular set. It is sometimes important to associate some information with an item after it is found. For instance, in a symbol table, it is important to associate some characteristics, such as a type declaration, with a symbol. In this case, the previous mapping can be extended to $T: X \rightarrow Y$ to accommodate this situation. When X is found, then an associated value of Y supplies some extra information. The search can be thought of as a partial mapping from values of X to values of Y.

The general form of searching can be represented by the mapping $T: i_1, i_2, \ldots, i_n \rightarrow (j_1, j_2, \ldots, j_m)$. For example, sometimes, X can be represented as a set of coordinates $(i_1, i_2, \ldots, i_n)$. For instance, when searching for the name SMITH, the name can be considered as the 5-tuple (S,M,I,T,H). There are searching techniques that use this type of representation, e.g., TRIE trees [Knuth, 1973]. Similarly, Y can be extended to contain more than one value. The variable Y can represent a set of values $(j_1, j_2, \ldots, j_m)$. However, the general form does not really differ substantially from the form $T:X \rightarrow Y$. There are always ways to encode $(i_1, i_2, \ldots, i_n)$ to one variable X, and $(j_1, j_2, \ldots, j_m)$ to another variable Y. For instance, it is possible to encode a set of integers $(i_1, i_2, \ldots, i_n)$ into one integer in such a way that the encoding is reversible. If the system is willing to do some encoding or pointer chasing, any mapping of the form $T: i_1, i_2, \ldots, i_n \rightarrow (j_1, j_2, \ldots, j_m)$ can be implemented as a mapping $T: X \rightarrow Y$.

Most of the data-structuring facilities used in the implementation of a DBMS are actually special cases of search mechanisms. Inverted files, which are used in DBMS's to implement content addressibility, are a form of searching. Namely, an inverted file is an implementation of the mapping $T: v \rightarrow (j_1, j_2, \ldots, j_m)$, where v is the attribute that is inverted, and $j_1, j_2, \ldots, j_m$ are the record identifiers of records containing the value v. In the hierarchical data model, the parent–child relationships consist of two search mappings. One mapping, $T_1 : j \rightarrow i$, is from a child to its parent, that is, given a record identifier of a record, the mapping determines the record identifier of its parent record, except for root records. The other mapping, $T_2 : i \rightarrow (j_1, j_2, \ldots, j_m)$, is from a parent to its children, that is, given a record identifier of a parent record, the mapping determines the record identifiers of its children records. A DBTG set can also be represented as two search mappings. The mapping $T_1 : j \rightarrow i$ relates the record identifier of a member record j to the record identifier of its owner record i. The mapping $T_2 : i \rightarrow (j_1, j_2, \ldots, j_m)$ relates the record identifier of an owner record i to the record identifiers of its member records, $j_1, j_2, \ldots, j_m$. In relational systems, joins can be represented as the two mappings $T_1 : j \rightarrow (i_1, i_2, \ldots, i_n)$ and $T_2 : i \rightarrow (j_1, j_2, \ldots, j_m)$ associating tuple identifiers of the two relations. Finally, general $N:M$ links can be represented as the two mappings $T_1: j \rightarrow (i_1, i_2, \ldots, i_n)$ and $T_2: i \rightarrow (j_1, j_2, \ldots, j_m)$. One mapping is needed for each direction of the link.

It seems, therefore, that many of the implementation considerations of a DBMS can be reduced to the problem of finding good methods of implementing mappings of the form $T: i_1, i_2, \ldots, i_n \rightarrow (j_1, j_2, \ldots, j_m)$, that is, good methods of searching. Figure 8.1−1 summarizes some of the mappings found in DBMS's.

The mapping $T: j \rightarrow (i_1, i_2, \ldots, i_n)$ can be effected in many different ways, e.g., linear lists, hashing, or trees [Knuth, 1973; Martin, 1975]. However, the particular implementation(s) of searching in a DBMS is very important for performance. The implementation should be efficient both for searching and for storage structure reorganization. Reorganization efficiency is necessary for effectively handling the modification operations, i.e., insertion, update, and deletion. For these reasons, different search requirements may be implemented by different search techniques. For instance, DBTG sets and inverted files are both search implementation problems, at least conceptually. However, in a particular system, their operational characteristics may be sufficiently different to warrant different implementations.

In this section, all search problems were considered together for conceptual reasons. In this way, the reader will realize that there is

Hierarchical relationship parent to child:

$\qquad T: \text{parent} \rightarrow (\text{child}_1, \text{child}_2, \ldots, \text{child}_n)$

Hierarchical relationship child to parent:

$\qquad T: \text{child} \rightarrow \text{parent}$

DBTG set owner to member(s):

$\qquad T: \text{owner} \rightarrow (\text{member}_1, \text{member}_2, \ldots, \text{member}_n)$

DBTG set member to owner:

$\qquad T: \text{member} \rightarrow \text{owner}$

General link each direction:

$\qquad T: i \rightarrow (j_1, j_2, \ldots, j_m)$

Join each direction:

$\qquad T: i \rightarrow (j_1, j_2, \ldots, j_m)$

Inverted file:

$\qquad T: v \rightarrow (j_1, j_2, \ldots, j_m)$

Fig. 8.1−1 Some search mappings in DBMS's.

some unity in concept and implementation throughout DBMS's. However, in a real system, many searching strategies are necessary, both software and hardware supported. By fitting the characteristics of a particular search problem to the best search technique, performance is improved.

As discussed in Chapter 3, data selection in DBMS's takes essentially two forms: content addressability and data relatability. Content addressability is usually provided by access paths as implemented, for instance, by inverted files. Data relatability deals with the implementation of associations and involves mechanisms implementing access paths between, for instance, record types. These access paths are related to the basic representation of associations in each data model, i.e., parent–child relationships, DBTG sets, joins, etc. In the rest of this chapter, the implementation of different kinds of access paths will be discussed in detail.

8.2 INVERTED FILES

In Chapter 3, an inverted file was discussed as a mechanism that can provide content addressability. An inverted file provides the access path corresponding to a mapping of the form $M: v \rightarrow (i_1, i_2, \ldots, i_n)$. In this section, some implementations of an inverted file will be outlined.

Consider an EMPLOYEE record type (relation) with data items (attributes) NUMBER, NAME, ADDRESS, AGE, DEPARTMENT, SKILL, and SALARY. It can be assumed, without loss of generality, that the EMPLOYEE record type (relation) is implemented by a file. Each data item (attribute) in the EMPLOYEE record type (relation) corresponds to a field in the records of the file. Therefore, each record of the file corresponds to a particular employee. It is usually necessary to select employees according to different qualifications, e.g., age, skill, or address. Even if the file implementing the EMPLOYEE record type (relation) is a direct access file, the records can be stored only according to the primary index, e.g., NUMBER. That is, the file system can find directly the record corresponding to an employee once the employee's number is specified. However, this facility does not help to satisfy user requests involving other data items (attributes), e.g., AGE, SKILL, or SALARY. In order to satisfy these requests, the system either has to search the EMPLOYEE file exhaustively, or else it has to provide content addressability on the basis of these other data items (attributes).

If the employee data is searched very often in terms of age, then it is worthwhile to construct an inverted file that facilitates requests on the data item (attribute) AGE. This inverted file is of the form M: $AGE \rightarrow (i_1, i_2, \ldots, i_n)$. That is, given a particular age, the inverted file supplies a means of locating the records (tuples) having that particular age. If the EMPLOYEE records (tuples) have been stored in a direct access file according to the data item (attribute) NUMBER, then i_1, $i_2, \ldots, i_n$ can be the employee numbers of the employees with that particular age.

An inverted file, for the data item (attribute) AGE can be implemented in many different ways. Consider the straightforward implementation for which a file AGEINVERSION is constructed (Fig. 8.2–1). Each record of the AGEINVERSION file contains a particular age and the NUMBER data item (attribute) value of records in the EMPLOYEE file with this age. A record in the AGEINVERSION file is often called an *inverted list* since each record in the file usually contains a list of several NUMBER data item values. A user request for EMPLOYEE records (tuples) in terms of the AGE data item (attribute) can now be reduced to a search of the AGEINVERSION file for the record

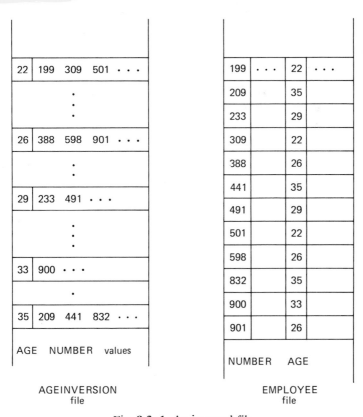

Fig. 8.2–1 An inverted file.

having the appropriate age. The employee records can then be obtained directly, using the NUMBER values associated with the specified age in the AGEINVERSION file. In this manner a search through the original EMPLOYEE file, for employees with a particular age, is reduced to a search in the AGEINVERSION file. This second search can be faster because the AGEINVERSION file can be organized to facilitate searching, e.g., sorted according to age or hashed on age.

Other implementations of content addressibility are possible. The main criteria for selecting a particular mechanism are the properties of the data and the frequency and types of requests. Another implementation of an inverted file using B-trees will be given as an example. B-trees have very nice properties both for searching and for reorganization.

A B-tree of order m is a tree with the following properties [Bayer and McCreight, 1972].

1. Each node has at most m sons.

2. Each node, except for the root node and terminal nodes, has at least $m/2$ sons.

3. The root node has at least two sons (unless it is a terminal node).

4. A nonterminal node with k sons contains $k-1$ values.

5. All terminal nodes appear on the same level and carry no information.

In this particular example, a value in the B-tree will consist of two parts. The first part, the *control field*, contains a particular age. The second part, the *information field*, contains a set of record identifiers of employee records having that age. For example, a B-tree inverting on the attribute age could contain the values shown in Fig. 8.2−2. Notice

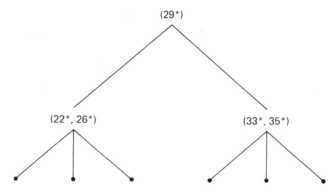

Fig. 8.2−2. A B-tree of order $m = 5$ inverting the attribute age. Asterisks denote the information fields.

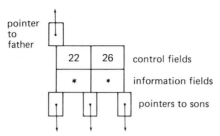

Fig. 8.2—3 A *B*-tree node structure for Fig. 8.2—2.

that all the age values of any subtree fall into the interval between the age values of two adjacent control fields in the node from which the subtree originates. The *B*-tree of Fig. 8.2—2 can be implemented using a combination of contiguity and pointers. For example, each node can have the structure shown in Fig. 8.2—3.

It is important to notice that, in this example, a search problem is reduced to a tree implementation problem. In Section 8.4, a tree implementation problem will be reduced to a search problem.

8.3 NETWORK IMPLEMENTATION

From Fig. 8.1—1, it would seem that the mapping for a link in one direction and an inverted file are similar. However, the nature of the mappings is quite different. Consider the mapping $T: i \mapsto (j_1, j_2, \ldots, j_n)$ of a link in one direction, where i is an identifier for a record occurrence and $j_1, j_2, \ldots, j_n$ are record identifiers of records connected to i according to the link. It is usually the case when exploiting this mapping that the user not only has a value for i, but that he also has the location of the record occurrence corresponding to i in the data base (implicitly via the system). Therefore, there is no need to search to determine where the record occurrence i is. On the other hand, an inverted file implies a search to determine the location of a given value v in the inverted file.

The distinction between the mapping for inverted files and that for links comes naturally due to the difference between content addressibility and data relatability. In the first case, it is necessary to search to establish the location of a record according to its contents. In the second case, the location of the record is known and the locations of other records connected to it are needed. If the other records are related directly to the record occurrence whose location is known, either through contiguity or pointers, then no search is needed. In the sequel, it will become apparent when discussing implementation techniques that some searching can be eliminated when using data relatability.

Data relatability in network systems is provided through connections between records according to links between record types. The implementation of the connections according to one link corresponds to an access path between records of the record types. An access path can take many forms, e.g., contiguity or pointers.

In Chapter 2, it was shown that a link can be information bearing or non-information bearing. In the case of an information-bearing link, a permanent access path must exist for the link. The access path is necessary since there is no other way of determining how the records should be connected. In the case of a non-information-bearing link, a permanent access path is optional. It is not strictly necessary since the connections among the records can be constructed algorithmically according to a closed-form predicate among the data items of the record types. That is, a temporary access path representing the connections can be constructed as required. If a permanent access path exists, its only purpose is to make the connection between record occurrences faster when using data relatability.

In most network systems, the definition of a link, whether information bearing or non-information bearing, implies the existence of a permanent access path. However, it should be kept in mind that the definition of a link and the creation of the access path that connects the records can be done separately [Tsichritzis, 1976]. In addition, for a general link, two access paths may be needed, one corresponding to each direction of the link. Each of these access paths may exist independent of the other. Sometimes, however, one of them may not be needed if the user always navigates in one direction of the link.

General $N{:}M$ links require two mappings of the form $T{:}\ i{\rightarrow}(j_1, j_2, \ldots, j_n)$. If a link is constrained to be $1{:}N$, then one of the mappings takes the simpler form $T{:}\ j{\rightarrow}i$, e.g., DBTG member to owner mapping. However, the other mapping still retains the general form $T{:}\ i{\rightarrow}(j_1, j_2, \ldots, j_n)$. It follows that an implementation technique for $1{:}N$ links has to be able to handle a mapping of the form $T{:}\ i{\rightarrow}(j_1, j_2, \ldots, j_n)$. Thus, the general form mapping $T{:}\ i{\rightarrow}(j_1, j_2, \ldots, j_n)$ has to be implemented for $1{:}N$ links, at least in one direction. Therefore, the discussion of link implementation techniques can be restricted to $1{:}N$ links without loss of generality. As a consequence, the emphasis in the rest of this section will be on implementation techniques for DBTG sets, i.e., 1:N links.

Various methods for implementing DBTG sets have been developed and used [Bachman, 1973a]. No one technique is best for all network data language operations. Some basic techniques will be described for implementing DBTG sets. The techniques may be used in combination. As a matter of fact, in some cases a technique by itself does not provide all the facilities needed for data base navigation. Some good and some poor features of each technique as regards data base navigation are also discussed.

8.3.1 Contiguity and Pointers

Contiguity alone can be used to represent a DBTG set. A *multiple level record array* consists of contiguous records whose organization resembles a hierarchy, the member records of a set occurrence physically following their owner record. If a member record is also an owner of a DBTG set, then its member records physically follow it as in Fig. 8.3.1−1.

This organization is not particularly good for either modification or retrieval unless the processing is always from owner to member records for all DBTG sets. For a record to be a member in more than one DBTG set, duplication of the record is required.

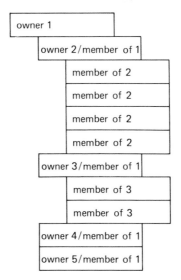

Fig. 8.3.1−1 Multiple level record array.

Contiguity and pointers can be combined to represent a DBTG set. In a *single-level record array*, all member records in a set occurrence are physically contiguous in one table. There is one such table for each set occurrence. Each owner record contains a pointer that points to the first member record in the table (Fig. 8.3.1−2). If member records are owners in another DBTG set, they in turn point to a table of member records.

Obviously, inserting new members, particularly in some order, into such an organization is not easy since members must be physically contiguous. Deleting a member in a table may eventually require reorganization of the table. Processing a set occurrence using a FIND NEXT command is quite simple since member records are physically adjacent. Unless a pointer to the owner is maintained in every member record, it is not possible to determine a member record's owner record. If a record is a member in more than one set occurrence, then it is physically duplicated in the table for each set occurrence in which it is a member record. Some types of set switching are very difficult in this organization. For example, set switching via a record that is a member in two set occurrences requires a search of the tables for the second DBTG set to find the corresponding member record.

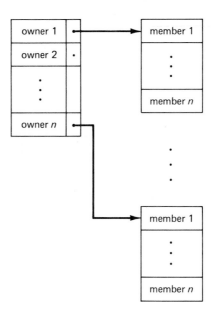

Fig. 8.3.1−2 Record array.

Pointers alone can be used to represent a DBTG set. In a *list*, the owner record and all member records of a set occurrence are connected via pointers. Each pointer points to the next member record in the set occurrence. The last member record in the list holds a null value in the pointer field to signal the end of the set occurrence (Fig. 8.3.1–3).

Note, however, that access to the owner record from a member record is not possible in a list. One way of solving this problem is to keep a pointer to the previous member record in each record. Another solution is to make the pointer in the last member record point back to the owner. Such a list is called a *chain* or *ring* (Fig. 8.3.1–4).

Inserting a new member in a list is fairly simple. However, maintaining an ordering on members requires searching through the members to determine where to place the new record and adjusting pointers accordingly. Deletion of a member may also require a search unless a backward pointer is also maintained. Retrieval is fairly simple except for FIND LAST and FIND PRIOR, which require chaining through all members.

The use of backward and owner pointers can alleviate some of the difficulties of lists. For example, a collection of pointers of the form shown in Fig. 8.3.1–5 can be associated with each record occurrence. There is one set of pointers for each DBTG set in which the record occurrence is an owner or a member.

Modification now becomes rather simple, since insertion involves moving pointers around. Although more expensive than contiguity,

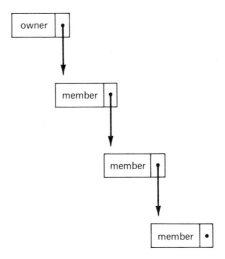

Fig. 8.3.1–3 List.

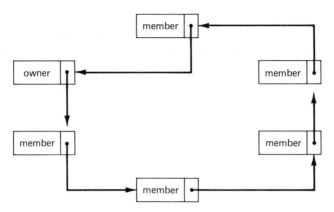

Fig. 8.3.1—4 Chain or ring.

retrieval is quite efficient except for <u>FIND</u> *n*th, which involves chaining through all member records. However, the price for this improved access is storage overhead in the form of pointers. On the other hand, the pointer storage required for each record type is fixed since, from the schema, it is known in how many DBTG sets the record type can be an owner or a member. Note that this organization is particularly good for set switching since the pointers are associated with the member records.

A pointer chain organization can involve a lot of pointer chasing if access to the members is random. In addition, the member records in a particular set occurrence can become widely scattered on secondary storage resulting in poor buffering characteristics. A better organization for random member access is a *pointer array* structure. For each set occurrence in the data base, an array of pointers is maintained as shown in Fig. 8.3.1—6. The pointer array is used to determine the owner record and member records of a set occurrence. The pointer array is stored independent of the records. In this way, all records of one type can be more easily stored as a unit and buffering characteristics improved.

Inserting a new member is fairly simple since only pointers need to be moved and not entire records. All types of retrievals are normally quite efficient since the pointer array can usually be kept in fast

DBTG set	pointer to next	pointer to prior	pointer to owner

Fig. 8.3.1—5 Pointer chain.

owner	member 1	member 2	· · ·	member n

Fig. 8.3.1—6 Pointer array.

memory, whereas the member records of a set occurrence probably could not. In addition, for an ordered representation, it is usually easier to order the pointers than to move entire records. Set switching, however, is not as easy as in a good pointer chain structure. The pointer arrays usually have to be scanned for the second DBTG set until a matching pointer is found.

Sometimes it is important to provide fast access to the owner record of a set occurrence. The *phantom* data structure provides each member record with a pointer that points to the owner record. The owner record does not have a pointer to any of its members. It may optionally hold a counter that indicates the current number of members. The counter is used to prevent the deletion of an owner while there are still members in the set occurrence. The phantom form may be used alone, but it is usually used in conjunction with one of the other forms to provide direct access to the owner record of a set occurrence.

8.3.2 Bit Arrays

Storage space savings can be achieved by replacing most pointers with a *bit* (Boolean) *array*. A bit array is maintained for each set occurrence and indicates whether a record of the member record type is a member in the set occurrence. The length of the array, in bits, is at least equal to the number of all record occurrences of the member record type. Each owner record of a set occurrence points to a bit array. A bit in the array is 1 if the record occurrence is a member in the set occurrence owned by the owner, 0 otherwise (Fig. 8.3.2—1). No two Boolean arrays, for a given set type, may have the same bit equal to 1.

Adding new members is fairly easy provided no ordering is desired. The bit array may have to be extended, which can cause storage reorganization problems. Retrieval characteristics for set occurrence members are similar to a pointer array structure except for FIND OWNER. It is not possible to find the owner of a member record with this organization alone. Also, set switching is very difficult.

In some instances, even further space savings can be effected by replacing long strings of 0 bits with a code signaling their absence. Since

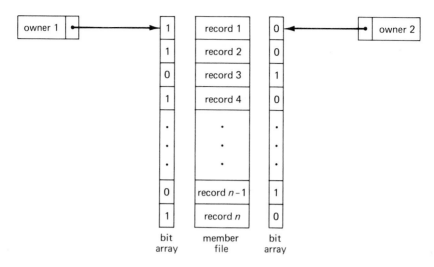

Fig. 8.3.2−1 Bit array.

the boolean arrays tend to be sparse, compressions of 100:1 can be effected [Bachman, 1973a].

8.3.3 Trees

In section 8.2, a tree data structure was used to provide a fast search mechanism. A tree data structure can also be used for DBTG sets that are to be maintained in some order based on the value of a data item in the member record type. However, the record type may only be ordered on the values of one data item in the record type.

There are several variations on this implementation form. The least complicated form uses binary trees and provides the owner record with one pointer field, and each member record with two pointer fields. The owner record points to the first member record inserted into the set occurrence (or some other member record if the tree has been balanced). The left pointer of each member record points to one member record and potentially a subtree of member records all with lower data item values than the member record doing the pointing. The right pointer points to one member record and potentially to a subtree of member records all with higher data item values. Both left and right pointers may be null (Fig. 8.3.3−1).

Insertion into a set occurrence requires searching the tree to determine where to place the new member record. On the average, however, the length of search is only $\frac{1}{2} \log n$, where n is the number of member

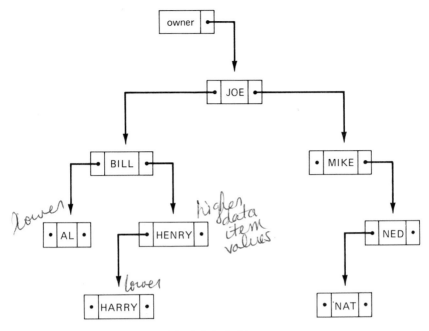

Fig. 8.3.3−1 Binary tree.

records in the set occurrence. This compares to an average search time of *n*/2 for a list organization. Searching for a member record with a certain data item value is quite fast since this is what the organization is designed to do best. However, most other types of retrieval are quite difficult. Other forms of trees such as *B*-trees or weight balanced trees can be used to improve retrieval time on a certain data item value further [Bayer, 1974].

8.3.4 Example Implementation

An example implementation of a DBTG set using contiguity and pointers will be outlined in this section. To simplify the example and the discussion, it is assumed that a DBTG set has only one member record type. However, the example can be extended to permit several member record types within a DBTG set.

The records for each record type are stored contiguously in a physical file. There is one file for each record type. It is assumed that the records in a file can be accessed by specifying the relative position of the record in the file. That is, the *i*th record in a file can be accessed simply by specifying the file name and the relative (*i*th) position.

The set occurrence data for each DBTG set is maintained via owner blocks and member blocks. One owner block and one member block is associated with, respectively, the member record type and the owner record type of a DBTG set. An owner block for a DBTG set contains one entry for each record in the member record type file. Each entry contains one pointer. If the corresponding record in the member type file is a member in a set occurrence of the DBTG set, then the pointer points to the owner record of the set occurrence in the owner record type file. Otherwise, the pointer is null.

A member block for a DBTG set contains one entry for each record in the owner record type file. Each entry contains one or more pointers. If the set occurrence identified by an owner record has no members, then the entry in the member block contains a single null pointer. Otherwise, the entry contains as many pointers as there are member records in the set occurrence. Each pointer points to a member record in the member record type file. The pointers in an owner or member block can be either direct addresses or record identifiers. An example representation of an owner and member block for one DBTG set is shown in Fig. 8.3.4–1.

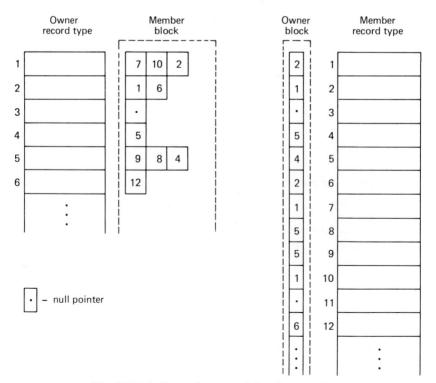

Fig. 8.3.4–1 Example network implementation.

The preceding implementation provides the necessary facilities for representing a DBTG network data base. Consider the various formats of the DBTG COBOL DML <u>FIND</u> command. Direct access to a record, in any record type, can be provided by means of content addressibility such as inverted files. Once a record has been located, one navigates in the data base according to the DBTG sets. Finding the owner record of a set occurrence from a member record is immediate via the owner block. Finding the next, prior, first, last, or nth member record from an owner record is also immediate via the member block. The same is true if the DBTG set currency indicator currently points at a member record in the set occurrence rather than the owner. However, in this case it may be necessary to go through the owner block to get to the member block for the DBTG set.

Set switching is also very easy. When switching sets, it is necessary to identify an occurrence of a DBTG set S_2, based on the current occurrence of a DBTG set S_1, via a member record M that is common to both the S_1 and S_2 set occurrence. To do this in the preceding implementation, one uses the owner block for DBTG set S_2 and the relative position of member record M in the member record type file. That is, using the relative position of member record M, the corresponding entry in the owner block for DBTG set S_2 is accessed. The owner record, for the S_2 set occurrence in which M is a member record, determines the S_2 set occurrence.

Inserting and modifying records present no problems. Deletion can be difficult if triggered deletes are allowed. However, in general, it is possible either to remove or delete member records in a set occurrence. In addition, this effect may be propagated to any number of levels, although the housekeeping required to keep track of which records to remove and/or delete may become involved.

Removing a member record from a set occurrence involves setting a pointer both in the member record block and in the owner block for the DBTG set to null. Including a member record in a set occurrence is more difficult. It may be necessary to expand the entry in the member block to accommodate the extra pointer. The representation of the owner and member blocks by a physical storage structure is one of the hardest design problems for this example. In general, the entries in a member block are of variable length. If the file system permits variable-length records, then the problem can be handled by the file system. Otherwise, it may be necessary to build a user-supported directory to the entries in a member block. In this way, entries can be moved if they need to be expanded. Another solution is to determine an optimum size for an entry in a member block. Entries that require additional space can be split into a base part and an overflow part. The overflow part is related to the base part via a pointer. However, entries that require only a small part of the base part will result in wasted space in the member block.

The owner block in Fig. 8.3.4–1 associated with each member record occurrence is much simpler than the member block associated with each owner occurrence. This situation is due to the $1:N$ restriction of a DBTG set. In the case of a general $N:M$ link, the blocks associated with both record types in the link will be similar to the member block in Fig. 8.3.4–1. In Section 8.5 this example implementation is extended to handle general $N:M$ links.

8.4 HIERARCHICAL IMPLEMENTATION

The implementation of a hierarchical data base requires access paths that connect the records according to the links in a hierarchical definition tree. Content addressibility can provide these access paths and some hierarchical systems are implemented on the basis of content addressibility, e.g., inverted files [Bleier and Vorhaus, 1968]. However, content addressibility was discussed in Section 8.2 and is common to all systems. Thus, specific mechanisms for content addressibility will not be discussed in detail in this section. Instead, some access paths that can be used to represent a hierarchical structure will be outlined. These access paths facilitate data relatability in a hierarchical data base.

In Section 8.3.1, many contiguity and pointer techniques were discussed that implement $1:N$ links. Parent–child relationships are certainly $1:N$ links. Therefore, all the DBTG set implementation techniques can be used for hierarchical implementation. In this section, these techniques will be outlined as they apply to a hierarchical data base. However, it should be noted that, in essence, they are similar to the contiguity and pointer techniques used for DBTG sets.

Physical contiguity of records can imply a connection according to a link. For example, the GET NEXT command in IMS processes a data base tree according to a preorder data base tree traversal. The records can be allocated to reflect this traversal order. For instance, they can be allocated according to the techniques outlined in Figs. 8.3.1–1 and 8.3.1–2. Such allocation saves space and increases access speed for GET NEXT type of processing. In addition, depending on the buffering characteristics of the operating system, the next record is often already in the buffer. Hence, no additional secondary storage access is necessary

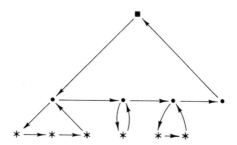

Fig. 8.4–1 Hierarchical pointer implementation.

in this case. However, data base reorganization problems arise for the cases where a record is inserted or deleted. Also, some overhead is involved in skipping groups of records when only a certain type of record is wanted.

Pointers between records can also imply a connection according to a link. Essentially the access path corresponding to a link between two record types in the hierarchical definition tree consists of a set of pointers, which implement the connections between the parent and child record occurrences. For example, there can be a forward and a backward pointer associated with every branch of a data base tree. This organization is similar to the DBTG set implementation of Fig. 8.3.1–5. In this type of organization, pointer chasing can be expensive, especially for upward or downward hierarchical normalization of more than one level. In addition, a great deal of space is required for pointers. The amount of space required for the pointers associated with a parent record varies as children are inserted and deleted. It would facilitate storage allocation if this space requirement were fixed. To this end, some systems limit the number of children of a given type that a parent may have [CII, 1973].

To reduce the space occupied by pointers, only one forward pointer plus one brother pointer can be used (Fig. 8.4–1) [Lowenthal, 1971]. Note that this technique is similar to the ring implementation of Fig. 8.3.1–4. In this organization, each record has a fixed amount of pointer overhead, but now even more pointer chasing is necessary. Whereas in the previous organization any child of a parent can be accessed by following one pointer, in this organization several pointers may need to be followed.

As for a network data base, pointers can also be combined with physical contiguity to implement a hierarchical data base. This approach results in many special purpose access methods for storing hierarchical data bases. In Part II of this book, some hierarchical oriented access methods will be discussed in the description of the IMS system.

8.4.1 Example Implementation

In this section, an example implementation of a hierarchical data base using contiguity and pointers will be considered. Contiguity is used to store a fixed number of brother records as a group. It can be assumed, without loss of generality, that the records of each record type are fixed size. The scheme can be extended to accommodate varying size records. Pointers are used to implement the connections between parent and child records according to the links in a hierarchical definition tree.

The children of each record are stored in one or more linked blocks. A block only stores records of one record type. In addition, each group of linked blocks stores the children for only one parent record. For each record type, a block is of fixed size, but it may be a different size for different record types. A block may contain a varying number of records. However, since the block size is fixed, it may not contain more than a certain maximum bound.

Within each block are also stored some presence bits and pointers (Fig. 8.4.1–1). The presence bits indicate whether a position in the block is currently occupied by a record. The pointers are used for data relatability. One pointer points to the parent block. Another pointer points to the next brother block or to the first brother block if this is the last block. The next brother pointers link blocks containing the children of the same parent record. The remaining pointers are grouped into collections of n pointers each, where n is the maximum number of records permitted in the block. The pointers in each group are associated one to one with the records in the block. They point to the first block containing the children, of one child record type, for the corresponding record in the block. There are c groups of pointers per block, where c is the number of children record types associated with the record type stored in the block. Notice the similarity between the node structure of the B-tree implementation in Section 8.2 and the example implementation in Fig. 8.4.1–1. The similarity should not be unexpected; after all, both implementations deal with trees.

This storage organization captures all the structure of a hierarchical data base. For example, to determine a record's parent, one follows the

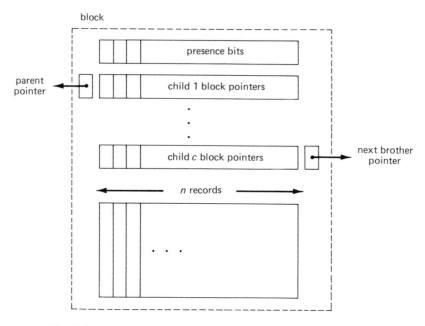

Fig. 8.4.1–1 Example pointer and contiguity implementation.

parent pointer in the block. To determine a record's descendants, one follows the appropriate child block pointer(s) to the desired level. Either one or all of a record's descendants can be determined in this way. Getting a record's brother is very fast since the brother record is either immediately contiguous or it is the first record in the next brother block.

Inserting the first child of a record requires the allocation of a new block, the setting of a presence bit, and the setting of the child pointer in the parent's block. Subsequent insertions of children merely require a search of the presence bits for an empty position and possibly the allocation and linking of a brother block. Deleting a record necessitates the setting of a presence bit and possibly the freeing of all descendant blocks of the record. Note that to avoid storage reorganization, free blocks can be kept in a free block list for each record type and reused when needed.

The major design decision in this scheme is the choice of an optimum block size for each record type (choice of n if records are fixed size). The value of n should be small enough so that the number of sparsely populated blocks is minimized. On the other hand, it should be large enough to reduce the number of linked blocks.

To summarize, a hierarchical implementation can utilize contiguity and pointers with the following objectives. First, it is important to have efficient retrieval by eliminating costly pointer chasing and resulting secondary storage accesses. Second, the space required both for the data and the pointers should be minimized. Third, costly reorganizations should be avoided by providing a flexible environment allowing easy expansion of the data base.

8.4.2   Tree-Addressing Techniques

As discussed in Section 8.1, a search can be reduced to the problem of transforming tuples of the form $(i_1, i_2, \ldots, i_n)$ to an address I where, for instance, a record is stored. One of the ways to implement the transformation $T: i_1, i_2, \ldots, i_n \rightarrow I$ is via a B-tree or TRIE data structure [Knuth, 1973]. Looking closely at these methods, it is obvious that the way they implement the searching mechanism is through a data structure similar to a hierarchical data base tree. Hence, in a sense, they transform a search problem into an implementation of a hierarchical data base. In this section, exactly the opposite will be effected. Namely, the implementation of a hierarchical data base will be reduced to a search problem. It will be shown that an effective way of transforming $T: i_1, i_2, \ldots, i_n \rightarrow I$ can be used to implement hierarchical data bases.

One way of implementing a hierarchical data base is to use a method of assigning a logical address to a record in a data base tree. This logical address can then be mapped into a physical one. A logical address to a record in a data base tree is called a *trace* [Lowenthal, 1971]. Some examples of assigning traces to records in a data base tree will be outlined.

Each record type, in a hierarchical definition tree, can be identified by a *type-number* as in Fig. 8.4.2–1a. Any record in a data base tree can then be identified by its type-number and a *generation tuple*. The generation tuple defines a path, in a data base tree, that leads to a record. For example, suppose that Fig. 8.4.2–1b corresponds to the third data base tree in a hierarchical data base. The root record type of this tree is identified by the trace 1(3). The number 1 is the type-number of the record type. The number 3 indicates that it is the third record of type-1. The first type-2 child of this root is assigned the trace 2(3,1). That is, it is the first type-2 child under the third root record. The first type-3 descendant under the first type-2 child of the third root record has as its trace 3(3,1,1). The first number identifies the

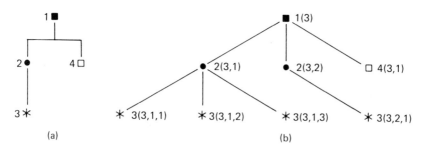

Fig. 8.4.2−1 Assigning traces to records.

record type. The numbers in parentheses define a path to a particular record. Using a type-number and a generation tuple, any record in a hierarchical data base can be uniquely addressed by the path to it.

Another way of representing a path to a record in a data base tree is to use a generation tuple only. However, the generation tuple is modified so that it contains a reserved position for every record type in a hierarchical definition tree. A zero in the position for a particular record type means that the record type does not lie in the path to the desired record. For the traces given earlier, their new representation would be:

$$1(3) \;\;\; \rightarrow (3,0,0,0)$$
$$2(3,1) \rightarrow (3,1,0,0)$$
$$3(3,1,1) \rightarrow (3,1,1,0)$$

This representation of traces contains some redundancy compared to the first representation. For this particular example, some tuples in the second representation are clearly invalid, e.g., (1,1,2,2) or any trace with all nonzero entries. In the first representation, all traces are valid, provided the bounds of the hierarchical definition tree are adhered to, i.e., type-numbers and levels. The second representation does have the advantage of being of a fixed length, whereas the first representation is of variable length. In either representation, traces may correspond to records that have not yet been inserted.

Given a trace, there is a straightforward algorithm to obtain the traces of ancestors, descendants, and brothers. The rules for the first representation of traces are:

1. *ancestor trace*—drop the appropriate (greater than level of ancestor) digits at the end of the generation tuple and change the type-number.

2. *descendant traces*—add the appropriate (descendant level minus current level) digits in the next generation tuple places and change the type-number.

3. *next brother trace*—add one to the last digit in the generation tuple.

4. *previous brother trace*—subtract one from the last digit in the generation tuple (if digit $\neq 1$).

Sometimes valid traces are restricted by specifying some bounds such as maximum number of levels in the hierarchical definition tree or maximum number of children at each level.

Traces for records already in a data base are kept in a trace table. A *trace table* gives a mapping between a trace and the location where the record is stored. This mechanism captures all the structure of a hierarchical data base. Given the trace of a record, one can find its ancestors, the record itself, its brothers, and its descendants.

Consider the problem of materializing the physical location of a record from a trace, i.e., the mapping given by the trace table. This mapping can, of course, be implemented by an actual physical table as mentioned earlier [Lowenthal, 1971]. In this case, it is necessary to search the table to arrive at the appropriate entry. The problem of implementing a hierarchical data base can therefore be reduced to a problem of searching.

Consider the simplified problem where each record type is stored in a separate file and the type-number is used to identify the file. A method is now needed of translating the generation tuple into a record identifier in the file. Such a method maps tuples of integers (the trace) into one integer (the record identifier in the file). It would be nice if the mapping were both one to one and onto. A one-to-one mapping means that for each generation tuple $(n_1, n_2, \ldots, n_t)$, there is only one record identifier x associated with it. An onto mapping means that all possible record identifiers have corresponding generation tuples.

One means of obtaining a file record identifier from the generation tuple is to apply a hashing function to it. Many different types of hashing functions are described in the literature, e.g., division or folding [Morris, 1968]. However, the mapping should preferably be close to one to one so that each trace can correspond to a different record. It should also preferably be close to onto since empty spaces in the file are undesirable. If a hashing scheme is one to one, then it will probably not be onto. Conversely, if it is onto, then it is probably not one to one. This tradeoff results from the fact that if the scheme is one to one, then to avoid collisions, the address space must be quite large compared to the number of different generation tuples. If the scheme is onto, then there are usually many collisions [Lum, 1973].

Consider now the function

$$I(x,y) = \tfrac{1}{2} (x+y-1) (x+y-2) + y$$

This function gives, for any pair of integers (x,y), a unique integer z such that the mapping $(x,y) \rightarrow z$ is both one to one and onto. The mapping can be expanded in a natural way to map n-tuples into one number, i.e., $P(x,y,w) = I(I(x,y),w)$. The resulting mapping is also both one to one and onto. This mapping, however, does not provide a practical solution. It does not work well if the data base grows or shrinks. In addition, it would be nice to make a distinction between an addressible node and an existing node. In this way, traces corresponding to records that are not present can be detected. The preceding mapping does not have these properties. As a result, at any point in time there will be one node (n_1, n_2, n_3) having the highest record identifier allocated to date. However, there may be "holes" (unused record identifiers) all through the file up to this maximum record identifier [Bernstein and Tsichritzis, 1975].

If it is assumed that for any tuple $(n_1, n_2, \ldots, n_t)$ $n_t \leqslant N_t$, i.e., every parent of a type-t node has at most N_t children of type t, the following scheme can be used (Fig. 8.4.2–2) [Lochovsky, 1973]. Every tuple $(n_1, n_2, \ldots, n_t)$ becomes an index into an array of dimension t. The slot in the array contains the record identifier in the file. An array is identified by the type-number of a record type. The result is that there are now no empty record spaces, but empty slots instead. Empty slots can result in a space saving if the space occupied by an empty record is much greater than that occupied by an empty slot. The mapping is quite simple, being according to coordinate addressing, and provides indirection. However, this scheme is impractical for any large-scale application. The arrays tend to become quite large as the number of levels increase and as the N_t become large.

To summarize, a mapping between traces and record identifiers is required such that the number of "holes" in a file is minimized. Therefore, the record identifier produced from the trace of a record with high probability of insertion should be small. On the other hand, the trace of a record with low probability of ever being inserted should produce large record identifiers for the file. This would allow the files to grow gracefully and reduce the amount of file storage overhead. However, such mapping schemes can become quite complicated [Bernstein and Tsichritzis, 1975].

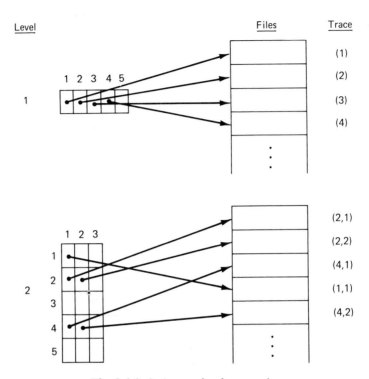

Fig. 8.4.2—2 A trace implementation.

In this section the implementation of a hierarchical data base was reduced to a searching problem. Solutions to the searching problem can therefore be used to implement a hierarchical data base, e.g., hashing or *B*-trees. The case of *B*-trees warrants further comment. On the surface, it only seems that trees can be used to implement trees. However, *B*-trees are quite different from hierarchical data base trees. *B*-trees can be thought of as controlled trees, e.g., the number of sons is restricted. Hierarchical data base trees are uncontrolled since they are constructed according to the relationships between data, which can be arbitrary. By using *B*-trees to implement a hierarchical data base, controlled trees can be used to implement uncontrolled trees. This observation becomes especially important when considered in the light of data base machines discussed in Section 8.6. Data base machines will probably implement, in hardware, a very specific and controlled type of environment that provides fast searching facilities. However, this controlled environment can be used to implement more general organizations just as controlled trees can be used to implement uncontrolled trees.

8.5 RELATIONAL IMPLEMENTATION

In network and hierarchical systems, data relatability is provided by access paths that implement the connections among records according to the links among the record types. The existence of a link between two record types usually implies the existence of an access path. Sometimes a very specific type of access path is implied, e.g., the set mode of the DBTG proposal. Thus, a user may have to be aware of the type of access path used to follow the connections between records and to exploit them properly and effectively.

In relational systems, data relatability is provided by the ability to construct new relations from existing relations by the use of the relational operators. The relational operators may require access paths to obtain or represent the derived relations. The access paths may exist in the system, or they may be constructed by the system as required. For instance, a join can be implemented as a separate file, as a set of pointers, or by storing the definition of the join and generating it as needed. However, no matter how it is implemented, the user is not aware of the exact representation and does not really care what it is.

Since a user is not explicitly aware of the access paths in a relational system, this may lead to the misconception that relational systems do not provide access paths. This is far from true. As in a hierarchical or a network system, a relational system may need specific fast access paths to take advantage of the querying activity of a specific nature. The existence, construction, and maintenance of these access paths may be hidden from the user. Nevertheless, they exist, and their implementation is one of the hardest design problems in a relational system [Codd, 1975].

Relational systems can be differentiated according to how they represent derived relations via access paths. If they only store the definition of a derived relation, then the access paths corresponding to the physical implementation of the derived relation are destroyed after every query. In this case, content addressibility may be sufficient to construct the access paths as required. For example, a join can be constructed using content addressibility by correlating tuple identifiers from the inverted files, for the two relations, according to the join condition. On the other hand, the system can retain and maintain the access paths corresponding to the definition of a derived relation. In this case, the maintenance of these access paths can become very involved.

In Chapter 7, two types of derived relations were discussed: snapshots and evolving views. The implementation of snapshots does not pose serious difficulties. Since snapshots become independent of the original relations after their creation, they can be handled in a manner similar to primary relations. Although their origin is different, their continuing properties are the same. Evolving views, on the other hand, must continue to reflect changes to the original relations. Therefore, they not only have problems of construction of an access path corresponding to the evolving view, but also of its maintenance. The system can maintain the access path either according to instructions provided by the DBA, or eventually, and hopefully, automatically by doing its own optimization.

The implementation of a DBMS can be very complex. In the previous sections, many different implementation techniques were discussed. In any one system, some combination of these techniques must be chosen to provide content addressibility and data relatability. In order to simplify implementation, it seems best to divide the system into smaller parts. This technique has been used extensively in operating system design [Dijkstra, 1969] and is being applied to relational implementation [Bjørner et al., 1973; Bracchi et al., 1974; Brodie et al., 1975; Held and Stonebraker, 1975; Schmid and Bernstein, 1975; Tsichritzis, 1975a]. In the rest of this section, the implementation of a relational system will be considered according to levels or layers of software. Each level of software uses the facilities provided by the next lower level and implements facilities used by the next higher level(s).

The very bottom level provides the basic facilities. At this level a programming language for implementation, an operating system and a file system are needed. It is helpful if the file system provides a direct access method so that records in the file can be accessed by a record identifier. That is, given the file name and the value of a record identifier, the access method returns the appropriate record. This level is not particularly unique to the implementation of relational systems. Any DBMS is usually based on similar types of facilities.

The next level, the *low level*, uses the basic facilities to provide a framework for the implementation of relations. Primary and snapshot relations can be implemented quite simply by making every relation correspond to a file and every tuple of a relation to a record in the file. Thus, the *i*th record in a file corresponds to the *i*th tuple of a relation. The relations at this level are not conceptual relations, but more closely resemble record types. For instance, order of tuples and copies are important at this level. Duplicates and order can be masked by the system at higher levels.

The next higher level, the *access path level,* provides facilities for fast access to and between relations. The access paths are essentially of two kinds, corresponding to content addressibility and data relatability. Content addressibility access paths are used to select and name sets of tuples based on their contents. Data relatability access paths are used to connect relations and to represent combinations of relations as constructed by relational operations, e.g., join.

The access path level of a relational system requires storage structures similar to those discussed for network and hierarchical implementation. For data relatability among primary relations the concept of a link is needed and can be implemented by any of the techniques discussed in Sections 8.3 and 8.4. For content addressibility the concept of an inverted file is needed as discussed in Section 8.2. As an example of an access path facility, a system will be outlined that is based on links and selectors [Tsichritzis, 1975a].

A *selector* corresponds to a qualification on a single primary or snapshot relation. The selector represents a subset of all tuples present in a relation. The definition of a selector uses attribute names and/or free variables. The creation of a selector results in the creation of an access path. The access path enables a user quickly to obtain the subset specified by the selector. The access paths corresponding to selectors can be created using existing inverted files.

A selector on a relation can be implemented by a pointer array [Czarnik *et al.,* 1975]. Each slot contains a pointer to a tuple that is selected by the selector. The relation name and the definition of the selector can be encoded in the header of the pointer array. Using selectors, one can represent subsets of relations obtained as the result of the selection, restriction, and projection operators.

Links, as discussed in Section 8.3, can be either automatic (according to a predicate) or manual (explicitly established by the user). Since all links in relational systems result as a representation of joins, which are defined according to properties between attributes of existing relations, all links are automatic. Manual links are not needed and are not allowed. Note that L_{ii} links are allowed. In relational systems there are join operations that relate tuples of the same relation.

A link can be implemented in many different ways depending on its characteristics. Many different implementations have already been discussed in the previous sections. Consider, for instance, a 1:1 link between relations X and Y. Such a link can be represented by two pointer arrays, such as the owner block in Fig. 8.3.4–1, considered in parallel. The corresponding slots point to the corresponding records of the relations according to the link. In the case of 1:N links, where N is bounded and small $N+1$ pointer arrays can be used in parallel. One pointer array is used in one direction of the link (functional) and N pointer arrays are used for the reverse direction. In the case where N is rather large and unbounded, one pointer array per tuple is needed. These pointer arrays are combined to represent the link as in the member blocks of Fig. 8.3.4–1. In the case of an N:M link, the implementation can take the form shown in Fig. 8.5–1. The implementation of a link can be represented as a separate binary relation connecting the two joined relations. As a matter of fact, binary relations have been used as the basis of relational system implementation [Lorie, 1974; Titman, 1974; Astrahan and Chamberlin, 1975; Astrahan and Lorie, 1975].

Links and selectors can be used to implement evolving views. However, the maintenance of the access paths that implement the links and the selectors can be very difficult [Chamberlin *et al.*, 1975; Schmid and Bernstein, 1975; Stonebraker, 1975b; Tsichritzis, 1975a]. On the other hand, the difficulty of the problem depends to a large extent on the way in which relational systems are used and the types of queries processed. In the face of much modification activity in a data base, it may be necessary to recreate evolving views when they are needed rather than to represent them explicitly. The existence of inverted files

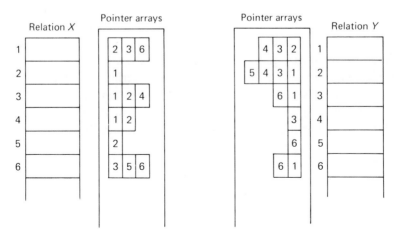

Fig. 8.5–1 Pointer array implementation of an N:M link.

for some of the attributes can be very helpful in recreating a view. In some relational languages the users tell the system when to create and maintain links. This is the case, for instance, in the net facility of SEQUEL [Boyce and Chamberlin, 1973].

The final level of a relational system, the *relational language,* implements relational operators. It can, for example, provide a query language like SEQUEL. The relational language is implemented using the facilities provided by the access path level. Consider, as an example, a relational language based on the relational algebra. Its implementation involves implementing the operators of the relational algebra at the access path level. Links and selectors can be used to implement the operators. The operators will be considered separately, and a sketchy outline of their implementation at the access path level will be given.

The union, intersection, and difference operators are implemented by manipulating sets of tuples. The access path level has facilities for naming sets of tuples using selectors. The selection and restriction operators involve the ability to select subsets of relations on the basis of their contents. The access path level has facilities for naming and selecting sets of tuples using selectors. The projection operator involves only the masking of certain attributes. This can easily be done by recording that only certain fields, of the files where the relations are stored, are pertinent. Finally, the join and cross-product operators involve the connection of different relations. These connections are represented by links at the access path level. The access path can take the form of the implementation of Fig. 8.5—1.

The implementation of relational systems is receiving a great deal of attention as a research and development effort. Many prototype systems have been proposed and are being developed. The interested reader is advised to consult the available literature for further details [Goldstein and Strnad, 1970; Bracchi *et al.,* 1972; Notley, 1972; Whitney, 1972; Lorie, 1974; Astrahan and Lorie, 1975; Czarnik *et al.,* 1975; Held *et al.,* 1975; McLeod and Meldman, 1975; Todd, 1975; Astrahan *et al.,* 1976; Stonebraker *et al.,* 1976].

8.6 DATA BASE MACHINES

Many of the searching facilities of DBMS's may be implemented directly in hardware. In fact, appropriate hardware may make the implementation of DBMS's considerably easier and more efficient than the implementations based on common hardware architectures. An example of a hardware proposal will be given that provides many of the search mechanisms needed by DBMS's.

The relational associative processor (RAP) is a nonnumeric processor designed to support data base management [Ozkarahan et al., 1975]. It is based on a rotating bulk memory and combines the features of associative and array processors [Dugan et al., 1966; Slotnick, 1970; Thurber and Wald, 1975]. The design consists of a controller, an arithmetic set function unit, and a parallel organization of cells. A *cell* consists of a memory component and a logic component. The memory component is one track of a rotating device such as disk, drum, or circular shift register. The logic component is a microprocessor that acts as a "search machine" on data, directs data manipulation, and performs limited numeric computations required by data base processing.

The cells are used to store a general data structure called a RAP relation, which is not a true relation as defined in Chapter 2. Instead, it corresponds more closely to a record type. The tuples of a RAP relation are stored one after another within one or more cells. Control information, specifying the relation and its domains, is stored at the beginning of each cell. Data are read or written via fixed heads—one pair for each cell—while the memory rotates under the heads. The entire contents of a cell can be read in one revolution.

Data base contents are manipulated directly on the cells by their processors. Search criteria are transmitted to all cells simultaneously. Evaluation is performed as the memory contents "pass by" and the contents that qualify are immediately manipulated or written out. Since the entire memory is processed for each instruction, search-aiding data structures, such as inverted files, do not enhance processing speed and can therefore be eliminated. The absence of search-aiding data structures also removes the overhead of their maintenance when modifying the data. This greatly enhances modification response as well as retrieval response.

A delete bit and four *mark* bits are stored with each tuple in a cell. Each mark bit can be thought of as a special domain of the RAP relation. If T is a combination of the four mark bits that are turned on, then a tuple is either T-marked (has the bits on) or T-unmarked. Markings allow the result of one instruction to be used by another instruction. For example, all tuples of a RAP relation can be marked according to whether or not they satisfy a qualification. The qualification consists of conditions involving the domains of the RAP relation and/or the mark bits. A marking, in effect, implements a selector as defined in Chapter 3 and used in Section 8.5. In fact, the four bits of the mark provide the means of encoding up to sixteen different selectors.

Besides the searching operations, RAP also provides commands to insert into, delete from, update, drop a domain from, create, and destroy relations. Set operations (intersection, union, etc.) are provided by marks. Statistical functions such as SUM, AVERAGE, MAX, MIN, and COUNT are also provided. All these commands interface directly with the microprocessor hardware.

RAP was initially conceived, as its name implies, for a relational implementation. However, its mechanisms can be used to support other kinds of organizations. In light of this, a more appropriate name for RAP would be data base associative processor. RAP is only one example of many efforts that are underway for providing hardware architectures that are appropriate for data base management [Rudolph, 1972; Su and Lipovski, 1975; Lin and Smith, 1976]. Hopefully, these architectures will alleviate some of the implementation problems of DBMS's. In the meantime, the implementation techniques will have to be developed, analyzed, and implemented in software. The "hardware around the corner" will not provide all the answers. In addition, the right hardware cannot be built before a thorough understanding of implementation techniques and DBMS architecture is achieved.

In this chapter, an effort was made to unify and present different techniques that can be used for the implementation of different DBMS approaches. Implementation techniques are not always elegant. Some of them can be rather "messy" and confusing. We remind the reader that a good implementation technique does not have to be conceptually pleasing. It just has to work!

EXERCISES

8.1 Consider AVL trees, TRIE trees, B-trees, and hashing as searching techniques [Knuth, 1973]. Associate with each case of a search mapping in Fig. 8.1−1 an appropriate searching technique. Justify your answer.

8.2 , Outline an implementation for the repeating group feature of the DBTG proposal. Try to take advantage of the special properties of this feature.

8.3 Propose a combination of the techniques outlined in Section

8.3.1, which are adequate to implement all the DBTG COBOL DML commands. Justify your choice.

8.4 For each category of implementation techniques discussed in Section 8.3, analyze the cost of the technique for retrieval purposes in terms of comparisons and disk accesses. Consider all forms of the DBTG COBOL DML FIND command. State any assumptions made.

8.5 Consider an implementation of DBTG sets as outlined in Section 8.3.4. How could you use this implementation to implement inverted files also? Are there any restrictions required?

8.6 How would you implement $N:M$ relationships directly?

8.7 What is the cost, measured in weighted comparisons and other machine instructions, of searching the Student Records data base of Chapter 5 if the hierarchical structure is implemented using (a) pointers and physical contiguity, (b) traces? To what extent would inverted files be helpful? How would you implement the inverted files?

8.8 Investigate in detail a hierarchical oriented access method [IBM, 1975].

8.9 How would you implement a GET PRIOR command in a hierarchical data language using a preorder tree traversal?

8.10 Consider the contiguity and pointer example of Section 8.4.1. Given some properties of a data base such as expected number of children per parent and record sizes, investigate the optimum selection of block sizes. Would two or more block sizes be advantageous? What relation should blocks and pages have in a virtual memory environment?

8.11 Outline a hashing algorithm mapping traces to record identifiers in a file. The hashing does not have to be one to one or onto. Investigate the properties of the algorithm. Under what circumstances will it perform well? Under what circumstances will it perform poorly?

8.12 Consider the proposed mapping between tuples representing traces and record identifiers in a file given by the function

$$p_1{}^{n_1} * p_2{}^{n_2} * \ldots * p_t{}^{n_t}$$

where p_i is the ith prime number. Is this mapping effective? What are the practical problems?

8.13 Consider an environment where the record occurrences are variable size. How would this fact affect the techniques discussed in Section 8.4? Outline an overflow technique capable of handling the problem.

8.14 What is the effect of virtual memory on the implementation of a hierarchical system [Denning, 1970] ?

8.15 Outline a series of tables and other structures that can be used to store a relational schema.

8.16 Outline a series of structures to implement evolving views. Discuss their relative advantages. Also propose ways to handle their maintenance in the presence of updates, insertions, and deletions to the relations involved [Schmid and Bernstein, 1975].

8.17 Investigate the meaning of an update, insertion and deletion on an evolving view. Are any restrictions necessary [Chamberlin *et al.*, 1975] ?

8.18 Outline a simple relational system that can be implemented on a minicomputer [McLeod and Meldman, 1975]. Assume that there is no special treatment for evolving views.

8.19 Consider a multilevel relational system as described in Section 8.5. Would you allow access to the lower levels from the relational language by privileged persons, e.g., DBA's? If so, what kinds of commands would you provide to access the lower levels?

8.20 Are relational systems inherently more or less efficient than hierarchical or network systems [Codd, 1975] ? Justify your answer.

8.21 Using *B*-trees, outline an implementation of:

    (a) selectors,

    (b) links,

    (c) inverted files.

8.22 Consider the natural join of a relation implemented as a link. Suppose further that all the attributes involved in the join are inverted. Outline an implementation of the link that does not require any extra maintenance as the relations are changed; namely, the maintenance of the link is guaranteed by the maintenance of the inverted files.

8.23 Suppose content addressibility is implemented in hardware. Discuss the effect on each of the approaches: hierarchical, network, and relational.

8.24 Consider the features of RAP discussed in Section 8.6. Outline a hierarchical and a DBTG set implementation based on RAP.

8.25 Suppose hardware content addressible memory is n times more expensive than conventional memory of the same speed. Investigate the trade-off between the cost of hashing in conventional memory using a good hashing algorithm, and the cost of content addressable memory.

How small should n be to make the hardware solution a viable and economical alternative? Can you make any predictions?

8.26 Suppose B-trees are implemented in hardware. Outline a hierarchical, network, and relational implementation based completely on B-trees.

8.27 Define a set of operations on pointer arrays. Use pointer arrays and their operations to implement the hierarchical and network example implementations given in Sections 8.3.4 and 8.4.1. Can the B-tree implementation given in Section 8.2 be implemented using pointer arrays?

Chapter 9

OPERATIONAL REQUIREMENTS

9.1 PERFORMANCE

The performance of a DBMS is a critical factor in its successful operation. DBMS performance is related both to reliability and to efficiency of operations. These factors, in turn, affect the cost effectiveness of a DBMS operation.

The reliability of a DBMS is a function of the reliability of both the hardware and software. Reliability is enhanced by the ability of the DBMS to recover from failures. Failures occur for different reasons, e.g., hardware malfunctions or software errors. The DBMS should be able to isolate the effects of the failures to small parts of the data base and to recover. Recovery is desirable without human intervention during the processing of a transaction. Between transactions, operator intervention can guide the system through the necessary steps to avoid complete breakdown.

A reliable DBMS implies a long interval between failures, and thus a high degree of *availability*. In addition, the system should be at least partially available even during failures. A particular failure should not affect the operation of the whole system. It should be isolated so as to minimize the amount of data affected by the failure. In this way, the rest of the data base is available for operation.

The efficiency of a DBMS is a function of both space and time. Space usually refers to the amount and type of memory needed for the data base and the DBMS. Time refers to both the CPU time and the real time required per transaction. In batch mode, DBMS's cannot be as efficient, per transaction, as conventional sequential file systems. DBMS's invariably add some overhead to an application. However, this overhead should be minimized. Some applications strain existing hardware either according to space or time, or both. Some extra overhead can affect not only the operation of an application, but the feasibility of implementing it using a DBMS.

The time aspect of efficient performance of a DBMS is affected by the order in which multiple searches are implemented. Given a general qualification, some conditions should be resolved before others. For instance, consider a Boolean expression of conditions of the form (data item = value) connected by AND Boolean operators (conjunctive form). It is much better first to evaluate the conditions that result in the selection of the fewest records. For example, if the qualification asks for people who speak English, German, and Greek, it is best to start by isolating persons who speak Greek since this will result in the selection of the fewest records (unless we are in Greece). The resolution of the subsequent search criteria then need only consider this small subset of all possible records. In addition, conditions that involve data items that have inverted files should be evaluated first. In this way, a search through the complete set of records is avoided. General algorithms that optimize searches can become quite complex [Farley and Schuster, 1975; Hammer and Chan, 1976].

Some DBMS's handle requests in an on-line environment. If the number of users currently on-line is very large, then the system has to process many transactions per second concurrently. Under these conditions, providing fast response time for each transaction is quite difficult. These systems need complex terminal monitors to coordinate on-line communication and data base access. As discussed in Chapter 1, they may also require special communication facilities and front-end hardware to handle a large number of users concurrently. Terminal-oriented systems face serious performance problems related to terminal communication and concurrent access of the data base. However, a good DBMS should perform well not only in a batch environment but also in an on-line environment.

The space aspect of efficient performance means that a DBMS has to provide storage capacity for efficiently storing large volumes of data. Most data storage problems, such as efficient access and searching of data on secondary storage, do not arise when handling small volumes. In these cases, efficient utilization of storage may not be an important consideration. However, for large volumes the optimization of storage structures and access paths is necessary to reduce storage costs and processing time. In order to reduce storage space, it is obviously desirable to minimize data redundancy. This implies that the same data are not duplicated just because two applications require different views. The DBMS should handle the different views, without unnecessary data duplication.

Data nonredundancy also reduces some of the consistency problems associated with multiple redundant copies of data. Modifications in a multiple-copy environment are particularly difficult to handle because the same data must be modified in many different copies. Ideally, an update should be reflected in all copies simultaneously. In practice, of course, this is technically impossible. It is not also always possible to modify all copies of the data since it may not be known that certain copies even exist. Inconsistency results when some copies are modified while others are not. To handle the problem of data redundancy and its associated consistency problems effectively, it is necessary to centralize, in the DBA, the capability to define data and to control their physical placement. The actual physical storage location of the data, however, need not be centralized. It can be distributed.

When evaluating a DBMS's performance, it is important that the performance of the entire information system be taken into account. People and external procedures should be included in the evaluation. DBMS's may add extra operational overhead, but hopefully they make better use of peoples's time and provide more timely information.

9.2 INTEGRITY

Preserving the *integrity* of data implies the safeguarding of the data from malicious or erroneous tampering, faulty equipment, etc. The emphasis in integrity provisions is on preserving all of the data and changes to the data so that the data base can be reconstructed in case of partial or total destruction. Thus, typical approaches to the problem include journalling, checkpoints, backtracking, access control, and monitoring to detect integrity breaches.

Journalling consists of saving requests to the DBMS, e.g., insertions, updates, deletions, and who accesses what and when. A *checkpoint* involves saving a specified part of the data base. Thus, by the use of checkpoints and journalling, a data base can be reconstructed from previous checkpoints up to the time of failure. This operation is different than backtracking. *Backtracking* involves reversing the effects of some of the transactions. Systems usually have a way of defining the limits, i.e., beginning and end, of a transaction. In addition, some systems can recover in the middle of a transaction and reverse the changes to the data base affected by that particular transaction. In this way, a particular transaction that produces undesirable side effects can be isolated. However, most systems cannot backtrack and eliminate the effects of several transactions, especially in an on-line environment.

Access control means restricting the type of access allowed to a data base by an application. For example, access may be restricted to retrieval only. By granting potentially destructive access, e.g., modification, only to "trusted" applications, the likelihood of data base contamination is reduced [Stonebraker and Wong, 1974; Chamberlin *et al.*, 1975].

Another integrity provision is to identify the mode of operation on the data base, e.g., test or production [Guide-Share, 1970]. The mode of operation determines the effect of a data language operation on the data base. For example, if the mode is "test," then a modification is not reflected in the data base.

An application should be able to instruct the DBMS to flag incorrect data [Guide-Share, 1970]. The flag makes the data inaccessible to other applications until corrective action is taken. For example, if an application detects an employee's salary to be $1,000,000, it should be able to flag such an error, even though it may not be able to correct it.

The system should provide the tools to the user to specify integrity constraints on the data base [Eswaran and Chamberlin, 1975; Stonebraker, 1975a]. Such integrity requirements capture semantic information that the user has about the data base. The DDL can have special commands to encode this information in the schema. For example, $10,000 can be distinguished from 10,000 feet. Such separation of data types is helpful in avoiding meaningless operations, e.g., adding 300 feet to $500.

Finally, a DBMS must be able to protect the integrity of the data during modifications. For example, if a data item is being modified, then the DBMS should prevent other applications from accessing the data item until the modification is complete. Search-aiding data structures also need protection to preserve the integrity and consistency of the data base. There should be a one-to-one correspondence between inverted files and the data in the data base for consistency purposes. Some techniques used to protect data during modification will be discussed in Section 9.4.

9.3 SECURITY

Recently, the privacy of data in large computerized data bases has received a good deal of attention [Gotlieb and Borodin, 1973; Martin, 1973]. The concern is that such data bases can store private information about people without their knowledge or consent. The same problem exists with manual or conventional EDP approaches. However, the scale of, and ease of access provided by DBMS's have focused much more attention on the privacy issue. Laws are being considered that may affect not only the possibility of storing private data, but the very mechanisms used for their storage and retrieval. For instance, in many countries citizens have the right to demand access to data about themselves stored in data bases. In this way, they can control the accuracy and nature of private data about themselves. In addition, some people argue that computer installations should be required to notify persons of the existence of such private data. Some of the mechanisms for storing private data may also be restricted. For example, it is possible that unauthorized installations will be forbidden to use social security numbers as an access key to their data. However, the main issue concerning privacy is the means of providing data security.

Data *security* concerns the protection of the data base against unauthorized access. Protection of the data base requires identifying and authenticating users whenever they access the data base. Identifying a user usually consists of entering a code that is recognized by the system. Authenticating a user means verifying that the user is actually the person who is allowed to use the identification code. For example, authentication can consist of specifying passwords that are supposedly known only to authorized users. In addition to user authorization, the system applies access control on the operations of the user. In this way, a user can be restricted to accessing only that part of the data base and using those data language operations for which he has been granted authorization. Some of the issues that complicate the protection problem in a DBMS environment will be outlined.

Since real data bases have between 10^8 and 10^{12} bits, the quantity of data requiring protection is very large. Different physical subsets of a data base can require different protection status. A query may select any part of the data base by means of a qualification. This qualified subset of the data base may require different access restrictions, according to its contents, than another subset, e.g., employee's with salary greater than $20,000 and less than or equal to $20,000 [Chamberlin *et al.*, 1975; Eswaran *et al.*, 1974]. The problem of protecting a large amount of data is therefore compounded when their subsets are considered.

The data organization facilities of a DBMS can be viewed on a variety of levels of detail. The protection mechanism has to work on any of these different logical levels. For example, at the view level, at the record type level, or at the data item level. The schema and subschemas of a data base also have to be protected. These are the most sensitive parts of the data base. Unauthorized use of a schema or subschema can be embarrassing and costly. For instance, the logical relationships of data, as described in a schema and the subschemas, often give much information. Knowing that there is a relationship between employees and national origin may allow one to determine an employee's national origin. One might be able to ask questions about employees or national origin, but not about the relationship between the two. In this respect, subschemas provide some data security by "masking out" parts of a schema which an application is not permitted to access. Unauthorized modification of a schema or subschema can be catastrophic. Modification to a schema can affect the entire data base, impacting all applications and perhaps resulting in a loss of data.

The additional search-aiding data structures provided by DBMS's should also be protected. Inverted files often contain as much information as the data. For example, if one inverted file exists for employee names and another for salaries, then an employee's salary can be determined without ever accessing the data base by judicious use of the inverted files. Another case of search-aiding data structures are general access paths. For instance, in DBTG network systems the programmer navigates through the data base from one record to another via DBTG sets [Bachman, 1973b]. The access paths between the records need protection checkpoints to prevent unauthorized users from gaining access to the data by clever manipulation of the access paths. The access paths connecting data are as important as the information present in the data since they usually reveal how data is related.

To summarize, in order to provide the necessary protection for a data base, a DBMS should be able to protect at least the following [CODASYL DBTG, 1971]:

1. the use of a schema or subschema;

2. the alteration of a schema or subschema;

3. any part of a schema or subschema, e.g., record type, data item, from a data language operation;

4. the physical occurrence of any part of a schema or subschema, e.g., record, data item value, from a data language operation.

In the preceding discussion, it is assumed that the DBMS has control over its data bases. Therefore it needs security mechanisms to protect its data. Another solution to the security problem is to view the DBMS as a utility of the operating system that provides a flexible interface to the data. The access control to the data is the domain of the operating system. In this manner, the code of the DBMS is not security sensitive. A user can take control of or infiltrate the DBMS, but this situation does not imply access to the real data. This solution of the security problem is attractive when security is of paramount importance. The security of the data bases is reduced to the security of the operating system, which can be further reduced to the security of a small part (kernel) of the operating system [Tsichritzis and Bernstein, 1974]. However, by adopting this solution, some of the flexibility of the DBMS is sacrificed.

9.4 CONCURRENCY

One of the major advantages of on-line terminal systems is fast response to user requests. As the number of terminals and the number of requests per unit time increase, some concurrency must be provided to handle all the requests and still maintain fast response time. Similarly, in an on-line DBMS environment, concurrent use of a data base must be allowed. If only one request at a time is allowed to access a data base, and if all other requests must wait until it has completed, then a bottleneck results. If requests arrive faster than they can be processed sequentially, then the time a request has to wait before being processed increases and response time suffers. However, if concurrent modification of the data base is permitted, then consistency problems can arise. The point will be illustrated by an example.

Consider an on-line airline reservation system. Clerks are continually booking reservations from many locations. Suppose that there is only one seat left on a particular charter flight and the following occurs. Clerk A requests that a seat on the flight be booked. At about the same time, clerk B makes the same request. If the timing of the requests is such that clerk B's request is processed before the seat count is decremented due to clerk A's request, then they will both book the same seat. What should have happened, of course, is that clerk B's request should have been delayed until clerk A's had been completed. This example illustrates one of many problems that can arise when applications are allowed to modify a data base concurrently. Such problems will be referred to collectively as the *concurrent update problem*. They are called update, as most of the problems arise when existing data are being modified.

As pointed out in the preceding example, one solution to the concurrent update problem is to control access by other applications to the data until a modification is complete. In a DBMS, three types of access to a data base are possible: unprotected, protected, and exclusive [CODASYL DBTG, 1971]. *Unprotected* access means that applications may retrieve and modify data concurrently. This situation usually never occurs in practice or, if it does, the DBMS provides some mechanism to warn an application that other applications are concurrently accessing the same data. *Protected* access means that any application may retrieve data, but only one application may modify it. For example, in the airline reservation example, if clerk B is merely curious as to the number of seats left on the flight, but does not want to book any, there is no reason to prevent clerk B's access to the data. *Exclusive* access means that all applications except one are prevented from accessing the data.

Whenever a data base is being modified and there are many applications accessing it concurrently, a combination of protected and exclusive access has to be provided. However, access need only be restricted during the time that the modification is being performed and then only to the data that are to be modified. Preventing access to data that are being modified is referred to as *locking* the data. The important consideration for concurrent modification is to decide what to lock and when to lock it. The solution to this problem is an important factor in a successful DBMS.

Consider a record type and concurrent modification of its records. The concurrent update problem does not seem formidable. If a specific record needs to be modified, then only that record needs to be locked. Assuming that each modification is only done on one record at a time, there is no need for very complicated locking procedures by the user. For example, the locking can be implicit in the modification command. The user does not explicitly lock anything. The system locks the pertinent record at the beginning of a modification and unlocks it at the end. If there is a conflict and the record cannot be locked, then the system tries again after a short delay. If it is unsuccessful after a specified length of time, it informs the user that the modification cannot proceed.

However, there are several issues that complicate locking. The complications that arise are due mainly to the amount of data that may need to be locked. Many modifications need to operate on more than one record at a time, for instance, according to a qualification that selects many records. All the records need to be locked for the completion of the modification. If one record at a time is modified, then the data base may be inconsistent during the modification. For example, when transferring funds among accounts, a preservation of all moneys is expected. In a DBMS, there are basically two ways of arriving at the same data: via content addressibility and via data relatability. Both these mechanisms should be consistent with the values of the data. Thus, a need may arise to lock more data than just the records themselves before the modification can be done. For example, any inverted files need to be changed when the corresponding values in a data base are modified. These must be locked while the modification is in progress.

Therefore, it is possible that many items may have to be locked while performing a modification to a data base. The number of items depends not only on the request, but on the level at which the locking is done. Locking can be done for an entire data base or at the view, at the record type, at the record occurrence, or at the data item value level [Gray et al., 1975]. If locking is done at a very high level, e.g., a data base, there is a possibility of locking nonessential parts of the data base. For example, if a data base contains EMPLOYEE and INVENTORY record types and locking is done at the data base level, then a modification to EMPLOYEE records also locks the INVENTORY records. Locking at a very high level affects frequent retrieval requests, which could proceed if the lock were not present. On the other hand, if locking is done at a low level, e.g., data item values, many more distinct items need to be locked. When the number of items that need to be locked is very large, the locking request is time consuming. Also, when performing a locking request at a low level, there is the possibility of a deadlock due to other concurrent locking requests.

Deadlock, in general, is the inability of a request to continue processing. Usually a request is unable to proceed because the resources it needs to continue are not currently available to it, nor will they be in the future. Such deadlock normally results from the incremental acquisition of resources. For example, request *A* gets resource 1 and request

B gets resource 2. Request A now asks for resource 2 while request B asks for resource 1. Unless there is some intervention, request A and B will wait for each other indefinitely. One solution is for a request to ask for all the resources it will need at one time. This solution, however, reduces the possible concurrent utilization of the resources. More on deadlock can be found in the literature [Habermann, 1969; Coffman *et al.*, 1971; Holt, 1972; Everest, 1974].

It is not possible to lock many unrelated items simultaneously and instantaneously, at least with current hardware. When they are locked one by one, they may need to be unlocked to avoid deadlock in the presence of a conflict with another locking request. For example, whenever a request A that is locking items encounters an item that has already been locked by another request B it unlocks all the items it has locked so far and starts again. This strategy allows other locking requests, which could continue if they had available some of the items locked by A, to proceed. However, unlocking items and restarting the locking request may give rise to an "accordion" effect, in which separate locking activities that require some of the same items collide and withdraw alternatively. For example, requests A and B both encounter items locked by each other, withdraw, try again, and the same thing happens. It is very hard for a DBMS to diagnose such a situation if the locking requests are independent.

To coordinate locking, all locking requests can be performed by a locking monitor. This type of locking involves a multilevel operation. First, exclusive use (lock) of the locking monitor is obtained, which later does the locking for the request. The locking monitor can arbitrate between conflicting requests, perhaps delaying one and informing it when it can proceed.

To maximize concurrent use of a data base, it is important that items are locked for the minimum amount of time possible. Therefore, it may be advantageous to claim items before locking. A *claim* on an item is analogous to protected access. Other locking requests may claim the items, but only one request may lock them at one time [Chamberlin *et al.*, 1974]. The items are only locked when all needed items can be locked. In this manner, retrieval requests are not interfered with during locking.

One of the most difficult problems relating to concurrent update concerns the action taken when a locking request cannot proceed. The request should obviously be blocked. The way in which a request is blocked depends heavily on the characteristics of the operating system. One way of blocking a request is to delay it by taking advantage of the

CPU scheduling algorithm. If a request is given a certain time slice in which to execute, the time slice can be terminated prematurely. The locking attempt proceeds again during the next time slice. Another way of blocking a request is to suspend it. Execution of the locking request is postponed until the request is given an alarm indicating that the locking can again be attempted.

Another alternative is to fake the modification request. No locking attempt or modification is actually done. Instead, the modification is posted in a pending modifications file. Every subsequent request accessing the data has to go through a "posted modifications" monitor, which checks the file to determine if a pending modification would affect the result of the request. The actual modifications to the data base can be done off-line when data base activity is minimal.

The level of locking and the method of locking and blocking are very important in any system. It is difficult to give general solutions since they depend heavily on the type of hardware, the properties of the operating system, the nature of the data base, and the type of requests. More on locking can be found in the literature [Shemer and Collmeyer, 1972; Everest, 1974; Stonebraker and Wong, 1974; Chamberlin *et al.*, 1975].

9.5 UTILITIES

DBMS's are intended to help people solve their increasingly complex data processing and information system problems. To achieve this goal a DBMS has to provide a complete set of facilities that enable users to implement their applications easily and efficiently. In addition, it has to provide a complete operational environment for processing the applications. Many utilities are needed for the successful generation and operation of a data base. The current software technology is adequate for the production of such utilities. However, some systems do not provide a complete set of utilities. Often users are not aware of what utilites are available on their systems or what utilities can be obtained from the manufacturers. In addition, they often do not know what utilities they need or how they should use them. Some utilities that are absolutely necessary for the successful operation of a DBMS will be outlined.

The initial loading of large volumes of data into a data base is a major problem. Data base loading can be a very costly operation because of the large amount of data involved and the need to convert it to machine-readable form. The use of data language operations to insert a large volume of data individually is often impractical because of the tremendous time and cost involved. A DBMS should provide a data entry and loading system to put the data initially in machine-readable form and load it into a data base.

A DBMS has to provide a complete facility that is able to answer any semantically meaningful user request and to provide the answer in an easy to digest format. To this end, good report generating facilities are very important. They are a major success factor in any DBMS operation. The users are able not only to get the information they want from the data base but to receive it in an understandable format [Curtice, 1974].

The naming of logical units of data in a schema and the subschemas can be a considerable problem in a large organization. There are many objects, items, concepts—all with accepted names in the organization. This situation reflects itself in a proliferation of names in the schemas and subschemas. The same name may be used in different applications to mean different things. All the names must be meaningful and unambiguous. A *data dictionary* that catalogs all the names and their meanings in any given context is often a necessity. Sometimes the creation and maintenance of a good data dictionary is beneficial even if there is no computer data base. It can be helpful in discovering the purpose of poorly documented applications. It also allows users to inquire about the meaning of names and prevents ambiguous use or definition of the same name. It is certainly a first step before generating a data base. A DBMS should provide utilities to make it easier for the DBA to construct and maintain data dictionaries [Curtice, 1974; Gradwell, 1975].

A data dictionary is a first step in specifying semantic information about the nature of the data base and its applications. Such semantic information is very important to enable the user to avoid meaningless operations on the data base. In the future, more semantic information will be introduced in DBMS's [Roussopoulos and Mylopoulos, 1975]. However, before semantic information is captured by DBMS's the users must thoroughly understand the nature and properties of their environment.

There are many operational problems that are critical, such as integrity, security, accounting, reorganization, and backup. Internal integrity and security measures were discussed in Sections 9.2 and 9.3. It is also necessary to provide external integrity and security procedures such as physical control of access to an installation [Martin, 1973].

Accounting is very important. In a sense, it is a form of monitoring that shows who the large users are and perhaps what their usage patterns are. It can be helpful in determining what services to provide and which services need upgrading. Performance monitors are very important. They provide the DBA with a very powerful tool to understand the operation of the system and to discover the bottlenecks in it. Reorganization utilities are necessary. Data usage patterns change and may require reorganization of the physical storage structure to improve processing efficiency and cost effectiveness. The DBA must be able to reorganize a data base to meet applications' changing needs. Backup in case of system crashes is essential. Checkpoint restart and journalling facilities are absolutely necessary. Systems frequently malfunction, for several reasons. Some lost processing can be inconvenient, but loss of information that cannot be regenerated can be catastrophic. Even loss of some data can be very expensive, especially if they must be re-entered.

9.6 CONCLUDING REMARKS

The DBMS user usually makes a tremendous initial and continuing investment in following the DBMS approach. The decision to use a DBMS for a company's information needs is as critical as the decision to introduce computers in the first place. It represents a large commitment in terms of money and human resources. Conversion to a DBMS can be costly. The continuous DBMS operation also requires substantial financial resources. As a result, the user expects many advantages and a relative low risk for the DBMS operation. A DBMS should provide a high operational performance for both the data processing installation and the users. In Part II, different commercial systems will be outlined and their facilities discussed. In this manner, the reader can relate the concepts discussed in Part I with existing systems. In addition, the DBMS facilities and operational requirements discussed in Chapters 4 and 9 can be contrasted with the features that are provided in commercial systems.

EXERCISES

9.1 Outline an algorithm for the optimization of the execution of general qualifications. Assume that you know which data items are inverted [Farley and Schuster, 1975].

9.2 Outline a method for deciding which data items to invert. Assume the existence of information about usage patterns of the data base.

9.3 Propose a set of packing schemes that can be used to encode, with great space savings:
  (a) the English language [Martin, 1975],
  (b) programs,
  (c) data structures, e.g., *B*-trees [Bayer and Metzger, 1976].

9.4 Investigate the backup facilities in three different commercial DBMS's. Can you say anything in general about these facilities?

9.5 What is the difference, if any, between the security mechanisms needed in an operating system and a DBMS? Are the two mechanisms related and, if so, how?

9.6 Compare the security of manually kept data bases to the security provided by DBMS's.

9.7 Outline a series of mechanisms by which a binary (protected/ unprotected) hardware-provided protection mechanism can be used eventually to implement data-dependent security in a DBMS.

9.8 Consider a typical mid-range IBM 370 business installation running OS/MVT or VS. Consider at least six DBMS's and the conversion problems for introducing the systems. Consider also the problem of converting from any one of these systems to another DBMS, or back to a conventional installation. Can you recommend a particular DBMS as a prime candidate for easy conversion? Distinguish between sales claims and technical reality.

9.9 Consider one of the performance issues discussed in Section 9.1. Expand on some of the problems associated with this issue.

9.10 How would you implement a locking mechanism at the record occurrence (attribute) level? Consider problems of deadlock, throughput, system overhead, and claim versus actual lock.

9.11 How would you implement locking in a system that allowed triggered delete operations, e.g., a hierarchical system? Try to minimize locking time and avoid deadlock.

9.12 Discuss some of the advantages and disadvantages of the methods of blocking a locking request given in Section 9.4. Can you give an alternative method?

9.13 Produce a list of utilities that you feel are important for data base generation and operation. Compare this list with a list of utilities of an existing system.

Part 2

DBMS EXAMPLES

Chapter 10

INTRODUCTION

DBMS's were developed to provide data independence for applications. Data independence is a noble goal, which is not completely achieved by any existing system. In reviewing current systems, one is struck by the absence of common terminology, many ad hoc techniques, different, incompatible facilities, extraordinary claims, extreme complexity, and dependence on physical properties of data storage.

Part II of this book is a survey of several different DBMS's. Its purpose is to shed some light on their functions and facilities. The survey is not a feature analysis; it is rather incomplete to serve that purpose. It is far from a comparative evaluation; that would be a complex research project. It merely describes the systems based on available documentation.

Five systems have been chosen for description mainly on the basis of their diverse features and wide use. An attempt has been made to choose systems that use different data models.

The survey includes examples of most of the types of DBMS's discussed in Part I. IMS and SYSTEM 2000 are hierarchical systems. IDMS is a DBTG network system. Total is also a network system, but does not conform to the DBTG specifications. ADABAS resembles a relational system, but is probably best described as a general network system. The original terminology of each system is retained wherever possible. In this way, the reader is able to go directly to the manuals for the systems and to recognize the systems from the descriptions presented in Part II.

The most striking absence concerning the systems described is the lack of an example of a truly relational system. There is some reason for this; there was no truly relational DBMS widely available on the commercial market at the time this book was written. Some commercial systems, however, are becoming available, e.g., the Tymshare system [Codd, 1975].

This survey will hopefully be useful for prospective users, educators, students, and in general anyone interested in obtaining a perspective of what real DBMS's are all about. Some prior knowledge of data management concepts as outlined in Part I is indispensible for understanding the descriptions of the systems.

A typical example of an application is used as a common thread throughout the descriptions of the systems. The example concerns a data base of employees, parts, suppliers, etc., related as follows [Boyce *et al.*, 1974; Date, 1975]. Each employee works in a department and has a manager and a salary. Each supplier company supplies different parts in certain volumes. Each department uses certain parts in certain volumes. Some queries that might be asked on this data base are:

1. Find the names of all employees working in department W.
2. Find the salaries of employees working in department W.
3. Find all departments that use at least two different parts supplied by the same company.

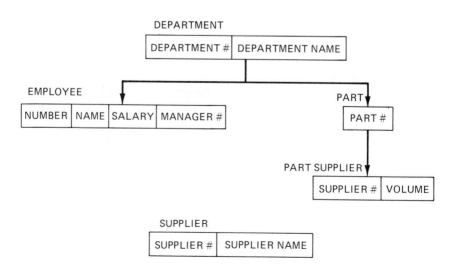

Fig. 10-1 Hierarchical definition trees of common application.

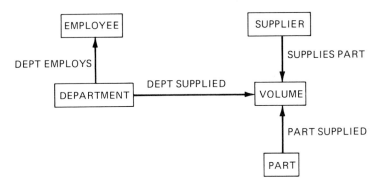

Fig. 10–2 Data structure diagram of common application.

A representation of the example data base, in terms of hierarchical definition trees, is shown in Fig. 10–1. The hierarchical representation of the example requires two definition trees to avoid redundancy in the data base. That is, if two data base trees are not used, then the supplier name would have to be repeated under every part supplied to a department by the supplier. If the example contained more data pertinent only to a supplier, such as the supplier location or status, then the problem of data redundancy is even more acute.

A network representation of the example allows departments, parts, and suppliers to be connected directly in the network via an intermediate VOLUME record as shown in the data structure diagram in Fig. 10–2.

The EMPLOYEE, DEPARTMENT, PART, and SUPPLIER record types contain the same data items as the EMPLOYEE, DEPARTMENT, PART, and SUPPLIER record types used in the hierarchical representation. The VOLUME record type contains only a volume data-item. Each VOLUME record occurrence pertains to a single part, department, supplier combination. That is, a VOLUME record occurrence owned by PART record P, DEPARTMENT record D, and SUPPLIER record S contains the volume of part P supplied by supplier S to department D.

A relational representation of the example data base is shown in Fig. 10–3.

EMPLOYEE (NUMBER, NAME, SALARY, DEPARTMENT#, MANAGER#)
PART (PART#, DEPARTMENT#, SUPPLIER#, VOLUME)
DEPARTMENT (DEPARTMENT#, NAME)
SUPPLIER (SUPPLIER#, NAME)

Fig. 10–3 Relational schema of common application.

Chapter 11

INFORMATION MANAGEMENT SYSTEM (IMS)

11.1 DATA MODEL

Information Management System (IMS) is a product of International Business Machines (IBM) Corporation [IBM, 1971, 1975; Date, 1975]. It uses the hierarchical data model. The smallest unit of logical data is called a *field* (data item). A *segment type* (record type) is a named collection of fields. Occurrences of segment types are called *segments* (records). Segments may be either fixed or variable length. The highest level segment in the definition tree is called the *root segment type*. All other segment types are referred to as *dependent segment types*. The relationship between two segments in the data base tree that are one level apart is called a *parent–child* relationship. Two segments of the same type under the same parent segment are referred to as *twins*. A *data base record* (data base tree) is one root segment and all of its dependent segments.

IMS supports both physical and logical data bases. A *physical data base* is represented by a single physical storage organization. IMS permits four types of physical data base storage organizations. These are discussed in Section 11.4. A *logical data base* consists of one or more physical storage organizations. That is, segment types comprising the data base are taken from one or more physical data bases. A parent–child relationship in a logical data base need not exist as a parent–child relationship in a physical data base.

For example, consider Fig. 11.1—1. The data bases corresponding to the hierarchical definition trees shown in Fig. 11.1—1a, b exist as physical data bases. In IMS, it is possible to define a logical relationship between PART SUPPLIED and PART as given by the dashed line. This relationship can be unidirectional or bidirectional. If the relationship is bidirectional, then it is possible to define the two logical data bases corresponding to the hierarchical definition trees shown in Fig. 11.1—1c, d. PART is called the logical parent of PART SUPPLIED and PART SUPPLIED is called the logical child of PART. The bidirectional nature of the relationship means that it is possible to get from SUPPLIER to PART as in Fig. 11.1—1c or from PART to SUPPLIER as in Fig. 11.1—1d. In Fig. 11.1—1c, the application views the logical parent of PART SUPPLIED, PART, as concatenated to each of its logical children, PART SUPPLIED. In Fig. 11.1—1d, the logical child of PART, PART SUPPLIED, is considered a physical child of its logical parent, PART, concatenated to its physical parent, SUPPLIER. In both cases the application views the relationship between PART and SUPPLIER as a physical parent/child relationship, although it is not implemented as a physical relationship. Much more complex and different views can be defined using logical relationships. For example, a parent—

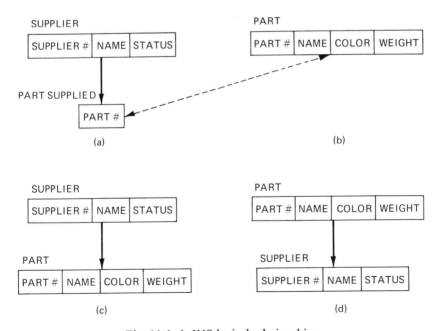

Fig. 11.1—1 IMS logical relationships.

child relationship in a physical data base can be defined as a child–parent relationship in a logical data base (inverted structure). In this way, many different views can be defined for the same physical storage organization.

11.2 DATA DEFINITION FACILITY

An IMS data base and its physical storage structures are described by a *data base description* (DBD). A DBD defines the schema for one physical or logical data base and consists of several statements.

A DBD statement names the data base and specifies its organization. The main organizations are those described in Section 11.4 or LOGICAL.

A DATASET statement defines the data set groups (files) for a data base.

A SEGM statement defines a segment type by naming it, by giving its position in the hierarchical definition tree, and by giving its relationship to other segment types, i.e., its parent segment type. It also specifies some of the physical characteristics of occurrences of the segment type such as its length in bytes, and its insertion, update, and deletion rules if applicable.

An LCHILD statement is used to define logical relationships.

A FIELD statement defines a field in a segment type that can be referred to by an application program. A field may be a key field (also called sequence field). Key field values are used to order segments and to store and retrieve segments in certain data base organizations (see Section 11.4). At most one key field may be specified per segment type and it may be either unique or nonunique. A unique key field means that the value for the key field is unique within the data base for root segments, or under a given parent for dependent segments. The FIELD statement also specifies the length, starting position within the segment, and optionally the data type of the field.

An XDFLD statement defines an indexed field. This causes an index data base (inverted file) to be created for the field. The index data base is similar to a regular data base in that it consists of a segment type called an *index pointer segment type*. The index points either at segments that contain the field or at ancestor segments. For example, if an index pointer segment exists for a field of a segment with the value 'RED', then the index can point at all segments with the value

'RED' or at all parents or grandparents, etc., of segments with the value 'RED'.

The DBDGEN, FINISH, and END statements indicate the end of the DBD definition.

Each application program views its data via a subschema defined by a *program specification block* (PSB). A PSB specifies the data bases and the segment types within the data bases that a program may access. A program may be key sensitive, data sensitive, or not sensitive to a segment type in a data base. If a program is not sensitive to a segment type, then it cannot access segments of the segment type or any segments of descendant segment types. If it is key sensitive, then it can specify key field values for the segment type in a qualification, but it cannot access segments of the segment type. For example, in Fig. 10–1 if an application is key sensitive to the DEPARTMENT segment type, then it can specify a DEPARTMENT# value in a qualification to determine all the employees in a certain department. However, it cannot retrieve DEPARTMENT segments. Data sensitivity means that a program may access a segment.

The PSB consists of subordinate *program communication blocks* (PCB's). Each PCB specifies the name of the DBD associated with a data base and names the segments within the data base to which a program is sensitive and the type of sensitivity, i.e., key, data, or not sensitive. It may also specify the type of data language operations permitted by the application on the segment type, e.g., retrieval only. When a PSB only concerns one data base, then it consists of a single PCB and the PCB is in fact the PSB. However, since an application may process several data bases at one time, the PSB can contain several PCB's, one for each data base. During data base processing, the PCB's act as communication buffers between IMS and the application program.

In addition, IMS provides several utility programs that load, reorganize, and recover a data base. Recovery facilities include checkpoints and journalling. It is also possible to remove changes made to a data base by selected application programs (backout).

11.3 DATA MANIPULATION FACILITY

IMS is a host data language system. The DML of IMS is called Data Language/1 (DL/1). DL/1 is invoked through procedure calls from application programs written in PL/1, COBOL or Assembler Language. It operates on one or more segments at a time and maintains one or more position pointers per data base. A position pointer marks an application program's progress through the data base according to a preorder data base tree traversal. If only one position pointer per data base is maintained, then answering certain queries is very cumbersome. This situation usually arises when we wish to retrieve segments that lie on two different hierarchical paths. For example, in Fig. 10—1 the EMPLOYEE and PART segment types lie on two different hierarchical paths. Consider now the query "Find all employees who work for a department that uses part number X." For each department, it is necessary to determine if it uses part number X. However, when this operation is done, the position pointer points at the PART segment, if one qualifies. The EMPLOYEE segments for the department now lie "behind" the part segment according to a preorder data base tree traversal. To retrieve the EMPLOYEE segments it is necessary to reset the position pointer to the DEPARTMENT segment and then retrieve the EMPLOYEE segments. To overcome this problem, IMS permits multiple positioning in a hierarchical data base. One position pointer is maintained for each possible path in the hierarchical definition tree. In the preceding example this means that we do not need to reposition the position pointer after the PART segment is found. Another position pointer marks the path from the DEPARTMENT segment to the EMPLOYEE segments and can be used to retrieve the EMPLOYEE segments. Note that multiple positioning is somewhat analogous to set currency indicators in a DBTG network system.

The format of DL/1 calls is as follows (assuming PL/1 is the host language):

CALL PLITDLI (parameter count, DL/1 function code, PCB name, I/O work area, segment search argument 1, segment search argument 2, . . .)

The *parameter count* is the address of a value representing the number of parameters to follow in the call statement.

The *DL/1 function code*, for data base calls, is one of the following:

GU	Get Unique
GN	Get Next
GNP	Get Next Within Parent
GHU	Get Hold Unique
GHN	Get Hold Next

GHNP	Get Hold Next Within Parent
ISRT	Insert
DLET	Delete
REPL	Replace

The data base calls will be described in detail later in this section. There are also several function codes for system service calls that deal with integrity and recovery procedures. These calls are not described here.

The *PCB name* is the name of the PCB that is to be used as a common message area between DL/1 and the application program. This common area has the following structure:

1. The name of the data base as given in the DBD.

2. The level number of the lowest segment type encountered in attempting to satisfy a DL/1 call.

3. The status code indicating the result (successful, unsuccessful) of the DL/1 call. This code can be checked by an application program after every DL/1 call.

4. A code that tells DL/1 the kind of calls that may be used by the program, e.g., get or insert.

5. A reserved area used by DL/1 for its own internal linkage with the application program.

6. The segment name feedback area containing the name of the lowest level segment type encountered when attempting to satisfy a DL/1 call.

7. The current active length, in bytes, of the key feedback area.

8. The number of sensitive segments in the data base.

9. The key feedback area containing the concatenated keys of each segment along the path to the requested segment, i.e., from the root segment down.

The *I/O work area* is an area in the application program where DL/1 is to place the retrieved segment(s) or to take the specified segment(s).

A *segment search argument* (SSA) specifies a qualification over one segment. There may be one SSA for each segment type in the path to a specified segment type. The structure of an SSA is

SEGMENT_NAME COMMAND_CODE (QUALIFICATION)

The SEGMENT_NAME is the name of a segment type in the data base. The COMMAND_CODE is optional and it specifies a variation to the DL/1 call. Some of the more important ones permit retrieval, update, or insertion of some or all of the segments from the root to a specified segment type in a single DL/1 call (path call); backing up to the first child under a segment at any or all levels (except at the root level); retrieving the last occurrence of a segment that meets all specified conditions under a parent; setting the parentage for a Get Next Within Parent call to a segment type other than the one retrieved in the preceding Get Unique or Get Next call.

The QUALIFICATION is a single condition or a Boolean combination of conditions on the fields of one segment type. Each condition is of the form

FIELD_NAME CONDITIONAL_OPERATOR VALUE

All the usual conditional operators, $<$, $\leqslant$, $>$, $\geqslant$, $=$, $\neq$, are allowed. Boolean operators permitted are AND and OR.

The set of SSA's in a command specifies a path from a root segment down a data base record to the desired segment. There may be at most one SSA for every segment type in the path and they must be ordered from highest level to lowest level. However, an SSA is not required for every segment type in the path.

An SSA may be either qualified or unqualified. A qualified SSA consists of a segment name, optional command code, and a qualification. An unqualified SSA consists merely of a segment name and an optional command code. If an SSA does not uniquely identify a segment, then IMS retrieves the next segment, which satisfies the SSA, according to a preorder data base tree traversal, except when modified by command codes.

The DL/1 function codes for data base calls are categorized into three general types: Get calls, Insert calls, and Delete and Replace calls. All calls may optionally include some form of SSA's. Any level for which an SSA is not specified is considered to have an unqualified SSA.

A *Get Unique* (GU) call retrieves a segment, as selected by the SSA's, independent of the current position in the data base. It is used for nonsequential processing or to establish a start position for sequential processing of the data base.

A *Get Next* (GN) call processes in a forward direction only, from the current position in the data base. Segments (optionally of a particular type) are retrieved according to a preorder data base tree traversal. Get Next can be used without SSA's to retrieve the segments in the data base sequentially. It can also be used to search for a particular segment if an SSA is included in the call.

A *Get Next Within Parent* (GNP) call obtains segments within the family of a parent segment. It can be used to obtain a particular segment within the family of the given parent if a qualified SSA is specified. Segments within the family of a given parent segment may also be obtained sequentially if no SSA is specified. The parent segment is established by the last Get Next or Get Unique call or by the COMMAND_CODE option in an SSA of a preceding Get Next or Get Unique call.

A *Get Hold* (GHU, GHN, GHNP) call is used to retrieve and hold a segment for a Delete or Replace call. Any field within the segment except the key field may be changed after the Get Hold call. The Get Hold call prevents other applications from modifying the segment while it is in hold.

An *Insert* (ISRT) call is used to add new segments to a data base. It requires at least one unqualified SSA. Qualified SSA's may be specified for segment types above the level at which insertion is to begin. The SSA's are used to select the position (in the data base record) where the segment is to be inserted.

A *Delete* (DLET) call deletes a segment and all of its descendant segments from the data base. It must be preceded by a Get Hold call. The segment at which deletion is to begin is the highest level retrieved in the Get Hold call. If more than one segment is retrieved in the Get Hold call, then one SSA may specify the level at which deletion is to begin.

A *Replace* (REPL) call updates segments in the data base. It must be preceded by a Get Hold call. Any nonkey field may be changed in the segment. If more than one segment is retrieved in the Get Hold call, then the COMMAND_CODE of SSA's in the Replace call may specify those segments that should not be updated.

11.4 STORAGE ORGANIZATIONS

IMS has two basic storage organizations: hierarchical sequential and hierarchical direct. Within each of these organizations, the access method may optionally use an indexed organization. The indexed organization, in its simplest form, orders the records by a key field value and divided them into blocks. Each block contains a fixed number of records. A directory indicates the highest key value stored in each block. In this manner, the block in which a record is stored can be quickly determined from its key value. For example, in Fig. 11.4—1 to find if 422 is in the file we first scan the index until we find a value greater than 422. We then use the pointer to the right of this value (438 in this case) to locate the appropriate block. The block is then scanned sequentially to find the desired record.

In the hierarchical sequential organization, segments are related by physical adjacency. The *hierarchical sequential access method* (HSAM) organization stores all segments in physically adjacent storage locations in hierarchical (preorder) sequence. Figure 11.4—2 shows two data base records for the hierarchical definition tree of Fig. 10—1 stored in hierarchical sequence. All segments must be of fixed length. To modify a HSAM data base, the entire data base must be reloaded.

The *hierarchical indexed sequential access method* (HISAM) organization is used for indexed access to a data base record. Each data base record is stored in physically contiguous locations in hierarchical sequence. The key field of the root segment is used to index each data base record. The storage area is divided into a primary and an overflow area. The primary area stores, in hierarchical sequence, a fixed size part of a data base record consisting of the root segment and as many segments of the data base record as can be accommodated. Additional

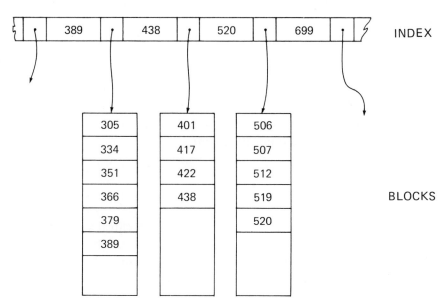

Fig. 11.4—1 Indexed sequential organization.

DEPARTMENT	EMPLOYEE	EMPLOYEE	EMPLOYEE	PART	SUPPLIER	SUPPLIER

PART	SUPPLIER	DEPARTMENT	EMPLOYEE	EMPLOYEE	PART	SUPPLIER

Fig. 11.4–2 HSAM organization.

segments of the data base record are stored, in hierarchical sequence, in the overflow area. A direct address pointer relates a data base record in the primary area with its extension in the overflow area. Figure 11.4–3 shows Fig. 11.4–2 organized according to the HISAM organization.

In the hierarchical direct organization, segments are related by pointers. There are two pointer organizations: hierarchical and physical child/physical twin. Hierarchical pointers relate segments in hierarchical (preorder) sequence as in Fig. 11.4–4a. Physical child/physical twin pointers relate all segments of a given type under a parent segment to

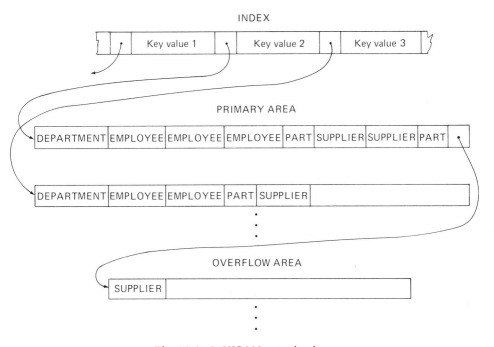

Fig. 11.4–3 HISAM organization.

each other, and the parent to its first child as in Fig. 11.4—4b. Both pointer organizations may optionally have backward pointers. It is possible to specify any combination of pointer organization within a data base and different organizations for different segment types within a data base. Note that both pointer organizations essentially relate segments according to a preorder data base tree traversal.

The pointers in the hierarchical direct organization are stored with each segment. The segment consists of two parts in this case: a prefix

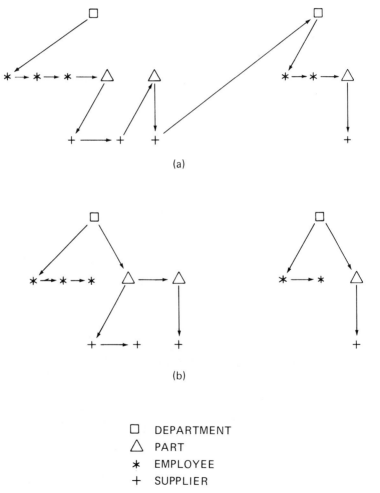

(a)

(b)

□ DEPARTMENT
△ PART
∗ EMPLOYEE
+ SUPPLIER

Fig. 11.4—4 Hierarchical direct pointer organizations. (a) Hierarchical pointers. (b) Physical child/physical twin pointers.

and a data part. The data part contains the segment data as supplied by the user. The prefix, which is system controlled and not available to an application, contains system data and the pointers. The system data consists of a segment code, delete flag, and a counter. The segment code identifies the segment type and the delete flag indicates whether the segment has been deleted. The counter is optional and is only present if the segment type participates in a logical relationship. A simple prefix consisting of the segment code and delete flag is stored with every segment in a multiple segment type HISAM data base.

Within the hierarchical direct organization, the *hierarchical direct access method* (HDAM) organization is used to access root segments via a hash algorithm. Segments are hashed into a primary storage area called the *root segment addressable area*. The hash is performed on the key field of the root segment. A fixed portion of a data base record, including the root segment, is stored in the root segment addressable area. Additional segments of a data base record are stored in an overflow area. A direct address pointer relates segments of a data base record in the root segment addressable area with its extension in the overflow area.

The *hierarchical indexed direct access method* (HIDAM) organization provides indexed direct access to segments in a data base. The index in this organization is a sequential file called INDEX. Each record in the INDEX file contains the key field value of a root segment and a pointer to the root segment in the data base. Root segments are accessed via the INDEX by searching for the key value in the INDEX and then following the pointer to the root segment in the data base. Segments in the data base are related by pointers as discussed previously.

11.5   EXAMPLE APPLICATION

The example application introduced in Chapter 10 is organized according to the hierarchical definition trees shown in Fig. 11.5—1. We first give the schema for the data base using the IMS DDL.

The first set of statements defines the data base containing the EMPLOYEE segment type. The DBD statement names the data base (EMPDB) and specifies the storage organization (HDAM). The DATASET statement names the physical file for the data base (EMPHDAM) and specifies the physical storage device (an IBM 3330

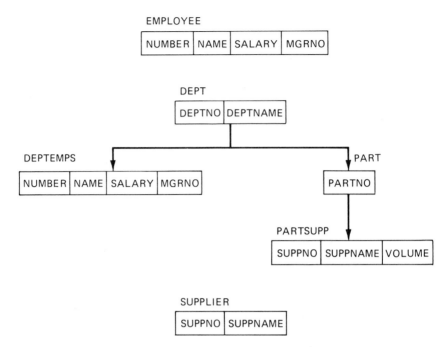

Fig. 11.5–1 Example application hierarchical definition trees.

disk). For the segment type EMPLOYEE we specify its name, total physical length in bytes, and an expected estimate of the number of occurrences of the segment type (FREQ). Finally, for each field we specify its name, physical length in bytes, and where in the segment the field begins, i.e., at which byte. The field NUMBER is specified as a sequence (key) field with unique values. The LCHILD statement specifies that this segment type is to have a logical child DEPTEMPS in the DEPTHDAM data base file.

```
DBD        NAME=EMPDB,ACCESS=HDAM
DATASET    DD1=EMPHDAM,DEVICE=3330

SEGM       NAME=EMPLOYEE,BYTES=54,FREQ=100
LCHILD     NAME=(DEPTEMPS,DEPTHDAM)
FIELD      NAME=(NUMBER,SEQ,U),BYTES=9,START=1
FIELD      NAME=NAME,BYTES=30,START=10
FIELD      NAME=SALARY,BYTES=6,START=40
FIELD      NAME=MGRNO,BYTES=9,START=46
```

```
DBDGEN
FINISH
END
```

Next, the data base containing the SUPPLIER segment type is defined. Its definition is similar to that for the EMPDB data base.

```
DBD        NAME=SUPPDB,ACCESS=HDAM
DATASET    DD1=SUPPHDAM,DEVICE=3330

SEGM       NAME=SUPPLIER,BYTES=35,FREQ=30
LCHILD     NAME=(PARTSUPP,DEPTHDAM)
FIELD      NAME=(SUPPNO,SEQ,U),BYTES=5,START=1
FIELD      NAME=SUPPNAME,BYTES=30,START=6

DBDGEN
FINISH
END
```

Finally, the data base containing the DEPT, DEPTEMPS, PART, and PARTSUPP segment types is defined. For the DEPTEMPS and PARTSUPP segment types a physical and a logical parent is specified (DEPT and EMPLOYEE for DEPTEMPS, and PART and SUPPLIER for PARTSUPP). In addition, the nature of the relationship (unidirectional) is specified by the POINTER option.

```
DBD        NAME=DEPTDB,ACCESS=HDAM
DATASET    DD1=DEPTHDAM,DEVICE=3330

SEGM       NAME=DEPT,BYTES=20,FREQ=15
FIELD      NAME=(DEPTNO,SEQ,U),BYTES=5,START=1
FIELD      NAME=DEPTNAME,BYTES=15,START=6

SEGM       NAME=DEPTEMPS,
           PARENT=( (DEPT,),
           (EMPLOYEE,VIRTUAL,EMPDB) ),
           BYTES=54,FREQ=20,POINTER=(,,LPARNT,,)
FIELD      NAME=(NUMBER,SEQ,U),BYTES=9,START=1
FIELD      NAME=NAME,BYTES=30,START=10
FIELD      NAME=SALARY,BYTES=6,START=40
FIELD      NAME=MGRNO,BYTES=9,START=46

SEGM       NAME=PART,PARENT=DEPT,BYTES=5,FREQ=20
FIELD      NAME=(PARTNO,SEQ,U),BYTES=5,START=1
```

```
SEGM         NAME=PARTSUPP,
             PARENT=( (PART,),
             (SUPPLIER,VIRTUAL,SUPPDB) ),
             BYTES=40,FREQ=5,POINTER=(,,LPARNT,,)
FIELD        NAME=(SUPPNO,SEQ,U),BYTES=5,START=1
FIELD        NAME=SUPPNAME,BYTES=30,START=6
FIELD        NAME=VOLUME,BYTES=5,START=36

DBDGEN
FINISH
END
```

The query that will be implemented requires only the DEPTDB data base. The subschema required is specified by the following PSB, which contains only one PCB. The PCB statement specifies the type of PCB (data base), the name of the associated data base, processing options (retrieval only in this case), the maximum possible length of the key feedback area described in Section 11.3, and the type of positioning (multiple in this case). Each SENSEG statement specifies a segment type accessible from this subschema and its parent. Finally, the PSBGEN statement specifies the host language and names the PSB.

```
PCB          TYPE=DB,DBDNAME=DEPTDB,PROCOPT=G,
             KEYLEN=15,POS=MULTIPLE
SENSEG       NAME=DEPT,PARENT=0
SENSEG       NAME=DEPTEMPS,PARENT=DEPT
SENSEG       NAME=PART,PARENT=DEPT
SENSEG       NAME=PARTSUPP,PARENT=PART
PSBGEN       LANG=PL/I,PSBNAME=QUERY
END
```

The query that will be implemented is, "Find the names of all employees who work for a department that is supplied parts by the company with supplier number X." The host language that will be used is PL/1. The first part of the program concerns various declarations that are needed for IMS to interface with PL/1. First, a skeleton for a storage area (PCB) must be defined. This area is used as a communications buffer between IMS and PL/1. It contains information (status code, key feedback area, etc.) needed to control the flow of execution in an application program. I/O buffers must also be declared. IMS places the data retrieved in these buffers and expects to find the new or updated data in these buffers. Finally, the SSA's must be declared if they will be used in the program. The variable QUERY_PCB is a pointer to the communications area used by IMS to communicate with the application program.

```
DLITPLI:PROCEDURE(QUERY_PCB) OPTIONS(MAIN);
   DECLARE PLITDLI ENTRY, QUERY_PCB POINTER;

/*  This is the PCB mask for the query */

DECLARE 1 PCB BASED (QUERY_PCB),
           2   DATA_BASE_NAME CHAR (8),
           2   SEGMENT_LEVEL CHAR (2),
           2   STATUS_CODE CHAR (2),
           2   PROCESSING_OPTIONS CHAR (4),
           2   RESERVED_FOR_DLI
               FIXED BINARY (31,0),
           2   SEMENT_NAME_FEEDBACK CHAR (8),
           2   LENGTH_OF_KEY_FEEDBACK_AREA
               FIXED BINARY (31,0),
           2   NUMBER_OF_SENSITIVE_SEGMENTS
               FIXED BINARY (31,0),
           2   KEY_FEEDBACK_AREA CHAR (15);

/*  The following are the three I/O areas needed for the query*/

DECLARE DEPT_IO_AREA CHAR (20),
       1   DEPARTMENT DEFINED DEPT_IO_AREA,
           2   NUMBER CHAR (5),
           2   NAME CHAR (15);

DECLARE EMPLOYEE_IO_AREA CHAR (54),
       1   EMPLOYEE DEFINED EMPLOYEE_IO_AREA,
           2   NUMBER CHAR (9),
           2   NAME CHAR (30),
           2   SALARY CHAR (6),
           2   MANAGER_NO CHAR (9);

DECLARE SUPPLIER_IO_AREA CHAR (40),
       1   SUPPLIER DEFINED SUPPLIER_IO_AREA,
           2   NUMBER CHAR (5),
           2   NAME CHAR (30),
           2   VOLUME CHAR (5);

/*  The following are the segment search arguments needed for
    the query                                           */
```

```
DECLARE 1 DEPT_SSA STATIC UNALIGNED,
           2   SEGMENT_NAME CHAR (8)
               INIT ('DEPT    '),
           2   LEFT_PARENTHESIS CHAR (1)
               INIT ('('),
           2   KEY_FIELD_NAME CHAR (8)
               INIT ('DEPTNO  '),
           2   CONDITIONAL_OPERATOR CHAR (2)
               INIT (' >'),
           2   SEARCH_VALUE CHAR (5) INIT ('     '),
           2   RIGHT_PARENTHESIS CHAR (1)
               INIT (')');

DECLARE 1 EMPLOYEE_SSA STATIC UNALIGNED,
           2   SEGMENT_NAME CHAR (8)
               INIT ('DEPTEMPS');

DECLARE 1 SUPPLIER_SSA STATIC UNALIGNED,
           2   SEGMENT_NAME CHAR (8)
               INIT ('PARTSUPP'),
           2   LEFT_PARENTHESIS CHAR (1) INIT ('('),
           2   KEY_FIELD_NAME CHAR (8)
               INIT ('SUPPNO  '),
           2   CONDITIONAL_OPERATOR CHAR (2)
               INIT (' ='),
           2   SEARCH_VALUE CHAR (5) INIT ('     '),
           2   RIGHT_PARENTHESIS CHAR (1)
               INIT (')');

/*  Finally, some necessary variables are declared */

DECLARE GU CHAR (4) INIT ('GU  '),
        GN CHAR (4) INIT ('GN  '),
        GNP CHAR (4) INIT ('GNP '),
        FOUR FIXED BINARY (31) INIT (4),
        SUCCESSFUL CHAR (2) INIT ('  '),
        SEGMENT_NOT_FOUND CHAR (2) INIT ('GE'),
        END_OF_DATA_BASE CHAR (2) INIT ('GB'),
        ABORT BIT (1) INIT ('1'B),
        PROCEED BIT (1) INIT ('0'B);

/*  The ERROR procedure handles IMS error conditions */
```

ERROR: PROCEDURE (ERROR_CODE);

.

.

.

END ERROR;

The various steps in the algorithm are:

1. Get each DEPT segment in turn (main procedure).
2. For each DEPT segment, determine if supplier number X supplies the department (CHECK_FOR_SUPPLIER procedure).
3. If supplier number X supplies this department then get all the employees for the department and print their names (PRINT_EMPLOYEES procedure); else go to step 1.

Calls to DL/1 are characterized by the starting sequence CALL PLITDLI. These calls may take a varying number of parameters, but in this example all calls require five parameters. The first parameter (FOUR) indicates the number of parameters to follow. The second parameter indicates the type of call (GU, GN, or GNP). The third parameter is a pointer to the PCB for the call. The fourth parameter specifies the address of the I/O area to be used. Finally, the last parameter specifies the SSA to be used.

After each call to DL/1, the STATUS_CODE entry in the PCB is checked to determine if an error or exceptional condition occurred. If an error occurred, then the ERROR procedure is called and processing terminated. Exceptional conditions that may arise are no more segments under a parent in a GNP call, no segment qualifies, or no more segments of specified type in the data base. These conditions are not errors, but are situations of which the program must be informed to properly control data base processing as in the following program.

```
/*  The PRINT_EMPLOYEES procedure retrieves all EM-
    PLOYEE segments under a department and prints their names*/

PRINT_EMPLOYEES:PROCEDURE RETURNS (BIT);
    /*  Get the first EMPLOYEE segment */
    CALL PLITDLI (FOUR,GNP,QUERY_PCB,
    EMPLOYEE_IO_AREA, EMPLOYEE_SSA);
    /*  Check if there are any employees */
```

```
IF PCB.STATUS_CODE=SEGMENT_NOT_FOUND
    THEN DO;
        PUT SKIP EDIT ('NO EMPLOYEES FOR THIS
        DEPARTMENT') (A);
        RETURN (PROCEED);
        END;
/*  Print the employee name and retrieve all department
employees */
DO WHILE (PCB.STATUS_CODE=SUCCESSFUL);
    PUT EDIT (EMPLOYEE.NAME) (X(10),A);
    CALL PLITDLI (FOUR,GNP,QUERY_PCB,
    EMPLOYEE_IO_AREA, EMPLOYEE_SSA);
END;
    /*  Check for error */
    IF PCB.STATUS_CODE=SEGMENT_NOT_FOUND
        THEN RETURN (PROCEED);
        ELSE DO;
            CALL ERROR (PCB.STATUS_CODE);
            RETURN (ABORT);
            END;
END PRINT_EMPLOYEES;

/*  The CHECK_FOR_SUPPLIER procedure determines if a
supplier with supplier number X supplies a department     */

CHECK_FOR_SUPPLIER:PROCEDURE RETURNS (BIT);
    /*  Check if the supplier supplies this department */
    CALL PLITDLI (FOUR,GNP,QUERY_PCB,
    SUPPLIER_IO_AREA, SUPPLIER_SSA);
    IF PCB.STATUS_CODE=SUCCESSFUL
        THEN DO;
            PUT SKIP EDIT ('DEPARTMENT',
            DEPARTMENT.NAME) (A,A);
            RETURN (PRINT_EMPLOYEES);
            END;
    /*  Check for error */
    IF PCB.STATUS_CODE=SEGMENT_NOT_FOUND
        THEN RETURN (PROCEED);
        ELSE DO;
            CALL ERROR (PCB.STATUS_CODE);
            RETURN (ABORT);
            END;
```

```
END CHECK_FOR_SUPPLIER;

/*  Begin main procedure by setting the search value for the
    SUPPLIER SSA                                              */
GET EDIT (SUPPLIER_SSA.SEARCH_VALUE) (A(5) );
/*  Set the search value for the DEPARTMENT SSA  */
DEPT_SSA.SEARCH_VALUE=LOW (5);
/*  Get the first DEPARTMENT segment */
CALL PLITDLI (FOUR,GU,QUERY_PCB,DEPT_IO_AREA,
DEPT_SSA);
/*  Loop processing all departments */
DO WHILE (PCB.STATUS_CODE=SUCCESSFUL);
        /*  Check if this department is supplied by a supplier with
            supplier# equal to X                                  */
        IF CHECK_FOR_SUPPLIER
            THEN RETURN;
        /*  Get the next DEPARTMENT segment */
        CALL PLITDLI (FOUR,GN,QUERY_PCB,DEPT_IO_AREA,
        DEPT_SSA.SEGMENT_NAME);
END;
/*  Check for error */
IF PCB.STATUS_CODE-=END_OF_DATA_BASE
    THEN CALL ERROR (PCB.STATUS_CODE);
END DLITPLI;
```

It should be noted that in this query, by the use of multiple positioning, it is possible to process two segment types (DEPTEMPS and PARTSUPP) under the same parent (DEPT) without the need for repositioning a data base position pointer.

11.6 CONCLUDING REMARKS

IMS is a data base management and data base communication system designed to operate on the IBM System 360/370 machines. The system consists of two separate packages. One is the data base facility, which is a batch data base management system. The other is the data base/data communications facility, which is essentially the data base facility with teleprocessing capabilities. Only the data base facility was described in this chapter.

IMS was designed to handle the general problem of avoiding redundancy when storing large amounts of data. Toward this end, IMS provides a great deal of flexibility in the definition of logical relationships between physical data bases. It is also possible to specify many different combinations of pointer relationships between segments. In this way, an almost networklike structure can be defined, although the interface is always hierarchical.

The implementation of the preceding query is quite complex. The complexity arises for two reasons. First, several communication buffers are necessary to permit IMS to interface with PL/1. These buffers must be explicitly declared by the user. Second, the DML of IMS is a very procedural one-record-at-a-time data language. In addition, retrieval must be according to a preorder data base tree traversal. The low-level commands are helpful at times, but the program can become quite involved when performing complex applications. DL/1 is also somewhat oriented to the storage organization of the data base. For example, in HISAM and HIDAM structured data bases, the data base records are ordered by the key field of the root segment. DL/1 makes use of this ordering when storing and retrieving segments and applications also implicitly use this ordering. In the next chapter, the same data base and query will be implemented using a set-oriented, high-level hierarchical data language.

In general, however, IMS provides a good set of facilities for defining, creating, manipulating, and maintaining hierarchical data bases. In addition, IMS provides numerous utilities for the DBA to organize and administer a data base.

Chapter 12

MRI SYSTEM 2000

12.1 DATA MODEL

SYSTEM 2000 is a product of MRI Systems Corporation of Austin, Texas [Datapro, 1972a; MRI, 1972; Evans, 1973c]. It uses the hierarchical data model. The smallest unit of logical data is called a *data element* (data item). A *repeating group* (record type) is a named collection of data elements. Occurrences of repeating groups are called *data sets* (records). A *logical entry* (data base tree) is a root data set and all of its descendants.

12.2 DATA DEFINITION FACILITY

The SYSTEM 2000 data definition language closely resembles that of COBOL file definition. A data base definition consists of entries called *components*. A *component* consists of a component number, a name, and some description of the component. A component may be either a data element, repeating group, string, or function definition.

The definition of a data element consists of specifying a unique name for the data element within the hierarchical definition tree, a data type, the repeating group it is a part of, and some options. SYSTEM 2000 supports six types of data: name, text, integer, decimal, date, and money. The options available in a data element definition are key, picture, and padding.

A data element may be either a key or a nonkey. The default is key. Note that the term key is not used here to mean a unique identifier. A key data element is one that is indexed. One or more data elements in a data base may be specified as key. The data element's associated repeating group occurrences can then be accessed directly without going through related repeating groups. The major part of data selection takes place by means of key data elements before any data element values in the data base are accessed. The degree of indexing is controlled by the DBA by means of the key option.

Nominal lengths for most data elements may be specified using the picture option. The user may design for the most likely character length and not pay the penalty for the worst case. Overflow of specified lengths is permitted for name and text data types. Decimal points can be positioned on printed output for decimal and money data types. Date data types require no picture specification. Money data types are automatically edited on output in standard COBOL money format.

The padding option reserves contiguous space for future additions to key data elements. It is useful for data elements that will have many multiple occurrences of the same data element value.

A repeating group definition merely consists of a unique name and the keywords REPEATING GROUP or RG. For a repeating group at a hierarchical level greater than two, the component number of the parent repeating group must also be specified.

A string definition is essentially a macro definition. During data base processing, the string can be invoked by specifying the label identifier of the string and possibly some parameters, e.g., data element values. A string can be nested within another string and can also address values located in other strings. For example, consider the definitions:

    10*   PURCHASES (REPEATING GROUP):
           11*ITEM (NAME IN 10):
           12*AMOUNT (MONEY IN 10):

    500*   ST1 (STRING/ADD PURCHASES EQ 11**1**
           12**2**END* WHERE CUSTOMER NAME EQ *3*
           AND CHARGE PLATE NUMBER EQ *4*:/:)

The component 500 defines a string called ST1. The request

    ST1 (FUR COAT,875.00,JACKSON A L,456-8944-2)

is equivalent to the update

<u>ADD</u> PURCHASES <u>EQ</u> 11* FUR COAT* 12* 875.00* END*
<u>WHERE</u> CUSTOMER NAME <u>EQ</u> JACKSON A L <u>AND</u>
CHARGE PLATE NUMBER <u>EQ</u> 456-8944-2:

Each data base consists of several files containing the data base definitions, inverted files, and the actual data. After the data base definition is loaded, these files are constructed in preparation for data base loading. For data base loading using the Natural Language feature, which is an English-like query language, SYSTEM 2000 requires the data base values to be laid out in a value string, with component numbers associated with each data element value. This enables data to be loaded from either a terminal or through batch input streams. The system scans the data, performs error checking, constructs the directories for the indexed values' file, and creates the data and tree structure files. Data may also be loaded using the Procedural Language Interface (see Section 12.3). Data formatting is not required with this method. The descriptions of the various files generated for a data base are shown in Table 12.2–1.

Table 12.2–1 SYSTEM 2000 Data Base Files

File	Description
Definition	The definition file contains the data base name, component names, component descriptions, function, and string definitions, etc.
Unique value	The unique value file stores the unique values for each key data element in the data base definition
Overflow	The overflow file contains all the overflow from the definition, unique values, and data files
Multiple occurrences	The multiple occurrences file contains pointers for the multiple occurrences of the unique values of each key data element
Hierarchical	The hierarchical file maintains the hierarchical definition tree structure and data set relationships
Data	The data file stores the contents of each data set in accordance with their defined picture size

12.3 DATA MANIPULATION FACILITY

SYSTEM 2000's data manipulation facility offers a variety of update and retrieval commands. There are four different qualification constructs that can be used in the DMF commands to specify which data elements are to be manipulated.

A <u>WHERE</u> <u>clause</u> specifies one condition or a Boolean combination of conditions. All data elements can be used in WHERE clauses with conditional operators such as EQ, NE, GT, GE, LT, LE, SPANS, FAILS, and EXISTS. Conditions may be combined with Boolean operators AND, OR, and NOT. Parentheses may also be used to nest the conditions. Examples of WHERE clauses are

<u>WHERE</u> AGE <u>EQ</u> 35 <u>AND</u> SALARY <u>GT</u> 20000:

<u>WHERE</u> BIRTH DATE <u>SPANS</u> 06/01/1927*12/31/41:

<u>WHERE</u> DATE RETURNED <u>FAILS</u>:

<u>WHERE</u> UNION MEMBERSHIP <u>EXISTS</u> <u>AND</u> AMOUNTDUE
    <u>SPANS</u> 0.00*5.00:

The <u>HAS</u>, <u>HAVE</u>, or <u>HAVING</u> feature allows data on one hierarchical level to be qualified on properties that data on any level below it may possess. For example, suppose that a STUDENT repeating group is an ancestor of a SUBJECT repeating group. The query

<u>PRINT</u> STUDENT NAME <u>WHERE</u> STUDENT <u>HAS</u> SUBJECT <u>EQ</u>
    MATH <u>AND</u> STUDENT <u>HAS</u> SUBJECT <u>EQ</u> SCIENCE:

will print a student's name only if he has two SUBJECT data sets, one for math and one for science. The query

<u>PRINT</u> STUDENT NAME <u>WHERE</u> SUBJECT <u>EQ</u> MATH <u>AND</u>
    SUBJECT <u>EQ</u> SCIENCE:

has an empty answer since there is no one subject called math and science (see also Section 5.2.2).

An <u>IF</u> <u>clause</u> also allows data elements to be specified in a qualification. The basic format is

<u>IF</u> conditions <u>THEN</u> operation (<u>ELSE</u> operation) <u>WHERE</u> clause

The additional qualification criterion stated in the IF clause operates only on those data sets selected by the WHERE clause. The qualification in the IF clause may use both key and nonkey data elements.

Qualification may be based on the relative logical position of the data in the data base. Keywords such as LAST and FIRST may be used to specify position so that the most recent or the oldest values that have been entered for a repeating group's data element may be retrieved, regardless of the data element's logical content. For example,

LIST SALARY WHERE SALARY EXISTS AT 0:

lists the most recent salary value entered.

SYSTEM 2000 provides the following DMF commands and options.

The PRINT command produces formatted, adjusted, and translated values for a single data element, a series of data elements, a repeating group, a repeating group and all its logical descendants, or an entire logical entry. The data elements printed are labeled with their associated component numbers. A qualification selects the appropriate repeating group. For example,

PRINT INSTRUCTOR NAME WHERE INSTRUCTOR HAS
    COURSE EQ 2510 AND INSTRUCTOR HAS COURSE EQ
    2204:

produces output in the format:

2*D. TSICHRITZIS

where 2 is the component number for INSTRUCTOR NAME. A variety of format options are provided.

The LIST command produces output in column format with user specified or default column headings.

The UNLOAD command produces values in a format suitable for subsequent reading by the LOAD command or the *DATA* option.

A retrieval command may specify that the output is to be ordered. The values may be sorted in ascending or descending order on the values of the data elements. Standard statistical functions such as COUNT, SUM, AVERAGE, MAXIMUM, and SIGMA, as well as user-defined functions may also be used. Functions may be defined in-line in the PRINT or LIST commands.

A data base is loaded with the LOAD command. The data are scanned for illegal data element values. All data satisfying the check are loaded. The total size of the data base is reported to the user.

The INSERT and APPEND commands are used for data insertion once the data base has been established.

The ADD, ASSIGN, and CHANGE commands are used to modify data element values. Data element values may be modified using algebraically calculated values, e.g., by user-defined functions.

The REMOVE command removes data element values from a repeating group. The effect is to set the data element value to null. The associated repeating group is not deleted. The REMOVE TREE command removes subtrees from a logical entry. The effect is to delete a repeating group and all of its descendants.

The appropriate data elements for modification commands are selected by a WHERE clause. In addition, INSERT commands may include an optional BEFORE/AFTER clause. This option may be used instead of a WHERE clause so that the insertion is performed logically before or after the data sets selected by the BEFORE/AFTER clause.

In addition, SYSTEM 2000 has the following two capabilities. The *DATA* keyword may be used anywhere a literal value is needed and causes the required data value to be read from a prespecified "data" file. The REPEAT command causes iterative processing until the end of a data file is reached.

SYSTEM 2000 offers four facilities by which retrieval and modification may take place. The *basic access module* is oriented toward high-volume data base maintenance and interrogation. It is suited to processing in batch and remote batch environments. The requests are organized into job queues. No processing occurs until all commands are scanned and arranged into access-processing sequence. To enhance efficiency, selection is done first against key data elements. Pointers to the selected data sets are sorted so that processing operations can take place against a single pass of the relevant portions of the data base. The commands that may be used in the basic access module are PRINT, UNLOAD, LOAD, APPEND, ADD, ASSIGN, CHANGE, REMOVE, REMOVE TREE, and REPEAT. The options allowed are WHERE clause, IF clause, and *DATA*.

The *immediate access module* is an optional feature that is oriented toward interactive use. It is designed for conversational "browsing" and for processing small batches of individual transactions. Unlike the basic access module, each command is processed individually and completely before the next command. The results of the immediately preceding WHERE clause processing may be reused with the SAME operator. In this case, WHERE clause results may be saved and do not need to be reprocessed. The commands available in this module include: PRINT, LIST, UNLOAD, INSERT, ADD, ASSIGN, CHANGE, REMOVE, and REMOVE TREE. A report on the number of data sets affected by a modification is printed. Options include the WHERE clause, SAME operator, and BEFORE/AFTER clause.

The *report writer* is an optional feature that enables a user to prepare report specifications according to a set of report-formatting conventions. Other capabilities permit the user to specify formats for data elements and accumulate subtotals and totals. The user can produce up to one hundred reports with one pass of the data base.

The *procedural language interface* is an optional feature. It provides the mechanism for accessing a data base from a program written in COBOL, FORTRAN, PL/1, or an Assembler Language. The program can retrieve data in a sequence and format suitable for processing by the host language, and update the data base. Interrelationships of two or more data bases can be established. This facility permits network data structures to be defined. The host language program is first passed through a SYSTEM 2000 precompiler, where SYSTEM 2000 commands are converted to appropriate calls to the procedural language interface. During execution, any request to access the data base must pass through the procedural language interface and then through SYSTEM 2000, which accesses the appropriate portion of the data base.

12.4 EXAMPLE APPLICATION

The example application introduced in Chapter 10 will be defined in terms of SYSTEM 2000's DDL. The data base contains information about a small company that is divided into departments. Each department may have a number of employees and use various parts, each of which may be supplied by several suppliers. The schema consists of two data bases—DEPARTMENT and SUPPLIER—as follows:

DATA BASE NAME IS DEPARTMENT:

```
1* DEPARTMENT # (NAME X(3) ):
2* DEPARTMENT NAME (NON-KEY NAME X(20) ):
3* EMPLOYEE (REPEATING GROUP):
    4* NUMBER (NAME X(4) IN 3):
    5* NAME (NON-KEY NAME X(25) IN 3):
    6* SALARY (NON-KEY MONEY 9(5).9(2) IN 3):
    7* MANAGER # (NAME X(4) IN 3):
8* PART USED (RG):
    9* PART# (NAME X(4) IN 8):
    10* PART SUPPLIER (RG IN 8):
```

11* SUPPLIER # (NAME X(4) IN 10):
12* SUPPLIER VOLUME (INTEGER 9(7) IN 10):

DATA BASE NAME IS SUPPLIER:

1* SUPPLIER NUMBER (NAME X(4)):
2* SUPPLIER NAME (NON-KEY NAME X(20)):

The query that will be implemented is, "Find the names of all employees who work for a department that is supplied parts by the company with supplier number X." Using SYSTEM 2000's Natural Language feature, the query is stated as

LIST NAME WHERE DEPARTMENT HAS SUPPLIER # EQ X:

12.5 CONCLUDING REMARKS

The reader should compare the implementation of the preceding query with the implementation in Chapter 11. Whereas the implementation in Chapter 11 required a tremendous amount of code, the preceding implementation required a single line. The major difference between the two implementations is the high-level query language of SYSTEM 2000 and its set-oriented nature. The user merely has to specify what is wanted and not how to get it as in IMS. In SYSTEM 2000 the DBMS uses the tree structure to select the data implicitly. In IMS the user must explicitly traverse the tree structure to select the data.

SYSTEM 2000 is implemented for IBM System 360/370, Univac 1100, CDC 6000, and CYBER 70 series computers. It provides a report writer, a query language with on-line or batch access, a procedural language interface, and sequential file processing. A teleprocessing monitor and a multiple-thread feature are also available. The teleprocessing monitor feature enables a user to use all of the system capabilities from a remote terminal. An extended version provides CRT "roll" and "scroll" scanning capabilities for conveniently displaying pages. The multiple-thread feature is used with teleprocessing to queue message traffic where the concurrent processing requirements exceed the message handling and processing speed of the system.

SYSTEM 2000 also provides many utilities that are useful to the DBA for data base maintenance and administration. Audit trail facilities preserve a machine-readable file of update transactions. This file can be used for backup when used in conjunction with an archival file. Periodic dumps are used to purge the audit trail file and update the backup copy. Security provisions employ passwords to give read and/or write access to selected users at the system, data base, command, or component levels. Security can also be provided at remote terminals through the use of terminal identification or passwords. Component level security enables the DBA to offer three types of access: retrieval, qualification, or update. Qualification access means that a user may specify a qualification involving a data element, but he may not retrieve or modify the data element unless he also has the associated permission. In addition, SYSTEM 2000 offers many optimization options and debugging aids. In general, it offers a good environment for either batch or on-line applications.

Chapter 13

INTEGRATED DATABASE
MANAGEMENT SYSTEM (IDMS)

13.1 DATA MODEL

Integrated Database Management System (IDMS) is marketed by the Cullinane Corporation [Cullinane, 1975]. It uses the DBTG network data model. The terminology used is similar to that of the DBTG proposal. A *data-item* (data item) is the smallest unit of named data. A *record type* is a named collection of data-items. Occurrences of record types are called *records*. A *set type* (DBTG set) is a named collection of record types consisting of one *owner* record type and one or more *member* record types. An occurrence of a set type is called a *set occurrence* and consists of one occurrence of the declared owner and zero or more occurrences of the designated members.

An *area* is a named logical subdivision of a data base composed of logical pages containing occurrences of record types. A *file* is a part of the secondary storage known to the operating system. It may contain one area, part of an area, or several areas. Each file is composed of physical blocks of secondary storage. Logical pages in an area are mapped to physical blocks in a file in a one-to-one correspondence. A *database-key* is a unique, permanent identifier assigned to a record occurrence. In IDMS, a database-key consists of a page number and a logical line number within the page.

A *database* consists of all occurrences of areas, records, and sets specified in one schema. A *schema* is a description of an entire data

300

base. A *subschema* is a description of part of a schema that is known to one or more application programs.

13.2 DATA DEFINITION FACILITY

The IDMS DDL is a COBOL-like language that describes a schema and its subschemas. Application programs only use subschemas when accessing the data base. A schema and its subschema descriptions are stored in a data dictionary for use by the DBMS.

The definition of a schema consists of five statement groupings: schema description, file description, area description, record description, and set description. The statements must appear according to the preceding order, and there is at most one grouping of each type.

The schema description statements name a schema and optionally specify the author, the date of creation, the installation, and any remarks.

The file description statements assign the files specified to physical datasets and optionally specify the type of storage medium for each file. A minimum of two files must be specified: one file is needed for the data base journal, and at least one file is needed for the data base. However, a data base may be stored on several physical files.

The area description statements name all areas, specify a range of logical pages for each area and a mapping of logical pages to physical blocks, within one or more files. The number of pages assigned to an area determines a size for the area. Whenever an area becomes full and requires more space, the entire area must be dumped, reallocated, and loaded again.

The record description statements specify the record types in a schema, their mode of storage, the area they are to be placed in, and their content. The description of a record type consists of specifying a record name, record id, location mode, area, and at least one data-item. The record name names the record type. The record id is an integer that numerically identifies a record type.

The location mode of a record type indicates how occurrences of the record type are to be stored and therefore how they may be retrieved. IDMS supports three location modes: DIRECT, CALC, and VIA. The DIRECT location mode is used to control the placement of a record in a specific page of an area. The user tells IDMS to assign a record a suggested database-key and IDMS attempts to assign the record the database-key if possible. The CALC location mode uses an IDMS supplied hashing function to assign a record a storage location within an area. The hash is performed on a specified data-item of the record type. The handling of duplicate CALC values must also be specified, i.e., first, last, or not allowed. The VIA location mode places records close to other member records in a specified set type. The distance (number of pages) of the member records from the owner record in a set occurrence can also be specified.

The description of a data-item consists of specifying a name and optionally a type for the data-item. IDMS allows character, binary, decimal, and floating-point data-items. The general format of the data-item is specified by a picture specification. An initial value may optionally be assigned to a data-item. Finally, a data-item may be a repeating group occurring a fixed or variable number of times.

The set description statements define the relationships between the record types in the schema. A set type is described by specifying a set name, set order, set mode, set membership, and the owner and member record types. The set name names the set type. The set order is the logical order in which member records should be placed in a set occurrence of the set type. The order first or last indicates that a new member record should become, respectively, the first or last member record in a set occurrence. The order next or prior means that a new member record should be inserted, respectively, immediately after or before the record pointed at by the set pointer for the set type. Finally, the order sorted means that a new member record is to be inserted in a set occurrence at a point where the order (ascending or descending), according to a data-item value, would be maintained. In this case, the manner in which duplicate values are to be handled (first, last, or not allowed) must also be specified.

IDMS only allows the chain set mode. A next pointer is always maintained for a set type. However, the user may optionally specify that a prior and/or an owner pointer also be maintained. Since IDMS stores the next, prior, and owner pointers with a record, and since a record type may be an owner and/or member in many set types, the user must also specify the relative position of each pointer in the pointer list associated with a record. Set membership is mandatory-automatic, optional-automatic, mandatory-manual, or optional-manual.

The definition of a subschema describes those parts of a schema required by one or more application programs. All or part of a schema may be described. However, before a subschema can be defined, at least one device media control language (DMCL) module must be defined. The DMCL module specifies some of the operational characteristics of schema and subschema use such as mapping of logical pages to physical blocks, buffer storage, and areas that are to be made available via the module.

The definition of a subschema consists of two parts: a subschema identification division and a subschema data division. The identification division names the subschema and the schema of which it is a part, and specifies the DMCL module to be used by applications invoking the subschema. The data division specifies the areas, record types, and set types to be made available in the subschema. For a record type, either the entire record type or only certain data-items of the record type can be included in the subschema. For each area, record type, and set type, privacy locks may optionally be specified for operations on the area, record type, or set type. Each operation can either be permitted (YES) or disallowed (NO).

All schemas, subschemas, and DMCL modules are stored in an IDMS base dictionary network (BDN). The BDN is used for control and documentation of an IDMS data base. There may be at most one schema in a BDN, but several subschemas and DMCL modules are allowed. The BDN is also used to monitor the use of all subschemas and to record who uses a subschema and the date of last access. IDMS provides various utilities for collecting and printing information from the BDN.

13.3 DATA MANIPULATION FACILITY

IDMS is a host data language DBMS. It may be used with any host language that supports a CALL macro statement, or equivalent. Processors for use with COBOL or PL/1 are available and allow access to a data base as a direct procedural extension to these two languages. This section will describe the IDMS COBOL DML, but similar facilities can be provided for any host language.

Every application program (run-unit) has associated with it one user working area (UWA), one set of system communication locations, and one set of currency status indicators. The UWA is a location in working storage where all data are placed and taken by the DBMS. There is one location in the UWA for every data-item in the subschema invoked by an application program. The data-item values in the UWA can be accessed and used like any other COBOL variables. The system communication locations are used by the DBMS to pass control and status information to an application program. Table 13.3–1 summarizes the

Table 13.3—1 System Status Information

Location	Contents
PROGRAM-NAME	The name of the application program
ERROR-STATUS	Indicates the outcome of the last DML statement
DBKEY	The database-key of the last record accessed
RECORD-NAME	The name of the record type last accessed
AREA-NAME	The name of the area last accessed
ERROR-SET	The name of the set type encountered during an operation that produced an error
ERROR-RECORD	The name of the record type encountered during an operation that produced an error
ERROR-AREA	The name of the area encountered during an operation that produced an error
DIRECT-DBK	Database data name field for location mode direct

system communication locations and their contents. There is one currency indicator for the application program, each record type, each set type, and each area in the subschema. IDMS currency indicators are the database-keys of the appropriate record occurrences. All relevant currency indicators are updated implicitly on the successful completion of a retrieval statement or modification statement. The currency indicators are associated with an application at execution time, but are not part of the application's storage.

IDMS DML statements fall into three categories: control, retrieval, and modification. Control statements are used to control processing within a data base as defined by a subschema. Retrieval statements are used to locate data in a data base and to make it available to an application program. Modification statements are used to change data or data relationships within a data base.

IDMS DML has four control statements: <u>INVOKE</u>, <u>OPEN</u>, <u>CLOSE</u>, and <u>IF</u>. Before any processing can be performed on a data base, a subschema must be invoked with the <u>INVOKE</u> statement and all areas that will be accessed must be opened with the <u>OPEN</u> statement. The <u>INVOKE</u> statement specifies a subschema for the program and reserves space for the UWA and system communication locations. The <u>OPEN</u> statement is used to open all or specified areas and to state the type of access desired. Each area may be opened in one of six usage modes: retrieval, update, protected retrieval, protected update, exclusive retrieval, or exclusive update. Retrieval and update usage modes permit other applications to open an area in any usage mode except exclusive.

Protected retrieval and protected update usage modes prevent the area from being updated concurrently, but allow concurrent retrieval. Exclusive retrieval and exclusive update usage modes prevent another application from opening an area in any usage mode. All areas that are open are closed at one time with the CLOSE statement. The IF statement is used to test if a set occurrence is (is not) empty, or if a record is (is not) a member in a set occurrence of a set type.

IDMS DML has three retrieval statements: MOVE, GET, and FIND/OBTAIN. The MOVE statement is used to move the currency indicator for the application (run-unit), a record type, a set type, or an area to a user-specified location in working storage. In this way, the database-key for the current record of the application, a record type, a set type, or an area can be saved for later use. The GET statement is used to transfer all data-items of the current record of an application to the UWA.

The FIND/OBTAIN statement is used to locate a record occurrence and make it the current record of the application, area, record type, and all set types in which it participates as an owner or a member record. The record occurrence may optionally be moved to the UWA with the OBTAIN form of the FIND statement. There are six formats of the FIND/OBTAIN statement: two to find a record independent of set types, one to reset currency indicators, and three to navigate according to set types. Each format will be described separately and only the FIND form discussed since OBTAIN is a combination of FIND and GET. Keywords that are required are underlined. All other notation is according to the DBTG report.

Direct-Access Form

FIND record-name RECORD USING identifier.

A record occurrence is located based on the value of its database-key. The variable identifier is a program variable containing a database-key.

FIND [NEXT DUPLICATE] record-name RECORD.

A record occurrence is located based on a CALC data-item. The location mode of the record-name record type must be specified as CALC in the schema. The user must initialize the CALC data-item value. If the NEXT DUPLICATE option is specified, then the next duplicate record must be the next duplicate for the current record of the application. In addition, a previous record with the same CALC value for the CALC data-item must be in the UWA.

Reset Currency Form

$$\text{\underline{FIND} \underline{CURRENT} OF} \begin{cases} \text{record-name \underline{RECORD}} \\ \text{set-name \underline{SET}} \\ \text{area-name \underline{AREA}} \\ \text{\underline{RUN-UNIT}} \end{cases}$$

A record occurrence is located and made the current record of the application, record type, area, and all set types in which it participates as an owner or a member record. This format is used, for example, to make a record that was previously located the current of the application, etc.

Set Navigation Form

$$\text{\underline{FIND}} \begin{cases} \text{\underline{NEXT}} \\ \text{\underline{PRIOR}} \\ \text{\underline{FIRST}} \\ \text{\underline{LAST}} \\ \text{integer} \end{cases} \text{[record-name] RECORD OF} \begin{cases} \text{set-name \underline{SET}} \\ \text{area-name \underline{AREA}} \end{cases}$$

A record occurrence that is the next, prior, first or last record occurrence of the named set type, or area is located. Optionally, a record of a specific type may be located. For a set type, the next, prior, first, or last record relative to the set order specified for the set type in the schema is located. For an area, the next prior, first, or last record according to database-key values is located.

FIND OWNER RECORD OF set-name SET.

The owner record of the current occurrence of the named set type is located.

FIND record-name RECORD VIA [CURRENT OF] set-name SET
    USING identifier.

This format of the FIND statement can only be used to locate a record occurrence that participates as a member in a set type for which the set order is specified as sorted in the schema. The identifier is the name of the data-item according to which the set type is ordered. The value of identifier specifies the value that the located record should have for the data-item represented by identifier. If no record has this value for the data-item, then the record occurrence with the next higher data-item value is located. The current occurrence of the named set is searched. If the CURRENT OF option is specified, then the search begins at the current record of the set occurrence as specified by the set type currency indicator. Otherwise, the search begins at the owner record. The search is always in the next direction.

IDMS DML has five modification statements: STORE, DELETE, MODIFY, INSERT, and REMOVE. The STORE statement is used to place a new record into the data base from the UWA. The new record is inserted into all set types for which its set membership is automatic. The set occurrences must be selected by the application prior to the STORE statement using appropriate FIND or OBTAIN statements.

The DELETE statement is used to delete a record from the data base. There are several options for handling member records of a deleted owner record. If no option is specified, then a record is deleted only if it has no member records. If the ONLY option is specified, then all mandatory member records are also deleted; optional member records are removed, but not deleted. The SELECTIVE option deletes all member records only if they are not participating members in an occurrence of another set type. Finally, the ALL option deletes all member records regardless of their set membership. In all cases, the DELETE statement propagates to member records as if the DELETE statement had been specified for the member record, and so on until a record occurrence is encountered that has no member records.

The MODIFY statement is used to replace a record in the data base from the UWA. Any data-item (including CALC key data-items) can be modified.

The INSERT statement is used to make a record a member of an occurrence of a set type. The set membership for the record type must be optional-automatic, optional-manual, or mandatory-manual. The record is inserted in the set occurrence in the position specified by the set order for the set type. The user must preselect the correct set occurrence using appropriate FIND or OBTAIN statements.

The REMOVE statement is used to cancel the membership of a record in an occurrence of a specified set type. The set membership for the record type in the set type must be optional.

13.4 EXAMPLE APPLICATION

The example application introduced in Chapter 10 will be implemented using the facilities of IDMS. The data base can be organized according to the data structure diagram shown in Fig. 13.4–1.

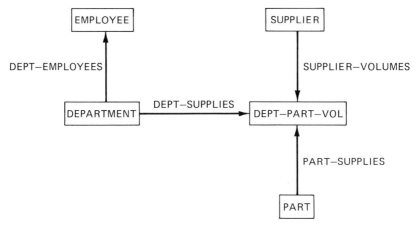

Fig. 13.4–1 Data structure diagram of example application.

The IDMS schema DDL that describes the data base follows:

SCHEMA DESCRIPTION.
SCHEMA NAME IS COMPANY.

FILE DESCRIPTION.
    FILE NAME IS COMP-FILE ASSIGN TO COMPDB.
    FILE NAME IS JOURNAL ASSIGN TO IDMSJRNL.

AREA DESCRIPTION.
    AREA NAME IS CMP-AREA
        RANGE IS 1001 THRU 1101
        WITHIN FILE COMP-FILE FROM 1 THRU 101.

For each record type a name, number, and location mode is specified. Occurrences of the record type are assigned to a specific area. Each data-item is then defined.

RECORD DESCRIPTION.
    RECORD NAME IS EMPLOYEE.
    RECORD ID IS 100.
    LOCATION MODE IS VIA DEPT-EMPLOYEES SET.
    WITHIN CMP-AREA AREA.
        03 EMPLOYEE-NUM   PIC X(4).
        03 NAME-LAST   PIC X(24).
        03 NAME-FIRST   PIC X(15).

```
    03  NAME-INITIAL    PIC X(1).
    03  SALARY          PIC 9(6) 9(2).
    03  MANAGER         PIC X(4).

RECORD NAME IS DEPARTMENT.
RECORD ID IS 200.
LOCATION MODE IS CALC USING DEPT-NUM
    DUPLICATES ARE NOT ALLOWED.
WITHIN CMP-AREA AREA.

    03  DEPT-NUM     PIC X(3).
    03  DEPT-NAME    PIC X(30).
    03  FILLER       PIC X(3).

RECORD NAME IS PART.
RECORD ID IS 300.
LOCATION MODE IS CALC USING PART-NUM
    DUPLICATES ARE NOT ALLOWED.
WITHIN CMP-AREA AREA.

    03  PART-NUM     PIC X(4).

RECORD NAME IS SUPPLIER.
RECORD ID IS 400.
LOCATION MODE IS CALC USING SUPPLIER-NUM
    DUPLICATES ARE NOT ALLOWED.
WITHIN CMP-AREA AREA.

    03  SUPPLIER-NUM     PIC X(4).
    03  SUPPLIER-NAME    PIC X(30).
    03  FILLER           PIC X(2).

RECORD NAME IS DEPT-PART-VOL.
RECORD ID IS 500.
LOCATION MODE IS DIRECT.
WITHIN CMP-AREA AREA.

    03  VOLUME       PIC S9(8).
```

For each set type a name, member ordering, set mode, owner record type, and member record type is specified. As discussed in Section 13.2, the pointers used to link records in set occurrences are stored with each record occurrence. The pointers form a pointer list and are numbered consecutively. The NEXT DBKEY clause specifies the relative position of the specified pointer in this pointer list.

SET DESCRIPTION.
    SET NAME IS DEPT-EMPLOYEES.
    ORDER IS SORTED.
    MODE IS CHAIN.
    OWNER IS DEPARTMENT   NEXT DBKEY POSITION IS 1.
    MEMBER IS EMPLOYEE   NEXT DBKEY POSITION IS 1
        ASCENDING KEY IS EMPLOYEE-NUM
        DUPLICATES ARE NOT ALLOWED
        OPTIONAL AUTOMATIC.

    SET NAME IS PART-SUPPLIES.
    ORDER IS FIRST.
    MODE IS CHAIN LINKED TO PRIOR.
    OWNER IS PART   NEXT DBKEY POSITION IS 1
                     PRIOR DBKEY POSITION IS 2.
    MEMBER IS DEPT-PART-VOL   NEXT DBKEY POSITION IS 4
                     PRIOR DBKEY POSITION IS 5
        LINKED TO OWNER   OWNER DBKEY POSITION IS 6
        MANDATORY AUTOMATIC.

    SET NAME IS DEPT-SUPPLIES.
    ORDER IS FIRST.
    MODE IS CHAIN LINKED TO PRIOR.
    OWNER IS DEPARTMENT   NEXT DBKEY POSITION IS 2
                     PRIOR DBKEY POSITION IS 3.
    MEMBER IS DEPT-PART-VOL   NEXT DBKEY POSITION IS 7
                     PRIOR DBKEY POSITION IS 8
        LINKED TO OWNER   OWNER DBKEY POSITION IS 9
        MANDATORY AUTOMATIC.

    SET NAME IS SUPPLIER-VOLUMES.
    ORDER IS FIRST.
    MODE IS CHAIN LINKED TO PRIOR.
    OWNER IS SUPPLIER   NEXT DBKEY POSITION IS 1
                     PRIOR DBKEY POSITION IS 2.
    MEMBER IS DEPT-PART-VOL   NEXT DBKEY POSITION IS 1
                     PRIOR DBKEY POSITION IS 2
        LINKED TO OWNER   OWNER DBKEY POSITION IS 3
        MANDATORY AUTOMATIC.

The following device media control language module will be used in this example. It identifies the associated schema and area within the schema, and defines an I/O buffer for the schema.

DEVICE MEDIA DESCRIPTION.
DEVICE MEDIA NAME IS SAMQUERY OF SCHEMA NAME
 COMPANY.

BUFFER SECTION.
 BUFFER NAME IS QUERY-BUFFER
 PAGE CONTAINS 1012 CHARACTERS
 BUFFER CONTAINS 5 PAGES.

AREA SECTION.
 COPY CMP-AREA AREA.

The following subschema will be used in this example.

SUBSCHEMA IDENTIFICATION DIVISION.
SUBSCHEMA NAME IS QUERY OF SCHEMA NAME COMPANY.
DEVICE MEDIA NAME IS SAMQUERY.

SUBSCHEMA DATA DIVISION.
AREA SECTION.
 COPY CMP-AREA
 PRIVACY LOCK FOR UPDATE IS 'NO'.

RECORD SECTION.

 01 EMPLOYEE
 PRIVACY LOCK FOR STORE IS 'NO'
 PRIVACY LOCK FOR DELETE IS 'NO'
 PRIVACY LOCK FOR UPDATE IS 'NO'.
 03 NAME-LAST.
 03 NAME-FIRST.
 03 NAME-INITIAL.
 COPY DEPARTMENT RECORD.
 COPY SUPPLIER RECORD.
 COPY DEPT-PART-VOL RECORD.

SET SECTION.
 COPY DEPT-EMPLOYEES SET.
 COPY DEPT-SUPPLIES SET.
 COPY SUPPLIER-VOLUMES SET.

Using this subschema, the query "Find the names of all employees who work for a department that is supplied parts by company X" will be implemented. In the following COBOL program, only those declarations required to interface with IDMS are given. It is assumed that the variable COMPANY has been set equal to the supplier number. An asterisk signifies a comment.

    IDENTIFICATION DIVISION.

        .

        .

        .

    ENVIRONMENT DIVISION.

        .

        .

        .

    DATA DIVISION.
    SCHEMA SECTION.
        INVOKE SUBSCHEMA QUERY OF COMPANY.

        .

        .

        .

    PROCEDURE DIVISION.

        .

        .

        .

        OPEN AREA CMP-AREA USAGE-MODE IS RETRIEVAL.
        MOVE 0 TO DEPT-COUNT.
        MOVE COMPANY TO SUPPLIER-NUM.
*
*   FIND THE SUPPLIER RECORD USING SUPPLIER-NUM AS
*   THE CALC KEY.
*

        FIND SUPPLIER RECORD.
*
*   EXAMINE ALL DEPT-PART-VOL RECORD OCCURRENCES
*   OWNED BY THE SUPPLIER RECORD. FOR EACH OF
*   THESE, FIND THE DEPARTMENT RECORD WHICH OWNS
*   IT AND SEE IF THIS DEPARTMENT HAS BEEN ENCOUN-
*   TERED BEFORE. IF NOT, THEN ENTER THE DEPART-
*   MENT NUMBER INTO THE ARRAY DEPT, INCREMENT
*   DEPT-COUNT AND PRINT THE NAMES OF THE EM-
*   PLOYEES IN THE DEPARTMENT.
*
*   LOCATE THE FIRST DEPT-PART-VOL RECORD.
*

```
      FIND FIRST RECORD OF SUPPLIER-VOLUMES SET.
*
*     PROCESS ALL DEPT-PART-VOL RECORDS OWNED BY
*     THE SUPPLIER.
*
      PERFORM PROCESS-DEPT-PART-VOL
          UNTIL ERROR-STATUS=0307.
      CLOSE ALL AREAS.
          .
          .
          .
      STOP-RUN.

      PROCESS-DEPT-PART-VOL.
*         FIND THE DEPARTMENT RECORD WHICH OWNS THE
*         CURRENT DEPT-PART-VOL RECORD.
*
          OBTAIN OWNER RECORD OF DEPT-SUPPLIES SET.
*
*         CHECK IF THIS DEPARTMENT HAS BEEN ENCOUN-
*         TERED BEFORE.
*
          MOVE 0 TO OLD-DEPT.
          MOVE 1 TO DEPT-INDEX.
          PERFORM DEPT-CHECK
              UNTIL ( (DEPT-INDEX>DEPT-COUNT) OR
              (OLD-DEPT=1) ).
          IF OLD-DEPT IS NOT EQUAL TO 1
              PERFORM NEW-DEPT.
*
*         LOCATE THE NEXT RECORD IN THE CURRENT
*         SUPPLIER-VOLUMES SET OCCURRENCE.
*
          FIND NEXT RECORD OF SUPPLIER-VOLUMES SET.

      DEPT-CHECK.
          IF DEPT-NUM=DEPT(DEPT-INDEX)
              MOVE 1 TO OLD-DEPT.
          ADD 1 TO DEPT-INDEX.

      NEW-DEPT.
*         THIS IS A NEW DEPARTMENT.
*
```

```
        ADD 1 TO DEPT-COUNT.
        MOVE DEPT-NUM TO DEPT (DEPT-COUNT).
  *
  *     GET THE FIRST EMPLOYEE RECORD FOR THE
  *     DEPARTMENT.
  *

        OBTAIN FIRST RECORD OF DEPT-EMPLOYEES SET.
        PERFORM PRINT-EMPLOYEES
            UNTIL ERROR-STATUS=0307.

    PRINT-EMPLOYEES.
        WRITE EMPLOYEE.
        OBTAIN NEXT RECORD OF DEPT-EMPLOYEES SET.
```

13.5 CONCLUDING REMARKS

The complexity of the query implementation is similar to that for IMS. Again the complexity is due to the procedural nature of the host language and the one-record-at-a-time navigation. However, in the IDMS implementation, communication buffers do not have to be defined explicitly by the application. They are defined instead in the DMCL module and by the DBMS. In addition, the form of the IDMS COBOL commands is more English-like than the IMS PL/1 commands.

IDMS is implemented for the IBM 360/370 and UNIVAC 70 computers. The IDMS DBMS is a subset of the April 1971 DBTG proposal for a network system. It includes most of the features specified in the report. In addition, some features have been added, e.g., the OBTAIN statement.

IDMS provides several utilities for data base administration. A utility is provided for initializing (preformatting) an area prior to use. In addition, part of an area or file can be reinitialized. All or part of a data base can be dumped, or all or part of a data base can be reloaded from a previous dump. In addition, transactions that change the data base are recorded on a journal file by saving a "before" and "after" page for all pages that are changed and by recording who altered the data base. In this way, a data base can be restored from the journal file either to a previous state (rollback) or from a previous state (rollforward).

IDMS permits the user to access the hashing routine used by IDMS to calculate CALC data-item values. In this way, a user can determine beforehand how the CALC data-item values will be distributed over the storage space. The user can then order his data so that more efficient access to secondary storage results. IDMS also provides on-line access to a data base, debugging tools, and a report generator (IDMS/CULPRIT).

Chapter 14

TOTAL

14.1 DATA MODEL

Total is a product of Cincom Systems, Inc. [Datapro, 1972b, 1974], which uses the DBTG network data model. However, its terminology and some of its restrictions are different from the guidelines of the DBTG report. A *data field* (data item) is the smallest unit of logical data. A *data element* is a collection of one or more data fields. A *data set* (record type) is a named collection of data elements. Occurrences of data sets are called *data records* (records).

There are two types of data sets in Total: *single-entry data sets* or *master* data sets, analogous to an owner record type, and *variable-entry data sets*, analogous to a member record type. *Linkage paths* (links) or *chains* may be specified between single- and variable-entry data sets and are analogous to DBTG sets. Membership of a variable-entry data set data record in a chain is automatic-mandatory according to the DBTG report specifications. Finally, a *data base* is a collection of data sets, usually related, and used as a family by application programs. A data set may be part of more than one data base.

14.2 DATA DEFINITION FACILITY

The DDL of Total is called data base definition language (DBDL). It is a self-contained, free-form coding language, which provides the input to the data base generation (DBGEN) program. The DBGEN program outputs an assembly language source deck, which is compiled and catalogued. The definition can then be used by application programs to access a data base. The disk area used by a data base may be preformatted with the FORMAT program.

The definition of a data base consists of three parts: an initial part, which names the data base and specifies some of its physical characteristics, descriptions of single-entry data sets, and descriptions of variable-entry data sets.

The initial part of the data base definition names the data base, specifies if access is to be shared, and allocates buffers.

The definition of a single- and a variable-entry data set consists of two parts: a data part and a physical characteristics part. The physical characteristics part specifies such things as storage device, physical record format, and physical storage structure characteristics such as record blocking. The data part specifies a control field (key data element), linkage paths for connecting data records together, and the data elements in the data set.

The control field of a single entry data set is used to hash a data record to a physical storage location. A single-entry data set can be the owner of several variable-entry data sets; this is indicated by specifying one linkage path in the single-entry data set definition for each variable-entry data set. A linkage path, in effect, reserves space for pointers in a data record. The pointers for each linkage path in a single-entry data set data record consist of a first and last pointer to, respectively, the first and last data record of the variable-entry data set in the chain.

A variable-entry data set contains one control field for every linkage path it is in. A control field value in a data record of a variable-entry data set corresponds to the control field value of the single-entry data set data record that is at the head of the appropriate chain. The data records in a variable-entry data set are stored serially by one of their control fields.

There is a linkage path definition for a variable-entry data set for every linkage path that the variable-entry data set is in. The linkage path, in effect, reserves space for a forward and backward pointer to variable-entry data set data records in the same chain. Thus, the combination of a control field and linkage path specifies a specific occurrence of a chain (set occurrence). These chains are defined with two statements in the DBDL: a CTRL statement identifies the chain and a LK statement reserves space for the pointers connecting the data records.

A single-entry data set can only have a single format. However, by splitting a variable-entry data set into two parts, different data formats are possible for the same variable-entry data set: a base data portion containing the control fields and linkage paths, and a variable-format section that can have several different formats. The different formats are identified by a record code statement. In this way, different data records can be part of the same chain. (This corresponds to the facility in the DBTG proposal of allowing several member record types in one DBTG set.)

14.3   DATA MANIPULATION FACILITY

The DML of Total is called data manipulation language (Total DML). It is a host language system using COBOL, FORTRAN, PL/1, or various Assembler Languages. Data sets may be accessed directly via hashing (single-entry data sets), pointers (variable-entry data sets), or serially. Serial access refers to the physical ordering of the data sets on the storage medium or in a chain according to a linkage path (analogous to DBTG set member access).

The general form of a request to the data base in PL/1 is

CALL DATBAS (operation,status,data set name,reference,
    linkage path,control field,element list,record area, 'END.')

All parameters are not always used. Their use depends on the operation specified.

The *operation* is the function being performed, e.g., read or insert. These will be discussed in more detail later in this section.

The *status* is a variable that contains an indication of the success of a call.

The *data set name* is the name of a data set as specified in the data base definition.

The *reference* is the relative position of a variable-entry data set data record in a chain. It is only used in variable-entry data set operations.

The *linkage path* is the name of a chain as specified in the DBDL definition. Since a variable-entry data set may be part of more than one chain, it is necessary to specify the chain for certain operations.

The *control field* is used in nonserial operations. For a single-entry data set it specifies the key to be hashed to determine a data set's location in the data base. For a variable-entry data set it specifies the key of the associated single-entry data set that is connected to the variable-entry data set.

The *element list* is a series of data element names concatenated together and terminated by 'END.'. It specifies the data elements that are to be retrieved. In addition, the data elements are retrieved in the order specified by the element list.

The *record area* is the name of the user area in memory where requested data is placed or specified data taken by Total.

The different DML operations will be grouped according to their function.

For *task management*, the procedure calls are of the form

CALL DATBAS (operation,status,base,taskname, 'END.')

There are four possible operations: TOTAL loads the entire Total DML; MPTOT loads the read and write subset of Total, which results in a 30% core saving; QUEST loads the read only subset of Total for a 60% core saving; finally, DEQUE detaches a task from the DML or DBDL phase of Total.

The *base* gives the name of the DBDL step to be loaded into memory.

The *taskname* is the name of the program using Total.

The procedure call for the *open* and *close* commands is of the form

CALL DATBAS (operation,status,data set name, 'END.')

There are three types of open and close operations: OPENM and CLOSM open and close a single-entry data set; OPENV and CLOSV perform the same operations as OPENM and CLOSM, but for variable-entry data sets; OPENX and CLOSX open and close a list of data sets.

The procedure call format for *serial access* is

CALL DATBAS (operation,status,data set name,element list,
    record area, 'END.')

There are six serial access operations: SEQRM serially retrieves all data records of a single-entry data set from first to last data record; SEQRV serially retrieves variable-entry data sets from first to last record by following the first linkage path of the variable-entry data set; SERLV serially retrieves all data records of a variable-entry data set

from first to last data record; SEQWV serially updates the variable-entry
data set data record previously retrieved by a SEQRV or a SERLV
command; RESTM and RESTV reset the reference pointer so that the
next access is to, respectively, the first single-entry data set or the first
variable-entry data set data record.

The format of the *direct-access* procedure call depends on the type
of data set accessed. For single-entry data sets the format is

>   CALL DATBAS (operation,status,data set name,control field,
>   element list,record area, 'END.')

There are five single-entry data set operations: READM retrieves a
single-entry data set data record whose control field value is equal to
the control field value specified; WRITM updates a single-entry data set
data record with the data record from the record area; ADD-M inserts
single-entry data set data records and checks for duplicate control field
values; DEL-M deletes a single-entry data set data record (all connected
variable-entry data set data records must be deleted first); LOADM is
the same as ADD-M but it does not check for duplicate control field
values.

For variable-entry data sets the call format is

>   CALL DATBAS (operation,status,data set name,reference,
>   linkage path,control field,element list,record area, 'END.')

There are nine variable-entry data set operations: READV and
READR retrieve a variable-entry data set data record by following the
linkage path specified in, respectively, a forward or backward direction.
The reference parameter is initially set by the user to 'LKxx' to point
to the first, last, or some other data record in the chain. Total then
updates the reference to either a binary number, which is the relative
position of the next or prior record in the chain, or 'END.', which
indicates the end or start of the chain has been reached.

READD retrieves a variable-entry data set data record in one of two
ways, depending on the reference parameter. If the reference is a
four-character numeric value, then the DML retrieves that relative data
record in the chain specified. The reference parameter can also redirect
the linkage path (set switching). In this case, a new linkage path must
be specified and the data record is retrieved again as part of the new
chain.

WRITV updates a variable-entry data set data record from the
record area. It acts on the previously retrieved data record.

ADDVC inserts a new variable-entry data set data record and places it at the end of all linkage paths of the variable-entry data set.

ADDVB inserts a new variable-entry data set data record before the previously retrieved record in the linkage path specified by the control field parameter. The record is automatically added to the end of all other chains it is in. ADDVA is the same as ADDVB except that the data record is inserted after the previously retrieved data record.

ADDVR disconnects all linkage paths of the variable-entry data set data record retrieved by the preceding retrieval command, inserts a new data record, and reconnects it. The new record is inserted in the same relative place for the linkage path specified. It is added to the end of all other chains it is in.

DELVD physically deletes the variable-entry data set record retrieved by the preceding retrieval command. Linkage path maintenance is performed automatically.

14.4 EXAMPLE APPLICATION

The example application introduced in Chapter 10 is implemented using the facilities of Total. Single-entry data sets are used for the department (DEPT), the supplier (SUPP), and the part (PART) data sets. Each is the head of a chain of volume (VOLM) data records. In addition, the DEPT single-entry data set is also the head of a chain of employee (EMPS) data records. The relationships are illustrated in the data structure diagram shown in Fig. 14.4–1.

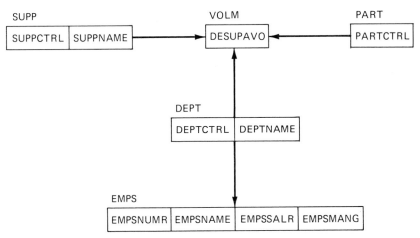

Fig. 14.4–1 Example application data structure diagram.

The following is the DBGEN section that defines the schema. It would be specified once for the data base and then catalogued. For each single-entry (master) data set we specify its name, a system required data field, a control (key) field, all linkage paths, and all data fields. The length, in bytes, of each data field is also specified. The physical characteristics of the storage area where the data records will be stored must also be specified.

```
BEGIN_DATA_BASE_GENERATION:
DATA_BASE_NAME=COMPAN
SHARE_IO:
IOAREA=GENN

BEGIN_MASTER_DATA_SET:
DATA_SET_NAME=DEPT
IOAREA=GENN
MASTER_DATA:
DEPTROOT=8                  REQUIRED BY TOTAL
DEPTCTRL=5                  DEPARTMENT NUMBER
DEPTLKVO=8                  LINK TO VOLM
DEPTLKEM=8                  LINK TO EMPS
DEPTNAME=15                 DEPARTMENT NAME
END_DATA:
DEVICE=2314                 PHYSICAL ENVIRONMENT
TOTAL_LOGICAL_RECORDS=39920
LOGICAL_RECORD_LENGTH=80
LOGICAL_RECORDS_PER_BLOCK=20
LOGICAL_BLOCKS_PER_TRACK=4
TOTAL_TRACKS=20
END_MASTER_DATA_SET:

BEGIN_MASTER_DATA_SET:
DATA_SET_NAME=SUPP
IOAREA=GENN
MASTER_DATA:
SUPPROOT=8
SUPPCTRL=5                  SUPPLIER NUMBER
SUPPLKVO=8                  LINK TO VOLM
SUPPNAME=30                 SUPPLIER NAME
END_DATA:
    .
    .                       PHYSICAL ENVIRONMENT
    .
```

```
END_MASTER_DATA_SET:

BEGIN_MASTER_DATA_SET:
DATA_SET_NAME=PART
IOAREA=GENN
MASTER_DATA:
PARTROOT=8
PARTCTRL=5              PART NUMBER
PARTLKVO=8              LINK TO VOLM
END_DATA:
    .
    .                   PHYSICAL ENVIRONMENT
    .

END_MASTER_DATA_SET:
```

For each variable-entry data set we specify its name, one control field/link path pair for each chain it is in, its data fields, and the length of each data field in bytes. The physical storage environment must also be specified as for single-entry data sets.

```
BEGIN_VARIABLE_ENTRY_DATA_SET:
DATA_SET_NAME=EMPS
BASE_DATA:
EMPSDEPT=5=DEPTCTRL     CONTROL FIELD FROM DEPT
DEPTLKEM=8              LINK FROM DEPT
EMPSNUMR=9              EMPLOYEE NUMBER
EMPSNAME=30            EMPLOYEE NAME
EMPSSALR=6             EMPLOYEE SALARY
EMPSMANG=9             EMPLOYEE MANAGER NUMBER
END_DATA:
    .
    .                   PHYSICAL ENVIRONMENT
    .

END_VARIABLE_ENTRY_DATA_SET:

BEGIN_VARIABLE_ENTRY_DATA_SET:
DATA_SET_NAME=VOLM
BASE_DATA:
VOLMDEPT=5=DEPTCTRL    CONTROL FIELD FROM DEPT
DEPTLKVO=8             LINK FROM DEPT
VOLMSUPP=5=SUPPCTRL    CONTROL FIELD FROM SUPP
SUPPLKVO=8             LINK FROM SUPP
```

VOLMPART=5=PARTCTRL	CONTROL FIELD FROM PART
PARTLKVO=8	LINK FROM PART
DESUPAVO=5	VOLUME OF PART SUPPLIED
	BY A SUPPLIER TO A
	DEPARTMENT

END_DATA:

.

.   PHYSICAL ENVIRONMENT

.

END_VARIABLE_ENTRY_DATA_SET:
END_DATA_BASE_GENERATION:

The query that will be implemented is, "Find the names of all employees who work for a department that is supplied parts by the company with supplier number X." The algorithm is as follows:

1. Sequentially retrieve all DEPT data records (PROCESS_ DEPARTMENTS procedure).

2. For each department, check if the department is supplied by supplier number X (CHECK_IF_SUPPLIED procedure).

3. If supplier number X supplies a department, then sequentially retrieve all employees of the department and print their names (PRINT _EMPLOYEES procedure); else go to step 1.

```
QUERY:PROCEDURE OPTIONS (MAIN);
    /*  Declare some needed variables */
    DECLARE X CHAR (5),
            STATUS CHAR (4),
            SUCCESSFUL CHAR (4) INIT ('****'),
            END_OF_CHAIN CHAR (4) INIT ('END.'),
            PROCEED BIT (1) INIT ('0'B),
            ABORT BIT (1) INIT ('1'B);

    /*  The ERROR procedure handles error conditions generated
        by Total */
ERROR:PROCEDURE (ERROR_CODE);
    .
    .
    .
END ERROR;
```

```
/*  The PRINT_EMPLOYEES procedure prints the names of all
    employees who work for a department supplied by the
    supplier with supplier number equal to X            */
PRINT_EMPLOYEES:PROCEDURE RETURNS (BIT);
    DECLARE REFERENCE CHAR (4),
            STATUS CHAR (4),
            EMPLOYEE_NAME CHAR (30);
    /*  Set REFERENCE to retrieve the first employee in the
        chain */
    REFERENCE='LKEM';
    /*  Get the first employee data record for this
        department */
    CALL DATBAS ('READV',STATUS,'EMPS',REFERENCE,
        'DEPTLKEM',DEPT.NUMBER,'EMPSNAMEEND.',
        EMPLOYEE_NAME,'END.');
    /*  Print all employee names */
    DO WHILE (STATUS=SUCCESSFUL);
        /*  Check if end of chain */
        IF REFERENCE=END_OF_CHAIN
            THEN RETURN(PROCEED);
        PUT EDIT (EMPLOYEE_NAME) (X(10),A);
        CALL DATBAS ('READV',STATUS,'EMPS',REFERENCE,
            'DEPTLKEM',DEPT.NUMBER,'EMPSNAMEEND.',
            EMPLOYEE_NAME,'END.');
    END;
    CALL ERROR(STATUS);
    RETURN (ABORT);
    END PRINT_EMPLOYEES;
/*  The CHECK_IF_SUPPLIED procedure checks the VOLM
    data set according to the DEPTLKVO chain to determine if
    supplier number X supplies a department            */
CHECK_IF_SUPPLIED:PROCEDURE (COMPANY)
    RETURNS(BIT);
    DECLARE COMPANY CHAR (5),
            REFERENCE CHAR (4),
            STATUS CHAR (4),
            SUPPLIER_NUMBER CHAR (5);
    /*  Set REFERENCE to retrieve the first VOLM data
        record in the chain linked to department        */
    REFERENCE='LKVO';
```

```
/*  Get the first VOLM data record in the chain */
CALL DATBAS ('READV',STATUS,'VOLM',
      REFERENCE,'DEPTLKVO',DEPT.NUMBER,
      'VOLMSUPPEND.',SUPPLIER_NUMBER,'END.');
/*  Check each VOLM data record in the chain until a
    supplier with supplier number equal to COMPANY is
    found */
DO WHILE (STATUS=SUCCESSFUL);
    IF REFERENCE=END_OF_CHAIN
        THEN RETURN (PROCEED);
    IF SUPPLIER_NUMBER=COMPANY
        THEN DO;
            PUT SKIP (2) EDIT
            ('DEPARTMENT',DEPT.NAME) (A,A);
            RETURN (PRINT_EMPLOYEES);
            END;
    CALL DATBAS ('READV',STATUS,'VOLM',
        REFERENCE, 'DEPTLKVO',DEPT.NUMBER,
        'VOLMSUPPEND.',SUPPLIER_NUMBER,'END.');
END;
CALL ERROR(STATUS);
RETURN (ABORT);
END CHECK_IF_SUPPLIED;

/*  The PROCESS_DEPARTMENTS procedure checks all
    departments and if a department is supplied by the supplier
    with supplier number equal to X, it prints the names of all
    employees who work for the department            */

PROCESS_DEPARTMENTS:PROCEDURE (COMPANY);
    DECLARE COMPANY CHAR (5),
            STATUS CHAR (4);

    DECLARE 1 DEPT BASED UNALIGNED,
            2    NUMBER CHAR (5),
            2    NAME CHAR (15);

    /*  Get the first department */
    CALL DATBAS ('SEQRM',STATUS,'DEPT',
        DEPTCTRLDEPTNAMEEND.',DEPT,'END.');
    /*  Check all departments */
    DO WHILE (STATUS=SUCCESSFUL);
```

```
            IF REFERENCE=END_OF_CHAIN
                THEN RETURN;
            /*  Check if this department is supplied by a supplier with
            supplier number COMPANY                              */
            IF CHECK_IF_SUPPLIED (COMPANY)
                THEN RETURN;
            /*  Get the next department */
            CALL DATBAS ('SEQRM',STATUS,'DEPT',
                'DEPTCTRLDEPTNAMEEND.',DEPT,'END.'):
        END;
        CALL ERROR(STATUS);
    END PROCESS_DEPARTMENTS;

    /*  Begin main procedure by loading the read only subset of
        Total */
    CALL DATBAS ('QUEST',STATUS,'DML','QUERY','END.');
    IF STATUS¬=SUCCESSFUL
        THEN DO;
            CALL ERROR ('UNSUCCESSFUL ATTACHING OF
            TOTAL');
            RETURN;
            END;
    /*  Open the DEPT, EMPS, SUPP and VOLM data sets */
    CALL DATBAS ('OPENX',STATUS,
        'DEPTEMPSSUPPVOLMEND.','END.');
    IF STATUS¬=SUCCESSFUL
        THEN DO;
            CALL ERROR ('UNSUCCESSFUL OPEN');
            RETURN;
            END;
    /*  Get the supplier number */
    GET EDIT(X) (A(5) );
    /*  Answer the query */
    CALL PROCESS_DEPARTMENTS(X);
    /*  Close the data sets */
    CALL DATBAS ('CLOSX',STATUS,
        'DEPTEMPSSUPPVOLM','END.');
    /*  Detach Total */
    CALL DATBAS ('DEQUE',STATUS,'DML','QUERY','END.');
END QUERY;
```

14.5   CONCLUDING REMARKS

The implementation of the query in Total is quite complex. The complexity is comparable to that of the IMS implementation and for the same reasons. Total requires the definition of communication buffers explicitly by the user and is oriented to one-record-at-a-time processing. In addition, Total does not allow one to express a qualification on a data record except for control fields, and even this facility is limited. Therefore, most processing is sequential via linkage paths.

Total is implemented for the following computers: IBM 360/370, IBM SYSTEM/3, NCR Century, UNIVAC 70 and 9000, Varian, PDP-11, CDC 6000/7000, CYBER 70/170, RCA SPECTRA/70, and Honeywell 1200. Although Total is a network system, it does not conform very closely to the DBTG report specifications. This is due no doubt to the fact that Total was implemented before the CODASYL DBTG report was published. For example, Total lacks completely the concept of set occurrence selection and different types of set membership as found in the DBTG report.

The data-structuring facility of Total, although somewhat cryptic, provides a great deal of flexibility due to its chains and unlimited interrelationships between single- and variable-entry data sets. It can handle virtually any association between its data sets.

Total also provides several utilities that are useful to the DBA for data base maintenance and administration. Utility programs are provided for initially loading a data base, logging transactions, recovering a data base, etc. Total can be used in an interactive mode by interfacing it with one of several terminal systems, e.g., ENVIRON I, CICS, or TASK-MASTER.

Chapter 15

ADAPTABLE DATA BASE SYSTEM (ADABAS)

15.1 DATA MODEL

Adaptable Data Base System (ADABAS) is a product of Software AG, West Germany [Software AG, 1971; Datapro, 1973; Evans, 1973d]. It uses a "flat file" data model with cross-linking of files. An ADABAS data base consists of one or more *files* (record types). A file is composed of *records*. Records are composed of *fields* (data items). Two or more ADABAS files may be *coupled* (linked) on a common attribute. The logical coupling of files permits the definition of data bases structured according to the hierarchical or network data model. ADABAS is not a relational system for it lacks many relational operations. However, it has some relational-like commands.

15.2 DATA DEFINITION FACILITY

The definition of a data base in ADABAS consists of specifying the files, the fields within the files, and any relationships between files. Relationships between files may also be specified after the data base has been created. A file is defined at load time and is assigned a number that uniquely identifies it.

Definition of fields can be done at load time or when the field is added to the file. Field definition employs the following format:

LN, FN, L, F, options

All elements are not always required. LN is a two-digit COBOL-like level number. FN is a two-character field name. L is the length of the field before compression. Data compression is a standard feature in ADABAS. F is a letter code for the field format (type). The options element specifies any special characteristics of a field. Some of the options available are: multiple-value fields (MU), descriptor or key fields (DE), null and empty field distinction (NU), and periodic fields (PE).

A multiple-value field may contain several values within the field, e.g., the name of a company may contain several words each of which is considered a single value. Multivalued fields permit retrieval of the name of a company, for example, if the user is only able to specify part of the company's name.

Periodic fields are like one-dimensional arrays. The first element of a periodic field "AA" would be referenced by "AA1", the second by "AA2", and so on.

A possible file definition might be:

01, SA	group field with name SA
02, P1, 5, P, DE	first field of group "SA" is "P1" with a length of 5, a packed decimal value and it is a descriptor
02, P2, 10, A	second field of group "SA" is "P2" with length 10 and an alphanumeric value

Associated with each record in a file is a unique internal sequence number (ISN). ISN's, once assigned to a record, never change and are used to access records and to couple files.

The logical relationships between coupled files are maintained by the ASSOCIATOR. The logical relationships are represented by tables of sorted ISN's. Using these ISN's the physical addresses of records are obtained using an address converter work file. To resolve queries efficiently, the ASSOCIATOR has four levels of indices: hyperindex, superindex, mainindex, and normalindex. The hyperindex is always in main memory and the superindex is usually in main memory. The normalindex consists of unique values and a list of ISN's of records having that value. The first three levels of indices are used to narrow the search in the normalindex.

The coupler routine permits a record to be connected to any number of other records in another file. Each file may be connected to up to 80 other files. Coupling may be done on-line. Therefore, hierarchical or network data bases may be constructed after the data base is loaded.

15.3 DATA MANIPULATION FACILITY

The ADABAS system consists of several disk resident subsystems, Their actions are coordinated by DANKEN (the *nucleus*). User programs can be linked directly to the nucleus, for single-user systems, or they can be linked to the nucleus by an ADABAS linkage routine. The nucleus itself is reentrant. It may reside in one region of memory and can concurrently support several application programs in other regions.

Large quantities of new records may be added to an existing file or a large file may be loaded a little at a time. A new file may be loaded at any time. Initially, before data base loading is possible, several system programs must first be link-edited and loaded into libraries. In addition, one special user routine must be added to allow concurrent communication with the nucleus.

ADABAS permits phonetic searching of the data base. Phonetic equivalents are found by dropping vowels and one letter of each double consonant. For example, "HILLS" becomes "HLS" and queries could retrieve the names "HILLS," "HOLLIS," "HALLS," and "HELOISE." Fields for which the phonetic search capability is needed must be specified at load time.

For batch operations, ADABAS can be interfaced with COBOL, FORTRAN, PL/1, or an Assembler Language. The data base commands are implemented as procedure calls to a procedure called "ADABAS". The procedure is passed the address of a control block and a number of buffers. The general format of a call, in COBOL, is

CALL "ADABAS" USING CONTROL-BLOCK, FORMAT-
    BUFFER, RECORD-BUFFER, SEARCH-BUFFER, VALUE-
    BUFFER, UPDATE-BUFFER.

Not all parameters are used by every command.

The *control block* specifies the command to be executed, user identification, the file number, buffer lengths, and special options such as sorting. A location in which ADABAS places a condition code indicating the result of the call (successful, unsuccessful, etc.) must also be defined. If an ISN is needed by the command, then it must be placed in the ISN field of the control block.

The *format buffer* specifies the format of the record or fields to be retrieved. ADABAS automatically converts fields to the format specified by the user. The buffer contains a string of field names, each two characters, followed by the length of the field for as many fields as are to be retrieved. Field types may be alphanumeric (A), binary right adjusted (B), fixed point (F), floating point (G), packed decimal (P) or unpacked decimal (U). Blanks may be inserted in the record by specifying the X format.

The *record buffer* contains the record retrieved by a retrieval command and formatted as specified by the format buffer.

The *search buffer* contains the identification number of a file, followed by a qualification involving only descriptor fields in the indicated file, followed by the identification number of a file, and so on for at most five files. Each descriptor field must be followed by a length. The conditional operator is always equality. Conditions on fields may be composed using the Boolean operators: AND (D), OR (O), TO (S), and BUT NOT (N).

The *value buffer* contains the value of descriptor fields specified in the qualification.

Finally, the *update buffer* contains values for fields to be updated or records to be inserted.

ADABAS has ten data base commands. All command names are two characters in length. ADABAS provides separate locate, called search, and access, called retrieval, commands as well as combined locate and access commands. In addition, the schema may be changed by means of a command that adds new fields to a file.

There are two search commands. The S1 command returns a list of ISN's of records satisfying the qualification specified in the Search Buffer. The S2 command is similar to the S1 command, but the ISN's returned can be sorted on the value of up to three descriptor fields. The ISN's of records satisfying the query are placed into an ISN buffer. If the buffer cannot hold all ISN's satisfying the query, then the overflow ISN's are stored in a temporary storage area. When the same query is repeated, a second set of ISN's will be loaded into the ISN Buffer from the temporary storage area. The total number of records satisfying the qualification is returned by ADABAS in a field of the control block. This allows the user to determine how many repeated calls must be made to obtain all record ISN's satisfying the query.

Below are shown the contents of the search and value buffers for the query:

"Find all records from file 5 (employee file) for which the field SA (salary) has a value greater than 10000 and less than 15000, or greater than 25000 but less than 30000 and linked to records in file 3 (Department) with DN (Department Name) not equal to 'HARDWARE'."

Search buffer:

$\overbrace{\qquad}$ length of SA (salary) field

/5/SA,5,S,SA,5,O,SA,5,S,SA,5,

file 5   to or to

$\overbrace{\qquad}$ length of DN (department name) field

/3/DN,8,S,DN,8,N,DN,8

file 3   to but not

Value buffer: 1000114999925001299996ƀƀƀƀƀƀƀ

ZZZZZZZHARDWARE

A ƀ represents a blank.

A record can be retrieved either following a search command or when its ISN is already known. The ISN must be placed in the ISN field of the control block. An L1 command will then read the record into the record buffer. Assuming that an L1 command was issued after the search for employees in the previous example, then the format of a record might be:

Format buffer: N1,15,N2,10,1X,N3,1,2X,SA,5,2X,DN,8

last first initial salary department

name name   name

Record buffer: HASSANƀƀƀƀƀƀƀƀƀTHOMASƀƀƀƀƀIƀƀ

20000ƀƀTOYƀƀƀƀ

The remaining retrieval commands do not follow search commands. The L2 command reads records in their physical storage sequence. An L3 command reads all or part of a file in the sequence of a specific descriptor field. Records are not sorted, but are retrieved starting with the ISN's for the lowest descriptor value. Finally, an L9 command retrieves all values of a particular descriptor field and the number of occurrences of each value. Only the ASSOCIATOR is accessed in processing the query. An L9 command can be used to determine how many records exist with a specific value for a given descriptor field.

The N1 command inserts a new record into the data base. Each field that is to be assigned a value must be specified in the update buffer and its format in the format buffer. ADABAS creates the record, assigns the values to corresponding fields, checking for type compatibility, converts it to standard form, compresses it if possible, and stores it as a new record. ISN's are added to the ASSOCIATOR for each field that is a descriptor.

To modify one or more fields in an existing record, the A1 command is used. Usually, a search command, which obtains the ISN's of the records to be modified, precedes an A1 command. The ISN of the record, the names of the field or fields to be changed, and their new values must be specified to use the A1 command. Again ADABAS checks corresponding values for type compatibility, updates the record, and changes the ASSOCIATOR if the values of descriptor fields are changed. The A2 command is used to add new fields to records, i.e., to change the schema. It does not add data to the records. This must be done by an A1 command.

The E1 command deletes the entire record specified by an ISN. That is, all ISN's in the ASSOCIATOR referring to the record are deleted. Note that if a field is modified to a null value by the A1 command, then it has effectively been deleted from the record.

For on-line operations, ADABAS can be interfaced with TSO, CICS, INTERCOMM, TASKMASTER, and ENVIRON I. In addition, ADABAS supports an interactive query system called ADASCRIPT. ADASCRIPT is a command language processor that allows a user to retrieve, update, and display fields in an ADABAS data base from an interactive terminal. The command language has a rigid syntax but permits a more attractive, English-like interface with ADABAS. Commands consist of from 1 to 12 lines with up to 72 characters per line. Facilities exist to redisplay or SHOW a command, to CHANGE a line, or to EXECUTE a command.

The FIND command is the basic command. It allows the user to retrieve and display records in a file based on a qualification. The file may optionally be coupled to other files, sorted, or updated. Using the FIND command and the facilities of ADASCRIPT, the query

> "Find all records from file 5 (employee file) for which the field SA (salary) has a value greater than 10000 and less than 15000, or greater than 25000 but less than 30000 and linked to records in file 3 (Department) with DN (Department Name) not equal to 'HARDWARE'."

would be expressed as:

> FIND ALL RECORDS IN FILE EMPLOYEE WITH SALARY
>   GREATER THAN 10000 AND SALARY LESS THAN 15000
>   OR SALARY GREATER THAN 25000 AND SALARY LESS
>   THAN 30000 AND

COUPLED TO FILE DEPARTMENT WITH DEPARTMENT-
NAME NOT EQUAL TO HARDWARE AND
DISPLAY IN FORMAT LAST-NAME, FIRST-NAME, INITIAL,
SALARY, DEPARTMENT-NAME.

The components of the FIND command can be identified with the
ADABAS control block and buffers in a natural way.

15.4 EXAMPLE APPLICATION

The sample application introduced in Chapter 10 will be implemented using the facilities of ADABAS. The data base consists of seven
files and their associated fields. The schema for the data base follows.
The names in parentheses are those that would be used in an
ADASCRIPT query; they are not part of the schema definition.

```
FILE 1 (EMPLOYEE)
    01, EN, 6, A, DE      (NUMBER)
    01, EZ, 30, A         (NAME)
    01, SA, 4, F, DE      (SALARY)
    01, DN, 8, A, DE      (DEPT-NO)
    01, MN, 6, A, DE      (MANAGER-NO)

FILE 2 (PART)
    01, PN, 5, A, DE      (PART-NO)
    01, DN, 8, A, DE      (DEPT-NO)
    01, SN, 6, A, DE      (SUPPLIER-NO)
    01, VO, 4, F          (VOLUME)

FILE 3 (DEPARTMENT)
    01, DN, 8, A, DE      (DEPT-NO)
    01, DZ, 30, A         (DEPT-NAME)

FILE 4 (SUPPLIER)
    01, SN, 6, A, DE      (SUPPLIER-NO)
    01, SZ, 30, A         (SUPPLIER-NAME)
```

The data base has a relational format although coupling of files
would permit the construction of a hierarchical or network data base.
The query "Find the names of all employees who work for a
department that is supplied parts by the company with supplier number

X" will be implemented. Using ADASCRIPT, the query could be formulated in two stages as follows.

First, find all departments supplied by supplier X:

FIND <u>ALL</u> RECORDS <u>IN</u> <u>FILE</u> PART <u>WITH</u> SUPPLIER-NO=X
    <u>AND</u>
DISPLAY <u>IN</u> FORMAT DEPT-NO, SUPPLIER-NO.

This performs an <u>S1</u> command search in the ASSOCIATOR followed by several <u>L1</u> command retrievals for the data. The associated search, value, and format buffers are shown below:

Search buffer: /2/SN,6

        file 2 ⎯⎯⎯┘   └⎯⎯length of SN

                      ┌⎯⎯⎯⎯⎯ SUPPLIER-NO field name

Value buffer: (value of X)

Format buffer: DN,8,SN,6

         DEPT-NO ⎯┘ └⎯⎯length of field

Taking the set of department numbers, with duplicates removed, from the first query, an ADASCRIPT <u>FIND</u> is now executed containing a qualification with several department numbers. If it is not possible to specify all department numbers in the search buffer, then more than one <u>FIND</u> needs to be specified. In terms of more basic ADABAS commands, this <u>FIND</u> command corresponds to executing an <u>S2</u> search command of the ASSOCIATOR and sorting on department number and within department on employee number. Several <u>L1</u> commands are then issued until all records are retrieved. For simplicity, assume that only one department is found that satisfies the qualification. If many departments are retrieved, then more than one <u>FIND</u> command may be needed as mentioned above. For the simplified case, the <u>FIND</u> command is

FIND <u>ALL</u> RECORDS <u>IN</u> <u>FILE</u> EMPLOYEE <u>WITH</u> DEPT-NO=i
    <u>AND</u>
SORT <u>THEM</u> <u>BY</u> DEPT-NO, NUMBER <u>AND</u>
DISPLAY <u>IN</u> FORMAT DEPT-NO, NUMBER, NAME.

where i is some department number.

    Search buffer: /1/DN,8
    Value buffer: i
    Format buffer: DN,8,1X,EN,6,1X,EZ,30

To demonstrate the usefulness of coupling, this query will be implemented again using coupled files. If File 1 (EMPLOYEE) is coupled to File 2 (PART) by the field DEPT-NO, then the preceding query can be expressed as follows:

FIND ALL RECORDS IN FILE EMPLOYEE AND
COUPLED TO FILE PART WITH SUPPLIER-NO=X AND
SORT THEM BY DEPT-NO, NUMBER AND
DISPLAY IN FORMAT DEPT-NO, NUMBER, NAME.

15.5 CONCLUDING REMARKS

The implementation of the query using ADABAS seems quite simple and straightforward. The simplicity is due to the query language ADASCRIPT and the simple data model used by ADABAS. If the query had been implemented using a host data language it would have been much more complex. The user would then need to set up all relevant buffers himself, using the facilities of the host language. It should also be noted that when coupling of files is not used, the complexity of the query also increases. File coupling lets the DBMS do some of the work that would otherwise need to be done by the user.

ADABAS is implemented for IBM 360/370, Siemens 4004, and UNIVAC 70 computers. It is designed for medium- to large-scale systems. ADABAS uses partially inverted files and a basic direct access method for retrieving records. Data compression is a standard feature.

ADABAS also provides many attractive features for data base maintenance and administration. High levels of data security are possible. Privacy and security features are implemented using passwords. Based upon a password supplied by an application program, a read or write priority of 0 to 15 is assigned to the program. The data are assigned a read and write access priority of 0 to 15. Therefore, depending on the application's priority and the data priority, access is permitted or denied.

An attractive facility provided by ADABAS is automatic data enciphering/deciphering. A four-digit cipher key may be used to encipher data when they are loaded or entered. Whenever data are retrieved, this same key must be supplied to decipher the data. Illegal browsing through the data base requires both interpretation of the compressed ADABAS storage tables and decoding of the cipher.

A checkpoint tape is maintained by a subsystem of ADABAS. This permits restoring the data base to the previous checkpoint in case of system failure. In the event that a track in the ASSOCIATOR becomes unreadable, the system automatically restores the track. For added security, before performing an update, the states of all records, tables, and fields to be changed are first saved.

A further feature is the automatic maintenance of a directory, or histogram, which records the range and frequency of occurrence of unique values assumed by each field name in the data base. An ADABAS command permits easy access to this information.

ADABAS's rigid and cryptic command structure may be its major drawback. However, it is an attractive system. Integration of existing files into an ADABAS data base is not difficult. Files may be automatically coupled in such a manner that hierarchical or network data bases can be constructed.

Appendix

DATA BASE EXERCISES AND GAMES

A.1 INTRODUCTION

In Part I, DBMS concepts were discussed and, in Part II, examples of some commercial DBMS's were outlined. A third aspect of a student's exposure to DBMS's concerns obtaining some "hands on" experience in using a DBMS. Ideally, this experience is best obtained in real-life data processing situations that employ a DBMS. However, in a teaching environment, availability and cost often preclude such use of a DBMS. At the University of Toronto, a DBMS has been designed and implemented specifically for use as a teaching tool. The Educational Data Base System (EDBS) is a DBMS implemented in and using as a host language APL [Lochovsky, 1973; Klebanoff, 1974; EDBS, 1975; Kanfer, 1975; Klebanoff *et al.*, 1975; Lochovsky and Tsichritzis, 1976]. Its primary purpose is to provide the "hands on" experience component of a course on DBMS's. EDBS actually consists of three DBMS's: hierarchical, network, and relational systems. In this way, the student is exposed to more than one type of DBMS approach, which would not be possible with most commercial systems.

A number of exercises are presented here that require the students to design and implement programs using the facilities of the EDBS systems [Klebanoff, 1974; EDBS, 1975]. The exercises are designed specifically for use with EDBS, but their use with other DBMS's is not precluded. The first set of exercises acquaints the student with the facilities of the DBMS. The next set of exercises consists of games that require the players to interact with the DBMS in more complex ways. Both the exercises and games are designed for use with an interactive DBMS.

The aim of the programming exercises is to acquaint the students with the DML of the DBMS. They involve simple queries and some simple modifications with as little interaction between users as possible. The modification exercises require a student to insert, change, and delete data that "belong" only to him. These first exercises give a comprehensive view of the DML and, yet, are not so numerous or lengthy as to burden or bore the student.

The data base games involve more complex interactions with the DBMS and between the students. In the type of games used, the data base contains the current state of the game. In order to plan his play, a player must query the data base to discover the state of the game. A player must modify the data base to actually participate in the game. The rules of the game constrain the players in the actions they may perform. In playing the game, the student gains experience both in retrieving information and in modifying the data base using a DBMS. Hopefully, the games will also illustrate what a DBMS can and cannot do for its users.

A.2 EXERCISES

A.2.1 Hierarchical Exercises

This set of exercises uses a data base for a small company. The data base contains data about the inventory, suppliers, departments, and employees of the company. The company is divided into several departments, each of which has a number of employees and uses a number of parts, which it gets from one or more different suppliers. The data base is structured according to the hierarchical data model to reflect this structure of the company. The hierarchical definition tree for the data base is shown in Fig. A.2.1–1.

The DEPARTMENT segment type contains the department name. The EMPLOYEE segment type indicates which employees work for a department. It contains the employee's number, name, salary, and the employee number of his manager. The PART segment type indicates the parts used by a department and contains the part name. Finally, the SUPPLIER segment type indicates the suppliers that supply a part to a

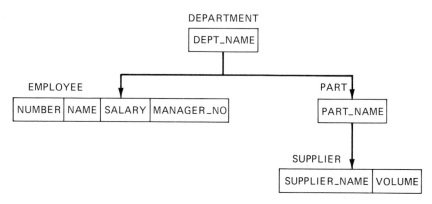

Fig. A.2.1–1 Corporate hierarchical definition tree.

department. It contains the supplier's name and the volume of the part supplied. The data base definition, in the EDBS DDL, follows.

```
DATA BASE CORPORATE HIERARCHICAL

    SEGMENT DEPARTMENT
        FIELD DEPT_NAME, STRING 15 : KEY
        SEGMENT EMPLOYEE
            FIELD NUMBER, NUMERIC (9,0) : KEY
            FIELD NAME, STRING 20
            FIELD SALARY, NUMERIC (9,2)
            FIELD MANAGER_NO, NUMERIC (9,0)
        END EMPLOYEE
        SEGMENT PART
            FIELD PART_NAME, STRING 20 : KEY
            SEGMENT SUPPLIER
                FIELD SUPPLIER_NAME, STRING 20 : KEY
                FIELD VOLUME, NUMERIC (7,1)
            END SUPPLIER
        END PART
    END DEPARTMENT

END CORPORATE
```

Exercises

1 The hierarchical schema of the CORPORATE data base can be translated into a relational schema in a straightforward manner. Give a relational schema for the CORPORATE data base.

2 Given the name of a department, design a program that finds the names of all parts used by the department, and the names of the suppliers that supply each part.

3 Given the name of a supplier, design a program that finds the names of all employees who work for a department that is supplied by the supplier.

4 Given the name of a department, design a program that inserts a new EMPLOYEE segment into the data base under the department.

5 Given an employee number, design a program that increments the value of the SALARY field of the corresponding EMPLOYEE segment.

6 Given an employee number, design a program that deletes the corresponding EMPLOYEE segment.

A.2.2   Network Exercises

This set of exercises uses a data base for a group of investors and businesses. The data base contains data about the investors, the businesses, the businesses in which an investor has investments, and the investors who have an interest in a business. In general, an investor may have interests in many businesses and a business may be financed by several investors. The data base is structured as a network that reflects the $N:M$ relationship between investors and businesses. The data structure diagram for the data base is shown in Fig. A.2.2–1.

The INVESTORS record type identifies an investor. It contains the investor id, name, birthdate, and the amount of capital available for investment. The BUSINESSES record type identifies a business. It contains the business name, location, the type of business, and the total assets of the business. The SHARES record type identifies the blocks of shares either held by an investor or for sale. It contains the percentage of total shares of the company represented by the SHARES record and the value of the shares.

The OWNS DBTG set groups all investments by one investor in various businesses in one set occurrence. The OWNED_BY DBTG set groups all shares of one business in one set occurrence. The sum of the percentage values for all shares in a company must equal 100%. Normally, all SHARES records are members in some occurrence of an OWNED_BY DBTG set. However, shares may be available to investors. This fact is indicated by the absence of a SHARES record as a member in

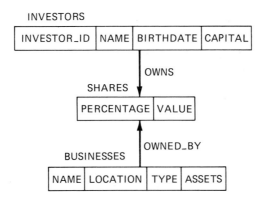

Fig. A.2.2–1 Investment data structure diagram.

an OWNS set occurrence. The data base definition, in the EDBS DDL, follows. All sets are optional-manual.

DATA BASE INVESTMENT NETWORK

    RECORD INVESTORS
        DATA-ITEM INVESTOR_ID, NUMERIC (9,0) : KEY
        DATA-ITEM NAME, STRING 20
        DATA-ITEM BIRTHDATE, DATE
        DATA-ITEM CAPITAL, NUMERIC (9,2)
    END INVESTORS

    RECORD BUSINESSES
        DATA-ITEM NAME, STRING 20 : KEY
        DATA-ITEM LOCATION, STRING 10
        DATA-ITEM TYPE, STRING 10
        DATA-ITEM ASSETS, NUMERIC (10,2)
    END BUSINESSES

    RECORD SHARES
        DATA-ITEM PERCENTAGE, NUMERIC (3,0)
        DATE-ITEM VALUE, NUMERIC (10,2)
    END SHARES

    SET OWNS
        OWNER IS INVESTORS
        MEMBER IS SHARES
    END OWNS

```
    SET OWNED_BY
        OWNER IS BUSINESSES
        MEMBER IS SHARES
    END OWNED_BY

END INVESTMENT
```

Exercises

1 Express the INVESTMENT schema as a relational 3NF schema.

2 Given an investor id, design a program that determines the businesses in which the investor has an interest, and the percentage and value of each interest.

3 Given the name of a business, design a program that finds the investors who have an interest in the business and the percentage and value of each interest.

4 Design a program that stores a new INVESTORS record.

5 Given the name of a business and an investor id, design a program that finds an available SHARES record, which is not currently a member in an OWNS set occurrence, for the business. Include this record as a member in the OWNS set occurrence owned by the given investor and subtract the amount of the investment from the investor's capital.

6 Given an investor id, design a program that deletes the corresponding INVESTORS record.

A.2.3 Relational Exercises

This set of exercises uses a small data base for a school. The data base contains data about the students, their marks, and the classes given in the school. The relations that comprise the data base are shown in Fig. A.2.3−1.

The STUDENT relation contains a student's number, name, and birthdate. Each student is uniquely identified by a nine-digit positive

```
STUDENT (NUMBER, NAME, BIRTHDATE)
CLASS (NUMBER, SUBJECT, LEVEL, TEACHER)
COURSE (STUDENT_NUMBER, CLASS_NUMBER, MARK)
```

Fig. A.2.3−1 School relational schema.

integer. There is one STUDENT tuple for each student in the school. The CLASS relation contains the class number, the subject, the level at which the subject is taught, and the teacher for the class. For each class given in the school, there is one CLASS tuple in the data base. Each class is identified by a four-digit positive integer. The classes are each taught a subject at a particular level. The level is denoted by a two-digit positive integer. The COURSE relation contains a student number, class number, and the mark received by the student in the class. Each mark is an integer between 0 and 100. One student may be in several classes. The data base definition, in the EDBS DDL, follows.

```
DATA BASE SCHOOL RELATIONAL

    RELATION STUDENT
        DOMAIN NUMBER, NUMERIC (9,0) : KEY
        DOMAIN NAME, STRING 20
        DOMAIN BIRTHDATE, DATE
    END STUDENT

    RELATION CLASS
        DOMAIN NUMBER, NUMERIC (4,0) : KEY
        DOMAIN SUBJECT, STRING 10
        DOMAIN LEVEL, NUMERIC (2,0)
        DOMAIN TEACHER, STRING 20
    END CLASS

    RELATION COURSE
        DOMAIN STUDENT_NUMBER, NUMERIC (9,0) : KEY
        DOMAIN CLASS_NUMBER, NUMERIC (4,0) : KEY
        DOMAIN MARK, NUMERIC (3,0)
    END COURSE

    END SCHOOL
```

Exercises

1 Is the SCHOOL schema in second normal form? What assumptions are necessary to ensure that the schema is in third normal form?

2 Given the name of a subject, design a program that finds the names of all the teachers teaching the subject and the level at which they teach the subject.

3 Given the name of a subject and the level at which it is taught, design a program that finds the average mark for the subject.

4 Design a program that inserts a new STUDENT tuple and COURSE tuples for that student into the data base.

5 Given a class number and a student number, design a program that changes the mark of the student for the class.

6 Given a student number, design a program that deletes all mention of the student from the data base.

A.3 GAMES

The games discussed in this section are designed to help the students understand data base management concepts and uses. The games simulate a real-world environment. In the first game—Stock Market—the players buy and sell shares in various imaginary companies. In the second game—Real Estate—the players buy, sell, and mortgage houses. In the third game—Production—each player owns a fictitious company and must secure enough supplies in order to produce finished products, which can then be sold.

Unlike "board" games where two to six people sit around a playing board for a few hours at a time, these games involve the entire class and are played over a period of a few weeks. The more the students participate and get involved, the more fun the games will become, and the better strategists they are, the more assets they will accumulate at the end.

The current state of the game is kept in a data base that all players can interrogate at any time (rules permitting). The format of the data within the data base is discussed with each of the games. Participation in the games involves making modifications to the data base.

What differentiates these games from standard programming exercises is that the games themselves are not concerned with the DBMS or data management, but with competitive play between players. The DBMS is just a tool needed to play the game. The enjoyment of the exercise comes from competition in the game.

For practical purposes, the games have been designed to be played in an intermittent mode. A game should be scheduled to be played over a period of time on the order of several weeks. Each player is allowed to make his moves intermittently at times convenient to him; there is no requirement to play in turn. This mode of play should alleviate the problem of scheduling times when both terminals and the students are available.

A.3.1 Stock Market Game

In this game the players buy and sell shares in various imaginary companies. A player starts out with $20,000 and no stocks in his portfolio. He can then make money by receiving dividends or by selling stocks for more than he paid for them. The object is to accumulate as valuable a portfolio as possible. At the end of the game each portfolio is evaluated by using the share price of the last sale of a company's stock as the value of the company's shares.

When a person wants to buy or sell shares he first sees if there is an offer that is acceptable in price and quantity. If so he accepts that offer, taking the whole quantity of the offer. Otherwise, he makes a bid, an offer to purchase, or an ask, an offer to sell, for a specific price per share and quantity and waits for someone to accept his offer. The player must decide what is the best price he can get and what quantities will be acceptable to the other players. He may decide to split his offer into several smaller offers, perhaps with different prices.

A player may base his strategy on several sources of information. He may see the last price of each stock and all the current bids and asks. He may also look at the number of shares outstanding and the dividend notices for the companies. Of course, he may also look at his own portfolio. However, he may not look at the state of any other player's portfolio.

The game administrator can offer for sale any shares to inflate or deflate the market artificially.

The Data Base

The stock market game uses a hierarchical data base. The data base definition, in the EDBS DDL, follows.

```
DATA BASE STOCK_MARKET HIERARCHICAL

    SEGMENT PLAYERCASH
        FIELD PLAYER, NUMERIC (9,0) : KEY
        FIELD CASH, NUMERIC (9,2)
    END PLAYERCASH

    SEGMENT COMPANY
        FIELD NAME, STRING 20 : KEY
        FIELD OUTSTANDING, NUMERIC (5,0)
        FIELD PRICE, NUMERIC (8,2)
```

```
SEGMENT BID
    FIELD PLAYER, NUMERIC (9,0) : KEY
    FIELD TIME, NUMERIC (14,0) : KEY
    FIELD QUANTITY, NUMERIC (5,0)
    FIELD PRICE, NUMERIC (8,2)
END BID
SEGMENT ASK
    FIELD PLAYER, NUMERIC (9,0) : KEY
    FIELD TIME, NUMERIC (14,0) : KEY
    FIELD QUANTITY, NUMERIC (5,0)
    FIELD PRICE, NUMERIC (8,2)
END ASK
SEGMENT SHAREHOLDER
    FIELD PLAYER, NUMERIC (9,0) : KEY
    FIELD QUANTITY, NUMERIC (5,0)
    FIELD PAID, NUMERIC (9,2)
    FIELD RECEIVED, NUMERIC (9,2)
    FIELD LAST_DIVIDEND, NUMERIC (14,0)
END SHAREHOLDER
SEGMENT PURCHASE
    FIELD PLAYER, NUMERIC (9,0) : KEY
    FIELD TIME, NUMERIC (14,0) : KEY
    FIELD QUANTITY, NUMERIC (5,0)
    FIELD PRICE, NUMERIC (8,2)
END PURCHASE
SEGMENT SALE
    FIELD PLAYER, NUMERIC (9,0) : KEY
    FIELD TIME, NUMERIC (14,0) : KEY
    FIELD QUANTITY, NUMERIC (5,0)
    FIELD PRICE, NUMERIC (8,2)
END SALE
SEGMENT DIVIDEND_NOTICE
    FIELD TIME, NUMERIC (14,0) : KEY
    FIELD AMOUNT, NUMERIC (6,2)
END DIVIDEND_NOTICE
END COMPANY

END STOCK_MARKET
```

The PLAYERCASH, COMPANY, BID, ASK, and DIVIDEND_ NOTICE segment types are fairly self-explanatory. The PLAYERCASH segment type gives the amount of cash on hand. The COMPANY segment type gives the company name, the number of shares outstanding, and the last price of the company's stock. The BID and ASK segment types give the players making bids and asks and the prices per share and quantities of the offers. The DIVIDEND_NOTICE segment type records the amount of the dividend and the time the dividend is payable.

The SHAREHOLDER, PURCHASE, and SALE segment types are more difficult. The information about a player's portfolio is spread among the various company segments. Within a company segment there is one SHAREHOLDER segment for each player who ever was a shareholder in the company. The SHAREHOLDER segment records the number of shares he currently holds, the total price he has paid for all his purchases of the company's stock, the total amount he has received from the company's dividends and the company's stock, and the time the last dividend he received was payable. A SHAREHOLDER segment is confidential; a player may not examine another player's SHARE-HOLDER segments. However, when a player effects a sale or purchase he must notify the other party. This is done by inserting a PURCHASE or SALE segment with the other player's number and the time, quantity, and price per share of the trade. Each player must do periodic housekeeping to collect his purchase and sale notices and update his SHAREHOLDER segments.

Rules

1. Each player starts out with $20,000 and no shares.

2. Initially all shares are held by the game administrator and will be sold in lots of approximately $500, with each share priced at about twenty times the first dividend.

3. Each player must make at least 10 and at most 25 transactions during the game.

4. Shares must be bought or sold in lots of 100 or more.

5. Shares are sold by accepting a bid or posting an ask and waiting for its acceptance. There are the following restrictions:

(a) A player may not sell shares he does not own.
(b) A bid is accepted by:
　　(i) deleting the bid from the data base;
　　(ii) inserting a PURCHASE segment giving the purchaser's number and the time, price per share, and quantity of the trade under the company's COMPANY segment;

(iii) updating the PRICE field of the COMPANY segment with the price per share of the trade;

(iv) updating the seller's own SHAREHOLDER segment;

(v) updating the seller's own PLAYERCASH segment.

(c) If there are two or more acceptable bids for the same price and quantity the earliest must be accepted before the rest.

(d) An ask is posted by inserting an ASK segment with the player number and the time, price per share, and quantity of the ask.

(e) A player may not post an ask if there is already an outstanding bid for the same price and quantity as the ask.

6. Shares are bought by accepting an ask or by posting a bid and waiting for its acceptance. There are the following restrictions:

(a) A player may not spend more money than he has.

(b) An ask is accepted by:

(i) deleting the ask from the data base;

(ii) inserting a SALE segment giving the seller's number and the time, price per share, and the quantity of the trade under the COMPANY segment;

(iii) updating the PRICE field of the COMPANY segment with the price per share of the trade;

(iv) updating the buyer's own SHAREHOLDER segment;

(v) updating the buyer's own PLAYERCASH segment.

(c) If there are two or more acceptable bids then the earliest must be accepted before the rest.

(d) A bid is made by inserting a BID segment with the bidder's number, the time, price per share, and quantity of the bid under the COMPANY segment of the company whose stock is being bid on.

(e) A player may not make a bid if there is already an outstanding ask for the same price and quantity as the bid.

7. A player must periodically collect any sale or purchase notices with his number on them and update his SHAREHOLDER and PLAYERCASH segments. A sale notice is collected by deleting the SALE segment, subtracting the quantity sold from the player's QUANTITY field of the SHAREHOLDER segment for that company, and adding the total price of the trade to the RECEIVED field of his SHAREHOLDER segment and to the CASH field of his PLAYERCASH segment. A purchase notice is collected by deleting the PURCHASE segment, inserting a SHAREHOLDER segment if necessary, adding the quantity bought to the QUANTITY field of the SHAREHOLDER

segment for that company, and adding the total price to the PAID field of the SHAREHOLDER segment and subtracting it from the CASH field of the PLAYERCASH segment.

8. At any one time a player may have at most a total of five BID and PURCHASE segments and a total of five ASK and SALE segments under any company.

9. A player may delete or modify a BID or ASK segment with his number on it. Otherwise BID and ASK segments may not be modified and may only be deleted to accept the bid or ask.

10. The game administrator announces dividends by inserting DIVIDEND_NOTICE segments. A player may claim a dividend for each share he owned at the time the dividend was payable. He receives the dividend by adding his total dividend (the amount in the dividend notice times the number of shares he owned in the company when the dividend was payable) to the RECEIVED field of his SHAREHOLDER segment for that company and to the CASH field of his PLAYERCASH segment.

11. The penalty for violating any of the rules, except for rule 3, is $1000 plus any gain made through the violation. Penalties will be assessed at the end of the game. The game administrator may correct any of the rule violations during the game. The penalty for violating rule 3 is $2000 times the number of transactions by which the minimum was missed. The penalty is $2000 for each transaction by which the maximum is exceeded plus any gain made.

12. The game administrator reserves the right to take whatever actions are deemed necessary to ensure the fairness, stability, and competitiveness of the game. This includes, but is not restricted to, amending existing or adding new rules, and changing the status of the game.

A.3.2 Real Estate Game

In this game, players buy and sell houses, mortgage houses, or issue mortgages on houses. A player starts out with $200,000 and no houses. He can then make money by buying houses and selling them at a higher price or by issuing mortgages and collecting interest on them. The object of the game is to accumulate as valuable a combination of real estate, mortgage holdings, and cash as possible. At the end of the game each player's assets are evaluated based on the current market value of his real estate and the cash value of his mortgage holdings and cash on hand.

Houses are bought and sold by players making bids on houses and the owners accepting one of the bids. Houses are mortgaged to raise capital in one of two ways. A player may offer a mortgage. This mortgage may then be accepted by any player who owns a house subject to certain constraints. On the other hand, an owner of a house may request a mortgage at a certain amount and rate of interest. Another player may then accept this request.

A player has access to a good deal of data on which to base his play. He may examine all the data on a particular house. These data include the area a house is in, its last selling price, the date last sold, and the current asking price. All outstanding mortgages and offers or requests for mortgages may also be examined. Mortgage information consists of the amount of the mortgage, the interest rate, and its due date. A player may also see the current bids on any house and the market history of the house. He does not have access to the current cash position, houses owned, mortgages held, or bids outstanding of another player.

The game administrator initially owns any excess houses and may from time to time build new houses and offer them for sale.

The Data Base

The real estate game uses a network data base. The data base definition, in the EDBS DDL, follows.

```
DATA BASE REAL_ESTATE NETWORK
    RECORD PLAYER
        DATA-ITEM NUMBER, NUMERIC (9,0) : KEY
        DATA-ITEM CASH, NUMERIC (8,2)
    END PLAYER

    RECORD HOUSES
        DATA-ITEM HOUSE_NO, NUMERIC (4,0) : KEY
        DATA-ITEM AREA_NAME, STRING 15 : KEY
        DATA-ITEM BUYING_PRICE, NUMERIC (8,2)
        DATA-ITEM DATE_BOUGHT, DATE
        DATA-ITEM ASKING, NUMERIC (8,2)
    END HOUSES

    RECORD MORTGAGES
        DATA-ITEM PRINCIPAL, NUMERIC (8,2)
        DATA-ITEM MATURES, DATE
```

```
            DATA-ITEM INTEREST, NUMERIC (4,1)
            DATA-ITEM PAYMENT, NUMERIC (8,2)
       END MORTGAGES

       RECORD BIDS
            DATA-ITEM AMOUNT, NUMERIC (8,2)
            DATA-ITEM HOUSE_NO, NUMERIC (4,0)
            DATA-ITEM AREA_NAME, STRING 15
       END BIDS

       RECORD AREA
            DATA-ITEM NAME, STRING 15 : KEY
       END AREA

       RECORD MARKET_VALUE
            DATA-ITEM DATE, DATE : KEY
            DATA-ITEM APPRECIATION, NUMERIC (4,1)
       END MARKET_VALUE

       SET OWNER
            OWNER IS PLAYER
            MEMBER IS HOUSES
       END OWNER

       SET MORTGAGOR
            OWNER IS PLAYER
            MEMBER IS MORTGAGES
       END MORTGAGOR

       SET MORTGAGEE
            OWNER IS HOUSES
            MEMBER IS MORTGAGES
       END MORTGAGEE

       SET PLAYER_BIDS
            OWNER IS PLAYER
            MEMBER IS BIDS
       END PLAYER_BIDS

       SET OFFERS
            OWNER IS HOUSES
            MEMBER IS BIDS
       END OFFERS
```

```
SET HOUSING
    OWNER IS AREA
    MEMBER IS HOUSES
END HOUSING

SET HISTORY
    OWNER IS AREA
    MEMBER IS MARKET_VALUE
END HISTORY

END REAL_ESTATE
```

The PLAYER record type indicates the amount of cash a player has on hand. The HOUSES record type contains all the data on a house. A house is identified by its house number and the area it is in. The other data-items give the price at which the house was bought, the date it was bought, and the current asking price. The OWNER DBTG set relates houses to their current owner. The MORTGAGES record type indicates the current offers and requests for mortgages as well as current mortgages held. An offer of a mortgage is identified by its membership in a MORTGAGOR set occurrence and its absence from a MORTGAGEE set occurrence. A request for a mortgage is identified by its membership in a MORTGAGEE set occurrence and its absence from a MORT- GAGOR set occurrence. The PAYMENT data-item is used to transfer interest and principal payments between the mortgagee and the mort- gagor. The interest is expressed as a percentage.

The BIDS record type indicates all bids on houses. The PLAYER_ BIDS DBTG set groups BID records by player, while the OFFERS DBTG set groups BID records by the house that the bid is on. The AREA record type is used to relate the market history of an area to its houses via the HISTORY and HOUSING DBTG sets. The MARKET_ VALUE record type depicts the history of house prices in an area. The APPRECIATION data-item is a percentage indicating the percent- age increase (decrease if negative) in the value of houses in an area on the date given. These data are used to calculate the current maximum allowable asking price for a house in a given area.

Rules

1. Each player starts out with $200,000 and no houses.
2. Houses are "built" by the game administrator and are placed on the market as they are completed.

3. Each player must make at least five and at most fifteen transactions. A transaction is considered to be the sale or purchase of a house or the holding of a mortgage.

4. All houses are considered to be for sale. A player indicates his intent to buy a house by placing a bid on the house. Bids are subject to the following constraints:

(a) The total value of all of a player's bids may not exceed the total amount of his cash reserves.

(b) A player may only have one bid on a house.

(c) A player makes a bid on a house by:
(i) inserting a BIDS record containing the amount of the bid and the house number and area name for the house;
(ii) including the BIDS record in the PLAYER_BIDS set occurrence owned by the bidder's PLAYER record;
(iii) including the BIDS record in the OFFERS set occurrence owned by the house on which the bid is being made.

(d) The bid may be for any amount that the bidder deems reasonable. It must not be for the same amount as another bid on the same house.

(e) Provided a bid has not been accepted, a player may withdraw his bid by deleting the appropriate BIDS record. A player may not delete another player's bid.

(f) A player may change the amount of his bid at any time prior to its acceptance. He may not change another player's bid.

5. A house is sold by the owner accepting one of the bids on it. The following restrictions apply:

(a) A player may not sell a house he does not own.

(b) Only one bid may be accepted.

(c) A bid is accepted and a house sold by:
(i) removing the acceptable bid from the OFFERS set occurrence owned by the house being sold;
(ii) adding the amount of the sale to the seller's cash reserves;
(iii) discharging any mortgages currently held on the house;
(iv) removing the house from the OWNER set occurrence owned by the seller's PLAYER record.

6. A player has bought a house when the bid he made on it is no longer a member of the OFFERS set occurrence owned by the house. A

house is bought by:

(a) deleting the purchaser's bid,
(b) subtracting the amount of the purchase from the purchaser's cash reserves,
(c) including the house in the purchaser's OWNER set occurrence,
(d) updating the buying price and date bought for the house,
(e) possibly updating the asking price for the house, which may not exceed the current market value of the house, although it may be less.

7. Houses may be mortgaged in order to raise capital. Mortgages may be either offered or requested. There are the following restrictions:

(a) A player may not offer a mortgage for more money than he has cash.
(b) A player may not request a mortgage for more than 80% of the current market value of his house.
(c) The value of all the mortgages on a house may not exceed the current market value of the house.
(d) A mortgage is offered (requested) by:
   (i) inserting a MORTGAGES record with the appropriate principal, due date, interest rate (in percentage), and a zero payment value;
   (ii) including it in the MORTGAGOR (MORTGAGEE) set occurrence owned by the player's PLAYER (HOUSES) record.
(e) A mortgage offer (request) is accepted by:
   (i) including the MORTGAGES record in the MORTGAGEE (MORTGAGOR) set occurrence owned by the player's HOUSES (PLAYER) record;
   (ii) adding (subtracting) the amount of the mortgage to (from) the player's cash reserves.

8. Interest on mortgages is payable at the end of every period. The interest is calculated based on the amount of the principal remaining at the *end* of the period. Interest is paid by:

(a) adding the amount (principal times interest rate) to the payment value of the MORTGAGES record;
(b) subtracting a similar amount from the player's cash reserves.

9. All or part of the principal of a mortgage may be paid at any time. If all of the principal is paid, then the mortgage is said to be *discharged*. The following conditions apply:

(a) A mortgage may not be discharged within its first period of tenure.

(b) If the principal outstanding on a mortgage has not been paid by the date that the mortgage matures, then a penalty of 10% of the amount outstanding will be charged for every day that the mortgage is overdue. This amount is payable to the mortgage holder.

(c) Overdue mortgages may be discharged by the game administrator. The ownership of the house reverts to the game administrator. The current owner will receive the sum of 50% of the current market value of the house minus the amount required to discharge all outstanding mortgages.

(d) Payments on the principal are made by:

    (i) subtracting the amount of the payment from the principal of the mortgage;

    (ii) adding the amount of the payment to the payment value of the mortgage;

    (iii) Subtracting the amount of the payment from the player's cash reserves;

    (iv) If the mortgage is being discharged, then removing the MORTGAGES record from the MORTGAGEE set occurrence.

10. The current market value of a house within an area is calculated from the MARKET_VALUE records of the area's HISTORY set occurrence. It is equal to the buying price of a house plus the product of the buying price and the appreciation value of the most recent MARKET_VALUE record containing a date *greater than* the date on which the house was purchased. Appreciation values may be positive or negative. The game administrator will reassess the market value of houses within an area from time to time.

11. A player must periodically perform some housekeeping duties. These consist of:

(a) collecting any payments made on mortgages he holds, adding such payments to his cash reserves, and setting the payment value to zero;

(b) determining if any outstanding bids he made have been accepted;

(c) deleting any mortgages he holds that have been discharged;

(d) adjusting the asking price for any houses he owns to reflect the market situation.

12. At the end of the game, a player's assets are determined as follows:

(a) Cash is valued at face value.

(b) Mortgages held are valued up to the portion of the principal that the mortgagee is able to pay from his assets.

(c) Houses are valued at their current market value.

(d) A player's mortgages are discharged and the amount subtracted from the total of (a), (b), and (c). If a player's assets are insufficient to discharge all his mortgages, then a portion proportionate to the principal outstanding will be paid on each mortgage from the player's assets.

13. The penalty for violating any of the rules, except rule 3, is $10,000 plus any gain made through the violation. The penalty for violating rule 3 is $20,000 times the number of transactions by which the minimum was missed. The penalty is $20,000 for each transaction by which the maximum was exceeded plus any gain made. Penalties will be assessed at the end of the game. The game administrator may correct any violations during the game.

14. The game administrator reserves the right to take whatever actions are deemed necessary to ensure the fairness, stability, and competitiveness of the game. This includes, but is not restricted to, amending existing or adding new rules, or changing the status of the game.

A.3.3 Production Game

In this game each player runs his own company. Each company has several projects, each requiring several different supplies and producing several different products. Each project has a deadline by which it must be completed, or the company will face a penalty.

The players each start out with $20,000 and no inventory. The game administrator initially offers for sale enough of the goods for the companies to start some of their projects. From then on the players may buy or sell any of the goods on an open market. Since each product will be used by several different companies and produced by several companies, the market should be fairly lively.

The object of the game is to accumulate the most assets by the end of the game. Cash will be valued at face value. Inventory will be valued using a weighted average of the prices paid for the goods during the game. The weighting is used to give the latest prices the most importance in the valuation of the goods.

The players will have access to a good deal of data. A history of all the transactions, requirements and products of the various projects, and records of all completed projects are all public data. The only private data are the project deadlines and company cash and inventory positions; a player will only know his own deadlines and cash and inventory positions. Each player will have to use these data to try to out-guess his opponents. He must time his purchases to buy the goods he needs at as low a price as possible and time his sales to get as high a price as possible. In addition, a player may try to speculate in goods that he does not use or produce.

The Data Base

The production game uses a relational data base. The data base definition, in the EDBS DDL, follows.

DATA BASE PRODUCTION RELATIONAL

    RELATION OFFER
        DOMAIN PART, STRING 10 : KEY
        DOMAIN SUPPLIER, NUMERIC (9,0) : KEY
        DOMAIN PRICE, NUMERIC (9,2) : KEY
        DOMAIN QUANTITY, NUMERIC (6,0)
    END OFFER

    RELATION SALE
        DOMAIN PART, STRING 10 : KEY
        DOMAIN SELLER, NUMERIC (9,0) : KEY
        DOMAIN PRICE, NUMERIC (9,2) : KEY
        DOMAIN QUANTITY, NUMERIC (6,0)
    END SALE

    RELATION TRANSACTION
        DOMAIN PART, STRING 10 : KEY
        DOMAIN SELLER, NUMERIC (9,0) : KEY
        DOMAIN PURCHASER, NUMERIC (9,0) : KEY

```
        DOMAIN TIME, NUMERIC (14,0) : KEY
        DOMAIN QUANTITY, NUMERIC (6,0)
        DOMAIN PRICE, NUMERIC (9,2)
    END TRANSACTION

    RELATION COMPLETION
        DOMAIN COMPANY, NUMERIC (9,0) : KEY
        DOMAIN PROJECT, STRING 10 : KEY
        DOMAIN TIME, NUMERIC (14,0)
    END COMPLETION

    RELATION REQUIREMENT
        DOMAIN COMPANY, NUMERIC (9,0) : KEY
        DOMAIN PROJECT, STRING 10 : KEY
        DOMAIN PART, STRING 10 : KEY
        DOMAIN QUANTITY, NUMERIC (6,0)
    END REQUIREMENT

    RELATION PRODUCT
        DOMAIN COMPANY, NUMERIC (9,0) : KEY
        DOMAIN PROJECT, STRING 10 : KEY
        DOMAIN PART, STRING 10 : KEY
        DOMAIN QUANTITY, NUMERIC (6,0)
    END PRODUCT

    RELATION INVENTORY
        DOMAIN COMPANY, NUMERIC (9,0) : KEY
        DOMAIN PART, STRING 10 : KEY
        DOMAIN QUANTITY, NUMERIC (6,0)
    END INVENTORY

    RELATION CASH
        DOMAIN COMPANY, NUMERIC (9,0) : KEY
        DOMAIN AMOUNT, NUMERIC (9,2)
    END CASH

    RELATION DEADLINE
        DOMAIN COMPANY, NUMERIC (9,0) : KEY
        DOMAIN PROJECT, STRING 10 : KEY
        DOMAIN DATE, DATE
    END DEADLINE

END PRODUCTION
```

The OFFER relation contains all current offers to sell goods. The SALE relation indicates sales of parts offered. The TRANSACTION relation contains a history of all transactions that have been made. Records of when and which projects have been completed are kept in the COMPLETION relation. The REQUIREMENT and PRODUCT relations give the parts required and parts produced by each project. The INVENTORY and CASH relations record the inventory and cash positions of all the companies. The DEADLINE relation indicates the date by which a company must finish a project.

Rules

1. Each player starts with $20,000 cash and no inventory.

2. Each player will be assigned a number of projects to be completed, each project with its own deadline. There will be a penalty of $500 per day or part of a day by which the deadline is missed. A project may not be completed more than once.

3. A player may complete a project when he has all the required supplies in his inventory and not committed for sale (see rule 4). A project is completed by:

(a) removing the required supplies from the company's inventory;
(b) entering the products in the company's inventory;
(c) inserting a COMPLETION tuple giving the company number, project number, and the time the project was completed.

4. Goods are offered for sale by inserting a tuple giving the part, the supplier number, the offered price per unit, and the quantity available in the OFFER relation. There are the following restrictions:

(a) A company must always have sufficient inventory to fill all its sales offers.
(b) A company may not have more than one sales offer for the same part and price at the same time.

5. Goods are bought by accepting an offer to sell. Each purchase may be for any quantity up to and including the quantity on the offer to sell. The price per unit must be that on the offer to sell and the purchaser must have sufficient cash to pay for the goods. The procedure for making a purchase is as follows:

(a) If the purchase is for the whole quantity of the offer then the

OFFER tuple is deleted. Otherwise the quantity of the purchase is subtracted from the quantity on the OFFER tuple.

(b) The total purchase price is removed from the purchaser's cash.

(c) The goods purchased are added to the purchaser's inventory.

(d) A tuple giving the part, seller's number, price, and quantity is inserted into the SALE relation.

(e) A tuple giving the part, purchaser and seller numbers, the time quantity, and price per unit of the purchase is inserted into the TRANSACTION relation.

6. A player may cancel any of his sales offers by deleting the OFFER tuple. A player may change the quantity or price of any of his offers by replacing the OFFER tuple. Any such change has no effect on any purchases previously made on that offer.

7. A player must periodically check the SALE relation to determine if he has made any sales. A sale is completed as follows:

(a) The SALE tuple is deleted.

(b) The total amount of the sale is added to the seller's cash.

(c) The quantity of the sale is subtracted from the seller's inventory.

8. A player may not change or cancel another player's offer to sell except to effect a purchase as set out in rule 5.

9. No player may replace, delete, or insert a tuple in the REQUIREMENT or PRODUCT relations.

10. No player may replace or delete a tuple in the TRANSACTION relation.

11. The object of the game is to have the most valuable inventory at the end of the game. At the end of the game a player's assets will be evaluated according to the following rules:

(a) Cash is valued at face value.

(b) Goods are valued using a weighted average of the prices paid for the goods. The transactions are numbered consecutively, in the order in which the transactions were made, with the first transaction given the number 1. If q_i is the quantity purchased in transaction i then the weight for transaction i is $i*q_i$. If p_i is the price per unit in transaction i, $T = \Sigma\ i*q_i*p_i$ and $W = \Sigma\ i*q_i$, where in both sums i ranges over the transactions involving part X, then each unit of part X will be valued at T/W.

(c) A player is penalized $1000 for each project that he has not completed.

12. The penalty for violating any of the rules, other than the missing of a deadline, is $1000 plus any gain made as a result of the violation. Any rule violations may be corrected by the game administrator during the game. Penalties will be assessed at the end of the game.

13. The game administrator reserves the right to take whatever actions are deemed necessary to ensure the fairness, stability, and competitiveness of the game. This includes, but is not restricted to, amending existing or adding new rules, and changing the status of the game.

REFERENCES

The following abreviations are used:

ACM   Association for Computing Machinery
AFIPS   American Federation of Information Processing Societies
CACM   Communications of the ACM
CODASYL   Conference on Data Systems Languages
FJCC   Fall Joint Computer Conference
IFIP   International Federation for Information Processing
NCC   National Computer Conference
SIGFIDET   Special Interest Group on File Description and Translation
SIGMOD   Special Interest Group on Management of Data (formerly SIGFIDET)

Abrial, J. R. [1974]. "Data Semantics," *in Data Base Management* (Klimbie, J. W., and Koffeman, K. L., eds.), pp. 1–59. North-Holland, Amsterdam.

ANSI/X3/SPARC [1975]. "Interim Report ANSI/X3/SPARC Study Group on Data Base Management Systems," *FDT* 7 (2).

Ashenhurst, R. L. [1974]. "A Great Debate," *CACM* 17, 360.

Ashenhurst, R. L., and Vonderohe, R. H. [1975]. "A Hierarchical Network," *Datamation* 21, (2) 40–44.

Astrahan, M. M., *et al.* [1976]. "System R: Relational Approach to Database Management," *ACM Trans. Database Sys.* 1, 97–137.

Astrahan, M. M., and Chamberlin, D. D. [1975]. "Implementation of a Structured English Query Language," *CACM* 18, 580–588.

Astrahan, M. M., and Lorie, R. A. [1975]. "SEQUEL-XRM, A Relational System," *Proc. ACM Pacific 1975*, 34–38.

Bachman, C. W. [1969]. "Data Structure Diagrams," *Data Base* 1 (2), 4–10.

Bachman, C. W. [1973a]. "Implementation Techniques for Data Structure Sets," *in Data Base Management Systems* (Jardine, D. A., ed.), pp. 147–157. North-Holland, Amsterdam.

Bachman, C. W. [1973b]. "The Programmer as Navigator," *CACM* **16**, 653–658.

Bachman, C. W. [1974a]. "The Data Structure Set Model," *Proc. ACM SIGMOD, Data Models: Data-Structure-Set versus Relational* (Rustin, R., ed.), pp. 1–10.

Bachman, C. W. [1974b]. "Summary of Current Work: ANSI/X3/SPARC/Study Group–Database Systems," *FDT* **6** (3), 16–39.

Bayer, R. [1974]. "Storage Characteristics and Methods for Searching and Addressing," *Proc. IFIP Congr. 1974*, pp. 440–444. North-Holland, Amsterdam.

Bayer, R., and McCreight, E. M. [1972]. "Organization and Maintenance of Large Ordered Indexes," *Acta Informat.* **1**, 173–189.

Bayer, R., and Metzger, J. K. [1976]. "On the Encipherment of Search Trees and Random Access Files," *ACM Trans. Database Sys.* **1**, 37–52.

Bernstein, P. A. [1975]. *Normalization and Functional Dependencies in the Relational Data Base Model.* Ph.D. thesis, Dep. Computer Science, Univ. of Toronto, Canada.

Bernstein, P. A., and Tsichritzis, D. C. [1975]. "Allocating Storage in Hierarchical Data Bases Using Traces," *Information Sys.* **1**, 133–140.

Bjørner, D., Codd, E. F., Deckert, K. L., and Traiger, I. L. [1973]. *The Gamma Zero N-ary Relational Data Base Interface: Specifications of Objects and Operations.* Tech. rep. RJ1200, IBM Res. Lab., San Jose, California.

Bleier, R. E. [1967]. "Treating Hierarchical Data Structures in the SDC Time-Shared Data Management System (TDMS)," *Proc. ACM Nat. Conf.,* 41–49.

Bleier, R. E., and Vorhaus, A. H. [1968]. "File Organization in the SDC Time-Shared Data Management System (TDMS)," *Proc. IFIP Congr. 1968,* Vol. 2, pp. 1245–1252. North-Holland, Amsterdam.

Boyce, R. F., and Chamberlin, D. D. [1973]. *Using a Structured English Query Language as a Data Definition Facility.* Tech. rep. RJ1318, IBM Res. Lab., San Jose, California.

Boyce, R. F., Chamberlin, D. D., King, W. F., III, and Hammer, M. M. [1974]. "Specifying Queries as Relational Expressions," *in Data Base Management* (Klimbie, J. W., and Koffeman, K. L., eds.), pp. 169–176. North-Holland, Amsterdam.

Bracchi, G., Fedeli, A., and Paolini, P. [1972]. "A Relational Data Base Management System," *Proc. ACM Nat. Conf.,* 1080–1089.

Bracchi, G., Fedeli, A., and Paolini, P. [1974]. "A Multilevel Relational Model for Data Base Management Systems," *in Data Base Management* (Klimbie, J. W., and Koffeman, K. L., eds.), pp. 211–223. North-Holland, Amsterdam.

Brodie, M. L. (ed.), Chan, S. S., Czarnik, B., Leong, E., Schuster, S. A., and Tsichritzis, D. C. [1975]. *ZETA: A Prototype Relational Data Base Management System.* Tech. rep. CSRG-51, Computer Sys. Res. Group, Univ. of Toronto, Canada.

Canadian Datasystems [1973]. "World's First Talking Computer for Shoppers," *Can. Datasys.* **5** (11), 32.

Canning, R. G. (ed.) [1971]. "Advanced Projects in Data Processing," *EDP Analyzer* **9** (11).

Canning, R. G. (ed.) [1972a]. "The Debate on Data Base Management," *EDP Analyzer* **10** (3).

Canning, R. G. (ed.) [1972b]. "The 'Data Administrator' Function," *EDP Analyzer* **10** (11).

Canning, R. G. (ed.) [1973a]. "Distributed Intelligence in Data Communications," *EDP Analyzer* **11** (2).

Canning, R. G. (ed.) [1973b]. "In Your Future: Distributed Systems?" *EDP Analyzer* **11** (8).

CDC [1970]. *MARS VI Multi-Access Retrieval System Reference Manual.* Control Data Corp., 44625500, Sunnyvale, California.

Chamberlin, D. D. [1976]. "Relational Data-Base Management Systems," *ACM Comput. Surveys* **8**, 43–66.

Chamberlin, D. D., and Boyce, R. F. [1974]. "SEQUEL: A Structured English Query Language," *Proc. ACM SIGMOD Workshop on Data Description, Access and Control*, pp. 249–264.

Chamberlin, D. D., Boyce, R. F., and Traiger, I. L. [1974]. "A Deadlock-Free Scheme for Resource Locking in a Data Base Environment," *Proc. IFIP Congr. 1974*, pp. 340–343. North-Holland, Amsterdam.

Chamberlin, D. D., Gray, J. N., and Traiger, I. L. [1975]. "Views, Authorization and Locking in a Relational Data Base System," *Proc. AFIPS* **44**, *NCC*, 425–430.

Chan, S. S. [1974]. *QLS: A Query Language Generator System.* M.Sc. thesis, Dep. Computer Science, Univ. of Toronto, Canada.

Chen, P. P.-S. [1976]. "The Entity-Relationship Model: Toward a Unified View of Data," *ACM Trans. Database Sys.* **1**, 9–36.

Childs, D. L. [1968]. "Feasbility of a Set-Theoretic Data Structure—A General Structure Based on a Reconstituted Definition of Relation," *Proc. IFIP Congr. 1968*, pp. 162–172. North-Holland, Amsterdam.

CII [1973]. *SOCRATE Manuel de Presentation.* Ref. document 4337 P/FR, Compagnie Internationale Pour l'Informatique, Louveciennes, France.

Clark, R. J. (ed.) [1974a]. "The Data Base Administrator: Part 1," *EDP In-Depth Rep.* **3** (12).

Clark, R. J. (ed.) [1974b]. "The Data Base Administrator: Part 2," *EDP In-Depth Rep.* **4** (1).

CODASYL [1969]. *A Survey of Generalized Data Base Management Systems.* CODASYL Sys. Committee tech. rep., ACM, New York.

CODASYL [1971]. *Feature Analysis of Generalized Data Base Management Systems.* CODASYL Sys. Committee tech. rep., ACM, New York.

CODASYL DBTG [1969]. *CODASYL Data Base Task Group Report, Conf. Data Sys. Languages,* ACM, New York.

CODASYL DBTG [1971]. *CODASYL Data Base Task Group Report, Conf. Data Sys. Languages,* ACM, New York.

Codd, E. F. [1970]. "A Relational Model of Data for Large Shared Data Banks," *CACM* **13**, 377–387.

Codd, E. F. [1971a]. "Normalized Data Base Structure: A Brief Tutorial," *Proc. ACM SIGFIDET Workshop on Data Description, Access and Control*, pp. 1–17.

Codd, E. F. [1971b]. "A Data Base Sublanguage Founded on the Relational Calculus," *Proc. ACM SIGFIDET Workshop on Data Description, Access and Control*, pp. 35–68.

Codd, E. F. [1972a]. "Further Normalization of the Data Base Relational Model," in *Data Base Systems, Courant Computer Sci. Symp. 6th* (Rustin, R., ed.), pp. 33–64. Prentice-Hall, Englewood Cliffs, New Jersey.

Codd, E. F. [1972b]. "Relational Completeness of Data Base Sublanguages," *in*

Data Base Systems, Courant Computer Sci. Symp. 6th (Rustin, R., ed.), pp. 65–98. Prentice-Hall, Englewood Cliffs, New Jersey.

Codd, E. F. [1974a]. "Seven Steps to Rendezvous with the Casual User," *in Data Base Management* (Klimbie, J. W., and Koffeman, K. L., ed.), pp. 179–199. North-Holland, Amsterdam.

Codd, E. F. [1974b]. "Recent Investigations in Relational Data Base Systems," *Proc. IFIP Congr. 1974,* pp. 1017–1021. North-Holland, Amsterdam.

Codd, E. F. (ed.) [1975]. *Implementation of Relational Data Base Management Systems.* Panel discussion, Nat. Computer Conf., AFIPS Press, Montvale, New Jersey.

Codd, E. F., and Date, C. J. [1974]. "Interactive Support for Non-Programmers: The Relational and Network Approaches," *Proc. ACM SIGMOD, Data Models: Data-Structure-Set versus Relational* (Rustin, R., ed.), pp. 11–41.

Coffman, Jr., E. G., Elphick, M., and Shoshani, A. [1971]. "System Deadlocks," *ACM Comput. Surveys* **3**, 67–78.

Cox, W. [1974]. "DBMS: Dangerous But Manageable Systems," *Proc. DPI/CIPS Conf. 1974,* pp. 295–299.

Cullinane Corp. [1975]. *Integrated Database Management System (IDMS)* publications: *Data Definition Languages, Utilities and GCI Reference Guide,* release 3.1; *Data Manipulation Language Programmer's Reference Guide,* release 3.1.

Cuozzo, D. E., and Kurtz, J. F. [1973]. "Building a Base for Data Base: A Management Perspective," *Datamation* **19** (10), 71–75.

Curtice, R. M. [1974]. "Some Tools for Data Base Development," *Datamation* **20** (7), 102–106.

Czarnik, B., Schuster, S. A., and Tsichritzis, D. C. [1975]. "ZETA: A Relational Data Base Management System," *Proc. ACM Pacific 1975,* 21–25.

Datapro Research Corp. [1972a]. "System 2000—MRI Systems Corporation," *Datapro 70,* April.

Datapro Research Corp. [1972b]. "Total, Cincom Systems, Inc.," *Datapro 70,* December.

Datapro Research Corp. [1973]. "ADABAS—Software AG," *Datapro 70,* April.

Datapro Research Corp. [1974]. "Environ/1, Cincom Systems, Inc.," *Datapro 70,* March.

Date, C. J. [1972a]. "Relational Data Base Systems: A Tutorial," *Proc. Int. Symp. Computer Informat. Sci. 4th,* pp. 37–54. Plenum Press, New York.

Date, C. J. [1972b]. *An Introduction to the April 1971 Report of the CODASYL Data Base Task Group.* IBM tech. rep. TR.12.104, IBM United Kingdom Lab. Ltd., Hursley Park, Winchester Hampshire, England.

Date, C. J. [1975]. *An Introduction to Database Systems,* Addison-Wesley, Reading, Massachusetts.

Date, C. J. [1976]. "An Architecture for High-Level Language Database Extensions," *Proc. ACM SIGMOD,* pp. 101–122.

Date, C. J., and Codd, E. F. [1974]. "The Relational and Network Approaches: Comparison of the Application Programming Interfaces," *Proc. ACM SIGMOD, Data Models: Data-Structure-Set versus Relational* (Rustin, R., ed.), pp. 83–113.

Date, C. J., and Hopewell, P. [1971a]. "File Definition and Logical Data Independence," *Proc. ACM SIGFIDET Workshop on Data Description, Access and Control,* pp. 117–138.

Date, C. J., and Hopewell, P. [1971b]. "Storage Structure and Physical Data Independence," *Proc. ACM SIGFIDET Workshop on Data Description, Access and Control*, pp. 139–168.

Denning, P. J. [1970]. "Virtual Memory," *ACM Comput. Surveys* **2**, 153–189.

Dijkstra, E. W. [1969]. "Complexity Controlled by Hierarchical Ordering of Function and Variability," *Software Engineering* (Naur, P., and Randell, B., eds.), pp. 181–185. NATO, Brussels.

Douque, B. C., and Nijssen, G. M. [1975]. "The Wepion Recommendations on the CODASYL DDL 1973," *in Data Base Description* (Douque, B.C., and Nijssen, G.M., eds.), pp. 369–371. North-Holland, Amsterdam.

Dugan, J. A., Green, R. S., Minker, J., and Shindle, W. E. [1966]. "A Study of the Utility of Associative Memory Processors," *Proc. ACM Nat. Conf.*, pp. 347–360.

Earley, J. [1973]. "Relational Level Data Structures for Programming Languages," *Acta Inform.* **2**, 293–309.

Earnest, C. P. [1974]. *A Comparison of the Network and Relational Data Structure Models.* Rep., Computer Science Corp., El Segundo, California.

Earnest, C. P. [1975]. "Selection and Higher Level Structures in Networks," *in Data Base Description* (Douque, B. C., and Nijssen, G. M., eds.), pp. 215–236. North-Holland, Amsterdam.

EDBS [1975]. *Educational Data Base System, Data Manipulation Facility User's Manual.* Tech. note 3, Computer Sys. Res. Group, Univ. of Toronto, Canada.

Emery, J. C. [1973]. "An Overview of Management Information Systems," *Data Base* **5**, 1–15.

Engles, R. W. [1971]. "An Analysis of the April 1971 Data Base Task Group Report," *Proc. ACM SIGFIDET Workshop on Data Description, Access and Control*, pp. 69–91.

Engles, R. W. [1972]. "A Tutorial on Data-Base Organization," *Annual Rev. Automat. Programming* **7**, 1–64.

Eswaran, K. P., and Chamberlin, D. D. [1975]. "Functional Specifications of a Subsystem for Data Base Integrity," *Proc. ACM Int. Conf. Very Large Data Bases* (Kerr, D. S., ed.), pp. 48–68.

Eswaran, K. P., Gray, J. N., Lorie, R. A., and Traiger, I. L. [1974]. *On the Notions of Consistency and Predicate Locks in a Data Base System.* Tech. rep. RJ1487, IBM Res. Lab., San Jose, California.

Evans, R. W. (ed.) [1971]. "File Management Systems," *EDP In-Depth Rep.* **1** (3).

Evans, R. W. (ed.) [1973a]. "Current Developments in Data Base Management," *EDP In-Depth Rep.* **2** (5).

Evans, R. W. (ed.) [1973b]. "Shared Processor Data Entry Systems," EDP In-Depth Reports **2** (6).

Evans, R. W. (ed.) [1973c]. "New Software For Data Base Management: Part 1," *EDP In-Depth Rep.* **3** (1).

Evans, R. W. (ed.) [1973d]. "New Software for Data Base Management: Part 2," *EDP In-Depth Rep.* **3** (2).

Everest, G. C. [1974]. "Concurrent Update Control and Database Integrity," *in Data Base Management* (Klimbie, J. W., and Koffeman, K. L., eds.), pp. 241–268. North-Holland, Amsterdam.

Everett, G. D., Dissly, C. W., and Hardgrave, W. T. [1971]. *Remote File Manage-*

ment System (RFMS) Users Manual. TRM-16, Computation Center, Univ. of Texas at Austin.

Fadous, R., and Forsyth, J. [1975]. "Finding Candidate Keys for Relational Data Bases," *Proc. ACM SIGMOD,* pp. 203–210.

Farber, D. J. [1975]. "A Ring Network," *Datamation* **21** (2), 44–46.

Farley, G. H., and Schuster, S. A. [1975]. *Query Execution and Index Selection for Relational Data Bases.* Tech. rep. CSRG-53, Computer Sys. Res. Group, Univ. of Toronto, Canada.

Flynn, R. L. [1974]. "A Brief History of Data Base Management," *Datamation* **20** (8), 71–77.

Frank, R. L., and Sibley, E. H. [1973]. *The Data Base Task Group Report: An Illustrative Example.* ISDOS working paper No. 71, U.S. Nat. Tech. Informat. Service, Document AD-759-267, Springfield, Virginia.

Fry, J. P., and Sibley, E. H. [1976]. "Evolution of Data-Base Management Systems," *ACM Comput. Surveys* **8**, 7–42.

Gohren, G. L. Von. [1973]. "User Experience with Integrated Data Store (IDS)," in *Data Base Management Systems* (Jardine, D. A., ed.), pp. 19–33. North-Holland, Amsterdam.

Goldstein, R. C., and Strnad, A. L. [1970]. "The MACAIMS Data Management System," *Proc. ACM SIGFIDET Workshop on Data Description, Access and Control,* pp. 201–229.

Gotlieb, C. C., and Borodin, A. [1973]. *Social Issues in Computing.* Academic Press, New York.

Gotlieb, L. R. [1975]. "Computing Joins of Relations," *Proc. ACM SIGMOD,* pp. 55–63.

Gradwell, J. L. [1975]. "Why Data Dictionaries," *Database* **6** (2), 15–18.

Gray, J. N., Lorie, R. A., and Putzolu, G. R. [1975]. "Granularity of Locks in a Shared Data Base," *Proc. ACM Int. Conf. Very Large Data Bases* (Kerr, D. S., ed.), pp. 428–451.

Gray, J. P., and Blair, C. R. [1975]. "IBM's Systems Network Architecture," *Datamation* **21** (4), 51–56.

Guide-Share Data Base Management System Requirements [1970]. Joint Guide-Share Data Base Requirements Group, New York.

Habermann, A. N. [1969]. "Prevention of System Deadlocks," *CACM* **12**, 373–377.

Hammer, M. M., and Chan, A. [1976]. "Index Selection in a Self-Adaptive Data Base Management System," *Proc. ACM SIGMOD,* pp. 1–8.

Hammer, M. M., and McLeod, D. J. [1975]. "Semantic Integrity in a Relational Data Base System," *Proc. ACM Int. Conf. Very Large Data Bases* (Kerr, D. S., ed.), pp. 25–47.

Hanold, T. [1972]. "An Executive View of MIS," *Datamation* **18** (11), 65–71.

Hardgrave, W. T. [1972]. *Theoretical Aspects of Boolean Operations on Tree Structures and Implications for Generalized Data Management.* TSN-26, Computation Center, Univ. of Texas at Austin.

Heath, I. J. [1971]. "Unacceptable File Operations in a Relational Data Base," *Proc. ACM SIGFIDET Workshop on Data Description, Access and Control,* pp. 19–33.

Held, G. D., and Stonebraker, M. R. [1975]. "Storage Structures and Access Methods in the Relational Data Base Management System INGRES," *Proc. ACM Pacific 1975,* 26–33.

Held, G. D., Stonebraker, M. R., and Wong, E. [1975]. "INGRES–A Relational Data Base System," *Proc. AFIPS* **44,** *NCC,* 409–416.

Heydon, M. J. [1974]. "How to Prepare for Effective Data Management," *Can. Datasys.* **6** (7), 60–61.

Holt, R. C. [1972]. "Some Deadlock Properties of Computer Systems," *ACM Comput. Surveys* **4,** 179–195.

Honeywell Information Systems [1972]. Integrated Data Store Reference Manual, Order No. BR69, Honeywell Information Systems, Wellesley, Massachusetts.

Houston, G. B. [1973]. "Trillion Bit Memories," *Datamation* **19** (10), 52–58.

Huhn, G. E. [1974]. "The Data Base in a Critical On-Line Business Environment," *Datamation* **20** (9), 52–56.

Huits, M. H. [1975]. "Requirements for Languages in Data Base Systems," *in Data Base Description* (Douque, B. C., and Nijssen, G. M., eds.), pp. 85–108. North-Holland, Amsterdam.

IBM [1971]. *Information Management System IMS/360, Application Description Manual (Version 2),* GH20-0765-1. IBM Corp., White Plains, New York.

IBM [1975]. *Information Management System/Virtual Storage (IMS/VS)* publications: *General Information Manual,* GH20-1260-3; *System/Application Design Guide,* SH20-9025-2; *Application Programming Reference Manual,* SH20-9026-2; *System Programming Reference Manual,* SH20-9027-2; *Operator's Reference Manual,* SH20-9028-1; *Utilities Reference Manual,* SH20-9029-2; *Messages and Codes Reference Manual,* SH20-9030-2. IBM Corp., White Plains, New York.

Jardine, D. A. [1974]. "Data Base Management Systems: The EDP Poker Game?" *Can. Datasys.* **6** (8), 46–49.

Kanfer, M. E. [1975]. *An Educational Network Data Base System.* M.A.Sc. thesis, Dep. Elec. Eng., Univ. of Toronto, Canada.

Kay, M. H. [1975]. "An Assessment of the CODASYL DDL for use with a Relational Subschema," *in Data Base Description* (Douque, B. C., and Nijssen, G. M., eds.), pp. 199–212. North-Holland, Amsterdam.

Kennevan, W. J. [1970]. "MIS Universe," *Data Management* **8** (9), 62–64.

Kent, W. [1973]. *A Primer of Normal Forms.* Tech. Rep. TR02.600, IBM Sys. Dev. Div., San Jose, California.

Kershberg, L., Klug, A., and Tsichritzis, D. C. [1976]. "A Taxonomy of Data Models," *in Systems for Large Data Bases* (Lockemann, P. C., and Neuhold, E. J., eds.), pp. 43–64. North-Holland, Amsterdam.

Klebanoff, J. L. [1974]. *Teaching Data Management.* M.Sc. thesis, Dep. Computer Sci., Univ. of Toronto, Canada.

Klebanoff, J. L., Lochovsky, F. H., and Tsichritzis, D. C. [1975]. "Teaching Data Management Using APL," *Proc. APL 1975,* Pisa, Italy.

Knuth, D. E. [1968]. *The Art of Computer Programming 1, Fundamental Algorithms.* Addison-Wesley, Reading, Massachusetts.

Knuth, D. E. [1973]. *The Art of Computer Programming 3, Sorting and Searching.* Addison-Wesley, Reading, Massachusetts.

Lefkovitz, D. [1969]. *File Structures for On-Line Systems* Spartan Books, New York.

Lias, E. J. [1974]. "On-Line vs. Batch Costs," *Datamation* **20** (12), 69–79.

Lin, C. S., Smith, D. C. P., and Smith, J. M. [1976]. "The Design of a Rotating Associative Array Memory for a Relational Data Base Management Application," *ACM Trans. Database Sys.* **1**, 53–65.

Lochovsky, F. H. [1973]. *An Educational Data Base Management System*. M.Sc. thesis, Dep. of Computer Sci., Univ. of Toronto, Canada.

Lochovsky, F. H., and Tsichritzis, D. C. [1976]. "An Educational Data Base Management System," *INFOR* **14** (3), pp. 270–278.

Lorie, R. A. [1974]. *XRM—An Extended (N-ary) Relational Memory*. Tech. rep. G320-2096, IBM Sci. Center, Cambridge, Massachusetts.

Lowenthal, E. I. [1971]. *A Functional Approach to the Design of Storage Structures for Generalized Data Management Systems*. Ph.D. thesis, Univ. of Texas at Austin.

Lum, V. Y. [1973]. "General Performance Analysis of Key-to-Address Transformation Methods Using an Abstract File Concept," *CACM* **16**, 603–612.

MacDonald, I. G. [1975]. "Univac's Interpretation of the CODASYL DBTG Proposals," *Database* **6** (2), 3–7.

McGee, W. C. [1972]. "Some Current Issues in Data Description," *Proc. ACM SIGFIDET Workshop on Data Description, Access and Control*, pp. 1–12.

McKeeman, W. M., Horning, J. J., and Wortman, D. B. [1970]. *A Compiler Generator*. Prentice-Hall, Englewood Cliffs, New Jersey.

McLeod, D. J., and Meldman, M. J. [1975]. "RISS: A Generalized Minicomputer Relational Data Base Management System," *Proc. AFIPS* **44**, NCC, 397–402.

Martin, J. T. [1973]. *Security, Accuracy, and Privacy in Computer Systems*. Prentice-Hall, Englewood Cliffs, New Jersey.

Martin, J. T. [1975]. *Computer Data-Base Organization*. Prentice-Hall, Englewood Cliffs, New Jersey.

Mealy, G. H. [1967]. "Another Look at Data," *Proc. AFIPS* **31**, FJCC, 525–534.

Meltzer, H. S. [1969]. "Data Base Concepts and Architecture for Data Base Systems," *IBM rep. to SHARE Information Systems Research Project, SHARE XXXIII*. Chicago, Illinois.

Meltzer, H. S. [1974]. "Relations and Relational Operations," *GUIDE* **38**. Chicago, Illinois.

Metaxides, A. [1975]. " 'Information bearing' and 'non-information bearing' Sets." *in Data Base Description* (Douque, B. C., and Nijssen, G. M., eds.), pp. 363–368. North-Holland, Amsterdam.

Michaels, A. S., Mittman, B., and Carlson, C. R. [1976]. "A Comparison of the Relational and CODASYL Approaches to Data-Base Management," *ACM Comput. Surveys* **8**, 125–151.

Morris, R. [1968]. "Scatter Storage Techniques," *CACM* **11**, 38–43.

MRI Systems Corp. [1972]. *SYSTEM 2000* publications: *General Information Manual, Basic Reference Manual, Immediate Access Feature*. MRI Systems Corp., Austin, Texas.

Murdick, R. G., and Ross, J. B. [1971]. *Information Systems for Modern Management*. Prentice-Hall, Englewood Cliffs, New Jersey.

Mylopoulos, J., Schuster, S. A., and Tsichritzis, D. C. [1975]. "A Multi-Level Relational System," *Proc. AFIPS* **44**, NCC, 403–408.

Nijssen, G. M. [1974]. "Data Structuring in the DDL and Relational Model," *in*

Data Base Management (Klimbie, J. W., and Koffeman, K. L., eds.), pp. 363–379. North-Holland, Amsterdam.

Nijssen, G. M. [1975]. "Set and CODASYL Set or Coset," *in Data Base Description* (Douque, B. C., and Nijssen, G. M., eds.), pp. 1–70. North-Holland, Amsterdam.

Notley, M. G. [1972]. *The Peterlee IS/1 System,* IBM UK Scientific Centre Report UKSC-0018, Peterlee, England.

Olle, T. W. [1974]. "Data Definition Spectrum and Procedurality Spectrum in Data Base Management Systems," *in Data Base Management* (Klimbie, J. W., and Koffeman, K. L., eds.), pp. 289–293. North-Holland, Amsterdam.

Olle, T. W. [1975]. "An Analysis of the Flaws in the Schema DDL and Proposed Improvements," *in Data Base Description* (Douque, B. C., and Nijssen, G. M., eds.), pp. 283–296. North-Holland, Amsterdam.

Ozkarahan, E. A., Schuster, S. A., and Smith, K. C. [1975]. "RAP: An Associative Processor for Data Base Management," *Proc AFIPS* 44, *NCC*, 379–387.

Palermo, F. P. [1972]. "A Data Base Search Problem," *Proc. Int. Symp. Computer Informat. Sci. 4th*, pp. 67–101. Plenum Press, New York.

Parker, J. L., and Jervis, B. [1972]. "An Approach for a Working Relational Data System," *Proc. ACM SIGFIDET Workshop on Data Description, Access and Control*, pp. 125–145.

Parker, R. W. [1965]. "The SABRE System," *Datamation* 11 (9), 49–52.

Philips-Electrologica B. V. [1974]. *Philips HOst LAnguage System (PHOLAS)* publications: *System and Operations*, pub. no. 5122 991 26071; *Schema DDL and SSL,* pub. no. 5122 991 25841; *Sub-Schema DDL and DML,* pub. no. 5122 991 25861. Philips Electrologica, B. V., Amsterdam.

Reside, K. D., and Seiter, T. J. [1974]. "The Evolution of an Integrated Data Base," *Datamation* 20 (9), 57–60.

Roberts, D. C. [1972]. "File Organization Techniques," *Adv. Computers* 12 (Rubinoff, M., ed.), 115–174.

Robinson, K. A. [1975]. "DMS-1100: An In-depth Evaluation," *Database* 6 (2), 8–14.

Roussopoulos, N., and Mylopoulos, J. [1975]. "Using Semantic Networks for Data Base Management," *Proc. ACM Int. Conf. Very Large Data Bases* (Kerr, D. S., ed.), pp. 144–172.

Rudolph, J. A. [1972]. "A Production Implementation of an Associative Array Processor—STARAN," *Proc. AFIPS* 41, *Part I, FJCC*, pp. 229–241.

Schafheitlin, D. W. [1974]. *A Study of Data Base Management System Structures: Hierarchical, Network and Relational.* M.Sc. thesis, Dep. Computer Science, Univ. of Toronto, Canada.

Schmid, H. A., and Bernstein, P. A. [1975]. "A Multi-Level Architecture for Relational Data Base Systems," *Proc. ACM Int. Conf. Very Large Data Bases* (Kerr, D. S., ed.), pp. 202–226.

Schmid, H. A., and Swenson, J. R. [1975]. "On the Semantics of the Relational Data Model," *Proc. ACM SIGMOD*, pp. 211–223.

Schubert, R. F. [1974]. "Directions in Data Base Management Technology," *Datamation* 20 (9), 48–51.

Senko, M. B., Altman, E. B., Astrahan, M. M., and Fehder, P. L. [1973]. "Data Structures and Accessing in Data-base Systems," *IBM Sys. J.* 12, 30–93.

Shemer, J. E., and Collmeyer, A. J. [1972]. "Database Sharing: A Study of Interference, Roadblock and Deadlock," *Proc. ACM SIGFIDET Workshop on Data Description, Access and Control*, pp. 147–163.

Sibley, E. H. [1974]. "On the Equivalence of Data Based Systems," *Proc. ACM SIGMOD, Data Models: Data-Structure-Set versus Relational* (Rustin, R., ed.), pp. 43–76.

Sibley, E. H., and Merten, A. G. [1973]. "Implementation of a Generalized Data Base Management System within an Organization," *Management Informat.* 2, 21–31.

Slotnick, D. L. [1970]. "Logic per Track Devices," *Adv. Computers* 10 (Alt, F. L., and Rubinoff, M., eds.), pp. 291–296. Academic Press, New York.

Software AG [1971]. *ADABAS* publications: *General Information Manual, Reference Manual, Utilities Manual*. Software AG, West Germany.

SPARC [1974]. *Outline for Preparation of Proposals for Standardization*. Document SPARC/90, CBEMA.

Steel, T. B. [1975a]. "Data Base Standardization: A Status Report," *in Data Base Description* (Douque, B. C., and Nijssen, G. M., eds.), pp. 183–195. North-Holland, Amsterdam.

Steel, T. B. [1975b]. "Summary of Recommendations," *in Data Base Description* (Douque, B. C. and Nijssen, G. M., eds.), pp. 373–376, North-Holland, Amsterdam.

Steig, D. B. [1972]. "File Management Systems Revisited," *Datamation* 18 (10), 48–51.

Stonebraker, M. R. [1975a]. "Implementation of Integrity Constraints and Views by Query Modification," *Proc. ACM SIGMOD*, pp. 65–78.

Stonebraker, M. R. [1975b]. *A Comparison of the Use of Links and Secondary Indices in a Relational Data Base System*, Memorandum No. ERL-M591, Electronics Research Lab., College of Engineering, University of California, Berkeley.

Stonebraker, M. R., and Held, G. D. [1975]. "Networks, Hierarchies, and Relations in Data Base Management Systems," *Proc. ACM Pacific 1975*, 1–9.

Stonebraker, M. R., and Wong, E. [1974]. "Access Control in a Relational Data Base Management System by Query Modification," *Proc. ACM Nat. Conf.*, pp. 180–186.

Stonebraker, M. R., Wong, E., and Kreps, P. [1976]. "The Design and Implementation of INGRES," *ACM Trans. Database Sys.* 1, 189–222.

Su, S. Y. W., and Lipovski, G. J. [1975]. "CASSM: A Cellular System for Very Large Data Bases," *Proc. ACM Int. Conf. Very Large Data Bases* (Kerr, D. S., ed.), pp. 456–472.

Sundgren, B. [1974]. "Conceptual Foundation of the Infological Approach to Data Bases," *in Data Base Management* (Klimbie, J. W., and Koffeman, K. L., eds.), pp. 61–96. North-Holland, Amsterdam.

Taylor, R. W. [1975]. "Observations on the Attributes of Database Sets," *in Data Base Description* (Douque, B. C., and Nijssen, G. M., eds.), pp. 73–84. North-Holland, Amsterdam.

Taylor, R. W., and Frank, R. L. [1976]. "CODASYL Data-Base Management Systems," *ACM Comput. Surveys* 8, 67–103.

Thurber, K. J., and Wald, L. D. [1975]. "Associative and Parallel Processors," *ACM Comput. Surveys* 7, 215–255.

Titman, P. J. [1974]. "An Experimental Data Base System Using Binary Relations," *in Data Base Management* (Klimbie, J. W., and Koffeman, K. L., eds.), pp. 351–360. North-Holland, Amsterdam.

Todd, S. J. P. [1975]. *Peterlee Relational Test Vehicle PRTV, a Technical Overview*, IBM UK Scientific Centre Report UKSC-0075, Peterlee, England.

Tsichritzis, D. C. [1974]. *On Implementation of Relations.* Tech. rep. CSRG-35, Computer Sys. Res. Group, Univ. of Toronto, Canada.

Tsichritzis, D. C. [1975a]. "A Network Framework for Relational Implementation," *in Data Base Description* (Douque, B. C., and Nijssen, G. M., eds.), pp. 269–282. North-Holland, Amsterdam.

Tsichritzis, D. C. [1975b]. *Features of a Conceptual Schema.* Tech. rep. CSRG-56, Computer Sys. Res. Group, Univ. of Toronto, Canada.

Tsichritzis, D. C. [1976]. "LSL: A Link and Selector Language," *Proc. ACM SIGMOD*, pp. 123–133.

Tsichritzis, D. C., and Bernstein, P. A. [1974]. *Operating Systems.* Academic Press, New York.

Tsichritzis, D. C., and Lochovsky, F. H. [1976]. "Hierarchical Data-Base Management: A Survey," *ACM Comput. Surveys* **8**, 105–123.

UCS [1970]. *UCS-VI UNIDATA Data Management System Reference Manual.* United Computing Systems, Inc. Kansas City, Missouri.

"University of Toronto Information System," [1973]. *Data Processor* **3**, 3–7.

Waghorn, W. J. [1975]. "The DDL as an Industry Standard?" *in Data Base Description* (Douque, B. C., and Nijssen, G. M., eds.), pp. 121–166. North-Holland, Amsterdam.

Weiner, B., Brevier, G., Britain, B., Clarkson, M., Fanucci, Jr., G., McKeeman, W., Sontz, S., Tsichritzis, D. C., and Welge, L. [1975]. *An Integrated Data Management Tool.* Unpublished manuscript. DBMS Inc., Miami, Florida.

Westgaard, R. E. [1975]. "A COBOL Data Base Facility for the Relational Data Model," *Proc. ACM Pacific 1975,* 132–139.

Whitney, V. K. [1972]. "A Relational Data Management System," *Proc. Int. Symp. Computer Informat. Sci. 4th,* pp. 55–66. Plenum Press, New York.

Woods, W. A. [1973]. "Progress in Natural Language Understanding—An Application to Lunar Geology," *Proc. AFIPS* **42**, *NCC*, 441–450.

Wulf, W., and Levin, R. [1975]. "A Local Network," *Datamation* **21** (2), 47–50.

Xerox Corp. [1972]. *Extended Data Management System (EDMS) Reference Manual.* 90 30 12A, Xerox Corp., El Segundo, California.

Yormark, B. [1976]. "The ANSI/X3/SPARC/SGDBMS Architecture," *SHARE XLIV,* Chicago, Illinois.

INDEX

Computer Science and Applied Mathematics

A SERIES OF MONOGRAPHS AND TEXTBOOKS

Editor
Werner Rheinboldt
University of Maryland

HANS P. KÜNZI, H. G. TZSCHACH, and C. A. ZEHNDER. Numerical Methods of Mathematical Optimization: With ALGOL and FORTRAN Programs, Corrected and Augmented Edition

AZRIEL ROSENFELD. Picture Processing by Computer

JAMES ORTEGA AND WERNER RHEINBOLDT. Iterative Solution of Nonlinear Equations in Several Variables

AZARIA PAZ. Introduction to Probabilistic Automata

DAVID YOUNG. Iterative Solution of Large Linear Systems

ANN YASUHARA. Recursive Function Theory and Logic

JAMES M. ORTEGA. Numerical Analysis: A Second Course

G. W. STEWART. Introduction to Matrix Computations

CHIN-LIANG CHANG AND RICHARD CHAR-TUNG LEE. Symbolic Logic and Mechanical Theorem Proving

C. C. GOTLIEB AND A. BORODIN. Social Issues in Computing

ERWIN ENGELER. Introduction to the Theory of Computation

F. W. J. OLVER. Asymptotics and Special Functions

DIONYSIOS C. TSICHRITZIS AND PHILIP A. BERNSTEIN. Operating Systems

ROBERT R. KORFHAGE. Discrete Computational Structures

PHILIP J. DAVIS AND PHILIP RABINOWITZ. Methods of Numerical Integration

A. T. BERZTISS. Data Structures: Theory and Practice, Second Edition

N. CHRISTOPHIDES. Graph Theory: An Algorithmic Approach

ALBERT NIJENHUIS AND HERBERT S. WILF. Combinatorial Algorithms

AZRIEL ROSENFELD AND AVINASH C. KAK. Digital Picture Processing

SAKTI P. GHOSH. Data Base Organization for Data Management

DIONYSIOS C. TSICHRITZIS AND FREDERICK H. LOCHOVSKY. Data Base Management Systems

WILLIAM F. AMES. Numerical Methods for Partial Differential Equations, Second Edition

B 7
C 8
D 9
E 0
F 1
G 2
H 3
I 4
J 5